History of American Thought and Culture

PAUL S. BOYER
General Editor

• *The Rights of Nature* •

A History of
Environmental
Ethics

RODERICK FRAZIER NASH

The University of Wisconsin Press

The University of Wisconsin Press
114 North Murray Street
Madison, Wisconsin 53715

The University of Wisconsin Press, Ltd.
1 Gower Street
London WC1E 6HA, England

5 4 3 2 1

Printed in the United States of America

Library of Congress Cataloging-in-Publication Data
Nash, Roderick.
The rights of nature.
(History of American thought and culture)
Bibliography: pp. 273–78.
Includes index.
1. Human ecology—Moral and ethical aspects—
History. 2. Human ecology—Philosophy. I. Title.
II. Series.
GF80.N36   1988   179'.1   88-17169
ISBN 0-299-11840-1

FOR HONEYDEW
◆
liberator of marmots
and dancer with the elk

· Contents ·

· *Foreword* ·

The Rights of Nature is a pathbreaking work on a timely subject by an eminently qualified scholar. The deepening of environmental consciousness represents a trend of the first importance in recent American thought and culture. This consciousness is rooted in the American past, of course, as the influence of such figures as Henry David Thoreau, John Muir, and Aldo Leopold makes plain. But in recent decades it has risen to an unprecedented level of cultural visibility, intellectual sophistication, and political influence.

Roderick Nash is particularly well qualified to explore the intellectual roots and development of environmental ethics. His 1967 work *Wilderness and the American Mind* is widely recognized as a classic treatment of the subject. And there is a special appropriateness in the appearance of *The Rights of Nature* under the imprint of The University of Wisconsin Press, since Professor Nash earned his doctorate at Wisconsin under Merle Curti, a founder of the field of American intellectual history. One of Nash's early published works was a short essay on "The Wisdom of Aldo Leopold" that appeared in the *Wisconsin Academy Review* in 1961.

The Rights of Nature is not only based on deep research, vigorous argument, and comprehensive coverage. It also reflects the perspective of a person who is himself firmly committed to environmentalism as an ethical imperative and who has acted on this imperative. Nash played a leading role in shaping the local response to the disastrous Santa Barbara oil spill of 1969, for example, and was the author of the widely publicized *Santa Barbara Declaration of Environmental Rights*. In future years, I suspect, *The Rights of Nature* will be read not only as a work of impeccable intellectual history, but also as a valuable primary source illuminating the ideological perspective of advanced environmentalist thinkers and activists in the closing years of the twentieth century.

Professor Nash's view of the widening circle of environmental awareness, and of the relationship of radical environmentalism to the larger evolution of liberal theory, natural-rights doctrine, and ethical consciousness in general, will provoke discussion and perhaps disagreement. Similarly, the book will stimulate reflections on the complex problems that arise when the impulse to protect and cherish the natural environment comes in conflict with other social values and competing claims of rights. The debate over whether anthropocentrism is as deplorable as many of the environmentalist thinkers considered by Nash apparently believe will doubtless be intensified by this work. But all those drawn into this discourse will, I feel confident, recognize *The Rights of Nature* as an important and seminal work by a gifted intellectual historian.

From the first, the Wisconsin Series in the History of American Thought and Culture was conceived as having a dual purpose: first, to offer the best and most original scholarship in the fields of American intellectual and cultural history; second, to contribute in meaningful and thoughtful ways to the ongoing discussion of public issues of contemporary interest and importance. *The Rights of Nature* fulfills both of these objectives admirably. I welcome it as a distinguished addition to the series.

Paul S. Boyer

◆ Preface ◆

I grew interested in the history of what came to be called "environmental ethics" as a graduate student assistant in the early 1960s when I began to collect and order the papers of Aldo Leopold in the archives of the University of Wisconsin–Madison. It was in Madison, in the 1930s, that Leopold began to formulate his land ethic. When he died in 1948, few outside of a small circle of conservationists knew of his writings. The dramatic growth of scholarly and popular interest in his work since 1965 is one indication of changing priorities within American civilization. After considering a biography of Leopold, I left that project to others,[1] preferring to concentrate on one of Leopold's primary interests: the significance of wilderness in American history.[2] Now it is exciting to return to a consideration of the history and implications of what I take to be one of the most remarkable ideas of our time: the belief that ethical standing does not begin and end with human beings.

The approach of this book to its subject matter requires a prefatory note. The process of jury selection theoretically weeds out persons with strong feelings about the case to be tried. The opposite is true in scholarship. It would be hard to find anyone qualified to write about recent American environmental history who did not have strong personal opinions about the controversial matters it concerns. I admit to such beliefs, but let me declare my intention in what follows to be an historian rather than a partisan. Although I have done so in other writings,[3] I will not here advocate the extension of ethics to include the natural world. I will not split logical hairs with the philosophers and theologians nor biological ones with scientists. It seems to me that the first responsibility of an historian of ideas must be to report accurately what was thought in the past. If those thoughts strike some readers as illogical, biased, emotional, unreasonable, or just plain wrong, the fault, if any, is that of the thinkers under discussion. In *The Rights of Nature* I am not trying to write philosophically about environmental ethics or natural rights or liberalism; I am not prescribing ways to think about the rights of human beings balanced against those of nature. I am not endeavoring to find universally acceptable definitions of tough words like "nature," "liberalism," and "rights." Many of the people I discuss do offer such prescriptions and definitions, but their ideas are not necessarily my ideas—or at least that is not the issue of concern in this book. I am, then, less concerned about whether a particular ethical position is politically responsible, philosophically correct, or scientifically valid than I am with the fact that it was expressed, the context in which the expression occurred, and its consequences for further thought and action. The biblical account of creation and the idea that the world is flat, for example, have been largely discredited, but they are vitally important to the historian of ideas. Of moment, after all, is not whether an idea won or lost, but how it functioned in history.

A history of environmental ethics necessarily involves many disciplines, some that transcend my professional competence. I am grateful to the philosophers, theologians, lawyers, and ecologists who have read portions of what follows and provided important suggestions for documentation and analysis. Among them, let me express special thanks to Thomas Attig, Richard Baer, Bill Devall, Edward Grumbine, Eugene C. Hargrove, J. Donald Hughes, Ernest Partridge, John Rodman, Holmes Rolston III, Donald Scherer, Paul Shepard, Kristin Shrader-Frechette, Christopher D. Stone, Michael Tobias, E. O. Wilson, and Donald Worster. J. Baird Callicott has supported this project for years, most recently in connection with his editorship of *Companion to* A Sand County Almanac (1987), which contains an abridgment of Chapters 2 and 3. George Sessions, who, with his publication of the newsletter *Ecophilosophy,* has done more than anyone to organize and clarify thinking about environmental ethics, provided continual encouragement. Indeed it was Sessions's 1980 observation that "a philosophically perceptive history of the shift from 'conservation' to 'ecological consciousness' in the 1960s and 1970s has yet to be written"[4] that led me into the often turbid seas of this subject. If I have not fully satisfied his plea for philosophical perception, I hope I have at least clarified some of the subject's main historical parameters.

My colleagues at the University of California, Santa Barbara, especially Daniel Botkin, Ray Ford, Nancy McCagney, Bill Powell, Arent H. Schuyler, and Inez Talamantez, and my friends Ron Hayes and Rick Smith, have offered helpful and repeated criticism. Bruce Stenslie contributed valuable research assistance and draft writing, particularly for Chapter 6. Alice Van Deburg and Anne Knowles of the University of Wisconsin Press took a personal as well as a professional interest in the quality of the manuscript and made many helpful suggestions. Marylee Prince's magic word processor accomplished the herculean task of keeping track of my revisions, additions, and second thoughts. A month's residency at the Rockefeller Foundation's Bellagio Study and Conference Center in Italy facilitated the start of this project. The dedication addresses my debt to Lindamel Murray, whose commitment to the rights of nature cheered and encouraged me along the scholarly trail.

Santa Barbara, California
May 1987

◆ THE RIGHTS OF NATURE ◆

Ethical Extension and Radical Environmentalism

———————◆———————

How narrow we selfish, conceited creatures are in our sympathies! How blind to the rights of all the rest of creation!
—*John Muir, 1867*

I believe in the rights of creatures other than man.
—*David R. Brower, 1971*

A kind of ultimate democracy is practiced. Plants and animals
are also people, and . . . are given a place and a voice in the
political discussions of the humans. They are "represented."
"Power to all the people" must be the slogan.
—*Gary Snyder, 1972*

What is crucial to recognize is that the human capacity for
empathy and identification is not static; the very process of
recognizing *rights* in those higher vertebrates with whom we
already empathize could well pave the way for still further extensions as we move upward along the spiral of moral evolution. It is
not only the human liberation movements . . . that advances
in waves of increased consciousness.
—*Laurence Tribe, 1974*

What is proposed here is a broadening of value, so that nature
will cease to be merely "property" and become a commonwealth. . . . If we now universalize "person," consider how
slowly the circle has enlarged . . . to include aliens, strangers,
infants, children, Negroes, Jews, slaves, women, Indians, pris-
oners, the elderly, the insane, the deformed, and even now we
ponder the status of fetuses. Ecological ethics queries whether

we ought to again universalize, recognizing the intrinsic value
of every ecobiotic component.
                                        —*Holmes Rolston, 1975*

We must constantly extend the community to include all. . . .
The other beings—four-legged, winged, six-legged, rooted,
flowing, etc.—have just as much right to be in that place as we
do, they are their own justification for being, they have inherent
value, value completely apart from whatever worth they have
for . . . humans."
                                        —*Dave Foreman, 1987*

This book concerns the history and implications of the idea that
morality ought to include the relationship of humans to nature. Focusing on American intellectual history, it traces the relatively recent
emergence of the belief that ethics should expand from a preoccupation with humans (or their gods) to a concern for animals, plants,
rocks, and even nature, or the environment, in general. One way to
think of this is as an evolution of ethics from the natural rights of a
limited group of humans to the rights of parts or, in some theories,
all of nature. The use of "rights" in this connection has created considerable confusion. Suffice it to say, for now, that while some use
the term in a technical philosophical or legal sense, others take it to
mean that nature, or parts of it, has intrinsic worth which humans
ought to respect.

From this perspective one can regard environmental ethics as
marking out the farthest limits of American liberalism. The emergence of this idea that the human-nature relationship should be treated
as a moral issue conditioned or restrained by ethics is one of the most
extraordinary developments in recent intellectual history. Some believe it holds the potential for fundamental and far-reaching change
in both thought and behavior comparable to that which the ideal of
human rights and justice held at the time of the democratic revolutions in the seventeenth and eighteenth centuries.

Two drawings may help clarify these thoughts, though at the inevitable risk of oversimplification. The first should be regarded as an
ideal type and not as an historical description of the actual thought of
any specific individual or group of people. Figure 1 attempts to show
what exponents of evolved or sequential ethics believe. The time line
along the figure's left margin suggests that ethics awaited the development of an intelligence capable of conceptualizing right and
wrong. And even then, for long periods of time, morality was usu-

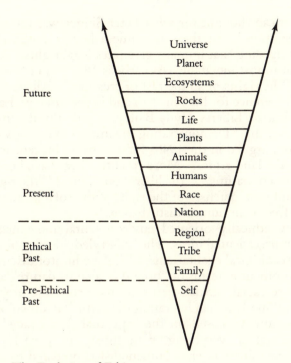

Future

Present

Ethical
Past

Pre-Ethical
Past

Universe
Planet
Ecosystems
Rocks
Life
Plants
Animals
Humans
Race
Nation
Region
Tribe
Family
Self

FIGURE I   *The Evolution of Ethics*

ally mired in self-interest, as for some it still is. Some people, however, pushed the circle of ethical relevancy outward to include certain
classes of human beings such as family and tribal members. At this
point it is important to remember that as self-imposed restraints on
conduct, ethics are ideals. Some humans, after all, commit suicide
and kill members of their families. Still, there is a concept of right
and wrong that applies to such behavior and laws that implement the
ideals of the community.

   Geographical distance eventually ceased to be a barrier in human-
to-human ethics, and in time people began to shake free from nation-
alism, racism, and sexism. The abolition of American slavery in 1865
marked an important milestone in this process. Humans could no
longer be owned, and ethics evolved beyond the level labeled "race."
Blacks, women, and all human beings gained a place in the sun of
ethical theory if not always in practice. But "speciesism"[1] or "human
chauvinism"[2] persisted and animal rights was the next logical stage
in moral extension. By the 1970s there was growing support in

Anglo–American thought for what Peter Singer was the first to call "animal liberation."[3] At the same time a lawyer raised the ethical stakes by proposing that humans give trees legal rights.[4] Further expansion was almost inevitable. As early as 1867 John Muir proposed respect for "the rights of all the rest of creation."[5] Albert Schweitzer discussed "reverence for life" in 1915 and in the same year an American horticulturist, Liberty Hyde Bailey, urged ethical consideration of "the holy earth."[6] Demonstrating the impact of ecology on ethics, Aldo Leopold argued in the 1940s for a holistic, biocentric morality he termed "the land ethic."[7] More recently there have been calls for "the liberation of nature,"[8] "the liberation of life,"[9] "the rights of the planet,"[10] and even defenses of the right of the solar system and universe to be free from human disturbance.[11]

The new ethically oriented environmental movement seethes with such unprecedented ideas. The self-styled "deep ecologists" are advancing "ecological egalitarianism."[12] An educator discusses abuse of the environment in terms of "prejudice against nature" and relates it explicitly to racial, sexual, national, and economic prejudice. He aspires to nothing less than liberating the earth.[13] Ecotheologians recommend a morality based on the "spiritual democracy" of God's creation, including everything from subatomic particles to spiral nebulae.[14] One Christian environmentalist is prepared to defend the "inalienable rights" of all the "citizens" in a Kingdom of God expanded to the entire ecosystem.[15] A Pulitzer prize–winning poet calls for an "ultimate democracy" in which plants and animals join people as rights holders.[16] The journal *Environmental Law* carries an essay proposing a constitutional amendment stating that wildlife must not be deprived of "life, liberty or habitat without due process of law."[17] Clearly the old boundaries that limited liberalism to *human* freedom are breaking down.

The second drawing, Figure 2, is a schematic view of the historical tradition of extending rights to oppressed minorities in Britain and then in the United States. At the center are the natural rights tradition and the concept of intrinsic value that date to Greek and Roman jurisprudence. The diagram lists the key document that codified each new minority's inclusion within the circle of ethical consideration. Figure 2 does not imply that the minority immediately attained full rights in practice as well as theory on the given date, nor that only the documents listed were important in establishing minority rights. Its purpose is merely to show that ethics have expanded over time and that some thinkers and activists now regard nature (or certain of its components) as deserving liberation from human domina-

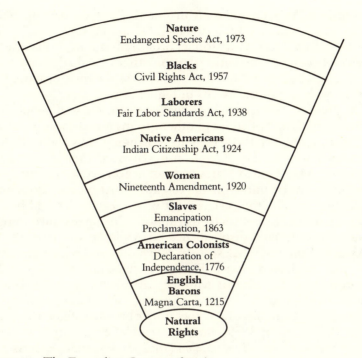

Nature
Endangered Species Act, 1973

Blacks
Civil Rights Act, 1957

Laborers
Fair Labor Standards Act, 1938

Native Americans
Indian Citizenship Act, 1924

Women
Nineteenth Amendment, 1920

Slaves
Emancipation
Proclamation, 1863

American Colonists
Declaration of
Independence, 1776

**English
Barons**
Magna Carta, 1215

**Natural
Rights**

FIGURE 2   *The Expanding Concept of Rights*

tion. For people of this persuasion natural rights has indeed evolved into the rights of nature.

Ideas like these, to be sure, are on the far frontier of moral theory. From the perspective of intellectual history, environmental ethics is revolutionary; it is arguably the most dramatic expansion of morality in the course of human thought. We will encounter confusion, contradiction, and inconsistency in many of the concepts explored in the following pages, but this, too, is part of the history of ideas. We might remind ourselves, however, that human-to-human ethics have not been entirely clarified. The important point for the historian is that in recent years many people have found compelling the notion that nonhuman life and nonliving matter have moral standing. The majority still regards this idea as incredible. But with an eye to the changes diagrammed in Figure 2, historians are aware that the same incredulity met the first proposals for granting independence to American colonists, freeing the slaves, respecting Indian rights, integrating schools, and adding an Equal Rights Amendment to the

Constitution. As John Stuart Mill put it, "every great movement must experience three stages: ridicule, discussion, adoption."[18] What happens in the process, Christopher Stone reminds us, is that the "*unthinkable*" becomes conventional—sometimes gradually and peacefully through legislative and legal processes, as Stone proposed, but often, as we know of the events in Figure 2, violently.[19]

The problem has always been that certain groups of people benefited from the denial of ethics to other groups (or to nature) and were reluctant to relinquish those benefits. Changing laws and institutions often required force. The American Revolution, after all, was a war, and slavery in the United States was not negotiated away. For similar reasons it might be unreasonable to expect that what Aldo Leopold was the first to call "the enslavement of . . . earth"[20] could be abolished without profound social disruption. The appearance in recent years of not only civil disobedience but violence and outright lawbreaking on behalf of whales, seals, redwoods, and wildernesses supports this conclusion. Earth First! rallied behind the slogan "No Compromise in Defense of Mother Earth!" A century and a half earlier William Lloyd Garrison shouted, "No Compromise with Slaveholders!" Contemporary liberators of animals liken themselves to John Brown in his 1859 raid on Harper's Ferry, Virginia. Harriet Beecher Stowe's *Uncle Tom's Cabin* (1852) and Rachel Carson's *Silent Spring* (1962) share a moral viewpoint. "Whether anyone likes it or not," a spokesman for Greenpeace declared in 1979, "force will eventually have to be brought to bear against those who would continue to desecrate the environment."[21] A participant in the raids of the Animal Liberation Front on animal-research laboratories explained her position as "like the Underground Railroad and slavery . . . sometimes people have to go outside the law. . . . Any movement for social change has required disobedience."[22] Henry David Thoreau would have understood her point. But even legal actions, such as the Marine Mammal Protection Act (1972) and the Endangered Species Act (1973), represent in some estimations the remarkable idea "that a listed nonhuman resident of the United States is guaranteed, in a special sense, life and liberty."[23]

An ethical rather than an economic approach to environmental protection lay behind ideas like these, and its. presence helps explain changes in the character of American conservation. One of the most useful insights into recent American history concerns the qualitative difference between "environmentalism," as it emerged in the 1960s, and what used to be called "conservation."[24] When Gifford Pinchot named it in 1907, conservation stood squarely in the American mainstream. The Progressive conservationists made every effort to plant their seedling notion in the fertile soil of national growth and strength. Utilitarianism and anthropocentrism marked the early movement. Time and again Pinchot, the first Chief of the U.S. Forest Service, pointed out that conservation did not mean protecting or preserving nature. On the contrary, it stood for wise and efficient *use* of natural resources. The idea was to control nature and serve the material interests of humankind but with an eye to long-term needs. Under this philosophy the dam-building Bureau of Reclamation and the timber-producing Forest Service became the showcases of early twentieth-century conservation. But a half century later these same agencies found themselves under heavy fire from a new breed of environmentalists. Impoundments and clearcuts, they alleged, infringed not only on the rights of people to experience and enjoy nature but on the rights of nature itself.

The change is explained in part by the rise of the science of ecology and its diffusion into a widespread popular enthusiasm. By creating a new conception of the meaning of biological community, the ecological sciences also suggested a new basis for moral community. Indeed, "ecology" tells us as much about the years after 1960 as "efficiency" does about the Progressive mind and the first surge of interest in the protection of what were called "natural resources" at the turn of the century. If, as Samuel Hays has shown, the conservationists of Theodore Roosevelt's and Gifford Pinchot's America believed in a "gospel of efficiency," then the new environmentalists could be said to subscribe to what I have called, elsewhere, a "gospel of ecology."[25] The quasi-religious fervor of the recent concern for nature, and some of its political muscle, can be understood as resulting from the introduction into traditional, utilitarian conservation of the idea that respecting the environment was an ethical, not just an economic, matter.

But what does it mean to say this? Speaking simply and in general terms for the time being, environmental ethics has come to signify two things. First, some people believe that it is right to protect and wrong to abuse nature (or certain of its components) from the standpoint of human interest. This idea gave an unprecedented moral dimension to the old prudential or utilitarian argument for conservation. But the more radical meaning, and the one that really pushes American liberalism to its conceptual limits (or, some say, beyond them), is that nature has intrinsic value and consequently possesses at least the right to exist. This position is sometimes called "biocentrism," "ecological egalitarianism," or "deep ecology," and it accords nature ethical status at least equal to that of humans. The antipode is "anthropocentrism," according to which humans are the measure of all value. The difference between the two viewpoints is the difference between feeling that cruelty to animals is bad for humans—as the old Anglo-American humanitarians believed[26]—and the recent belief that cruelty violates animals' rights. From these perspectives environmentalists can either think that people have a right to a healthy ecosystem or that the ecosystem itself possesses rights.

Of course, nature does not demand rights, and some moral philosophers even question whether anything so general as the "rights of nature" can exist at all. But, as we shall see, others use the term confidently. At the same time they recognize that wolves and maples and mountains do not petition for their rights. Human beings are the moral agents who have the responsibility to articulate and defend the rights of the other occupants of the planet. Such a conception of rights means that humans have duties or obligations toward nature. Environmental ethics involves people extending ethics to the environment by the exercise of self-restraint. In what follows, one of the central concerns is to analyze the significance of these ideas for ecology, theology, and philosophy, their implication for action, and their impact on the American environmental movement since World War II.

Another concern is the character and influence of American liberalism. Few would disagree that liberty is the single most potent concept in the history of American thought. The product of both Europe's democratic revolutions and, following Frederick Jackson Turner's hypothesis, the North American frontier, liberalism explains our national origins, delineates our ongoing mission, and anchors our ethics. Natural rights is a cultural given in America, essentially beyond debate as an idea. The liberal's characteristic belief in the goodness and intrinsic value of the individual leads to an endorsement of freedom, political equality, toleration, and self-determination. The most successful reform efforts in American history have occurred in the context of this liberal tradition.[27] When environmentalists began in the 1960s to talk about the rights of nature and the need to liberate this new oppressed minority from human tyranny, they used the language and ideals of liberalism. Old-style conservation, recast in ethical terms and plugged into the American liberal tradition, became the new, radical environmentalism.

Critics of the new environmentalism attacked the movement's negativism, charging it with not only being un-American but anti-human. The new "ecofreaks" and "druids" were said to set themselves squarely in the path of the American dream. Interestingly, many environmentalists accepted, even welcomed, this negative image. "Naturalists," Paul Shepard said with pride in 1969, "seem always to be *against* something."[28] Shepard's statement appeared in a book with the word "subversive" in its title. In fact, as early as 1964 Paul Sears had employed that word to characterize the broader implications of ecology, and seven years later political scientist Lynton Caldwell referred to "the subversive implications of ecology."[29] The point of the strong adjective was that the American propensity for unlimited growth, intense competition, and the domination of nature ran directly counter to ecological ideals such as stability, interdependence, and a community consciousness extended to include nonhuman beings and biophysical processes. So Shepard could conclude with reference to traditional American values and behavior that "the ideological status of ecology is that of a resistance movement. Its Rachel Carsons and Aldo Leopolds are subversive."[30]

Pushing this point still further, contemporary environmental philosophers such as Murray Bookchin called for a full-scale dismantling of America's "institutional and ethical framework." Without these "revolutionary changes" and the resulting establishment of an anarchistic "ecological society", Bookchin grimly predicted "the end of humanity's tenure on the planet."[31] Herbert Marcuse felt that the "liberation of nature" depended on the "coming revolution" against American economic and political traditions.[32] And William R. Catton, Jr., wrote about the inevitable crash of modern civilization that could be prevented only if it underwent "revolutionary change."[33] Theodore Roszak likewise called for sweeping and fundamental changes in American ideals and institutions on behalf of the rights of the planet. He, too, labeled contemporary environmentalism "profoundly subversive" because its aim was nothing less than the "disintegration" of contemporary American society and culture.[34] The deep ecologists added that meaningful reform was predicated on restructuring the nation's dominant social paradigm. From these points of view there seemed little about American culture worth building the brave new ecological world upon.

Much of the new environmentalists' criticism of American traditions is warranted, but in adopting a subversive, countercultural stance, they overlooked one important intellectual foundation for protecting nature that is quintessentially American: natural-rights philosophy, the old American ideal of liberty that they themselves were applying to nature. Conceived of as promoting the liberation of exploited and oppressed members of the American ecological community, even the most radical fringe of the contemporary environmental

movement can be understood not so much as a revolt against traditional American ideals as an extension and new application of them.
The alleged subversiveness of environmental ethics should be tempered with the recognition that its goal is the implementation of liberal values as old as the republic. This may not make modern environmentalism less radical, but it does place it more squarely in the
mainstream of American liberalism, which, after all, has had its revolutionary moments, too. Finally, from this point of view the goals
of the ethically oriented environmentalists may be more feasible
within the framework of American culture than even they themselves
believe.[35]

CHAPTER I

From Natural Rights to
the Rights of Nature

The American war is over: but this is far from being the case
with the American revolution. On the contrary, nothing but the
first act of the great drama is closed.
—*Benjamin Rush, 1787*

We are finally coming to recognize that the natural environment
is the exploited proletariat, the downtrodden nigger of every-
body's industrial system. . . . Nature must also have its natural
rights.
—*Theodore Roszak, 1978*

*I*t began, appropriately enough, outdoors—in a June-green meadow
called Runnymede alongside the River Thames. The English barons
who gathered there in 1215 forced King John to accept a lengthy list
of concessions which came to be known, in the Latin in which it was
written, as *Magna Carta*. Although the barons hardly thought of it in
such terms, they were in fact dealing with ethical dynamite that revolutionaries five centuries later would call "natural rights." The tendency of this concept to take on expanded meaning is one of the most
exciting characteristics of the liberal tradition. Whether this tradition
should expand to include nonhuman interests—perhaps even nature
as a whole—is the proposition under examination in the present
volume.

While it is easy to overstate and modernize the significance of
Magna Carta, there are some reasons for regarding it as the corner-
stone of liberty in Anglo-American culture. Set forth in this document for the first time was the idea that a certain segment of society,

in this case some twenty-five barons, possessed rights by virtue of their existence, independent of the will of England's king. Clause thirty-nine, for example, prohibited imprisonment or banishment except in accordance with law and as a result of the judgment of one's peers. *Magna Carta* placed other limitations on the royal power to tax property and confiscate land without the consent of the Great Council.[1] The concept of natural rights, and even some of the charter's wording, later figured in the making of the American government. Of course the barons at Runnymede would have been appalled at such extension of their principles. They had no conception of the rights of anyone save a male in the upper crust of English nobility. But time was on the side of ethical expansion.[2]

The thought of English philosopher John Locke (1632–1704) became the most important source of American natural-rights tradition.[3] As outlined in his *Two Treatises of Government* (1690), Locke's ideas contained a logic particularly compelling to a people engaged in building a society in a wilderness. The "state of nature" that underlay Locke's ethical system was a pre-social, pre-government condition in which all people were equal and free before God and each other. The natural or fundamental law that existed in this situation consisted of absolute and unchanging or, as Americans preferred, "unalienable" moral axioms. The most important of them was that every person, by the simple virtue of their existence, shared a natural right to continue existing. From this Locke derived his list of the natural rights of mankind: "Life, Liberty, Health, Limb or Goods."[4] In regard to "Goods," or what he alternately called "Property or Possessions," Locke believed a person had a right to that which he labored to produce. This principle would later prove troublesome in the case of slaves, and Thomas Jefferson, as we shall see, neatly avoided the difficulty in his 1776 formulation by the substitution of "happiness." Much later the sanctity of property would create a problem when environmentalists sought to treat the environment itself as having rights superior to ownership.

Locke did not go so far as his fellow philosopher Thomas Hobbes (1588–1679) in characterizing life in the state of nature as "solitary, poor, nasty, brutish and short,"[5] but he did acknowledge sufficient insecurity in nature to persuade rational people to organize a society and a government. He called the process a "social contract." Through it each individual surrendered some of the complete freedom characteristic of the state of nature, but retained the natural, pre-social or God-given rights to life, liberty, and property. Indeed the whole point of social and political organization was to safeguard these fundamental values. From this recognition stemmed one further right, revolution. If the government acted in ways that menaced the natural rights of the people, they were justified, according to Locke, in renouncing its power. Through revolution individuals reclaimed the protection of natural rights they had entrusted to the state through the social contract.

It followed that subscribers to Lockean principles favored constitutional forms of government (democracies and republics) over monarchies, where concentrated power was susceptible to corruption. Locke wrote his *Treatises* as a defense of England's "Glorious Revolution" of 1688, which tempered royal power with a written statement of the people's rights.

The potency of natural-rights ideology is such that one revolution breeds another. So it was that soon after the Glorious Revolution, and increasingly after 1760, English colonists in America began to flex their ethical muscles against yesterday's revolutionaries, now consolidated as the government of the mother country. What Bernard Bailyn calls "the transforming radicalism of the [American] Revolution"[6] was the idea that the English Parliament and monarchy were denying the colonists their natural rights. Going back five hundred years for justification, American revolutionaries like James Otis contended that "Magna Carta itself is a . . . proclamation" of the people's uncompromised possession "of their original, inherent, indefeasible, natural rights."[7] Time and time again, as independence approached, Americans employed words such as "tyranny," "slavery," and "oppression" to describe their condition. Liberty was the objective, and the revolutionary mind elevated it to the status of a sacred and secular mission.

The Declaration of Independence of 1776 marked the fullest flowering to that date of natural-rights philosophy. As Carl Becker was among the first to understand, Jefferson's manifesto was not so much original thought as it was a compilation of ideals that had circulated widely in England, France, and North America for at least a century. But Jefferson's phraseology was especially felicitous. "The laws of nature and of nature's God," he wrote, are the foundations from which reason and conscience reveal "self-evident" truth, namely, "that all men are created equal" in their possession of "certain unalienable rights." The three Jefferson chose to enumerate were, of course, "life, liberty, and the pursuit of happiness."[8]

But Jefferson did not really mean what he wrote. In practice some people were more equal than others. Women, for example, were not full partners in the spirit of 1776. Neither were slaves nor Indians,

and most of the states initially required even white males to be property holders and taxpayers. Most of the restrictions on white male
suffrage withered away in the early nineteenth century,[9] but blacks
were not constitutionally enfranchised until 1870 and a half century
more elapsed before females (1920) and Indians (1924) achieved suffrage. Civil rights for blacks dominated social protests in the 1950s
and 1960s. Clearly the American Revolution did not create an egalitarian product so much as it started a process.[10] Two centuries after
Jefferson's articulation of America's preeminent ideal its fullest implications were still being discovered in the movement for the rights of
nature.

    Natural-rights principles exploded into Western thought in the
seventeenth and eighteenth centuries. They spawned one revolution
in Massachusetts which, in turn, helped inspire a powerful wave of
liberalism throughout the Western world. The magic circle of rights
holders was widening. This was the sense of Benjamin Rush's 1787
comment, above, about the ongoing American Revolution. Subsequent acts in Rush's "great drama" would take the democratic impulse far beyond what the eighteenth-century revolutionaries imag-
ined possible or even desirable. According to Robert R. Palmer, the
liberal leaders in revolutionary America were "groping toward a new
kind of community."[11] Only the most radical among them understood that the concept of community might be extended beyond the
confines of the human race. The idea, however, was not entirely new.

    Greek and Roman philosophers had a clear conception of natural,
as opposed to man-made, law. Although they did not speak about
"rights," they understood that people had existed prior to government or indeed any civil order. This state of raw nature was organized according to certain biological principles centered on the facts
of existence and survival. In Latin these principles were called *jus na-
turae* or *jus naturale*. In contrast, the ideas of justice that humankind
overlaid on this basic order were thought of as the *jus commune,* the
common law applied to the people and embodied in the laws of states
and nations.[12] But where did nonhuman beings fit? It was obvious to
classical thinkers that humans had not been alone in the wilderness,
Eden, or whatever state of nature one chose to place at the dawn of
history. Animals were there, too, not to speak of less sophisticated
forms of life, along with the inanimate components of the environment. What, then, was the right relationship of humans to these fellow travelers in the stream of time?

    Concerned about these questions, Romans found it logical to as-
sume the existence of another body of moral precepts: the *jus ani-*

malium. It implied that animals possessed what later philosophers would call inherent or natural rights independent of human civilization and government. As the third-century Roman jurist Ulpian understood it, the *jus animalium* was part of the *jus naturale* because the latter includes "that which nature has taught all animals; this law indeed is not peculiar to the human race, but belongs to all animals." [13] Granted, Ulpian included only animals in his concept of justice, but it derived from the idea that nature as a whole constituted an order that humankind should respect.

After the decline of Greece and Rome and the advent of Christianity, nature did not fare well in Western ethics. [14] Increasingly people assumed that nature, animals included, had no rights, and that nonhuman beings existed to serve human beings. There was no extended ethical community. It followed that the appropriate relationship of people to nature emphasized expediency and utility. There need be no guilty consciences because the only values of nature were instrumental or utilitarian—defined, that is, in terms of human needs. The Christian version of this argument turned to Genesis for evidence that God gave humankind dominion over nature and the right to exploit it without restraint. Understandably, early philosophers such as Hugo Grotius (1583–1645) and Samuel Pufendorf (1632–1694) could believe that the human relationship to the environment was not a subject for ethical concern. Departing from Ulpian, they argued that natural rights did not derive from a pre-social state of nature but only from *human* nature. This meant that law did not originate in fundamental principles of justice common to people and animals. Rather it represented a set of manmade rules that reflected human interests. So Pufendorf could conclude, "there is no common rights/law between man and brutes." John Rodman has identified this seventeenth-century rejection of animal rights as a "turning point in the history of thought." [15]

In the early modern period discussion of the extent to which ethics should be applied to nature swirled around the question of vivisection. At its worst this practice involved cutting up unanesthetized animals that had been tied or nailed live to a board. As medical science emerged in the seventeenth century, it relied on vivisection to study the workings of the body. But the practice drew the wrath of early humanitarians, and the vivisectors turned to René Descartes (1596–1650) to justify their research methods. A celebrated mathematician, physiologist, and psychologist, Descartes provided a general philosophy of the irrelevance of ethics to the human-nature relationship. Animals, according to Descartes, were insensible and irrational machines. They moved, like clocks, but could not feel pain. Lacking minds, animals could not be harmed. They did not suffer. They were, in Descartes's sense of the term, unconscious. Humans, on the other hand, had souls and minds. Thinking, in fact, defined the human organism. "I think, therefore I am" was Descartes's basic axiom. This dualism, the separateness of humans and nature, justified vivisection and indeed any human action toward the environment. Descartes left no doubt that people were the "masters and possessors of nature."[16] The nonhuman world became a "thing." Descartes understood this objectification of nature as an important prerequisite to the progress of science and civilization.

An alternate, but extremely minor, train of Western thought that challenged anthropocentrism derived in part from the classical Greco-Roman idea that animals were part of the state of nature and the subjects of natural law. Although Christianity weakened the ideas of an extended community, the principle of *jus animalium* persisted in European thought. Intriguing but fragmentary evidence suggests that from time to time in the Middle Ages courts of law conducted criminal trials of animals that, for instance, killed humans.[17] This practice makes the argument of the 1970s that trees and other natural objects should have standing before the law less novel than it might appear at first glance.[18]

Interestingly, the first record of a law respecting the rights of nonhuman beings, or at least human duties toward them, appeared in the Massachusetts Bay Colony. The author of "The Body of Liberties," which the General Court adopted in 1641, was Nathaniel Ward (1578–1652). A lawyer and later a minister, Ward came to New England in 1634, settling in Ipswich. At the request of the court he prepared the first codification of the colony's statutes. Ward's list of "rites," by which he meant "rights," contained as the ninety-second item the stipulation that "no man shall exercise any Tirranny or Crueltie towards any bruite Creature which are usuallie kept for man's use." The ninety-third "rite" obliged persons who "leade or drive Cattel" to rest and refresh them periodically.[19] Obviously, utilitarianism is evident here—only domestic creatures are protected— but it is significant that in 1641, at the height of Descartes's influence in Europe, the first New Englanders endorsed the idea that animals were not unfeeling machines. And the use of the word "Tirranny" seems to imply the idea of the natural rights or freedoms of nonhuman beings in the tradition of *jus animalium*. Perhaps the task of creating a new society in a wilderness made the Puritans more mindful of comprehensive ethical principles derived from a state of nature similar to the one they occupied.

The treatment of animals was not a major concern with John Locke but property was, and the fact that animals could be owned resulted in their acquiring some rights in his philosophy. These, of course, derived from the rights of the owner, not the animal, and were otherwise related to human interests. In *Some Thoughts Concerning Education* (1693) Locke reasoned, in opposition to Descartes, that animals can suffer and be harmed and that harming them needlessly is morally wrong. It becomes clear that this is not due to the natural rights of animals but to the effects of cruelty to animals on people. Locke notes that many children "*torment,* and treat very roughly young Birds, Butterflies, and other such poor Animals, which fall into their Hands." He feels this behavior should be stopped and corrected because it "will, by Degrees, harden their Minds even towards Men." People, Locke continues, "who delight in the Suffering and Destruction of Inferiour Creatures, will not . . . be very compassionate, or benign to those of their own kind." Locke concludes this discussion with a commendation of a mother of his acquaintance who made sure her children took responsibility for the welfare of their "Dogs, Squirils, Birds," and other pets. He felt these children were on their way to becoming responsible members of society. In his 1693 discourse, then, Locke moved beyond a strict concept of utility. Not only customarily owned and useful animals like cattle and horses should be well treated, but also squirrels, birds, insects— indeed "any living Creature."[20]

Nathaniel Ward and John Locke were not alone in opposing cruelty to animals. As early as the fifteenth century, and increasingly in the seventeenth and eighteenth, protests sounded over practices such as vivisection, cock-fighting, staged fights with dogs known as bull- and bear-baiting, fox hunting, and the sort of purposeless brutality Locke addressed in 1693. Two arguments appeared most frequently. The early English humane movement pointed, like Locke, to the adverse effects of cruelty to animals on its human perpetrators. It also contended that since animals were part of God's creation, humans, as the most favored and powerful form of life, had the responsibility of being good trustees or stewards of their welfare on God's behalf. Some formulations of this argument even hinted that God would keep account of cruelty and dole out appropriate punishments. The first humanitarian protests in no way questioned the assumption that nature existed for mankind. But they did call for the human dominion to be as gentle as possible.[21]

Amidst the undeniable potency of anthropocentrism and dualism in Western thought in the seventeenth and eighteenth centuries, one finds a weaker yet persistent notion that leads directly to the concept of expanded community on which environmental ethics rests. It was the revolutionary idea that the world did not exist for humanity alone. Pre-ecological thinkers generally set this idea in a religious context. All of nature existed because of and for the glory of God, the Creator. He cared as much about the welfare of the most insignificant being as about human beings. Another source of this humbling concept was the philosophy of animism or organicism, the belief that a single and continuous force permeated all beings and things, making the world, in effect, one large organism.

For Henry More (1614–1687), an animist who taught at Cambridge University, there was a "Soul of the World, or Spirit of Nature" (he called it the "Anima Mundi") present in every part in nature. This mysterious "plastical power" literally held the world together.[22] In Germany Gottfried Leibnitz (1646–1716) not only discarded the distinction between humans and nature so dear to Descartes but also rejected the separation of the living from the nonliving. Everything, he believed, was interconnected. But recent ecophilosophers, notably George Sessions, point to Baruch Spinoza (1632–1677) as the organicist who most closely anticipated both ecological consciousness and environmental ethics. In marked contrast to his anthropocentric contemporaries such as Descartes, the Dutch thinker put forward the pantheistic notion that every being or object—wolves, maple trees, humans, rocks, stars—was a temporary manifestation of a common God-created substance. When a person died, the matter that was his body became something else: soil and food for a plant, for instance, which might nourish a deer and, in turn, a wolf or another person. Spinoza's understanding of these interrelationships made it possible for him to place ultimate ethical value on the whole, the system, rather than on any single and transitory part. There was no "lower" nor "higher" in his philosophy. His idea of community had no bounds and neither, it followed, did his ethics. A tree or a rock had as much value and right to exist as a person.[23]

The English botanist John Ray (1627–1705) learned about animistic philosophy from his mentor Henry More. Ray spent a lifetime collecting and categorizing plants. The result was *Historia Generalis Plantarum* (1686–1704), a three-volume survey of the world's flora regarded as one of the high points of British natural science. In the course of his research Ray developed a global perspective as well as a profound admiration for natural processes. He became convinced that the idea that the whole natural world existed only for people's benefit was an unsupportable conceit. So, at the age of sixty-four,

John Ray turned from botany to philosophy and wrote *The Wisdom of God Manifested in the Works of Creation* (1691). His thesis distilled to a single sentence: "It is a generally received opinion that all this visible world was created for Man; that Man is the end of the Creation, as if there were no other end of any creature but some way or other to be serviceable to man . . . yet," Ray continued, "wise men nowadays think otherwise."[24] Ray believed that animals and plants exist to glorify God or, as his friend More put it, "to enjoy themselves."[25] Their value, their right to life, in other words, did not depend on their utilitarian function. This way of thinking neatly dethroned humans from the dominant status accorded them by traditional Christianity and Cartesian science. At least in the theory of the animists the circle was clearly widening.

It remained for the gifted British poet Alexander Pope (1688–1744) to summarize thousands of pages of animist philosophy in a few pointed lines. In his *Essay on Man* (1733) Pope wrote that living things

> Are all but parts of one stupendous whole,
> Whose body Nature is, and God the soul.

Drawing the implications of organicism for the human-animal relationship, he continued:

> Has God, thou fool!, work'd solely for good,
> Thy job, thy pastime, attire, thy food? . . .
> Know, Nature's children all divide her care;
> The fur that warms a monarch, warm'd a bear.[26]

With "Nature's children" defined as everything alive, Pope laid the intellectual foundation for an expanded ethic.

It is helpful to remember that Spinoza, Ray, and Pope wrote during a time of rapidly widening scientific horizons and related challenges to anthropocentrism. Telescopes suggested that the earth was hardly the center of the universe. John Ray, for one, thought it conceivable that there were living beings on other planets, possibly even on the moon. How could such ideas square with the notion that all life served humankind? At the other end of the scientific spectrum, the microscope revealed a complex community on which people seemed to depend rather than the other way around. Anton van Leeuwenhoek (1632–1723), the pioneer microbiologist, knew that there were more tiny creatures in his mouth than there were people in Holland.[27] Explorers revealed the existence of vast uninhabited wildernesses on the face of the earth that were teeming with life, perfect and complete in and of themselves and never even seen by humans. In sum, the more humans learned about nature, the more difficult it became to entertain the notion that the universe, or even the vacant field down the street, existed *for* humans. Humanity did not seem to be the master of nature so much as one of the members of the natural community. Charles Darwin, as we shall see, would put the capstone on this line of reasoning in 1859.

Donald Worster has argued persuasively in *Nature's Economy* that it would be a mistake to read an environmental ethic into the work of the seventeenth- and eighteenth-century organicists. Although they questioned anthropocentrism, they remained convinced of the legitimacy of human control of the natural world. As the most advanced form of life, human beings would continue to use other beings and modify the environment. The point was to do so carefully, according to the principles of good stewardship, and always mindful of the fact that other interests—God's, other life-forms'—were involved. From this point of view the impact of people on the planet carried with it some disturbing ethical problems. John Bruckner (1726–1804), for example, worried about English expansion into the New World. In *A Philosophical Survey of the Animal Creation* (1768) he wondered if the transformation of the American wilderness was not breaking the "web of life" (Bruckner was among the first to use this term, so central to later ecological science) and "the whole plan of Providence." [28] It occurred to Bruckner that many species would be seriously harmed, perhaps rendered extinct, in the process of settling the virgin land. This reduction in the completeness of God's creation troubled Reverend Bruckner, but he shied away from the possible conclusion that it would be morally wrong. Nor did Bruckner address the question of what Americans should do. Instead, he expressed confidence that God's wondrous plan would accommodate even thoughtless human action.

Although the eighteenth century was clearly not ready for an environmental movement, the matter of the ethics of humankind's relationship to at least parts of the environment surfaced with increasing frequency at the same time that democratic revolutions swept America and France. Evidently all the commotion about the rights of man caused at least a few intellectuals to take the next logical steps. In 1776 Dr. Humphrey Primatt opened the English discussion of animal rights with a treatise entitled *A Dissertation on the Duty of Mercy and Sin of Cruelty to Brute Animals*. A minister, Primatt argued that all creatures, being works of God, deserved humane treatment. It was clear to him that since pain was *"Evil,"* cruelty to any form of life was "ATHEISM" and "INFIDELITY."[29]

Writing in 1789, England's Jeremy Bentham used familiar liberal rhetoric to argue for an end to cruelty toward animals. "The day *may* come," he declared, "when the rest of the animal creation may acquire those rights which never could have been withholden from them but by the hand of tyranny."[30] Bentham's ethics stemmed from his "greatest happiness principle." Pain was bad, pleasure good. It followed that the rightness or wrongness of an act stemmed from the degree to which it caused pleasure or pain. Bentham referred to these consequences of an action as its utility. His doctrine was known as utilitarianism, but it contained the potential of transcending a narrowly anthropocentric sense of the term. Bentham understood how the logic of the maximization of happiness could extend from colonists to slaves to nonhuman beings. He reasoned that "the blackness of the skin is no reason why a human being should be abandoned without redress to the caprice of a tormentor. It may come one day to be recognized, that the number of the legs, the villosity of the skin, or the termination of the *os sacrum* [i.e., spinal base], are reasons equally insufficient for abandoning a sensitive being to the same fate." Bentham rejected the ability to reason or to talk as an ethical dividing line between people and other forms of life. "The question," he concluded in a passage much-quoted by later humanitarians, "is not, Can they *reason?* nor Can they *talk?*, but Can they *suffer?*"[31]

According to Bentham's utilitarianism the most unethical action was that which caused the most pain. It followed for him, as it did for his student John Stuart Mill, that cruelty to people, whose nervous systems were the most refined, was worse than cruelty to lower forms of life, but this was a quantitative difference only. An ethical individual or society should strive to maximize pleasure and minimize pain in general, wherever it existed. And animals, he disagreed with Descartes, felt pain. So, Bentham asked, "Why should the law refuse its protection to any sensitive being?" An encouraging example in support of his challenge came from one form of human liberation: "We have begun by attending to the condition of slaves; we shall finish by softening that of all the animals which assist our labours or supply our wants." Apparently, for Bentham, animals useful to people, like horses and chickens, occupied an ethical status below slaves but superior to other life forms. Yet in an earlier statement in the same passage he predicted, "The time will come, when humanity will extend its mantle over every thing which breathes."[32]

The "mantle" to which Bentham referred meant moral status and legal protection.

Bentham's philosophy, and the eighteenth- and nineteenth-century English humane movement in general, treated cruelty to animals as a *human* wrong or, from a religious perspective, a sin. But some of Bentham's contemporaries advanced to a still more radical position, attributing rights to animals and discussing their treatment in terms of justice. John Lawrence, a little-known English country gentleman and a self-styled literary farmer, is one instance. Lawrence's liberal political persuasion led him to approve of the principles of the American and French revolutions, favor the abolition of the slave trade, and support women's rights. And Lawrence went further. In 1796 he wrote *A Philosophical Treatise on Horses and on the Moral Duties of Man towards the Brute Creation.* He began a chapter entitled "On the Rights of Beasts" with a look at the reason for "the barbarous, unfeeling and capricious conduct of man to brute creation." The problem, in a nutshell, was that animals were "utterly devoid of rights and placed without the pall of justice." Lawrence rejected this idea and the Cartesian view that animals were "merely for the use and purposes of man." Drawing on the principles of natural law, he argued that "life, intelligence, and feeling necessarily imply rights." What he meant was that animals were, in these respects, like people and that "the essence of justice" was not "divisible."[33]

For John Lawrence in the 1790s the root of the trouble was "a defect in the constitution of all communities." He went on to say that no human government had ever recognized "the *jus animalium,* which surely ought to form a part of the jurisprudence of every system founded on the principles of justice and humanity." Then Lawrence issued his manifesto, remarkable even in an age when declarations of the rights of man appeared frequently: "I therefore propose that the Rights of Beasts be formally acknowledged by the state, and that a law be framed upon that principle, to guard and protect them from flagrant and wanton cruelty."[34]

In the seven hundred pages of his book Lawrence had plenty of space to explain his position. He was not, he made clear, opposed to killing animals for food provided it was done in a quick and humane manner. He detested bull-baiting and cock-fighting, but he accepted fox hunting. Reflecting Bentham's utilitarianism, he thought it was more merciful to destroy an overabundance of animals than to let them starve and die slowly and painfully. In short, Lawrence was not a purist. He recognized the presence in England of people "a step beyond me" who would not eat meat. And he satirized still more radical humanitarians who would "build hospitals for lice and fleas." Essentially, Lawrence's ethics centered on the animals humans used, especially horses, but his concept of "the Rights of Beasts" marked a significant ethical evolution in Western thought.[35]

The translation of humanitarian ideals into law can be traced to a 1596 ordinance in the English community of Chester that prohibited bear-baiting. Cock-fighting became the subject of local English regulation in the seventeenth century. The 1641 "Body of Liberties" of Massachusetts Bay was the earliest general law respecting cruelty to domestic animals in Anglo-American jurisprudence.

Broader, more substantive, and better-enforced laws arrived with the liberating revolutions of the late eighteenth century, which alerted humanitarians to the logic of an extended philosophy of natural rights. In 1800 the English Parliament considered, but did not pass, a nationwide ban on the baiting of bulls. Nine years later, Lord Thomas Erskine, a friend of Bentham's, rose in Parliament to propose legislation prohibiting cruelty to domestic animals. Its passage, he predicted, would launch a new era of benevolence in world history. But the new era had to wait until June 22, 1822, when Richard "Humanity Dick" Martin (1754–1834), an Irish landlord and friend of both John Lawrence and Thomas Erskine, pushed through to adoption the Ill-Treatment of Cattle (or Martin's) Act. Although Martin hoped for a broader scope, the final version of this action concerned only the larger domesticated animals. English society in 1822 was not prepared to go further. A sense of the possible also dictated that Martin's Act be phrased in terms of the injury to other person's animals. The lawmakers, in other words, were reluctant to take on the issue of *owner*-caused cruelty to animals. (The same reluctance appeared in early attempts to improve master-slave and husband-wife relationships.) Property remained too sacrosanct, too much a natural right in itself, to be challenged by the natural rights of nonhuman beings. Nonetheless, Martin's Act stands out as the first instance of a modern legislature making cruelty to an animal a punishable, nationwide offense.[36]

In 1824 Richard Martin and other English humanitarians organized a Society (after 1840, the Royal Society) for the Prevention of Cruelty to Animals (RSPCA). It is significant from the standpoint of natural rights extension that several of the founders of the RSPCA, notably William Wilberforce, had been leaders in the English abolition of slavery and the slave trade. Evidently the idea of liberating oppressed beings was not easily confined to humankind. John Stuart Mill, the nineteenth century's preeminent philosopher of liberalism, wrote in 1848 that the laws making it a crime for parents to abuse their children should be extended to "apply not less strongly to the case of those unfortunate slaves and victims . . . the lower animals."[37] Mill later declined an offer to become the vice-president of the RSPCA on the grounds that this upper-class organization ignored the transgressions of its own members (fox hunting, for example, and the use of feathers and furs in high fashion) and concentrated instead on the vices of the poor. In support of Mill's analysis, the initial successes of England's friends-to-animals groups concerned the nationwide abolition of lower-class diversions such as bear- and bull-baiting (1835) and cock-fighting (1849).[38]

The struggle for humanitarian legislation in England reached a high point in 1876 with the passage of the British Cruelty to Animals Act. Vivisection was at issue, and it elicited strong opinions from the leading members of England's scientific and humanitarian communities. The motives of the antivivisectionists were complex. For Frances Power Cobbe, hostility toward medical science and a desire to gain political power for women figured prominently, but so did her belief in animal immortality and in a sentimental, anthropomorphic cult of pets. The antivivisectionists did not talk about *animals'* rights; rather they stressed that it was wrong for humans, particularly those who fancied themselves members of the world's most advanced society, to dissect living animals in the name of science. The 1876 act emerged as something of a compromise: vivisection could continued but only in licensed medical centers and only if animal pain was minimized with anesthetics. There were many loopholes through which experimenters with animals could escape. But the whole vivisection issue raised as never before the moral dilemmas inherent in extending ethics beyond the human-to-human dimension.[39]

The late Victorian era produced a flurry of ethical writings notable for the radical nature of their arguments. The celebrated British historian Arthur Helps, for example, extended his ethics to include insects. The following conversation occurred in his 1873 volume, *Some Talk about Animals and Their Masters:*

MILVERTON: I distinctly hold that every living creature has its rights, and that justice, in the highest form, may be applied to it.

ELLESMERE: Every animal has its rights . . . why stop there? Every reptile then; every insect?

MILVERTON: Certainly. . . . Look there: you see, at this moment, in front of the open window, a number of flying creatures . . . whirling about in a mazy dance, and, as far as we can judge enjoying themselves very much, and doing us no harm. They are not even touching any of that "property" which the lawyers love so well. If you were to kill any of them at this moment, I think it would not merely be cruelty, but an invasion of right.[40]

Edward B. Nicholson, a librarian at the London Institution, dedicated his 1879 contribution to the animal rights literature to Arthur Helps and to John Lawrence, along with the better-known Jeremy Bentham. The book began with an attack on the prevailing arguments against ethical extension. Nicholson dismissed the view that animals have no powers of reason as inconsistent with common observation of household pets. Granted an animal's "functions of mind are fewer and its feeling more limited than that of a man." But so are those of a human idiot, Nicholson continued, and no ethical person proposes to deny such a person's rights to life and, as appropriate, to liberty. (Animal rights advocates a century later would frequently use this line of argument.) As for the issue of the souls that allegedly survive after human deaths, Nicholson argued that the proposition is incapable of being proved and hence "cannot be used to bar a natural right" to animals.[41]

Turning to a refutation of the philosophy of Descartes, Nicholson contended that animals have nervous systems just as people do and are certainly capable of experiencing pain and pleasure. He concluded that *"animals have the same abstract Rights of Life and Personal Liberty with man."* Nicholson qualified this assertion on the grounds that people's need for sustenance and living space justifies killing animals for food and where their numbers threaten to overcrowd the earth. But in other respects the London librarian made bold to accord animals not a lower order of natural rights but *"the same"* rights as humans'.[42]

If the thought of Primatt, Bentham, Lawrence, Martin, Mill, and Nicholson launched the English consideration of an extended ethical community, the idea reached a nineteenth-century crescendo in the mind of Henry S. Salt. So complete was Salt's rejection of English mores that when he gave up a comfortable career as a schoolmaster at Eton in 1885 and retreated to a life of deliberate simplicity in the Surrey countryside, he used strips cut from his academic gowns to tie up his vines and vegetables. A multifaceted thinker and activist, Salt, like his hero Henry David Thoreau, delighted in being out of step with the dominant values of his age. He advocated socialism at a time of rampant capitalism, vegetarianism in a culture that celebrated roast beef, nonviolent resistance during World War I, and animal rights. In 1891 Salt took the lead in founding the Humanitarian League, and the next year he published *Animals' Rights Considered in Relation to Social Progress,* the most sophisticated treatment of the issue since John Lawrence's 1796 tract and one that continues to influence American environmental thought.[43]

Salt made his position clear at the outset: if humans have rights to life and liberty, so do animals. Both derived from natural rights, *jus animalium* in the case of animals. Martin's Act of 1822, according to Salt, marked the initial appearance of *jus animalium* in English law, but he dryly noted it had been applied "rather in the interests of *property* than of *principle.*" What was lacking in English and American attitudes, Salt felt, was "a true sense of kinship" with nonhuman beings. The community had to be widened. There followed a remarkable statement for Salt's time and place: "If we are ever going to do justice to the lower races [i.e., animals], we must get rid of the antiquated notion of a 'great gulf' fixed between them and mankind, and must recognize the common bond of humanity that unites all living beings in one universal brotherhood." In several instances Salt extended natural-rights philosophy so far as almost to imply that humans and animals should and would ultimately participate together in a common government. Anticipating Gary Snyder by eight decades, he called for the perfection of democracy by the inclusion of "all living things within its scope." And again he declared, "it is not human life only that is loveable and sacred, but *all* innocent and beautiful life: the great republic of the future will not confine its beneficence to man."[44]

Critics of Salt's ideas in the 1890s jumped on his homogenization of living things into one "great republic." British philospher David G. Ritchie, for example, argued that animals were not members of human society. While we should be kind to them, it was incorrect to treat animals "as if they had rights against us." Continuing his argument that ethics were entirely one-sided—a gratuitous extension by humans to animals—Ritchie engaged Salt on the concept of animal protection laws. Salt maintained that these proved animals had rights. Ritchie disagreed. "Because a work of art or some ancient monument is protected by law from injury, do we speak of the 'rights' of pictures or stones?"[45] In Ritchie's view, clearly not. Joseph Rickaby, a Jesuit, went further in his criticism of Salt. "Brute beasts," he thundered, "cannot have any rights. . . . They are of the number of *things.*" Consequently "we have no duties of charity, nor duties of any kind, to the lower animals, as neither to sticks and stones." Animals, he concluded, "exist for us, not for themselves."[46]

Henry Salt could not ignore such arguments, and he was too acute a thinker really to believe that humans and animals could have reciprocal ethical and political relationships. He knew that right and wrong were human concepts. Animals might have rights in the sense of being the beneficiaries of ethical extension, but they could not be expected to act ethically themselves. So in other parts of *Animals' Rights* (1892) Salt made it clear that the liberation of animals would depend on human beings reaching their full ethical potential, becoming, as Salt put it on his final page, "truly man." In this way Salt adroitly turned the animal rights movement into a movement for human improvement with which few could disagree. The key passage read: "To advocate the rights of animals is far more than to plead for compassion or justice towards the victims of ill-usage; it is not only, and not primarily, for the sake of the victims that we plead, but for the sake of mankind itself. Our true civilisation, our race-progress, our *humanity* . . . are concerned in this development; it is ourselves . . . that we wrong, when we trample on the rights of the fellow-beings, human or animal, over whom we chance to hold jurisdiction."[47] In this way Salt paradoxically transcended anthropocentrism by its reemphasis. He also marked himself as a transitional figure whose ethics stopped short of the radical nonanthropocentrism of modern animal rightists.

Salt had no problem linking animal rights to reforms of human-to-human relationships. In an essay in *Cruelties of Civilization* (1897) he stated, "The emancipation of men from cruelty and injustice will bring with it in due course the emancipation of animals also. The two reforms are inseparably connected, and neither can be fully realized alone." He envisioned democracy expanded to include all people and all nonhuman beings. In Salt's view "it is only by the spread of the same democratic spirit that animals can enjoy the 'rights' for which even men have so long struggled in vain."[48] Salt was interested in a full-scale overhaul of his civilization. He contributed to the growing interest in socialism among late nineteenth-century English and American intellectuals. Indeed, Henry David Thoreau, whose biography Salt wrote in 1890, interested him more as an exponent of the release of human potential from a repressive political and economic system than as a naturalist.[49] The Social Democratic Federation and the Fabian Society attracted Salt's attention. So did the ideas of the American tax reformer Henry George, whose *Progress and Poverty* (1879) challenged private ownership of the earth. From Salt's perspective, capitalism victimized both nature and people. In his autobiography, *Seventy Years among Savages* (years, that is, in England), Salt recalled his reasons for leaving the posh Eton subculture in 1885:

"We Eton masters . . . were but cannibals in cap and gown—almost literally cannibals, as devouring the flesh and blood of the higher nonhuman animals so closely akin to us, and indirectly cannibals, as living by the sweat and toil of the classes who do the hard work of the world."[50]

Henry Salt had no doubt that injustice to nonhuman beings was part of a general social malaise. "The present unequal and inequitable social system . . . where commercial profit is avowed to be the main object of work" could never give appropriate consideration to the well-being of men and women, much less to that of animals. Reform, he believed, would never come voluntarily from those who held and benefited from economic and political power. Socialism might help in this respect. But society also needed, perhaps as a preliminary to socialism, a sweeping program of education in the true meaning of "humanism." Not only children needed instruction in the reasons for techniques of humane behavior, but "our scientists, our religionists, our moralists, and our men of letters." Once education had transformed society's ethics, Salt assumed, the law would change because "legislation is the record, the register, of the moral sense of the community; it follows, not precedes, the development of . . . moral sense."[51]

The bulk of *Animals' Rights* is a diatribe against the customs and institutions of Victorian England of the early 1890s. Salt attacked the "murderous millinery" industry that was bringing numerous species to the brink of extinction so that "idle gentlemen and ladies may bedeck themselves . . . in borrowed skins and feathers." He railed against sport hunting as "amateur butchery" and in a ten-year campaign led the Humanitarian League in a successful fight against the Royal Buckhounds, the Queen's own pack of elite hunting dogs expert in chasing down deer released from carts. The Buckhounds had existed in England for seven centuries, and Salt's victory attracted widespread public attention. "Experimental Torture" headed another Salt chapter, this one concerning cruelty to animals in the name of science. Salt rejected the "moral . . . short cut" that held a wrong to be right if it benefited posterity. He concluded his book with a forty-page section by Albert Leffingwell, a New York physician and humanitarian, on vivisection in America. England had regulated the practice in 1876, but in the United States the dissection of living animals went unchallenged until the Animal Welfare Act of 1966. Leffingwell's discussion included a paean to William Wilberforce and William Lloyd Garrison and a plea that their example in crusading against slavery in England and America stimulate a later generation to abolish the torture of animals.[52]

Despite Salt's bitter criticism of his society (a 1926 collection of his poetry bore the title *Homo Rapiens*), he remained confident that progress would be made toward the elevation of human morality and the consequent liberation of animals. The capacity for moral growth "of such men as St. Francis and Thoreau" reminded him of "what far-reaching possibilities still lie before us." Salt took still more encouragement from his reading of history. He found in William E. H. Lecky's *History of European Morals* (1869) the following passage under the heading "The Natural History of Morals": "At one time, the benevolent affections embrace merely the family, soon the circle expanding includes first a class, then a nation, then a coalition of nations, then all humanity and finally, its influence is felt in the dealings of man with the animal world."[53] From this Salt generalized that "every great liberating movement" had progressed from a vague sense of sympathy to a clear conception of rights. The necessary precondition was for the oppressors to recognize the oppressed as members of their community.

Salt had no problems with this extension. He understood that humans and the "lower races" were one in being animals, in possessing natural rights, and in their status as parts of nature. Not surprisingly, Salt drew parallels between abolitionism and humanitarianism. "The present condition of the highly organized domestic animals," he wrote, "is in many ways very analogous to that of the negro slaves of a hundred years ago." Both suffered "exclusion from the common pale of humanity" and experienced "the same deliberate stubborn denial of their social 'rights'". Clearly Salt hoped that the moral evolution that liberated colonists and freed slaves in the nineteenth century would continue toward the emancipation of animals. Summarizing his life's work in 1935, he expressed the hope that "the religion of the future will be a belief in a Creed of Kinship, a charter of human and sub-human relationships."[54]

It is true that Lawrence, Bentham, Nicholson, Salt, and other nineteenth-century English humanitarians might have gone further. Their emphasis was strictly on animals and domesticated ones at that. "Environment" did not figure in their vocabulary, but their humanitarianism was an ideological building block leading to environmental ethics. Further development awaited the science of ecology and the proof that the "kinship" or "brotherhood" Salt and his colleagues idealized signified a dependency grounded in scientific fact. Meanwhile, Salt's achievement in *Animals' Rights* was to fuse the ancient doctrine of natural rights with eighteenth- and nineteenth-century liberalism, and to advance the concept to its fullest expression before the twentieth century.

Henry Salt was one of the small group of Anglo-American intellectuals who created Henry David Thoreau's modern reputation.[55] In the process his own reputation and influence grew. Just as Salt hoped, the twentieth century became increasingly sympathetic to the idea of including at least some parts of nature in an ethical system. Salt's original 1892 tract appeared in book editions in 1894, 1899, 1915, and, revised to address criticism, 1922. It was widely known in the United States. The 1894 edition, which included the essay on vivisection by the American physician Leffingwell, appeared as the result of financial subsidy by a "Miss Eddy" of Providence, Rhode Island. Salt and his benefactress distributed the book, free, to libraries throughout the United States. The latest American edition of *Animals' Rights* appeared in 1980, from the Society for Animal Rights.

While Salt's work was hardly popular in the 1890s, he struck chords that subsequent advocates of animals and the environment would echo. A few years after Salt, University of Michigan professor Edward P. Evans argued that any attempt to set humankind apart from nature is "philosophically false and morally pernicious,"[56] and in 1910 W J McGee described Progressive conservation as a way to perfect American liberty or, as he put it, "to round out the American Revolution."[57] In 1949, after ecology had begun to widen the ethical circle, Aldo Leopold advocated a "land ethic" that "changes the role of *Homo sapiens* from conqueror of the land community to plain member and citizen of it."[58] By this time the cutting edge of environmental philosophy was beginning to transcend Salt's fixation on animals. Michael W. Fox, an officer of the Humane Society of the United States, declared in 1978 that "if a human has a natural right, by virtue of his very being, to be free, . . . then surely this right should be accorded to all other living creatures."[59] In the same year Theodore Roszak followed Salt in seeing the emancipation of slaves and the laboring classes as stages in moral evolution pointing to the realization "that nature must also have its natural rights."[60] Indeed, books like Peter Singer's *Animal Liberation* (1975) and Tom Regan's *The Case for Animal Rights* (1983) built directly on Salt's arguments. The difference was that Singer, Regan, and the holistic environmental ethicists labored in a more sympathetic intellectual and political context. A century after Salt's 1885 rebellion against the English establishment, the idea of extending natural rights to include the rights of nature could no longer be brushed aside as a perversion of liberalism. For increasing numbers it was the new frontier of that philosophy.

CHAPTER 2

Ideological Origins of American Environmentalism

We are launced on the ocean of an unchained democracy.
—*Wendell Phillips, 1859*

The world, we are told, was made especially for man—a presumption not supported by all the facts. . . . Why should man value himself as more than a small part of the one great unit of creation?

—*John Muir, 1867*

*B*ernard Bailyn's *The Ideological Origins of the American Revolution* (1967) called attention to the fact that for the late eighteenth century, natural-rights philosophy and the concept of democratic liberty it inspired were a "contagion" so powerful it surprised even its advocates. The liberal impulse, Bailyn wrote, "swept past boundaries few had set out to cross, into regions few had wished to enter."[1] The American Revolution may have settled the issue of propertied, white, male colonists' rights, but in clarifying those rights it left other categories of human beings outside the pale of ethics. Those whose ethical status was undefined remained vulnerable to those with clearly defined rights. The interests of these oppressed minorities, however, would gradually receive attention, as would, in time, the whole human relationship to that other component of John Locke's state of nature: nature itself.

The United States played a major role in expanding the definition of democracy. Americans took freedom to be the basis of their national mission. John Adams believed his country was "designed by Providence [as] the Theater" in which humankind would crusade for liberty.[2] The boundaries of the stage expanded most dramatically after 1960 to admit actors and beneficiaries totally unanticipated by the revolutionaries of 1776. It is revealing to consider the radical environmentalists of the 1960s, 1970s, and 1980s as occupying the same role in the spread of liberalism as did the political radicals of the 1760s, 1770s, and 1780s. Both groups of Americans used natural rights ideology to reach revolutionary conclusions. Both, at times, exhibited confusion and contradiction. And both experienced quite heated resistance from more conservative members of their society. At least one of the environmentalists followed John Adams in using the rights of nature as the core of a new national mission. "Perhaps," Michael W. Fox wrote in 1978, "America may come to lead other nations and show them alternative values . . . that will benefit not only all people of one earth, but also all of earth, including all sentient beings and habitats, since all are interrelated and interdependent."[3]

Bernard Bailyn was interested in knowing where the intellectuals of the American Revolution got their ethical ideas and how they applied them to a major problem of their time: the relationship of the American colonists to Great Britain. The same questions arise in examining the thought of the new environmentalists, although for them the compelling problem was the relationship of nature to human civilization. How was it that people could begin to talk seriously in the middle of the twentieth century about environmental ethics and the rights of nature? Where did the idealism come from that led environmental activists to blockade lumber roads, throw their bodies in front of seal clubbers, and chain themselves to the banks of rivers scheduled for damming? What inspired them to burn billboards, destroy bulldozers, free laboratory animals, and at least talk about blowing up dams to "liberate" rivers? What were the ideological origins of radical environmentalism in the United States?

In the United States the greatest gains in conservation or environmentalism occurred after 1960. But in the eighteenth and nineteenth centuries England went far beyond her former colony in expounding an ethical philosophy of human-nature relationships and in beginning its legal implementation with respect to animals. There was no Jeremy Bentham or John Lawrence in the United States and no Martin's Act. The few Americans who did talk about nature in ethical terms in the nineteenth century were not even dignified by ridicule; most often, they were ignored completely. It is well to remember in this regard that Thoreau did not become an environmental hero until well into the twentieth century. Significantly, his modern reputation depended in large part on his discovery and popularization by English animal rightists, notably Henry S. Salt.[4]

With full awareness of the risks of broad cross-cultural generalizations, three observations help explain the lag time between American and English consideration of the rights of nature. First, for much of the nineteenth century the majority of territory claimed by the United States was wilderness. The inexhaustibility of resources was the dominant American myth for a century after independence. Even utilitarian conservation seemed unnecessary, much less any viewpoint that challenged anthropocentrism. Even people critical of resource exploitation could not escape the feeling that there was, after all, plenty of room for people *and* nature in the New World. Consider, for instance, that until May 10, 1869, one could not cross the continent without having to go at least part of the way on foot or with the aid of animals. On May 24, 1869, two weeks after the first railroad linked the coasts, John Wesley Powell rode the new train to Green River, Wyoming, and started in boats down a thousand miles of unmapped river. The Indian wars were in full cry then; much of the West was wild. In this geographical context, progress seemed synonymous with growth, development, and the conquest of nature. The idea of living ethically and harmoniously with nature was incompatible with nineteenth-century American priorities.[5]

A second reason for the lack of American interest in the rights of nature until well into the twentieth century was the dominant concern of earlier intellectuals and reformers with the rights of people. The Revolution released a flood of idealism based on natural-rights principles, but for a century it focused almost exclusively on social problems such as slavery. For almost a century after 1776, the oppression of black people diverted American eyes from other wrongs. As far as natural rights idealists were concerned, slavery was the firebell in the night that had to be answered first. It would have been incongruous for Congress to pass legislation forbidding cruelty to cattle while millions of human beings existed as unprotected livestock. So a Wendell Phillips or a William Lloyd Garrison devoted himself to abolitionism. In England, on the other hand, slavery was on the way to legal abolition in 1792, and a John Lawrence or a Richard Martin could turn his attention to righting other kinds of wrong.

Third, when Americans at last began protecting nature in the nineteenth century, it was through a very anthropocentrically defined national park ideal. Americans preserved Yellowstone (1872), the Adirondacks (1885), and Yosemite (1890) for people's pleasure and for utilitarian purposes such as water and game supply. England in the same period had no wilderness and consequently directed its environmental ideals to a component of nature closer to its experience: animals, especially domesticated ones. Henry Salt's Humanitarian League and John Muir's Sierra Club, founded within a year of each other in the early 1890s, had vastly different objectives related to the particular experience of their respective cultures with nature.

In choosing the Fourth of July for his 1845 departure to Walden Pond, Henry David Thoreau intended to make what a later generation would call a "statement." The Massachusetts naturalist-philosopher saw little to celebrate about his nation's first sixty-nine years. Americans seemed to be obsessed with what his Concord colleague, Ralph Waldo Emerson, called "things."[6] Going to a shop to buy a blank notebook in which to record his thoughts, Thoreau could only find ledgers ruled for dollars and cents. His countrymen appeared to be oblivious to any but utilitarian values. Nature was merely an object—a resource—and they exploited it with a vengeance. Thoreau observed the rapid recession of the New England forest and commented: "Thank God, men cannot as yet fly, and lay waste the sky as well as the earth!"[7] He was one of the first Americans to perceive inexhaustibility as a myth.

As Donald Worster has explained, there were ecologists before "ecology." Thoreau was among them. The word itself dates to 1866, but the idea that the many parts of nature fit together into a single unit—or were so fitted by a creative God—appeared frequently in scientific and religious circles since the seventeenth century.[8] Holistic thinkers such as Henry More and John Ray wrote about nature from this point of view, as did the renowned Swedish botanist Carl von Linne (or Linnaeus), whose 1749 treatise *The Oeconomy of Nature* popularized the phrase the pre-ecologists favored. In 1793 the Reverend Nicholas Collin asked the American Philosophical Society to support the protection of little-known birds, apparently on the verge of extinction, until naturalists discovered "what part is assigned to them in the oeconomy of nature."[9] God had created the creatures, Collin implied, and for humans to remove them from the natural scheme of things would be both imprudent and irreverent. This line of reasoning forecast the way the ecological perspective would provide an intellectual basis for environmental ethics. The central idea was community membership and its attendant rights.

As a Transcendentalist, Thoreau's holism stemmed from his belief in the existence of an "Oversoul" or godlike moral force that permeated everything in nature. Using intuition, rather than reason and science, humans could *transcend* physical appearances and perceive "the currents of the Universal Being" binding the world together.[10] Thoreau expressed the resulting perception: "The earth I tread on is not a dead, inert mass; it is a body, has a spirit, is organic and fluid to the influence of its spirit."[11] In this holism, Thoreau professed what might be termed "theological ecology"—God held things together. Still, the scientist in Thoreau emerged every day as he walked the Concord countryside. His journals are crammed with data about how organisms relate to each other and to their environment, and he followed the Linnaean tradition in using the phrase "economy of the universe."[12]

Thoreau's organicism or holism, reinforced by both science and religion, led him to refer to nature and its creatures as his society, transcending the usual human connotation of that term. "I do not," he wrote in his journal for 1857, "consider the other animals brutes in the common sense."[13] He regarded sunfish, plants, skunks, and even stars as fellows and neighbors—members, in other words, of his community. "The woods," he declared during an 1857 camping trip in Maine, "were not tenantless, but choke-full of honest spirits as good as myself any day."[14] There was no hierarchy nor any discrimination in Thoreau's concept of community. "What we call wildness," he wrote in 1859, "is a civilization other than our own."[15] Such ideas are remarkable for their total absence in previous American thought.

Although he did not use the term, an environmental ethic sprang from Thoreau's expanded community consciousness. It began with the axiom that "every creature is better alive than dead, men and moose and pine trees"[16] and went on to question the appropriateness of human domination (kindly or not) over nature. "There is no place for man-worship," he declared in 1852; and later, "The poet says the proper study of mankind is man. I say, study to forget all that; take wider views of the universe."[17] Thoreau's own expanded vision led him to rant against the Concord farmers engaged in the quintessentially American activity of clearing the land of trees and underbrush: "If some are prosecuted for abusing children, others deserve to be prosecuted for maltreating the face of nature committed to their care."[18] Here Thoreau seemed to imply that nature should have legal rights like other oppressed minorities. On another occasion, he pointed out the inconsistency of the president of an anti-slavery society wearing a beaver-skin coat.

While Thoreau avoided the word "rights," his association of abused nature with abused people placed him squarely in the path that the new environmentalists would later follow. But in the middle of the nineteenth century, Thoreau was not only unprecedented in these ideas, he was virtually alone in holding them. In fact, it is likely that no more than a handful of Americans even read these icono-

clastic journal entries until the first complete edition of Thoreau's unpublished work in 1906. Of course Henry Salt, Thoreau's first biographer, knew about them, but Salt's perspective, as noted, was
English. He would have at least partially understood what Thoreau
meant about muskrats being his brothers.

In 1864, as the Civil War worked toward the resolution of one
moral problem, two Americans began to pose another: How could
human beings reconcile their voracious use of nature with their
need—and duty—to preserve it? George Perkins Marsh approached
the question through a magnum opus; John Muir stumbled onto his
answer in a Canadian swamp.

Marsh's book *Man and Nature; Or, Physical Geography as Modified by Human Action* (1864) was the first comprehensive description
in the English language of the destructive impact of human civilization on the environment. Marsh (1801–1882) spoke twenty-one languages, traveled widely abroad as a U.S. diplomat, studied the history of past civilizations in detail, and wrote with passion. In the
manner of subsequent ecologists, Marsh discussed the "balances"
and "harmonies" of nature, but unlike Thoreau, he did not move on
to challenge anthropocentrism. He was perfectly content with the
idea of human dominion over nature, provided that it was careful and
far-sighted. That it had not been was the subject of his book. "Man
has forgotten," Marsh wrote, "that the earth was given to him for
usufruct alone, not for consumption, still less for profligate waste."
Anticipating the ecological perspective of the twentieth century,
Marsh warned that the interrelatedness of "animal and vegetable life
is too complicated a problem for human intelligence to solve, and we
can never know how wide a circle of disturbance we produce in the
harmonies of nature when we throw the smallest pebble into the
ocean of organic life." As a corrective to previous human careless-
ness, Marsh proposed "geographical regeneration," a great healing
of the planet beginning with the control of technology. This, he continued, would require "great political and moral revolutions."[19]

Marsh's enormously influential book was the first published in
America to discuss nature protection in ethical terms. Granted,
Marsh's work contained nothing about the rights of nature; the welfare of people was constantly uppermost in his mind. But he did suggest that human custodianship of the planet was an ethical or "moral"
issue, not just an economic one. It was right, in other words, to take
care of nature, wrong to abuse it.

John Muir's first encounter with the idea that nature had rights
came as a consequence of draft-dodging. President Abraham Lincoln

asked for 500,000 more men to defend the Union on March 10, 1864. Muir, who was twenty-six and single, felt certain he would be called, and he apparently had no interest in fighting to save the Union or free the slaves. However, he was learning to care greatly about nature. So Muir left his Wisconsin home in June and vanished into the Canadian wilderness north of Lake Huron. He followed a lonely trail into a wet and darkening swamp, where he suddenly came upon a cluster of rare white orchids, miles from anywhere and so beautiful that he "sat down beside them and wept for joy." Reflecting later on the experience, Muir realized his emotion sprang from the fact that the wilderness orchids did not have the slightest relevance to human beings. Were it not for Muir's chance encounter, they would have lived, bloomed, and died unseen. Nature, he generalized, must exist first and foremost for itself and for its creator. Everything had value. "Would not the world suffer," he concluded, "by the banishment of a single weed?"[20]

For Muir, as for Thoreau and the earlier organicists, the basis of respect for nature was to recognize it as part of the created community to which humans also belonged. God permeated Muir's environment. Not only animals, but plants (like the orchids) and even rocks and water were "sparks of the Divine Soul."[21] But civilization, and particularly Christianity with its dualistic separation of people and nature, obscured this truth. To reemphasize it, Muir deliberately chose organisms at the bottom of the Christian's hierarchical chain of being. "What good are rattlesnakes for?" he asked rhetorically, and replied that they were "good for themselves, and we need not begrudge them their share of life."[22] On one occasion during his 1867 walk from Wisconsin to the Gulf of Mexico Muir remarked that "if a war of races should occur between the wild beasts and Lord Man I would be tempted to sympathize with the bears."[23] In several other places Muir used the phrase "the rights of animals."[24]

But Muir's morality did not stop with animals. On the hike to the Gulf he encountered alligators, commonly regarded as ugly and hateful vermin, but Muir preferred to understand the giant reptiles as "fellow mortals" filling the "place assigned them by the greater Creator of us all" and "beautiful in the eyes of God." The moral implication followed: "How narrow we selfish, conceited creatures are in our sympathies! How blind to the rights of all the rest of creation!" Although a few Americans, notably Henry Bergh, had previously conceived of the rights of animals (see below, p. 46), this entry in Muir's 1867 journal was the first association of rights with what a later generation would call "environment." Its basis lay in Muir's

perception of people as members of the natural community. "Why,"
he asked, "should man value himself as more than a small part of the
one great unit of creation?"[25]

Muir recognized that this point of view would not be popular
among his contemporaries: "A numerous class of men are painfully
astonished whenever they find anything, living or dead, in all God's
universe, which they cannot eat or render in some way . . . useful to
themselves." These people never thought that "Nature's object in
making animals and plants might possibly be first of all the happiness
of each one of them, not the creation of all for the happiness of one."
Muir's first published statement of this radical idea appeared in 1875:
"I have never yet happened upon a trace of evidence that seemed to
show that any one animal was ever made for another as much as it
was made for itself."[26] He also gave unprecedented American articulation to the organicists' vision: "When we try to pick out anything
by itself, we find it hitched to everything else in the universe."[27]

In sharp contrast to Thoreau, Muir became a hero to his contemporaries for defining the values of a vanishing wilderness and cham-
pioning the national park idea. He focused his energies on California's High Sierra, where the trail that now serves thousands of
backpackers each summer bears his name. The establishment of
Yosemite National Park in 1890 was Muir's greatest political achievement. Two years later a group of Californians organized around
Muir for the purpose of defending the new park. They called themselves the Sierra Club. In 1908 the club began an unsuccessful five-
year campaign to prevent San Francisco from taking a portion of
Yosemite National Park—the Hetch Hetchy Valley—as a municipal
water and hydropower facility.[28]

It seems surprising at first glance that John Muir did not emphasize the intrinsic value and rights of nature in his defense of the Sierra
and other wild places in the American West and Alaska. His essays
consist, in almost equal parts, of elaborate descriptions of the beauty
and spirituality of wilderness and diatribes against the mean, commercial spirit of his age that would sacrifice such environments to
"the Almighty Dollar."[29] Occasionally he also tossed in a pinch or
two of the "watershed" argument that Marsh first elaborated in 1864
in *Man and Nature*. Highly utilitarian, it urged care of the nation's
mountainside forests in the interest of regulating the hydrologic
cycle and preventing the lowlands from becoming deserts. Although
Muir had written passionately about the rights of orchids, rattlesnakes, alligators, and "all the rest of creation" before arriving in
California, his later work skirts this issue almost completely. Nature

is valuable, an older Muir says, for *people:* for rest and recuperation, for aesthetic satisfaction, for spiritual nourishment, and for the protection of mountain watersheds. Granted that Muir broke sharply with Gifford Pinchot and the utilitarian conservationists of the Progressive Era, but his aesthetic variety of conservation (better termed "preservation") was, in its own way, equally anthropocentric.[30]

Why did Muir abandon the environmental ethics approach? The reason, it seems clear, is that he got into politics and became pragmatic. Muir believed the only way to save the American wilderness was to persuade the American people and their government of its worth to them. Consequently he tempered his biocentricity and the ethical system it implied, hiding them in his published writing and speeches under a cover of anthropocentrism. It is important to recall that Muir's remarks about the rights of nature appeared first in his private, unpublished journals and not in book form until after his death. Muir knew very well that to go before Congress and the public arguing for national parks as places where snakes, redwood trees, beavers, and rocks could exercise their natural rights to life and liberty would be to invite instant ridicule and weaken the cause he wished to advance. So he camouflaged his radical egalitarianism in more acceptable rhetoric centered on the benefits of nature for people. Later ecologists used the same technique whenever politics was involved. Aldo Leopold could be very utilitarian; and witness the cure-for-cancer arguments more recently used in defense of rare and endangered species, or the Sierra Club's reliance in the 1960s upon the economics of hydropower production to save the Grand Canyon from dams.

But Muir held nothing back when it came to attacking people who would destroy the wilderness. Nature was his church, the place where he perceived and worshipped God, and from that standpoint protection of nature became a holy war. Muir lashed out at the "temple destroyers" who would dam/damn (the pun occurred frequently) the Hetch Hetchy Valley. San Francisco became "the Prince of the powers of Darkness" and "Satan and Co."[31] Muir's was a manichaean world of black and white, good and evil, vying for the American environment. As William Lloyd Garrison had understood, compromise was difficult when ethics was involved. One's opponents were not merely in error but morally wrong. This orientation gave the preservation crusade a certain moral intensity, but in the political arena Muir stopped short of the fullest implications of his early ethical ideas.

The more radical parts of John Muir's philosophy received needed intellectual support from the work of his contemporary, the English naturalist Charles Darwin (1809–1882). Darwinism took the conceit out of humanity by putting humans back into nature. The evolutionary explanation of the proliferation of life on earth undermined dualistic philosophies at least two thousand years old. Darwin extended the boundaries of kinship to the limits of life. No more special creation in the image of God, no more "soul," and, it followed, no more hierarchy, dominion, or expectation that the rest of nature existed to serve one precocious primate. The books in which Darwin developed his thesis, *On the Origin of Species* (1859) and *The Descent of Man* (1871), became important sources of environmentalism and environmental ethics.

The overarching concept that emerged from Darwin and his popularizers was the unity and continuity of life. The prime movers of evolution—species—may have changed often, but the process itself ran back in an unbroken chain (Darwin preferred the metaphor of the branches, trunk, and roots of a tree) to the first life-forms. At this point even Darwin stopped. He did not care to lift the ultimate veil. Let God explain creation. Leave the amino acids and lightning flashes to a later generation of life scientists. Darwin, after all, referred to the origin of *species* in his title, not *life*.

After his trip to the Galapagos Islands in 1835, Darwin returned to England and arrived at an astonishing conclusion: "Man in his arrogance thinks himself a great work, worthy the interposition of a deity. More humble and, I believe, true to consider him created from animals."[32] But so out of keeping was this idea with what people wanted to believe about themselves that another two decades elapsed before Darwin dared to publish his magnum opus. Even then he pulled its hardest punches as far as human evolution was concerned. But the implications were clear enough, and Darwin finally drew them in 1871 in *The Descent of Man*. Humans, he declared, evolved from primates, which they still closely resembled. Even human mental processes, the bulwark of dualism for a millennium, did not strike Darwin as particularly distinguishing. "My object," he wrote, "is to show that there is no fundamental difference between man and the higher mammals in their mental faculties." On another occasion Darwin scribbled himself a memo to guide his thinking about evolution: "Never use the words *higher* and *lower*."[33]

Partially because it built upon a holistic philosophy familiar from several centuries of organicist and animist philosophy, Darwinism spread rapidly and exerted an immediate impact on Western ethics. After reading Darwin in 1867, John Muir noted, "this star, our own good earth, made many a successful journey around the heavens ere man was made, and whole kingdoms of creatures enjoyed existence and returned to dust ere man appeared to claim them." Then, looking ahead, he extrapolated an idea that few among even the most enthusiastic Darwinians dared to think: "After human beings have also played their part in Creation's plan, they too may disappear without any . . . extra ordinary commotion whatever."[34] For Muir evolution was an enormously humbling idea, suggesting that every creature on the planet had a right to exist—or at least the right to struggle to exist—equal to that of every other creature.

But other minds took Darwinism in quite antipodal directions. For them the catch phrases "struggle for existence" and "survival of the fittest" led to the conclusion that might made right. Human beings' position atop the tree of life gave them an open invitation to lord their achievement over the rest of creation. Progress depended upon it. Civilized humans had a duty to conquer and control the other species that, left alone, would constantly try to pull humans down and take their place.

Crude and self-serving as this interpretation of Darwin was, it gave rise to several highly influential essays around the turn of the century. Thomas Huxley, the London anatomist and foremost advocate of Darwin in England, stated in *Evolution and Ethics* (1893) that the latter ended at the boundary of civilization. The human relationship to nature was amoral.[35] The American philosopher William James reached similar conclusions in "The Moral Equivalent of War" (1910). James's equivalent, to be precise, was conquering nature, and he urged American youth to become "a part of the army enlisted against Nature."[36] The so-called Social Darwinists even removed less advantaged humans from the ethical circle that restrained the rich and powerful.[37] But there was yet another way to understand Darwinism. In the same year as James's essay, Thomas Hardy, the English novelist, wrote in *The Humanitarian*, "the most far-reaching consequence of the establishment of the common origin of all species is ethical." Hardy believed Darwinism "logically involved a readjustment of altruistic morals, by enlarging . . . the application of what has been called 'The Golden Rule' from the area of mere mankind to that of the whole animal kingdom."[38]

Darwin himself appeared to favor Hardy's interpretation. As early as 1837 he referred to animals as "our fellow brethren" and remarked that "we may be all melted together."[39] True, Darwin described fierce competition, but he saw a commonality among all the competitors. Living and dying together over the eons, everything alive participated in a universal kinship or brotherhood. It was not far from there to the idea of respect for humans' fellow creatures. Darwin believed that this respect characterized a civilized people. Moreover, he made it plain in *The Descent of Man* that moral sensibilities (or, as Darwin preferred, "sympathies") were a product of evolution. Darwin recognized rudimentary ethics in the "social qualities" of animals, and argued that cooperation or "mutual aid" within a species had direct survival value and hence was naturally selected.[40] Once human societies appeared and morality or ethics began to evolve from "social instincts," it was extended by education and emulation. "As soon as [a] virtue is honoured and practiced by some few men," Darwin wrote, "it spreads through instruction and example to the young, and eventually becomes incorporated in public opinion."[41]

Over time, Darwin continued, humans broadened their ethical circle to include "small tribes," then "larger communities," and eventually "nations" and "races." They gradually reached out still farther "to the imbecile, maimed, and other useless members of society." Finally, humans would put aside "baneful customs and superstitions" and might eventually reach "disinterested love for all living creatures." Darwin thought that as ethics evolved all "sentient beings" would ultimately come to be included in the moral community.[42] But the route to such moral enlightenment would be long and difficult. Darwin understood that the greater the biological differences between humans and other life-forms, the longer the time lag before we would regard them as morally considerable.

Darwin himself did not push his 1871 scheme beyond animals. Despite attempts to read into his work an "all-embracing reverence for life,"[43] it is more accurate to see his ethical horizon defined by his time and place. In Victorian England that horizon ended with animal rights. And even there Darwin expressed some ambivalence. In 1875 he made a rare public appearance before the Royal Commission studying the vivisection problem. Although he advocated kindness to animals and never personally experimented on a live animal, Darwin the scientist defended the importance of such experimentation to physiology. He told the commissioners that the excesses of the vivisectionists should be curbed, and the 1876 Cruelty to Animals Act expressed Darwin's point of view. While not outlawing vivisection, as the extreme animal rightists advocated, it attempted to regulate the practice through a system of licensing and inspection and mandated the use of anesthetics on laboratory animals.[44]

Darwin believed that the higher a society advanced in civilization, the wider its ethical field of vision. Indeed, one criterion for the fully civilized person was his or her extended sympathies or ethics. This preeminent Victorian ideal allowed advocates of extended ethics, in Darwin's time and later, to contend that their opponents were not fully civilized and that they partook of some of the bestiality of the creatures they excluded from their ethical circle. Darwin himself reacted this way to the colonists he encountered in South America in the 1830s after his visit to the Galapagos. They beat their slaves to death, slashed each other with knives, and devastated the native flora and fauna. In Darwin's view they were ethically retarded. In defense of Hetch Hetchy Valley, John Muir and his colleagues applied a similar logic against the "devotees of ravaging commercialism" who wanted the dam.[45] And the new environmentalists would lash out at the "insensitive colossalism" that "must grind people into statistical grist for the market place and simultaneously destroy the biosphere."[46] Like Darwin, they hoped their contemporaries could attain an elevated ethical perspective embracing nature as well as people.

In shaping his view on the evolution of ethics, Darwin drew, as his footnotes in *The Descent of Man* indicate, on the work of William E. H. Lecky. This distinguished Irish intellectual historian published his *History of European Morals from Augustus to Charlemagne* in 1869, when Darwin was in the final stages of writing *Descent*. Lecky endeavored to show that "there is such a thing as a natural history of morals, a defined and regular order, in which our feelings are unfolded." As Lecky saw it, this process had produced improvement in moral standards since Roman times. The nineteenth-century efforts to include animals in the ethical circle were an important part of Lecky's evidence for this hypothesis. In a footnote Darwin stated that Lecky "seems to a certain extent to coincide" with his own conclusions.[47] In point of fact Lecky anticipated Darwin on this point almost completely, and in 1892, when Henry Salt discussed animal rights "considered in relation to social progress," it was the historian rather than the naturalist whom he quoted (see above, p. 31).

Although dominated for almost a century by the American slavery issue, natural rights ideology held great potential for nonhuman beings. Thomas Paine saw the connection in 1793 when he declared that "everything of persecution and revenge between man and man, and everything of cruelty to animals, is a violation of moral duty."[48] For Paine, a Deist, it was simple and straightforward: God had created and apparently reverenced a wide variety of life-forms. The ethical person respected them all. This conjunction of theology and

democratic ideology was powerful enough to inspire a few state anti-
cruelty laws in the early nineteenth century. But the American efforts
paled in comparison to those of England and its vigorous Royal Society for the Prevention of Cruelty to Animals. Then, within eighteen months, Charles Darwin published *On the Origin of Species*
(1859) and a war began that would end slavery in the United States.
Thereafter it would be easier to advance the cause of nonhuman
rights in the United States.

In 1865 a wealthy and somewhat eccentric New Yorker named
Henry Bergh (1811–1888) retired as the secretary of the American
legation to Russia and returned to the reunited American states with
unusual ambitions. On the way home Bergh had conferred with
leaders of the RSPCA in London. His plan was to organize an
American equivalent.[49] Bergh launched his crusade in New York City
early in 1866 with several public meetings. Following John Locke, he
contended that cruelty to any living creature demoralized and bru-
talized the perpetrator. A nation that did not stop cruelty to animals
ran the risk of cruelty extending to people and, ultimately, of decline
and decay as a civilization. Bergh pointed to the history of Rome,
with its staged animal fights, and Spain's bullfighting, as cases in
point. With slavery recently abolished, he urged his countrymen to
move on to the next frontier of humanitarianism: abuse of animals.

On April 10, 1866, Bergh secured a charter for the American Society for the Prevention of Cruelty to Animals (ASPCA). It contained
an unprecedented "Declaration of the Rights of Animals," which
Bergh described as "a species of Declaration of Independence."[50] He
believed the document would come to be venerated in the same manner as Jefferson's famous statement. Moving quickly, Bergh next
wrote and pushed a law through the New York legislature. The April
19 statute was far-reaching in scope. Going beyond even Martin's
Act, it forbade cruelty to all animals, wild as well as tame.[51] In practice the law applied mostly to domestic draft animals. Bergh, ele-
gantly attired in top hat and tails, made headlines roaming the streets
of New York and reminding drivers that overloading, beating, starv-
ing, and otherwise abusing their animals was now illegal. Bergh
understandably received abundant abuse in return. But time was on
his side, and other Americans came to his support.

On February 22, 1868, two of the strongest horses in Massachusetts were loaded with two men each and raced over forty miles of
rough road. There was no winner; both animals died. Reading about
the event the next day, George T. Angell, a prominent Boston lawyer, became infuriated. He called together several dozen well-

connected friends, some of them former abolitionists, and organized the Massachusetts Society for the Prevention of Cruelty to Animals. It distributed newsletters, built public drinking fountains for livestock, and pressed for humane legislation concerning the care, transport, and slaughter of animals. Realizing in 1882 that changing laws depended on changing values, Angell created the first American Band of Mercy for schoolchildren and, for himself, the inevitable sobriquet "Angell of Mercy." An English organization also known as the Band of Mercy was his inspiration. The American Humane Education Association appeared, under Angell's leadership, seven years later. Its motto was impressively broad: "Glory to God, Peace on Earth, Kindness, Justice and Mercy to Every Living Creature." Horses, however, had a special place in Angell's concern. In 1890 Angell discovered *Black Beauty: His Grooms and Companions,* written by Anna Sewell, an Englishwoman, in 1877. The book was, in Angell's mind, "the 'Uncle Tom's Cabin' of the Horse." Printing and distributing a quarter-million copies, he looked forward to its exerting "as widespread and powerful [an] influence in abolishing cruelty to horses as 'Uncle Tom's Cabin' had on the abolition of human slavery."[52]

Underscoring this continuity in American moral thought, the author of *Uncle Tom's Cabin,* Harriet Beecher Stowe, joined the humane movement, writing to Henry Bergh in 1877 of her distress at the treatment of Florida's animals and birds. Stowe called the cages in which the latter were packed for shipment "veritable slave ships," and she told Bergh she was ready to "do *any* thing that can benefit the cause." Stowe's equally famous brother, the minister Henry Ward Beecher, became the first prominent American theologian to argue for an expanded ethic that would include nonhuman life. As early as 1873 Beecher publicized Bergh's ASPCA and urged that "all good people help on his humane mission," which Beecher defined as advancement of "the rights of animals." Taking a larger view than even Bergh, Beecher urged his congregation to "teach children not to abhor insects, worms, and harmless reptiles." But the minister had more difficulty with Bergh's belief that animals might be immortal and coinhabitants of heaven with people.[53]

While slower to develop than their counterparts in England, the nineteenth-century American humane movement and related reform movements such as vegetarianism and antivivisectionism deserve more recognition than they have received as intellectual precursors of environmental ethics.[54] True, nineteenth-century anti-cruelty efforts in the United States were largely confined to domesticated animals.

Pain in familiar creatures was the evil to be eradicated. Moreover, the humanitarians defined the problem from a human perspective. The humane movement frequently focused not so much on the suffering of the animals as on the apparent enjoyment of that suffering by callous people, who were in danger of moral atrophy. The humanitarians echoed Locke's concern that cruelty to animals could easily extend to cruelty to other people. The ethical principle behind nineteenth-century humanitarianism was that it is wrong for humans to be cruel, rather than that cruelty violates the rights of animals.

Seizing on this point, one present-day philosopher of environmental ethics, J. Baird Callicott, goes so far as to argue that in their limited moral perspective, nineteenth-century humanitarians and the more recent animal liberationists are quite irrelevant to the new environmentalism. He quotes an advocate of holistic environmental ethics as saying that "the last thing we need is simply another 'liberation movement.'"[55] If pain is the problem, Mark Sagoff has recently joked, the humanitarians should attempt to end it in wild as well as domestic contexts. Why not, he asks tongue in cheek, try to feed and shelter the millions of wild creatures who die horrible deaths in the wilderness every day?[56]

This somewhat ahistorical contemporary criticism does injustice to the old humanitarians. Granted they lacked a holistic ecological consciousness as well as philosophical consistency. Clearly the people concerned about animals in the nineteenth century were not biocentric; they did not consider natural systems so much as individual organisms in moral terms. Yet they deserve credit for making the first stumbling steps away from a definition of moral community that began and ended with human beings. Logically, those first steps were sequential, starting with the domesticated or captured laboratory creatures most familiar to humans and closest to them biologically. As Lecky and Darwin understood, there was an historical progression in the evolution of morality that began closest to home. Animals were the next in line to people. It is not particularly helpful for Callicott and Sagoff to fault the humanitarians, past and present, for not widening the circle further than they did. Their ideas were revolutionary enough in terms of the main currents of Western ethical thought.

From the standpoint of intellectual history, the humanitarians compare to the radical environmentalists as the nineteenth-century opponents of slavery to civil rights activists. Crude and incomplete as the abolitionists' efforts might have seemed to black activists of the 1960s, William Lloyd Garrison and his colleagues opened the way for

Martin Luther King, Jr., and Jesse Jackson. The essential first step was the idea that enslaved black people were not "things" and that relations to them should be considered ethically, not just in terms of white convenience. Humanitarians took the same pioneering step on behalf of at least some nonhuman life-forms. Their shortcomings are undeniable but should be judged in the light of the fact that, despite the deep ecologists, a full-blown, philosophically consistent environmental ethic is still inchoate in its conceptualization and, especially, its institutionalization.

Early American conservation existed quite independently of the humane movement, but parts of it also nourished the seeds of an ethical relationship to nature. The main thrust of early conservation was economic and utilitarian. Timber-producing forests and useful game species of animals, birds, and fish attracted the most attention. Progressive conservation became the showpiece of a philosophy of efficient progress.[57] But late nineteenth- and early twentieth-century conservation movements occasionally transcended traditional utilitarianism. One instance was the movement to protect nongame birds. The American Ornithologists Union began the effort in the 1880s and, after 1886, received the support of George B. Grinnell's Audubon Society. Grinnell, the publisher of *Forest and Stream* magazine, wished to protect "any wild birds not used for food."[58] These included song birds and those sought by the plumage hunters. Grinnell called the slaughter of birds for millinery purposes "unholy work."[59] The implied linkage of nature protection and religion paralleled John Muir's defense of Yosemite's Hetch Hetchy Valley and pointed the way toward an ethical conception of conservation. In the late 1890s Grinnell's friend, Congressman John F. Lacey, sponsored legislation designed to stop shipment of plumage from Florida to the New England fashion centers. The Lacey Act of 1900, which made interstate transport of illegally killed wildlife a federal offense, institutionalized the idea that even nonutilitarian species should be allowed to coexist with people. This identification of the right to life and habitat would eventually flower into endangered species legislation.

Another root of the moral orientation in conservation runs back to the resource democracy of late nineteenth-century land-use reformers such as Lester Frank Ward, Edward Bellamy, and especially Henry George. In *Progress and Poverty* (1879), George argued against the political and economic policies and institutions that permitted a fortunate few who owned the land to skim off enormous profits. For him this violated natural rights (of people) and worked against the nation's democratic ideals. "The reform I have proposed," he wrote at the end of *Progress and Poverty,* "is . . . but the carrying out in letter and spirit of the truth enunciated in the Declaration of Independence." The ideal of liberty, he explained, meant more than extending citizenship and suffrage. "We cannot go on prating of the inalienable rights of man and then denying the inalienable right to the bounty of the Creator."[60] The thrust of George's tax-reform proposals was to challenge absolute ownership of the environment in a manner comparable to the abolitionists' challenge of the ownership and exploitation of people. Significantly, among the many contemporary reformers attracted to George's ideas was the English animal rightist, Henry Salt.[61]

A self-educated Iowa geologist named W J McGee (he avoided both full names and periods) extended Henry George's point of view into the early twentieth century. He believed that Progressive conservation meant equal access to natural resources, that national (rather than private) ownership was essential, and that more than economics were at stake in the matter. "On its face the Conservation Movement is material," McGee explained in 1910, "yet in truth there has never been in all human history a popular movement more firmly grounded in ethics, in eternal verities, in the divinity of human rights!" He went on to argue that the intellectual basis of conservation had as its most fundamental goal perfection of "the concept and the movement started among the Colonists one hundred and forty years ago—to round out the American Revolution."[62] In this paper McGee was referring to the right of people to use nature, not the rights of nature, but he demonstrated how natural-rights ethics derived from the American Revolution could be an integral and explosive part of conservation ideology. It is plausible that what gave conservation its special hold on the Progressive mind was this injection of ethics into what ordinarily involved only economics. The same assessment might be made of the new environmentalism, except by that time the issue had broadened from equal rights to use the land to the rights of the land itself.

A century after the English humanitarian, John Lawrence, urged attention to "The Rights of Beasts," Edward Payson Evans (1831–1917) made the first extensive American statement of what would come to be called environmental ethics. A multifaceted scholar who taught modern languages at the University of Michigan from 1862 to 1867 and then moved to Germany, Evans wrote books about animal symbolism and about the prosecution of animals in medieval courts of justice.[63] The first product of Evans's research into ethics and psychology was an article in *The Popular Science Monthly* for September

1894, entitled "Ethical Relations between Man and Beast." It begins with a statement of Evans's intent to correct the "anthropocentric assumption" in psychology and ethics just as it had been corrected over the past several centuries in astronomy and, more recently, in biology.

Evans's initial task was to attack the religious basis of anthropocentrism. Anticipating Lynn White's thesis by seventy years, Evans developed a remarkably full case against "the anthropocentric character of Christianity." That faith made humans "a little lower than the angels" when, in reality, they are "a little higher than the ape." Evans criticized the "tyrannical mandate" contained in Genesis to conquer the earth, and he unfavorably compared Judeo-Christian beliefs to the biocentric religions of the East such as Buddhism and Brahmanism.[64] Taken for granted by environmentalists after the 1960s, this exposure of the shortcomings of Western religious tradition with regard to nature had been unknown in the 1890s even in the writings of so sharp a critic of orthodox Christianity as John Muir.

In the 1894 essay, and more extensively in a book published three years later entitled *Evolutional Ethics and Animal Psychology,* Evans proceeded to demonstrate the commonality of humans and animals on "strictly scientific grounds." Drawing on the new field of animal psychology, he discussed "metempsychosis" or reincarnation, communication abilities, the aesthetic sense, and the universality of "consciousness" or what he called "mind." Evans often skated boldly over ice that later psychologists and philosophers would find thin. But his real purpose was to exhort, and this he accomplished with unprecedented enthusiasm: "Man is as truly a part and product of Nature as any other animal, and [the] attempt to set him up on an isolated point outside of it is philosophically false and morally pernicious." On this basis Evans branded as wrong "maliciously breaking a crystal, defacing a gem, girdling a tree, crushing a flower, painting flaming advertisements on rocks, and worrying and torturing animals." The only hints of such a far-reaching perspective in America's past were John Muir's comments about the divine spark in plants, rocks, and water. Organicists such as John Ray and Muir had posited a spiritual kinship between all things in the universe, but Evans stood alone in using this as the basis for "ethical relations."[65]

Evans, who was, after all, a linguist, not a scientist, proved a better philosopher than psychologist. He carefully deflated the argument that mistreatment of animals was wrong only because it tended to degrade humans. For Evans, nonhuman life-forms held intrinsic rights that humans ought not violate. On the same grounds Evans criticized the legal practice of regarding animal suffering as an injury done to the animal's owner. The payment of fines, he declared, did not right this wrong.

Evans devoted considerable attention in his 1897 book to the changes in morality over time. He believed he was riding the crest of an intellectual wave. "In tracing the history of the evolution of ethics," he declared, "we find the recognition of mutual rights and duties confined at first to members of the same horde or tribe, then extended to worshippers of the same gods, and gradually enlarged so as to include every civilized nation, until at length all races of men are at least theoretically conceived as being united in a common bond of brotherhood and benevolent sympathy, which is now slowly expanding so as to comprise not only the higher species of animals, but also every sensitive embodiment of organic life." [66] Evans's indebtedness, even stylistically, to Charles Darwin and William Lecky is obvious here. But in degree Evans was unprecedented. Even the most vigorous of the nineteenth-century humanitarians and natural rightists stopped with animals. Evans went far beyond, to every "sensitive" living thing and even to inanimate objects like rocks and minerals.

American interest in and concern for wild animals rose in Edward Evans's generation to near-cult status. [67] Ernest Thompson Seton and other "nature writers" thought about wild creatures in the same way that Henry Bergh and George Angell regarded domestic ones. In 1898, after describing a partridge dying in a snare, Seton asked, "Have the wild things no moral or legal rights? What right has man to inflict such long and fearful agony on a fellow-creature simply because [it] does not speak his language?" [68] Edward Evans, who based part of his argument for "ethical relations" on the communicative abilities of nonhuman beings, would have been in full agreement with Seton's answers to these rhetorical questions. And so would the recent advocates of reforms of the laws regulating trapping.

Along with Edward Evans, the turn-of-the-century American who dealt most extensively with ethical extension was a Chicago high school teacher. John Howard Moore (1862–1916) came from Missouri and attended Oskaloosa College in Iowa in the 1880s. He married a sister of the renowned trial lawyer and defender of evolutionary theory, Clarence Darrow. In 1898 Moore began teaching at Crane Manual Training High School in Chicago, and from this unlikely vantage point published a series of books on evolutionary biology and ethical philosophy that attracted international attention. Most of them are short and undocumented, apparently originating as course lectures at Crane. Moore's major statements appeared in 1906 and 1907 under the titles *The Universal Kinship* and *The New Ethics*. Henry Salt's Humanitarian League published the first book, undoubtedly with the hope of closing the gap between America's nascent animal rights movement and England's well-established one. An American edition of *The Universal Kinship* came out two years later. Salt and Moore never met but were closely acquainted through correspondence until the American's death, by suicide, in 1916. Seven years later the Englishman dedicated *The Story of My Cousins* to Moore.[69] The book concerned Salt's intimate relationships with cats, dogs, and birds.

Along with Darwinism, misanthropy was the driving force behind Howard Moore's ethical philosophy. A human, in his eyes, was "not a fallen god, but a promoted reptile." In fact, people were worse than snakes: "the most unchaste, the most drunken, the most selfish and conceited, the most miserly, the most hypocritical, and the most bloodthirsty of terrestrial creatures." Gradually and incompletely, Moore felt, people had tried to transcend their innate selfishness, but they were still mired in what he termed the "larval stage." The extension of ethics beyond humans was a hopeful sign. Moore, in fact, understood his "new ethics" to be the cutting edge of what he grandiloquently styled "the great task of reforming the universe."[70]

The starting point for Moore's ethical system, as his title implied, was universal kinship. To Moore this meant that "all the inhabitants of the planet Earth" were related "physically, mentally, morally." He took pains to explain that his sense of ethical community applied "not to creatures of your own anatomy only, but to *all* creatures." It followed for Moore that the Golden Rule, or what he termed "The Great Law," was "a law not applicable to Aryans only, but to *all* men; and not to men only, but to *all beings*." Moore thought of this principle as "simply the expansion of ethics to suit the biological revelations of Charles Darwin."[71]

Moore could adopt a far-reaching ethical stance. "All beings are *ends*," he wrote. "*No* creatures are *means*." And again: "All beings have not equal rights, but *all have rights*." But it soon becomes clear that Moore's ethical circle had definite limits. He respected the rights of domestic animals, and also of mice, turtles, insects, and fish. But plants have no status in Moore's moral system. In *The New Ethics* he explained, following Bentham and anticipating Feinberg, that plants lacked "*consciousness*"—they were alive but did not "*feel*." Consequently, neither could they be harmed nor their rights violated. Plants were "outsiders," "mere things," and not beings or creatures.[72]

At times Moore strikes contemporary ethicists as rather ridiculous, arguing, for instance, against meat-eating even by wild animals. It is likely that Moore's ardent vegetarianism contributed to
this attitude. It is also pertinent that in the 1910s he would not have
had the benefit of the ecologists' sense of the legitimacy of natural
processes, including killing and eating prey. Nonetheless, much of
what Moore wrote is impressive even by the standards of latter-day
biocentric ecologists such as Aldo Leopold, a college student when
Moore's books appeared. For example, Moore wrote about "earth-
life as a single process . . . every part related and akin to every other
part." And he could say "the *Life Process is the End—not man.*"[73]
Clearly Moore's ideas, like those of Edward Evans, were stepping
stones toward holistic environmental ethics.

Good evolutionists as they were, both Evans and Moore saw
themselves as part of an unfolding intellectual process. Their own
age might be ethically unenlightened, but they could be optimistic
about the future. Charles Darwin, their mentor, had been confident
about the spread of altruism through natural selection. The relatively
recent abolition of slavery and gains in rights for laborers and women
encouraged them. Moore made the links explicit: "the same spirit of
sympathy and fraternity that broke the black man's manacles and is
today melting the white woman's chains will tomorrow emancipate
the working man and the ox." Moore understood that this would not
occur overnight. "New ideas," he wrote in *The New Ethics*, "make
their way into the world by generations of elbowing." But despite
lack of respect for his opinions by his contemporaries, Moore could
look forward to a time when "the sentiments of these pages will not
be hailed by two or three, and ridiculed or ignored by the rest; *they
will represent Public Opinion and Law.*"[74] Evans also forecast a day
when "our children's children may finally learn that there are inalienable animal as well as human rights."[75] His use of natural rights
theory and even Jeffersonian rhetoric showed the ease of transferring
those concepts from humanity to at least part of nature. And his
sense of timing was uncanny. The "children's children" of Evans's
generation lived after 1960, and some of them became radical environmentalists and animal liberationists.

• CHAPTER 3 •

Ecology Widens the Circle

The land ethic simply enlarges the boundaries of the community
to include soils, waters, plants, and animals, or collectively:
the land.

—*Aldo Leopold, 1949*

And the thing which is missing is love, some feeling for, as well
as some understanding of, the inclusive community of rocks and
soils, plants and animals, of which we are a part.

—*Joseph Wood Krutch, 1954*

The Greek word *oikos,* meaning house, is the root of both "economics" and "ecology." Over time the significance shifted from the
house itself to what it contained: a living community, the household.
Economics, the older of the two concepts, concerns the study of how
the community manages its time, labor, and material resources.
Ernst Haeckel, the German Darwinian, coined the term "oecologie"
in 1866. The modern spelling appeared in the 1890s along with the
first sophisticated ecological monographs by European botanists. By
that time ecology meant the study of how organisms (of any sort)
interacted with each other and with their total environment. From its
beginnings, ecology concerned communities, systems, wholes.[1] Because of this holistic orientation, the discipline proved to be fertile
soil for environmental ethics. Aldo Leopold, one of the pioneers
in American wildlife ecology, was among the first to see the connection clearly. "All ethics," he wrote in 1949, "rest upon a single
premise: that the individual is a member of a community of interdependent parts."[2]

With national origins steeped in the social contract theory of John
Locke, Americans were especially apt to understand the concept of
community or society as replete with strong ethical overtones. Once
an American conceded that something was a member of his or her

community, the argument for its rights was hard to deny. Each time democratic ideology broadened since 1776 it was to accommodate new groups as members of Jefferson's ambiguous community of equal "men." The abolition of slavery was the most dramatic nineteenth-century instance. By the turn of the century the rights of Indians, laboring people, and women had become pressing social and political issues. And the idea had at least surfaced in the thought of John Muir, Edward Evans, and John Howard Moore that the community to which human beings belong did not end with people. Ecology, the study of interdependent communities, would aid this cause, providing striking new scientific reasons for yet further widening the circle of ethical relevancy.

One of the characteristics of the "theological ecology" of John Ray or Henry David Thoreau was its basis on faith rather than fact. God provided the ultimate glue that bound things together. Darwin, of course, offered abundant scientific reasons for believing all life to be interrelated in its origins, but he did not push on to explore the ways in which living things were presently interrelated. He, too, let the vague presence of a creator do what science could not yet accomplish. The ecologists, however, went into the field, looked at nature as a whole, and used interrelationships and interdependencies to explain how it functioned as a community.

Henry C. Cowles, for instance, walked along the southern shore of Lake Michigan in the 1890s and observed the change in vegetation as he moved back from the beach and dunes to more stable land. His subsequent research at the University of Chicago documented the complex environmental factors that went into determining the distribution of plant communities.[3] About the same time, out on the Nebraska prairies, Frederic Clements investigated what he called the "succession" of plants. He was interested in the process that led to a "climax" vegetation, which he described as a "complex organism." What Clements meant was that many living things functioning together resembled a single being. They were mutually dependent. Just as the heart, head, and lungs of an animal could only exist together, plants interrelated with climate, soil, and each other to form a predictable vegetative association such as a grassland. The whole, Clements was starting to appreciate, was more than the sum of the parts. There was something special about communities. In 1914 the Scotch biologist J. Arthur Thompson first described this quality with the phrase "web of life."[4]

The next year in Ithaca, New York, Cornell University horticulturist Liberty Hyde Bailey concluded three decades of what he termed a "biocentric" approach to his subject with the publication of *The Holy Earth*. The book followed a well-worn intellectual path in arguing that abuse of the earth was morally wrong because it was God's creation. Bailey went on to advocate abandoning "cosmic self-ishness" and developing instead a sense of "earth righteousness." This, he felt, would help human beings "put our dominion into the realm of morals. It is now in the realm of trade."[5] Because of the holistic orientations of their discipline, ecologists frequently leaped from science to moral philosophy.

In the 1930s Frederic Clements teamed with a student of Henry Cowles named Victor Shelford to write *Bio-Ecology*. As a zoologist, Shelford thought that if Clements's conception of a "climax" excluded animals, it was too narrow. Searching for a phrase to designate all life-forms in an environment, Clements and Shelford hit upon "biotic community" or "biome."[6] The circle was widening.

Meanwhile, in 1927, Charles Elton coined the phrase "food chain." His ecological research revealed nutritional dependencies that started with the sun, proceeded through plants to plant eaters and then to the carnivores. Elton also used the metaphor of a pyramid: the simplest organisms with the shortest food chains were the most numerous and, as the base of the structure, the most important. Remove the top of the food pyramid—a hawk, say, or a human—and the system was hardly disturbed. But take away bases like plant life or soil bacteria and the pyramid collapsed. In one sense the food chain idea corroborated the old notion of the lower orders of nature existing for the higher. But ecologists turned this logic upside down. In reality, humans depended on the bacteria which sustained the grass which fed the cattle which became steaks. As the top link in the chain humans were not so much exalted as they were vulnerable. The least sophisticated life-forms stabilized the entire community and were the most vital to its continuation. Ecology took still more conceit out of humanity.[7]

Some pioneer ecologists did not favor describing nature as a community. The English ecologist Arthur G. Tansley, for instance, disliked the anthropomorphic connotations of the term. Nature was not a society or a neighborhood as those words were commonly understood. Instead Tansley used hard physical science, reduced nature to chemicals and energy, and described how these flowed through living things according to the laws of physics. Instead of "community" Tansley, in 1935, proposed "ecosystem," and the word caught on. In the 1940s Aldo Leopold used the metaphor of a "round river" to characterize the flow. More recent quantitative ecologists, such as David Gates and Eugene Odum, understood dependency in terms of energy transfer. By any name, what Tansley was describing was a relationship or association of living things, their nonliving context, and solar energy. From this perspective it would not be hard to draw ethical implications concerning human impacts on an integrated system that sustained life on earth.[8]

Another intellectual innovation of the ecologists was the concept of ecological "niche." Charles Elton coined the term in the late 1920s to designate the place a species occupied in the biotic community. Specialization, through evolution, filled the opportunities for various ways of living within a given environment. The concept of niche helped ecologists throw light on the ancient debate about the purpose of nonhuman life. Their research provided increasing evidence that an organism did not exist to help or hinder humans but simply to perform a role that their characteristics, and those of their environment, necessitated.

One of the earliest applications of the new ecological understanding was to the predator problem. Ecologists tended to oppose efforts of the federal government to control—actually, in the early years, to exterminate—large meat-eating animals that shared a link with humans in the food chain. Charles C. Adams led the American Society of Mammalogists in several decades of resistance to the relentless poisoning, trapping, and shooting of wolves, coyotes, mountain lions, bears, and even eagles and prairie dogs. Why not, Adams and his colleagues said, attempt to find ways of coexisting with the continent's native fauna?[9] Olaus Murie, a wildlife ecologist who worked somewhat uneasily with the federal predator programs survey for a quarter century, put his disagreement with their philosophy succinctly: "I dislike no animal because he eats." On another occasion Murie suggested that "we should go beyond proving the rights of animals to live in utilitarian terms. Why don't we just admit we like having them around? Isn't that answer enough?"[10] A later generation of environmentalists would have replied, "No, it isn't." Murie's logic, based on human pleasure in animals, was unabashedly anthropocentric. But at the root of his viewpoint was the feeling, however inchoate in the 1920s and 1930s, that predators had a right to exist if only because they did exist in the North American ecosystem.

Ecology, almost inevitably, led to the idea of interdependence. William Morton Wheeler, a Harvard biologist, began to think about it early in the present century when he studied social insects such as

ants and termites. Groups of these creatures acting together constituted what Wheeler called, as early as 1910, a "superorganism." In
the next two decades he generalized that there existed in nature "an
inexplicable 'social' tendency for wholes to combine . . . with wholes
to form wholes of higher orders." So it was that atoms formed molecules, molecules cells, and cells organisms. Organisms, it followed,
could cooperate with each other to form societies. Darwin and Kropotkin had understood this in the nineteenth century. Wheeler was
especially interested in the next step: a society of societies or an ecological community. He believed that every organism, humans included, existed as a member of such an extended community and was
dependent upon it.[11] At the University of Chicago a noted group of
ecologists headed by Warder Allee spent much of the 1930s documenting the existence of cooperative communities in nature. One of
Allee's colleagues, Alfred Emerson, thought that in its study of how
individual interests gave way to those of the group, ecology had the
potential to provide "a scientific basis for ethics."[12] The text upon
which Emerson, Allee, and others collaborated, *Principles of Animal
Ecology* (1949), became a basic source of a new scientific organicism.
It pointed toward an ethical philosophy based on the legitimacy of
everything alive.

Interdependence, as a description of nature and as a basis for determining human conduct toward nature, rose with ecology. Walter
P. Taylor, the president of the Ecological Society of America, commented that "there is little rugged individualism in nature" and went
on to depict the ecosystem as a "closely organized cooperative commonwealth of plants and animals."[13] In 1936 Secretary of Agriculture
Henry Wallace remarked that his generation needed a "Declaration of
Interdependence" just as the colonists had required a Declaration
of Independence.[14] The secretary's observation was perceptive. In the
1770s democratic-republican theory provided the rationale for extending the notion of rights, at least in theory, to "all men." In the
early twentieth century ecology suggested reasons for broadening
the concept of community, and the consequent notions of rights and
ethical behavior, still further.

During the interwar period the holism inherent in ecology received support from several lines of philosophical and theological inquiry. Together they helped lay the groundwork for environmental
ethics. The most all-embracing philosophy of interdependence was
unquestionably that of Alfred North Whitehead (1861–1947), the
English metaphysician who joined William Morton Wheeler on Harvard's faculty in 1924. Utilizing new findings that constantly inter-

acting electromagnetic particles were the essence of matter, White-head contended that the identity and purpose of every object in the universe arose from its relationship to everything else. All things were in flux at all times. This continuing interaction at the molecular level of all matter—animate and inanimate—defined reality. It followed for Whitehead that every organism, indeed every atom, had intrinsic value if only for the contribution it made to the ongoing reality of the universe, or what he called "process." Although not an ecologist, Whitehead used words like "interlocked" and "interwoven" to describe a view of the world that was ecological in the most fundamental sense.[15] Whitehead himself hoped that science would embrace his new organicism, abandon objectivity, and lead humankind to a recognition of the intrinsic worth of every component of the environment.

Probably because he couched his philosophy in simpler terms and lived it dramatically in the heart of Africa, Albert Schweitzer had far more influence than Whitehead on the popular understanding of a wide-ranging environmental ethic in the United States. Born in the Alsace-Lorraine region between France and Germany in 1875, Schweitzer, like Thoreau, Muir, and Henry Salt, broke sharply from the expectations of his associates and the assumptions of his culture. For him the year was 1905. Schweitzer abruptly resigned his university appointments (he held doctorates in both philosophy and theology) and ceased performing as a concert organist in order to train for a career in medicine. His hope was to serve the natives in what was then French Equatorial Africa. God, he said, told him to go.[16]

In September 1915, after two years at his African medical outpost, Schweitzer found himself on a small steamer moving slowly up the Ogowe River. It was sunset and the boat had just passed through a herd of hippopotamuses. Schweitzer was on deck, thinking about a problem that had puzzled him for years: What was the most valid basis for ethics? Suddenly "there flashed upon my mind, unforeseen and unsought, the phrase, 'Reverence for Life.'" The German word Schweitzer actually used was *Ehrfurcht,* which has the connotation of awed humility in the face of a vast and mysterious power. From this mystical starting point and from his study of the ethical teachings of India, China, and Tibet, Schweitzer built a theory of value based on the "will-to-live" that he understood every living being to possess. Right conduct for a human consisted of giving "to every will-to-live the same reverence for life that he gives to his own." The preservation, promotion, and enhancement of life in general became the anchor of Schweitzer's ethics.[17]

Schweitzer made it abundantly clear that his reverence for life did not end with human beings. In fact he wrote that "the great fault of all ethics hitherto has been that they believed themselves to have to deal only with the relations of man to man." In his eyes "a man is ethical only when life, as such, is sacred to him, that of plants and animals as that of his fellow men."[18] Elsewhere Schweitzer went still further, apparently extending his ethics, in the manner of Whitehead, to all matter. The ethical person, Schweitzer wrote in 1923, "shatters no ice crystal that sparkles in the sun, tears no leaf from its tree, breaks off no flower, and is careful not to crush any insect as he walks."[19]

But if all life, and perhaps even crystals of ice, were equally valuable, if they had equal significance as part of the universe, how was the ethical person to live? How could Schweitzer eat, and, as a doctor, how could he justify taking the lives of germs? Schweitzer's answer to such problems was that in the process of living one did on occasion kill other forms of life. But this should happen only when absolutely necessary to enhance another life and then only with a compassionate sense of "responsibility for the life which is sacrificed."[20] Whenever another life had to be taken, Schweitzer would pass the decision through this ethical filter. He provided an example: "The farmer who has mowed down a thousand flowers in his meadow in order to feed his cows must be careful on his way home not to strike the head off a single flower by the side of the road in idle amusement, for he thereby infringes the law of life without being under the pressure of necessity."[21]

On these same grounds Schweitzer approved the killing of animals for medical research but only when "really and truly necessary" and then only with the maximum alleviation of their pain. He added that this "sacrifice" of a life for humanity, as well as all the needless cruelty humans perpetrated, created an obligation for everyone "to do as much good as we possibly can to all creatures in all sorts of circumstances." So Schweitzer would place a worm, washed onto pavement by a rainstorm, back into the grass and remove an insect struggling in a pool of water. He explained that, "when I help an insect out of his troubles all that I do is to attempt to remove some of the guilt contracted through [humanity's] crimes against animals." For the same reason Schweitzer championed the animal protection or humane movement. In a 1935 essay he called for "making kindness to animals an ethical demand, on exactly the same footing as kindness to human beings." The powerful and privileged status humans enjoyed in the natural community entailed for Schweitzer not a right to exploit but a responsibility to protect.[22] This demanded "so great a revolution for ethics" that philosophers had hitherto resisted the conceptual leap. This was particularly the case in Europe and North America, where ethics traditionally concerned only relationships between people. Schweitzer made it his lifework to think through the details of "the ethic of love for all creation."[23]

Like William Lecky and Charles Darwin, Schweitzer concerned himself with the history and future of ethics. He believed in the potential of ethical evolution. He wrote that the thoughtful person must "widen the circle from the narrowest limits of the family first to include the clan, then the tribe, then the nation and finally all mankind." But this was only the beginning for Schweitzer. "By reason of the quite universal idea . . . of participation in a common nature, [one] is compelled to declare the unity of mankind with all created beings." Schweitzer understood that so fundamental an intellectual revolution as the extension of ethics to new categories of beings was not easy. World War I reminded him of the shortfall in even interhuman ethics. But he took hope from the history of ideas: "It was once considered stupid to think that colored men were really human and must be treated humanely. This stupidity has become a truth." In the same manner Schweitzer predicted in 1923 that the ethical circle would continue to widen: "Today it is thought an exaggeration to state that a reasonable ethic demands constant consideration for all living things down to the lowliest manifestations of life. The time is coming, however, when people will be amazed that it took so long for mankind to recognize that thoughtless injury to life was incompatible with ethics."[24]

Albert Schweitzer's ideas reached the United States in English translations of his books in the 1920s and 1930s. Although his was a mystical holism, it coincided remarkably with the ecologists' concept of a biotic community. No life was worthless or merely instrumental to another life; every being had a place in the ecosystem and, some philosophers and scientists were beginning to think, a right to that place.

Understanding that ethics had expanded before, Schweitzer anticipated its expanding again. One encouraging sign was the expansion of his own reputation and influence. The image of the kindly, craggy-faced doctor stepping around an insect or assisting a worm back to the soil stuck in people's minds. In 1952 Schweitzer received the Nobel Peace Prize; a decade later Rachel Carson dedicated a book to him entitled *Silent Spring*. When Schweitzer died at the age of ninety, in 1965, the environmental movement was starting to lengthen its stride along the course he had outlined.

Few today would challenge Aldo Leopold's reputation as one of the seminal thinkers in the modern American development of environmental ethics. Yet his statement of "the land ethic," and the basis of his enormous reputation, amounts to but twenty-five small and undocumented pages at the conclusion of a book he did not live to see in print: *A Sand County Almanac* (1949). Nevertheless, within two decades Leopold's manifesto became the intellectual touchstone for the most far-reaching environmental movement in American history. In 1963 Secretary of the Interior Stewart L. Udall declared that "if asked to select a single volume which contains a noble elegy for the American earth and a plea for a new land ethic, most of us at Interior would vote for Aldo Leopold's *A Sand County Almanac.*"[25] J. Baird Callicott has called Leopold "the father or founding genius of recent environmental ethics," a writer who created the paradigm of an ethical system that included the whole of nature and nature as a whole.[26] Wallace Stegner considered *A Sand County Almanac* "one of the prophetic books, the utterance of an American Isaiah," and intellectual historian Donald Fleming called Leopold "the Moses of the New Conservation impulse of the 1960s and 1970s, who handed down the Tablets of the Law but did not live to enter the promised land." In a similar vein, another tribute singled out Leopold as "an authentic patron saint of the modern environmental movement," and *A Sand County Almanac* as "one of its new testament gospels." Dave Foreman, a founder of the radical environmental group Earth First!, called Leopold's work "not only the most important conservation book ever written, it is the most important book ever written."[27] Van Rensselaer Potter dedicated a 1971 volume to Leopold as an intellectual pioneer "who anticipated the extension of ethics to Bioethics." *A Sand County Almanac,* which Leopold thought might never even find a publisher, went on after his death to sell a million copies in several paperback editions. René Dubos felt it was "The Holy Writ of American Conservation."[28]

Aldo Leopold was born in comfortable circumstances in Burlington, Iowa, in 1887. His early experience with hunting and ornithology inclined him toward an outdoor profession. He pursued it at Yale, graduating from the School of Forestry in 1909. It was an exciting time to launch this kind of career. President Theodore Roosevelt and his Chief Forester Gifford Pinchot had just succeeded in making a new idea called "conservation" a keystone of Progressive politics. Their well-publicized governors' conference on the conservation of natural resources, held at the White House, took place just as Leopold graduated from Yale. Indeed, the graduate program in forestry he entered in the fall of 1908 owed its existence to the generosity of Gifford Pinchot. Understandably Leopold absorbed much of the utilitarianism of Pinchot and the pioneer conservationists. Nature was to be used—albeit wisely and efficiently—for the greatest good of the greatest number (of people) over the longest possible run. Management was the mecca of utilitarian conservation, and Leopold started his professional life in 1909 as a manager of national forests in Arizona and New Mexico. One of his first projects was a campaign for the complete extermination of "bad" predators (chiefly wolves and mountain lions) in the interest, he then believed, of helping the "good" animals (cattle and deer).

But the emergence of the ecological sciences brought a new perspective, and as he matured Leopold absorbed its import. He came to believe that "the complexity of the land organism" was "the outstanding scientific discovery of the twentieth century," and he realized that predators were part of the whole. By 1933, when he assumed a professorship of wildlife management at the University of Wisconsin, Leopold could tell his students that the entire idea of good and bad species was the product of anthropocentric and utilitarian bias. One of his lecture notes stated that "when we attempt to say that an animal is 'useful,' 'ugly' or 'cruel,' we are failing to see it as part of the land. We do not make the same error of calling a carburetor 'greedy.' We see it as part of a functioning motor." On another occasion he advised those who would modify the natural world that "to keep every cog and wheel is the first precaution of intelligent tinkering."[29]

This organic conception of nature, which Leopold came to share with his friend Olaus Murie, saw species functioning like organs within a body or, following one of Leopold's favorite metaphors, like parts of an engine. This insight was one of the hallmarks of twentieth-century ecology and a foundation of environmental ethics. Groping for another way to make the point, Leopold chose as the title of a 1944 essay the arresting phrase "thinking like a mountain." It described an afternoon, probably in 1909, when Leopold and his Forest Service crew were lunching on a cliff overlooking a New Mexico river. They saw a wolf cross the current, and, operating under the old ethical criteria, instantly opened fire. "I was young then," Leopold remembered, "and full of trigger-itch; I thought that because fewer wolves meant more deer, that no wolves would mean hunters' paradise." The wolf fell, but Leopold scrambled off the rimrock in time to "watch a fierce green fire dying in her eyes."[30] The green fire haunted his thought for thirty years. It started him toward the realization that wolves and other predators were necessary for the healthy herds of game animals humans prized. This was a utilitarian viewpoint, but Leopold transcended it to understand that the wolf was a legitimate part of the southwestern ecosystem. Its presence had ecological and ethical, if not economic, justification. Gradually Leopold realized that in his predator-extermination phase he had not taken what Thoreau called "the wider view." For Leopold this transcendence of anthropocentrism was thinking like a mountain.

Leopold's first exploration of the ethics of the human relationship to nature appeared in a paper unpublished until 1979 but written in 1923, when he was an assistant director of the national forests in Arizona and New Mexico. The essay began traditionally enough by assuming the need for the "development" of the region and the importance of "economic resources" in that process. For most of his paper Leopold drew on the familiar Pinchot-inspired position that conservation was necessary for continued prosperity. But in an unusual conclusion he turned to "conservation as a moral issue." Pinchot, Roosevelt, and especially W J McGee had used similar rhetoric, but only in the sense of the morality of equal *human* rights to resources. This amounted to the familiar democratic rationale for Progressive conservation. Leopold, however, had something else in mind. The argument that the earth was humankind's "physical provider" and hence worthy of ethical consideration left him unsatisfied. He wondered if there was not a "closer and deeper relation" to nature based on the idea that the earth itself was alive.

With this concept Leopold moved into uncharted waters. The humanitarians in England and the United States were clearly concerned with living things, but what about geographical features such as oceans, forests, and mountains? Were they animate or inanimate, living or merely mechanical? Intuitively, Leopold rebelled against the idea of a "dead earth." He already knew enough about ecology to understand the importance of interconnections and interdependencies, which rendered hollow the traditional distinction between the organic and inorganic.[31]

In his search for help with these concepts Leopold found, rather surprisingly, the Russian philosopher Peter D. Ouspensky (1878–1947). Almost an exact contemporary of Leopold, Ouspensky published *Tertium Organum* in 1912. An English translation appeared in the United States in 1920, and Leopold quoted from it in his 1923 essay. What excited Leopold about Ouspensky was the Russian's conviction that "there can be nothing dead or mechanical in Nature . . . life and feeling . . . must exist in everything." The philosopher continued "*a mountain, a tree, a river, the fish in the river, drops of water, rain,*

a plant, fire—each separately must possess a mind of its own." Ouspensky wrote about "the mind of a *mountain*," and it is likely that
Leopold remembered this phrase twenty years later when he chose a
title for one of his best-known essays, "Thinking Like a Mountain." [32]

Ouspensky believed that everything in the universe had a "phe-
nomenal," or visible, appearance, and a "noumenal" essence. The
latter was hidden to humans. Ouspensky variously described it as
life, emotions, feeling, or mind. Leopold had sufficient confidence in
his intuition to grasp this idea and went on to accept Ouspensky's
argument that combinations of objects and processes could also be
said to have a life of their own. The whole was greater than the sum
of the parts. So cells functioned together to make organs and arrangements of organs made organisms possible. But Ouspensky did
not stop here. Many organisms working together in the context of
air, water, and soil constituted a superorganism with its own particular noumenon. Such functioning communities could not be divided
without destroying their collective lives; or, as Ouspensky put it in a
phrase Leopold quoted, "anything indivisible is a living being." Take
away the heart, for example, and you kill the greater life of the wolf.
Remove the wolf from the ecosystem and you alter the noumenon of
the biotic community of which it was a part. The erosion of soil
produces a similar alteration. The conclusion Ouspensky drew and
Leopold applauded was that the earth itself (or, as Leopold came to
prefer, "land") was not dead but alive. Leopold came to the Russian's
aid in expressing the concept: The earth was alive, "vastly less alive
than ourselves in degree, but vastly greater than ourselves in time
and space—a being that was old when the morning stars sang together, and, when the last of us has been gathered unto his fathers,
will still be young." [33]

For Leopold in 1923 the assumption that the earth was "an organism possessing a certain kind and degree of life" offered reason
enough for an ethical relationship. "A moral being," he wrote, "respects a living thing." This proposition, of course, could and would
receive intensive scrutiny by later philosophers. But Leopold, already probing the scientific basis of a functioning earth-organism,
did not pursue the philosophical puzzles. As he saw it, the "indi-
visibility of the earth—its soil, mountains, rivers, forests, climate,
plants, and animals" was sufficient reason for respecting the earth
"not only as a useful servant but as a living being." [34]

For the historical record, Ouspensky's philosophy had many precursors. Leopold, as the administrator of a remote forest in New

Mexico, would have had little reason to read them extensively, but the organicists and animists of the seventeenth and eighteenth centuries, and the nineteenth-century Transcendentalists like Thoreau, assumed the same all-pervading force that made nature a vast, living, interconnected being. Leopold also ignored the Eastern faiths when he wrote in 1923 that "most religions, insofar as I know" assumed a dead earth created expressly for human beings. Neither did the forester reveal any familiarity with the work of William Morton Wheeler on superorganisms. But Leopold did refer in his 1923 essay to John Muir's challenge to anthropocentrism in the 1860s, quoting his opinion that even rattlesnakes were parts of creation and, as such, worthy of respect regardless of human bias. On the same point he cited the natural historian John Burroughs, who wrote in 1920 that "creation is no more exclusively for [humans] than for the least of living things."[35] Leopold ended this discussion with perhaps the oldest defense of the rights of nonhuman beings in the history of thought. In a rare reference to the deity, Leopold concluded that "God started his show a good many million years before he had any men for audience . . . and . . . it is just barely possible that God himself likes to hear birds sing and see flowers grow."[36]

Ten years passed before Aldo Leopold wrote again about the ethical dimension of conservation. When he did so, Susan Flader thinks, he wrote "in a strikingly different manner"—as an ecologist rather than as a philosopher and theologian.[37] Her assessment is true in part. As Leopold turned in the early 1930s from government to an academic career and associated with renowned ecologists like his friend Charles Elton, he absorbed a new vocabulary of chains, flows, niches, and pyramids. The glue holding the earth together consisted of food and energy circuits rather than divine forces or Ouspensky's noumena. But striking continuities carry over from the 1923 essay. The seeds of the key concepts in Leopold's land ethic are all present in the 1923 paper. He had discovered the idea that a life community extended far beyond traditional definitions. He had argued for an ethical relationship to the community's component parts and to the whole. And he had found that a strictly economic posture toward nature created serious ecological and ethical problems. Leopold's plunge into ecology represented not so much a switch as an extension. He never stopped working on the borderline between science and philosophy, using each to reinforce the other. When science lost sight of the broad picture in a welter of detail, philosophy adjusted the focus. Perhaps Leopold remembered Ouspensky's warning that scientists "always study the little finger of nature."[38] Ecologists, at any rate, were the scientists most likely to meet holistic-thinking theologians and philosophers half-way.

The next building block in Aldo Leopold's land ethic was a paper read in New Mexico on May 1, 1933. Published as "The Conservation Ethic," its major contribution was the idea of ethical evolution. Like so many commentators on this subject, Leopold noted the parallels between human slavery and unconditional ownership of land. The fact that slavery had been challenged and abolished encouraged him with regard to nature. "The Conservation Ethic" begins with a reference to "god-like Odysseus" who returned to his Greek homeland to hang, on a single rope, a dozen slave-girls accused of misbehavior during his absence. Yet, Leopold explained, Odysseus was an ethical man and he did not condone murder. The point was that slaves were property, and as such were outside Odysseus's ethical community. Relations with them were strictly utilitarian, "a matter of expediency, not of right and wrong." With the passage of time, Leopold continued, an "extension of ethics" occurred. Slaves became people, the abolition of slavery followed. But, Leopold continued, "there is as yet no ethic dealing with man's relationship to land and to the non-human animals and plants which grow upon it. Land, like Odysseus' slave-girls, is still property." The progress of civilization still entails "the enslavement of . . . earth." Leopold hoped that the conservation movement represented an awareness that "the destruction of land . . . is wrong." And, Leopold made clear, he did not mean "wrong" in the sense of inexpedient or economically disadvantageous. He meant it in the same sense that abuse of another human being was wrong.[39]

Aldo Leopold gave no specific indication in his 1933 statement (or, for that matter, in *A Sand County Almanac*) that anyone had ever thought about ethical expansion before his time. Yet he must have known that Charles Darwin had written extensively on the subject. In fact, in identifying "the tendency of interdependent individuals or societies to evolve modes of cooperation" known as ethics, Leopold nearly plagiarized Darwin. He also ignored the anticipation of his ideas by William Lecky, Henry Salt, Edward Evans, J. Howard Moore, Liberty Hyde Bailey, and Albert Schweitzer. Yet the work of these men was readily available when Leopold was in college or early in his professional career. Granted that as an ecologist Leopold took his ethics further than most of these thinkers—to collections of organisms and habitats organized as ecosystems, and to the extent of defending them scientifically—but it is disconcerting that this scientist, so meticulous in his recording of biological facts, would play so loosely with historical ones. Similarly surprising is the occasional tendency of Leopold scholars to aggrandize their subject at the expense of historical accuracy. The contemporary philosopher J. Baird Callicott, for example, overstated the case with his opinion that Leopold's ideas are "the first self-conscious, sustained and systematic attempt in modern Western literature to develop an ethical theory which would include non-human natural entities and nature itself in the purview of morals." More recently, however, Callicott has modified his position in an essay which argues that "Leopold's *unique* contribution . . . was to provide a sound *scientific* foundation for a land or environmental ethic."[40]

Probably in July 1947, Leopold reviewed his 1923 and 1933 essays, added insights from subsequent papers,[41] and wrote for *A Sand County Almanac* a final chapter entitled "The Land Ethic." It begins with the story of Odysseus and the slave-girls, lifted with only minor changes from the 1933 paper, and the concept of ethical evolution. But then Leopold turns with fresh insights to the origin and meaning of ethics. Ethics, he explains, is the body of self-imposed limitations on freedom of action that derive from the recognition that "the individual is a member of a community of interdependent parts." The land ethic, then, "changes the role of *Homo sapiens* from conqueror of the land-community to plain member and citizen of it. It implies respect for his fellow-members, and also respect for the community as such." Behind this sentence lies Leopold's recognition that while, in one sense, humans are simply members of a "biotic team," in another their technologically magnified power to affect nature sets them apart from the other members. As it became more powerful human civilization increasingly needed the restraints afforded by a land ethic. Just as concepts of right and wrong had made human society more just, Leopold felt they would enhance justice between humankind and the earth. The entire import of *A Sand County Almanac,* Leopold writes in his foreword, is directed to helping land "survive the impact of mechanized man." His statement of the basic problem and solution is characteristically pithy and powerful: "We abuse land because we regard it as a commodity belonging to us. When we see land as a community to which we belong, we may begin to use it with love and respect."[42]

Frequently in *A Sand County Almanac* Leopold takes an instrumental view of the land ethic. It is prudent for people to be ethical with regard to the natural order that sustains the human one. A battle-scarred veteran of conservation-policy wars, Leopold knew this was the best way to sell his philosophy in the 1930s and 1940s. He also knew it was not the full story. His most radical ideas, and his greatest significance for the 1960s and beyond, concern the intrinsic rights of nonhuman life-forms and of life communities or ecosystems. Early in "The Land Ethic" Leopold affirms "the right to continued existence" of not only animals and plants but waters and soils as well. The life-forms that share the planet with people should be allowed to live "as a matter of biotic right, regardless of the presence or absence of economic advantage to us." This means "there are obligations to land over and above those dictated by self-interest," obligations grounded on the recognition that humans and the other components of nature are ecological equals.[43]

This idea of biotic right was the intellectual dynamite in *A Sand County Almanac,* the ingredient that set it apart from the traditional conservation movement in the United States. The Darwinian evolutionists and the old-style humanitarians had occasionally glimpsed the idea of a morality that extended beyond human society, but Leopold, with the aid of ecology, gave the concept its most dramatic articulation up to at least the late 1940s. Most of the earlier advocates of extended ethics dealt almost exclusively with individual organisms, and then mainly with the higher animals. Leopold's achievement was to follow the road to its logical termination—in ecosystems, environment, or "land." For him individual organisms, humans included, were always subordinate in importance to what he styled "the biotic community."[44] While he had several predecessors in the idea of ethical extension, Leopold is rightly regarded as the most important source of modern biocentric or holistic ethics.

If Darwin killed dualism, the ecologists presided over its burial. Humans were simply one group of many in a greatly expanded biotic community. The moral implications of this idea for human behavior were, to say the least, problematic, and philosophers after Leopold continued to struggle with the subject. But Leopold was quite clear about what he thought the land ethic mandated in terms of conduct. It did not mean having *no* impact on one's environment. As a biologist Leopold knew this was an impossibility for any organism. He might have chuckled at vegetarians such as Henry Salt and extreme right-to-life sects such as the group in India called the Jains who, following the philosophy of *ahimsa,* breathed through gauze so as not to inhale insects or microorganisms. Even Albert Schweitzer's assistance to struggling worms and insects would have struck Leopold as naïve and beside the main point of land health. Leopold's concept of Schweitzer's reverence-for-life principle was precisely that—respect for life *en toto,* not so much for the individual players in life process. Of course Leopold approved of Schweitzer's principle of taking life only for essential purposes and with reverence for that which was killed. Hunting, meat eating, and even, in Leopold's words, "the alteration, management and use" of the ecosystem were acceptable impacts of humans on nature. The essential proviso, Leopold wrote as early as 1933, was that any human action be undertaken in such a way as "to prevent the deterioration of the environment." By 1948, when he finished "The Land Ethic" for *A Sand County Almanac,* Leopold had refined this principle into what has become his most widely quoted precept. A land-use decision "is right when it tends to preserve the integrity, stability, and beauty of the biotic community. It is wrong when it tends otherwise." [45]

This functioning definition of a land ethic, shaped by the insights of ecology and by Leopold's lifelong involvement with game management, should have eased the qualms of humanitarians about the suffering of individual organisms. Leopold seldom thought in these terms and he expressed no interest in opposing vivisection or easing the lot of domestic animals. His ethic operated on the species level and, more comfortably, in the realm of congregations of species and ecosystemic processes. Donald Worster notwithstanding, [46] Leopold never wrote about the natural rights of particular organisms nor used classic Jeffersonian rhetoric in defending nonhuman beings. A game manager most of his professional life, he advocated killing thousands of animals if their population exceeded the carrying capacity of their environment. Culling the herd by intelligent human managers was necessary for its "stability," and, in a sense, its "beauty." The reason shooting the wolf in New Mexico had been ethically wrong was that there were very few wolves in that area. Their extermination destroyed the integrity of the biotic community. Moreover, wolves helped control deer populations and thus exerted a stabilizing influence. But, Leopold would be quick to add, too many wolves (or, presumably, humans) was just as unfortunate as too many deer. Let the natural dynamic balances, calculated by ecological research, determine the appropriate human action. The end product for Leopold was always the "healthy functioning" of the "biotic mechanism." [47]

Leopold knew that this matter of natural balances was another way his species differed from other species. Predation did not check the human population as it did others. To make the point in his 1923 essay, Leopold drew on John Burroughs's *Accepting the Universe* (1920). Burroughs, Leopold wrote, explained that a potato bug "exterminated the potato, and thereby exterminated itself." [48] But parasites

checked the potato bug population before this occurred. Humans
had no significant predators to control their numbers, and their technology enabled them to disrupt nature virtually without limit. This
was where the land ethic played a vital role. Leopold took it to be a
restraint on humankind's capacity to modify the environment beyond levels conducive to its own survival and the biotic rights of
other species.

Leopold was well aware of the massive obstacles standing in the
way of introducing morality into human-environment relations.
"No important change in ethics," he wrote in *A Sand County Almanac,* "was ever accomplished without an internal change in our intellectual emphasis, loyalties, affections, and convictions." The conservation movement of his day, the 1940s, had not, in his view,
touched these "foundations of conduct." As proof Leopold submitted that "philosophy and religion have not yet heard" of "the
extension of social conscience from people to land." In this belief
Leopold was both correct and in error. Although evidently unrecog-
nized by Leopold, philosophy, biology, history, religion, and even
law (the humane legislation) had all "heard" of the extension of ethics; if not as far an extension as Leopold's proposal, at least beyond
human-to-human interactions. In 1944, four years before Leopold
wrote "The Land Ethic," Chauncey D. Leake told the American Association for the Advancement of Science that "whatever preserves
the 'balance of nature' is . . . good."[49] But Leopold was correct in
assuming that Western thought in general contained little approaching the holistic character of his moral philosophy. In matters of
slowly shifting attitudes and values, however, he knew the value of
patience. Ethics, after all, was comprised of ideals, not descriptions
of how people actually behaved. "We shall never achieve harmony
with land," Leopold believed, "any more than we shall achieve justice or liberty for people. In these higher aspirations the important
thing is not to achieve, but to strive."[50]

The parallel Leopold drew here between human-to-human and
human-to-nature ethics informed many of his final essays. In 1947 in
"The Ecological Conscience" he noted that it "has required nineteen
centuries to define decent man-to-man conduct and the process is
only half done; it may take as long to evolve a code of decency for
man-to-land conduct." His prescription for such progress was not to
allow economics to dictate ethics: "Cease being intimidated by the
argument that a right action is impossible because it does not yield
maximum profits, or that a wrong action is to be condoned because
it pays." "That philosophy," Leopold concluded, "is dead in human
relations, and its funeral in land-relations is overdue."[51]

Aldo Leopold's pessimism concerning public comprehension, not to speak of acceptance, of the land ethic was supported by the early history of *A Sand County Almanac*. As an unpublished typescript it was sent to and rejected by a number of publishing houses; the author despaired of ever seeing his work in print. Leopold did not live to see the reviews of *Sand County,* but they probably would have disappointed him. Most critics understood the book to be just another collection of charming nature essays. Very few reviewers recognized the ideas that a later generation would find compelling. Initial sales of the slender green volume were slow; before its renaissance in the 1960s, it sold only a few thousand copies.

The most obvious reason for the initial lack of public interest in Leopold's ideas was their truly radical nature. What he proposed would have necessitated a complete restructuring of basic American priorities and behavior. His philosophy also involved a radical redefinition of progress. The conquest and exploitation of the environment that had powered America's westward march for three centuries was to be replaced as an ideal by cooperation and coexistence. The land ethic, in short, placed unprecedented restraints on a process that had won the West and lifted the nation to at least temporary greatness as a world power. Leopold's philosophy abruptly curtailed the accustomed freedom with which Americans had hitherto dealt with nature.

Americans of the late 1940s and early 1950s were not likely to receive Leopold's proposals with enthusiasm. The deprivations of the Great Depression fed immediately into those of World War II. Emerging from fifteen years of frustrated materialism, the United States pursued the main chance with extraordinary vigor. The postwar decade was a time for building homes and families. Upholding the integrity, stability, and beauty of the ecosystem and granting even nonutilitarian species biotic rights made little sense to parents of the first wave of baby boomers. Moreover, most ecologists rejected Leopold's ideals. Ecology after World War II became increasingly abstract, quantitative, and reductionist.[52] Crop yields and mathematical modeling, not the ethical implications of the organic wholeness of life and matter, dominated the new research agenda. Interdependence gave way as an organizing concept to production efficiency. Meanwhile, a substantial proportion of life scientists turned their attention inward, to cells and molecules. The kind of integrative natural history at which Aldo Leopold excelled seemed to many hopelessly old-fashioned. In this relatively hostile climate of opinion the ecological perspective and environmental ethics took what shelter they could find in the humanities, in religion, and in the so-called counterculture. This intellectual climate resembled that of two or three centuries earlier, when organicism and interrelatedness were the exclusive concern of theologians, philosophers, and poets. But by the 1980s, as Robert P. McIntosh helps explain,[53] a new breed of ecologists sensitive to the ethical implications of their science picked up Leopold's emphasis once again.

It would have been hard to predict from the first half of Joseph Wood Krutch's life that he would become a major spokesman for Leopold's ideas. But, as the title of his autobiography put it, he had *More Lives than One.*[54] Born in 1893 in Knoxville, Tennessee, Krutch studied English at Columbia University's graduate school and emerged in the 1920s as one of America's leading young intellectuals of the "lost generation" era. Krutch systematically rejected religion, mythology, art, and ethics as grounds for human faith. In 1929 he concluded, in a widely acclaimed book entitled *The Modern Temper,* that the human spirit faced a tooth-and-claw world stripped by science of moral and spiritual values. Yet Krutch still felt his species should try to maintain a distinction from the rest of nature and "rather die as men than live as animals." Here was the old dualism that had impeded environmental ethics for so long. The young Krutch clung to the idea that he was not part of the natural community. As for nature itself, he confessed that his principal feeling about it was terror.[55]

Following T. S. Eliot's imagery in *The Wasteland* (1922), Krutch wrote in 1929 of his despair over the "desert" of human values.[56] But when he encountered the actual desert he began to change his mind. The process began in 1938 when Krutch vacationed for the first time in the Southwest. As had happened to Aldo Leopold thirty years earlier, the wildness of Arizona, New Mexico, and Utah changed his way of thinking. For Krutch, whose previous interest in nature centered on his Connecticut bird feeders, the deserts of the Southwest were austere, brooding, and awesome. Here he perceived an environment that existed, and existed splendidly, without the slightest reference to humans and their civilization. From this starting point in the wilderness Krutch began to formulate a new philosophy based on the importance of the nonhuman world.

The next step in Krutch's intellectual odyssey was his rediscovery of Henry David Thoreau. As a college student he had read and rejected Thoreau as completely irrelevant to the quest for meaning and value in the human endeavor. But by the 1940s Krutch was ready to concede that Thoreau pointed to one way out of the bleak despair of modern intellectuals. Humans could find comfort in their membership in the greater community of living things. With this insight

Krutch reevaluated Thoreau's relationship to sunfish and wood-chucks at Walden Pond and, in 1948, published a biography of the New England naturalist. In this he followed the example of Henry Salt, whose biography of Thoreau appeared in 1890 on the verge of his own plunge into transhuman ethical philosophy.

In the early 1950s, after many trips to renew his spirit in the Southwest, Krutch published *The Desert Year*. It was a collection of nature essays similar in format to the opening sections of Aldo Leopold's *A Sand County Almanac,* which also traced a landscape through the seasons. In 1952, at the age of fifty-seven, Krutch completed his pilgrimage by retiring from Columbia University and moving to a lightly settled area near Tucson, Arizona. There followed a series of books reflecting Krutch's new-found joy in nature: *The Voice of the Desert* (1956), *Grand Canyon* (1958), and *The Forgotten Peninsula: A Naturalist in Baja California* (1961). A common theme ran through these works: "The wilderness and the idea of wilderness is one of the permanent homes of the human spirit." [57]

Aldo Leopold had preceded Joseph Wood Krutch in discovering the Southwest and recognizing the value of wilderness. In the 1950s Krutch followed Leopold's example once again, into environmental ethics. His most succinct statement appeared in a 1954 essay entitled "Conservation Is Not Enough." The point of the title was that old-style utilitarian and anthropocentric resource management was insufficient to save nature (and, ultimately, humankind) from human selfishness. Krutch argued the need for "love, some feeling for, as well as understanding of, the inclusive community of rocks and soils, plants and animals, of which we are a part." [58] Of course this was almost a paraphrase of Leopold, and Krutch credited *A Sand County Almanac* as "subtle" and "seminal"; he also cited Leopold's little-known 1933 essay in the *Journal of Forestry*.

Krutch, to be sure, was not a trained scientist. His instinct as a humanist was to draw on the theological organicism of John Ray, whom he quoted in "Conservation Is Not Enough." But Krutch understood the relevance of the ecologists' findings to his ethics. "The science of ecology," he explained, "is every day making [clear] . . . those . . . interdependencies which, no matter how remote, . . . are crucial even for us." From this starting point Krutch could develop one of the main tenets of ecology, namely the irony of modern men and women's "too successful participation in the struggle for existence." Krutch meant that the modification of nature was beneficial up to the point where it did not interfere too drastically with the ecosystem as a whole. Everything in nature had limits, even human progress, and if humanity "insists upon trying to go beyond those limits, nature will have the last word."[59]

All this underscored for Krutch the need for a "large morality" predicated on the realization that people "must be part not only of the human community, but of the whole community, . . . the natural . . . community." Like Leopold, Krutch left some ambiguity as to whether his extended ethic was pure, in the sense of respecting the rights of other parts of existence, or instrumental to the successful continuation of human existence. Pragmatically he knew, as did Leopold, that the latter had a better chance to win public favor in the 1950s. But Krutch made clear his belief in the "right to live" of creatures that had no direct bearing on human welfare. Still, the main thrust of his philosophy, as of Leopold's, centered on the idea that an ethical attitude toward nature was "better in the longest run for [humans] also."[60]

In 1956 Krutch continued developing his philosophy of respect for nature in a book, *The Great Chain of Life*. It explored one of the oldest ideas in Western (especially Christian) thought, namely, the concept that every part of creation has purpose, importance, and value to the creator.[61] Krutch understood the science of ecology to say the same thing in nontheological terms, but he deplored the disrespect many modern scientists showed for life and life process. College biology, with its emphasis on the collection and dissection of specimens, seemed to teach little love of nature. Killing a creature without real need, Krutch agreed with Schweitzer, "is at least a small murder." The revolutionary new ethics implicit in such a statement also appeared when Krutch declared that "the wanton killing of an animal differs from the wanton killing of a human being only in degree." In 1956 Krutch did not pursue this philosophical distinction, but in the manner of the animal rightists, and in contrast to Leopold, he came out strongly against sport as well as subsistence hunting, vivisection, and the fur and feather trades.[62]

Although Krutch was the most popular American writer to publicize Leopold's ideas about ethical extension, he received help from several scientists who retained broad philosophical perspectives in an age of increasing emphasis on economics. One was the biologist Olaus Murie, an early opponent of predator control and a collaborator with Aldo Leopold in the formation of the Wilderness Society in 1935. In 1954, the same year as Krutch's essay on the limitations of conservation, Murie published "Ethics in Wildlife Management." He criticized anthropocentric wildlife "technicians" whose goal was only the maintenance of game populations. He hoped for more "thoughtful" scientists who would endeavor "to understand our place in Nature." Murie's own "groping for a code of ethics toward . . . nature" led him to try to formulate "a sense of neighborliness in the Nature of which we are a part." Referring to Leopold, Thoreau, and Ralph Waldo Emerson, Murie called for "a big-hearted code of ethics" that granted nature a "right to exist." He approved of sport hunting provided it included love of the wilderness context and respect for the prey. This had been Leopold's essential position. As for "meat hunters" who killed indiscriminately, Murie condemned them as strongly as Krutch, helping set the stage for continuing controversy over the ethics of hunting.[63]

With an ecologist's sense of the importance of every living "cog and wheel" to the healthy functioning of the land, Aldo Leopold had stressed the necessity of saving all of the biotic mechanism. In other words, every living thing had a right to "continued existence." This land ethic held the implicit idea that a too-complete human victory in the struggle for existence carried ironic consequences for the victors. "The conqueror role," wrote Leopold, "is eventually self-defeating." A natural world tailored too closely to human needs could bring ruin to the tailors. Leopold's primary case in point had been the eradication of predators such as wolves; his recommendation was to think like a mountain—that is, holistically and not anthropocentrically. He saw evolution as a great equalizer. "Men," he said, "are only fellow-voyagers with other creatures in the odyssey of evolution."[64]

In the 1950s the scientist who went furthest with the idea of the integrity of the ecosystem was René Dubos (1901–1982). A brilliant bacteriologist who would win a Pulitzer Prize, Dubos dedicated his early career to killing a particular form of life: germs. His research contributed significantly to the identification and application of antibiotics. Like predator-control programs and insecticides such as DDT, the new "miracle" drugs such as penicillin tempted humanity with the edenic vision of a sanitized world. But as he matured Dubos experienced doubts about the ends his research helped make possible. By the 1950s he was well acquainted with ecology and was prepared to say that even germs should not be eradicated. Let the antibiotics control disease-causing germs but not exterminate them. A healthy human organism, Dubos believed, could and should rely on natural resistance to infection. People and germs should coexist, just like people and wolves. Here was a completely new point of view. As one of Dubos's colleagues remarked, these ideas "marked the first time that anyone grasped the point that disease is part of the total harmony."[65]

Dubos never quite said that germs had a right to exist which humans should respect. His point was that people would actually be better off with a full complement of germs in the world if only because extermination might lead to unforeseen health problems. But this was far from the old dualistic egocentrism. In *A God Within* (1972) Dubos explained the difference between "crude" anthropocentrism, which held that "man is the only value to be considered in managing the world," and what he called "enlightened anthropocentrism." The latter acknowledged that over the long run "the world's good always coincides with man's own most meaningful good." Echoing Krutch, about whom he wrote an admiring essay,[66] Dubos argued that effective earth stewardship depended on loving nature "for her own sake."[67] Thinking ecologically, Dubos arrived at the conclusion that germs, too, were residents of Leopold's mountain, fellow travelers in the evolutionary process, and, as such, were entitled to continuing passage on the planet.

Remarkably, in a male-dominated field, the two books that proved most effective in extending American ethics were the work of women. Harriet Beecher Stowe's *Uncle Tom's Cabin,* published in 1852, was the catalyst around which antislavery thought crystallized. Its argument was simple and pointed: blacks were not commodities to be exploited, but members of the moral community. This idea proved to be the intellectual explosive that blew American society apart at the seams.[68] There was considerable truth in Abraham Lincoln's characterization of Stowe as the lady who caused the civil war. One-hundred and ten years after *Uncle Tom's Cabin* Rachel Carson wrote another book that exploded against traditional American assumptions. It argued that all life-forms, even insects, were not commodities but deserved ethical consideration. Carson's *Silent Spring* (1962) was a landmark in the development of an ecological perspective. It did much to accelerate the new environmentalism and generated the most widespread public consideration of environmental ethics to that date.

Like Aldo Leopold, Rachel Carson never earned nor cared to earn a Ph.D. Her forte was not original research but old-fashioned natural history, colored in every respect with something many modern ecologists had forgotten: love of nature. Carson's birthdate, 1907, came as Leopold was completing college, and her maturation coincided with that of the science of ecology. In 1935, after completing a master's degree in biology, Carson joined the U.S. Bureau of Fisheries (later melded into the Fish and Wildlife Service) as a writer and editor.[69] Her first book, *Under the Sea Wind* (1941), attracted comparatively little attention, but her next, *The Sea Around Us* (1951), was a publishing sensation. It appeared on nonfiction best-seller lists for nearly two years, won a National Book Award, enjoyed translations into thirty-two foreign languages, and, incidentally, provided Carson with sufficient royalty income to retire from government bureaucracy. With her new leisure she completed *The Edge of the Sea* in 1955. The marine ecology books profess no overt environmental ethic, but they testify on almost every page to the author's awe in the face of the vast community of life centered on the oceans. Carson emphasized not just well-known forms of sea life but species that humans never use and seldom see. Respect for these creatures and for the life process suffused Carson's thought and behavior. Paul Brooks, her editor at Houghton Mifflin, recalled how after examining living specimens with her microscope, Carson would conclude the day by placing them in a basket and returning them, alive, to the sea. It came as no surprise to her colleagues and friends that Carson chose to honor Albert Schweitzer in the dedication of *Silent Spring*. "In one form or another," Brooks recalled, Schweitzer's principle of reverence for life "lies behind everything that Rachel Carson wrote."[70]

Rachel Carson's concern about insecticides dated to 1945 and a potent poison known as DDT. The popular term for such chemicals was "pesticides," but Carson discerned a covert anthropocentrism in the word. A creature was a "pest" only from the human perspective. In nature it had a legitimate role as part of what ecologists knew as the web of life. Carson preferred to think about DDT and the like not as pesticides but as biocides—killers of life. And she knew that the poisons seldom stopped working at a convenient or expected point in the food chain. Creatures that ate the poisoned insects sickened and died. Other forms of life became unintended victims of indiscriminate sprayings. Ultimately the insecticides infected the entire ecosystem. A "silent spring" where no birds sang was a distinct possibility. And so, Carson reasoned, was a sick human society, poisoned as an ironic side-effect of the drive to conquer and dominate nature. The realization that insecticides menaced human health made *Silent Spring* headline news.[71]

The ethical philosophy displayed in *Silent Spring* is a blend of old ideas and new ones. Carson intended the book to shock Americans into awareness and action. She was angry. Her objective was to outlaw insecticides or at least greatly constrain their use. Like Muir and Leopold, she wanted to be effective in the political arena, and she knew she would lose her audience if she stepped too far ahead of public opinion. As a result there is no direct mention in *Silent Spring* of the rights of insects, birds, fish, and other victims of the poisons.

The only reference to natural rights is Carson's suggestion that had the founding fathers been aware of chemical insecticides they surely would have included freedom from poisoning in the Bill of Rights. When she mentions a poisoned ground squirrel writhing in agony, her point, like that of earlier humanitarians, is that such cruelty diminishes us as human beings. She says nothing about the ethics of diminishing the squirrel.[72]

Although it is hard to separate Carson's personal convictions from her role as an explainer and persuader, there is much traditional anthropocentrism in *Silent Spring*. For instance, she takes the time-worn approach of dividing the insect world into "friends" and "enemies" of humankind. The friendly insects have value for their contribution to "keeping at bay a dark tide of enemies" that would otherwise "overrun us." Insecticides, which kill the good insects as well as the bad, thus pose a threat to human welfare. The same unabashed utilitarianism appears in Carson's advocacy of "keeping the balance of nature tilted in our favor."[73]

There was, however, another side to Rachel Carson. Buried only slightly beneath the anthropocentrism of her book, and quite clear in her personal correspondence and public speeches, was a much broader ethical perspective. As she started writing *Silent Spring*, she reported to her editor that, while it had "always been my intention to give principal emphasis to the menace to human health," she was increasingly persuaded that the disruptions insecticides caused to "the basic ecology of all living things . . . outweighs by far . . . any other aspect of the problem."[74] These words do not appear in *Silent Spring*, but Carson does mention the "web" and integrated "fabric" of life, and the "arrogance" humans displayed in "'eradicating' any creature that may annoy or inconvenience us."[75] Here was an attitude parallel in many respects to John Muir's toward rattlesnakes and alligators, Aldo Leopold's to wolves, and René Dubos's to germs. Carson brought insects into the circle.

The basis of Rachel Carson's moral philosophy was her conviction that "life is a miracle beyond our comprehension, and we should reverence it even where we have to struggle against it." This Schweitzerian attitude gives perspective to Carson's remark about tilting nature's balance in the human direction. Like any form of life, humans had to compete for food, for shelter, for habitat. Insects sometimes challenged humans in this competition. Insecticides were the latest human response, but in Carson's opinion they escalated the conflict to a dangerous level. Her book tried to make people understand that the growing ability to dominate and control nature could prove counterproductive. Humans needed what she called "humbleness" and an ethic that stressed "sharing our earth with other creatures." *Silent Spring* made it abundantly clear that human welfare was at stake, but that so, also, was the welfare of our living companions on the planet. It was only a step from this position to a full-blown philosophy of the rights of nature.[76]

The closest Rachel Carson came to making that step was on January 7, 1963, when she accepted the Schweitzer Medal from the Animal Welfare Institute. She was moribund at the time, depleted by the cancer she knew she had even as she finished *Silent Spring*. But Schweitzer was special; *Silent Spring* had been dedicated to him and to his idea that people must restrain themselves or destroy the earth. At the ceremony, Carson compared Schweitzer's experience with the hippos on the African river to her own "sight of a small crab alone on a dark beach at night, a small and fragile being waiting at the edge of the roaring surf, yet so perfectly at home in its world." Albert Schweitzer, Carson continued, "has told us that we are not being truly civilized if we concern ourselves only with the relation of man to man. What is important is the relation of man to all life." Carson meant an ethical as well as biological relation, and on another occasion she stated her belief that "man will never be at peace with his own kind until he has recognized the Schweitzerian ethic that embraced decent consideration for all creatures—a true reverence for life." The concluding paragraph of *Silent Spring* made the same point another way. "The 'control of nature,'" Carson wrote, "is a phrase conceived in arrogance, born of the Neanderthal age of biology and philosophy, when it was supposed that nature exists for the convenience of man." In its place Carson proposed "reasonable accommodation" between insects and people; ethics, as a restraining device on technological man, was a means to that end.[77]

Silent Spring appeared in serial form in *The New Yorker* magazine in the summer of 1962; Houghton Mifflin released the book in the fall. It enjoyed extensive sales but, like Darwin's *Origin of Species,* was one of those books that was more talked and written about than read.[78] At any rate *Silent Spring* generated a heated nationwide controversy, revealing, again like Darwin, that Carson had touched some very raw intellectual nerves. She was most intensely vilified by persons, corporations, and government agencies engaged in agriculture. These parties assumed they would lose economically by limiting pesticides and resented any extension of the ethical circle that promoted this end. Agribusiness was unsympathetic to Carson's proposals for biological controls (the encouragement of insect "friends" to control insect "enemies") as inconvenient and untested. But the root of the matter was that Carson enraged people who were unwilling, perhaps ashamed, to think in ethical terms about their relation to other life-forms. She challenged the right of humans to own and abuse nature just as Harriet Beecher Stowe and the abolitionists challenged that right with regard to black people. Carson especially angered those persons who sincerely believed that such exploitation was right or at least a matter beyond the province of morality.

But for other Americans, Carson was a courageous heroine, an ethical pioneer willing to use the final energy of her life (she died April 14, 1964, at the age of fifty-six) to advance a new relationship with the environment and a new ethics. For many in Carson's large following her most compelling idea was the danger chemical insecticides posed to human health. In this sense the public interest in *Silent Spring* supports Samuel Hays's thesis that post–World War II America evinced a new interest in conservation causes that enhanced the quality of the human environment and the quality of human life.[79] But Carson also publicized the idea that it was right to include all forms of life, and even the ecosystem as a whole, in humankind's moral community. Conversely, she argued that it was wrong to regard any creature as an expendable and exploitable commodity. Leopold had said as much in the 1940s, but Carson's much greater visibility as an author and the climate of opinion two decades later brought unprecedented attention to the idea of ethical extension. Carson led the way in acquainting the American public of the 1960s with the fundamentals of the ecological perspective and its ethical implications.

For Edward O. Wilson, as for his predecessor at Harvard, William Morton Wheeler, the study of the social insects led to a concern for kinship ties and ethical responsibility. Wilson, writing in the 1970s and 1980s, was also interested in the history of science and philosophy. As he saw it, the first ecologists raised ethical questions. The subsequent increase of knowledge in the field produced a focus on facts that Wilson called "amoral." But "finally, as understanding became sufficiently complete, the questions turn ethical again." Wilson hoped the environmental sciences were, at the conclusion of the twentieth century, ready to proceed to this third phase. Indeed he believed that "the future of the conservation movement depends on such an advance in moral reasoning."[80]

Hoping to contribute to this development, Wilson addressed the origin and meaning of ethics in *Sociobiology: The New Synthesis* (1975). He began with the premise that ethics had a place in nature that, like everything else in the biota, should be explained in evolutionary terms. It followed that ethics arose as an aid to survival, was transmitted genetically, and changed with changing circumstances. At the present time, Wilson reasoned, modern technological humans' survival is threatened by their ability to reduce biological diversity. The wholesale extermination of species, Wilson felt, "is the folly our descendants are least likely to forgive us." How could ethics help in this situation? Wilson first argued on the instrumental level: it was wrong to eliminate species because humankind might find them useful in the future, for foods, medicines, and the like. Wilson regarded this as a "surface ethic" but, like Leopold, he was fully prepared to use it to advance the conservation cause. "The only way to make a conservation ethic work," he believed, "is to ground it in ultimately selfish reasoning. . . . People will conserve land and species fiercely if they foresee a material gain for themselves, their kin and their tribe." At the instrumental level, then, ethics springs from the struggle for existence.[81]

But Wilson, like Krutch, did not personally believe this rationale for conservation was enough. In 1984 he wrote about a "deep conservation ethic" based on "biophilia," which he defined as the tendency of the human mind to "affiliate" with other forms of life and with the life process. He was speaking here about psychological, not physical, survival, a subject still cloaked in mystery. The core of the issue was that the human mind evolved in association with myriad life forms and needed them, even if subconsciously, for the continued survival of "the human spirit." It was a question of kinship, Wilson explained, and respect for the ten billion "bits" of genetic information in even the humblest living creature. Borrowing Schweitzer's term, Wilson concluded that "reverence for life" will one day be understood in terms of evolutionary biology and evolutionary psychology. His definition of community ranged not only across the entire contemporary ecosystem but backwards in time to the beginning of evolution. Humans belonged, physically and psychologically, to both past and present ecosystems; Wilson's achievement was to use this expanded definition of community as a reason for respecting the rights of the other members.[82]

The impact of ecology on modern ethical philosophy can, finally, be illustrated by the work of David Ehrenfeld. A professor of ecology at Rutgers University and associate editor of *Human Ecology*, Ehrenfeld's career bears out Wilson's point that a scientific discipline tends to shift over time toward a philosophical orientation. Ehrenfeld's doctoral research concerned a narrow biochemical problem, but in the late 1970s he began to explore the ethical implications of ecological science. The problem, he felt, could be distilled into a single phrase: "the arrogance of humanism." Ehrenfeld used "humanism" here to denote a bias in favor of the human species and against other species. It had the same connotation as racism or sexism, and the antidote in each case was to widen the ethical community.[83]

Ehrenfeld, like Wilson, was prepared to concede that protection of the human interest was a useful rationale for conservation. "Selfishness, within bounds," he believed, "is necessary for the survival of any species, ourselves included." But Ehrenfeld perceived technologically enhanced anthropocentrism to have "grown ugly and dangerous. Humanism . . . must now be protected against its own excesses." This is the point at which ethics becomes relevant as a restraining device. Capping several centuries of Anglo-American thought on the matter, Ehrenfeld declared that "long-standing existence in Nature" carries with it "the unimpeachable right to continued existence." He stressed that this ethical precept is not in the least predicated on the usefulness of a species to humans. This, in fact, is where "resource" conservation, with its economically oriented arguments, failed. What Ehrenfeld wanted was recognition of the rights of "non-resources," including species that have no significance to people or even to the healthy functioning of the ecosystem. Leopold had made much of the healthy-functioning argument, but Ehrenfeld saw himself as going further. He wanted a land ethic that would include even those members of the biotic community whose disappearance could not possibly affect land health. As an example, Ehrenfeld put forward the furbish lousewort, "a small member of the snapdragon family which has probably never been other than a rare constituent of the forests of Maine." In its case Ehrenfeld thought the only firm base for ethical respect was "existence value," a kind of ecological because-it-is-there attitude.[84]

To make this point most dramatically, Ehrenfeld cited a 1976 article by an English physician, Bernard Dixon, on smallpox. He pointed out that this virus, once the scourge of humankind, had been so effectively pursued by world health organizations that it only existed as a carefully guarded specimen in three research laboratories. Vaccination programs had eliminated the germ in its only natural habitat: human beings. Dixon pointed out that "this is the first time in history when man has been able to obliterate—for all time and by conscious rational choice—a particular form of life," and he wondered, was there "a case for the conservationists to move in and call a halt?" Both Dixon and Ehrenfeld believed that such a case could be made but for different reasons. The physician pointed to the research value of smallpox and its potential use in fighting other human diseases. The ecologist noted that smallpox, as part of the biotic community, was a product of evolution as were wolves and whales and redwood trees. According to the biocentric reading of environmental ethics, there was no logical reason for discriminating against the virus just because it was small and harmful to humans.[85] Such reasoning drew the fullest implications of the ideas René Dubos introduced twenty years earlier. It was ethically appropriate, from Ehrenfeld's perspective, to protect the right to life of even an organism whose only function was to prey on people. Here, surely, was the ultimate submergence of the human ego in the ecological community.

Aldo Leopold felt that acceptance of a land ethic depended on changing long-established cultural attitudes, and in the 1940s he was not optimistic about the prospects for such a change. But in the next two decades a dramatic rise in public understanding of ecological realities created a favorable climate for the growth of environmental ethics. Ecology substituted a new biological basis of community for the old mystical and theological organicism. It suggested many practical reasons for enlarging the moral circle to include nature, but also created an argument for the intrinsic rights of other species and even of the environment as a whole.

Had he lived beyond 1948 Leopold undoubtedly would have been both surprised and pleased at the appearance of "bioethics" as a scholarly field,[86] the rise of ecophilosophy and ecotheology, and the appearance of journals such as *Environmental Ethics* and *Ecology Law Quarterly*. He would have applauded the Wilderness Act of 1964 and the Endangered Species Act of 1973, which some take to mean that certain nonhuman members of an extended American community have, quite literally, a right to life, liberty, and the pursuit of happiness. Leopold certainly would have been sympathetic with the counterculture's questioning of traditional American definitions of progress and with the "deep ecology" movement.[87] While it was not his style, he would have supported in principle some aspects of radical environmentalism as interpreted by action-oriented groups such as Earth First! and Greenpeace. Leopold would have read with satisfaction Christopher Stone's 1972 essay "Should Trees Have Standing? Toward Legal Rights for Natural Objects," which singled him out as the source of the no longer unthinkable idea that the land had rights which deserved recognition in courts of law just as those of human litigants.

. Although Leopold died discouraged about ethical extension, the next generation of ecologists felt that "the idea of rights conferred by other-than-human existence is becoming increasingly popular" and looked forward to continuing expansion of "the circle of altruism."[88] Indeed, by the centennial of his birth, 1987, Aldo Leopold would have seen clearly that, thanks in large part to the emergence of an ecological perspective, increasing numbers of Americans were extending the limits of their nation's traditional liberalism to include nature.

◆ CHAPTER 4 ◆

The Greening of Religion

A theology of the natural world . . . asserts the intrinsic worth
of the non-human world. Such a theology declares that the
non-human world has just as much right to its internal integrity
as does the human world, that human beings transgress their
divine authority when they destroy or fundamentally alter the
rocks, the trees, the air, the water, the soil, the animals—just as
they do when they murder other human beings.
                                                    —*Allan R. Brockway, 1973*

"Do people have ethical obligations toward rocks?" . . . To
almost all Americans, still saturated with ideas historically
dominant in Christianity . . . the question makes no sense at all.
If the time comes when to any considerable group of us such a
question is no longer ridiculous, we may be on the verge of a
change of value structures that will make possible measures to
cope with the growing ecologic crisis. One hopes that there is
enough time left.
                                                    —*Lynn White, Jr., 1973*

*A*s he concluded his pioneering delineation of a land ethic in *A Sand
County Almanac,* Aldo Leopold despaired at the shallowness of the
American conservation movement of the 1940s. Economic, not ethical, criteria still determined policy. "In our attempt to make conservation easy," Leopold wrote, "we have made it trivial." The reason,
he believed, was that human beings were not prepared intellectually
for "the extension of the social conscience from people to land." As
proof Leopold submitted his opinion that "philosophy and religion
have not yet heard" of including nature in an expanded morality. The
next generation of theologians and philosophers, however, would
pay a significant amount of attention to this problem. Indeed by the
1980s it is possible to discern, borrowing Charles Reich's word, a
"greening" of both fields. Just as John Locke's ideas underlay the first

87

wave of democratic revolutions, environmental philosophy and what is called "ecotheology" provided the intellectual foundations for a revolutionary expansion of the meaning of conservation.[1]

The church has always been the chief custodian of ethics. Even in the secular modern era, most Americans continue to derive their ideas of right and wrong, directly or indirectly, from one religion or another. Harold W. Wood, Jr., has noted, "insofar as ordinary people are concerned, it is religion which is the greatest factor in determining morality."[2] The morals of intellectual and political leaders also spring from a perception of reality that, if not related to established churches, could still be characterized as religious. Therefore when American religion began to consider the relations between humans and nature, it lent important support to environmental ethics. Formidable theological obstacles thousands of years old stood in the way of such a reorientation, but recognizing the obstacles was a start in the "greening" process.

The modern discussion of the resistance of Western religion to environmental ethics crystallized around a 1967 essay by the medieval historian Lynn White. In "The Historical Roots of Our Ecologic Crisis," White set himself the task of understanding why his civilization had exploited nature to such a degree that its own quality, if not its survival, was at stake. Granted that the rise of science and technology provided tools for wholesale ecological disruption, but why were they used so destructively? White found the explanation for this pattern in the history of ideas, in particular the concept that although it was wrong to exploit people, exploiting nature was perfectly right and proper. Where, then, did Western society find a dualistic ethical system that discriminated so sharply between people and the environment? White's answer was the Judeo-Christian tradition.[3]

Judaism and Christianity, White maintained, posited a dichotomy between people and nature. According to the sacred texts of these religions, people were masters, not members, of the natural world. Created in the likeness of God, unique in their possession of a soul and the expectation of salvation, humans clearly stood above other forms of life. Moreover, according to White, Jews and Christians traditionally believed that the rest of creation existed solely for human benefit. Referring to the creation account in the Bible, he wrote: "God planned all of this explicitly for man's benefit and rule; no item in the physical creation had any purpose save to serve man's purposes. . . . Christianity is the most anthropocentric religion the world has seen."[4] For evidence White needed to look no further than the first pages of the Old Testament where, after shaping man "in his own image," God commands his favorite artifact to "be fruitful and multiply, and fill the earth and subdue it; and have dominion over the fish of the sea and over the birds of the air and over every living thing that moves upon the earth."[5] Every creature was assumed to be created to serve a human need. Human beings were, quite literally, the kings of beasts; every other being was inferior in the Judeo-Christian hierarchy. In case any doubt remained, God reaffirmed his alleged promise of dominance to Noah after the great flood and the new beginning: "The fear of you and the dread of you shall be upon every beast of the field, and upon every bird of the air, upon everything that creeps on the ground, and all the fish of the sea; into your hand they are delivered . . . I give you everything."[6] Human dominion, in other words, was complete and unqualified. Nature had good reason to fear humankind. As White saw it, this was all the rationale Christians and Jews needed to exploit nature at will. Meaningful change in human-nature relations would not occur "until we reject the Christian axiom that nature has no reason for existence save to serve man."[7]

Pausing at one point in his indictment, White observed that he seemed "to be headed toward conclusions unpalatable to many Christians."[8] In this opinion, at least, he had abundant support. Large numbers of environmentally conscious Jews and Christians challenged White's thesis. Frequently this response took on strong emotional overtones. White emerged in his critics' eyes as something of a heretic; they tended to forget that he was writing primarily as an historian.

As a scholar concerned with the history of ideas, White knew the relevant question was not, what does Christianity mean? but what did it mean to a particular society at a given time and place? His approach, in other words, was pragmatic: How was the Judeo-Christian tradition used? White was perfectly willing to concede that Christians of the 1960s might form a commitment to environmental responsibility from their reading of Genesis. He agreed that there was a biblical basis for environmentalism. But his point was that for nearly two thousand years the Christian tradition had not been so construed. Instead people used Scripture to justify the exploitation of nature in the same way that defenders of slavery used it to justify ownership and exploitation of certain classes of humans. Modern Christians, White observed, no longer viewed the Bible as a justification for holding slaves, and a similar reinterpretation with regard to nature might be under way. Revelation, after all, was supposed to be an unending process. "Perhaps," White concluded, "the Holy Ghost is whispering something to us."[9]

The best place to search for confirmation of Lynn White's contention that traditional Christianity opposed an ethical attitude toward nature is in the original significance of the language employed in the Bible. Hebrew linguists have analyzed Genesis 1:28 and found two operative verbs: *kabash,* translated as "subdue," and *radah,* rendered as "have dominion over" or "rule." Throughout the Old Testament *kabash* and *radah* are used to signify a violent assault or crushing. The image is that of a conqueror placing his foot on the neck of a defeated enemy, exerting absolute domination. Both Hebraic words are also used to identify the process of enslavement.[10] It followed that the Christian tradition could understand Genesis 1:28 as a divine commandment to conquer every part of nature and make it humankind's slave. Certainly such an interpretation proved useful over the centuries as intellectual lubrication for the exploitation of nature. Indeed, was this not one of the main reasons for its initial appearance and persistence in Christian thought?[11]

Along with positing a dualism that separated humans from nature and gave them the right to exploit it, the other principal argument in Lynn White's 1967 critique was Christianity's rejection of animism. This ancient body of ideas, typical of most pre-Christian cultures and persisting in non-Christian ones into the present era, held that every part of the environment, living and nonliving, had a consciousness or spirit. Pantheists, for example, identified deities with natural objects and processes. The god of the sea—Poseidon to the Greeks and Neptune to the Romans—remains the best known of a full spectrum of gods. For people of this persuasion nature was holy. White reasoned that this belief conditioned human behavior toward nature in the direction of reverence and respect.

One way to understand animism is as an expanded circle of moral considerability. Ethical relevancy did not end with God, angels, saints, and other people. Everything had a sacred quality. Nothing, to use Martin Buber's terminology, was an "it." People thought of nature as something with which a personal relationship was possible, as with another human being. With animism what Buber called an "I-Thou" relationship characterized human interaction with the entire environment.[12]

Judaism and Christianity changed all this.[13] Rigidly monotheistic, the first commandment of these religions was to worship no other gods or idols or spirits except Yahweh/God/the Heavenly Father. Even Jesus was the *son* of this supreme deity, and thus hierarchy (that villain of contemporary environmental and social reformers) was thoroughgoing in Christianity. Natural objects might be created by

God, but they were not gods, nor did they possess souls or spirits of any sort. Modern Christians contend that the fact of divine creation of nonhuman beings and inanimate objects should be sufficient reason for respect and reverence, but their ancient and medieval predecessors took the absence of animism as a license to exploit. Since they had objectified nature and were now dealing with something outside their religious and ethical community, the restraints previously provided by fear or morality were no longer operative. As White put it, "by destroying pagan animism, Christianity made it possible to exploit nature in a mood of indifference to the feelings of natural objects."[14] Significantly, early Christian evangelists felled the sacred groves of northern Europe where pagans worshipped a multiplicity of deities. The contemporary custom of cutting Christmas trees may have vague ties to that ancient ritual.

White's brief 1967 essay could not involve more than a cursory examination of Christian ideas about the environment. He might have expatiated on that religion's deep hostility to metempsychosis. The soul of the good Christian was destined only for heaven, never for the body of a plant or animal. A grizzly bear or redwood tree could never be one's late grandmother reincarnated. This belief effectively removed another of the constraints that held pagan appetites for the exploitation of nature in check. Severed from the human community and its ethical protection, nature was fully exposed to human greed. Interestingly, one of the first American expositors of the rights of nature, Edward P. Evans, based part of his expanded moral philosophy on the possibility of metempsychosis.

White also said nothing about the traditional Christian view of wilderness as a cursed land, the antipode of paradise. But this idea, so pervasive in both the Old and New Testaments, contributed significantly to the absence of respect for the nonhumanized landscape for more than two thousand years. As the Puritans demonstrated at the beginning of the American experience, the only appropriate Christian response to wild country and its wild inhabitants was conquest, subjugation, and, in the case of the more fortunate Indians, conversion.[15]

Neither did Lynn White find space in his short essay to note the pervasive otherworldliness of Christianity. Christians' aspirations were fixed on heaven, the supposed place of their origins and, they hoped, their final resting. The earth was no mother but a kind of halfway house of trial and testing from which one was released at death. Ludwig Feuerbach, a nineteenth-century theologian, repre-

sented the Christian perspective that "nature, the world, has no
value, no interest for Christians. The Christian thinks of himself and
the salvation of his soul."[16] Indeed Christians expected that the earth
would not be around for long. A vengeful God would destroy it, and
all unredeemed nature, with floods or drought or fire. Obviously
this eschatology was a poor basis from which to argue for environmental ethics in any guise. Why take care of what you expected to be
obliterated?

Faced with growing misgivings about the environmental implications of the Judeo-Christian tradition, modern leaders of American religious thought and practice had essentially three options. They
could turn to the East, to Asian faiths that had never abandoned a
sense of the unity of nature and subscribed to an ethical philosophy
that did not begin and end with people. They could incorporate the
strong animist traditions of American Indians, which rendered the
entire ecosystem sacred and therefore worthy of ethical consideration. Or the reformers could go back to basic Jewish and Christian
beliefs and reinterpret them to accommodate demands for an ethical
system that did not exclude nature. Most of the "greening" of recent
American religion—the development of what is called ecotheology—
involves the explication and, to some extent, the synthesis of these
three options.

A starting point for exploring the theological frontiers of the new
environmentalism might be Lynn White himself. Despite the com-
prehensiveness of his critique of Western religious traditions, he was
not prepared to abandon them as a key to easing the ecologic crisis.
He laughed at his reputation in conservative Christian circles as "a
junior Anti-Christ, probably in the Kremlin's pay, bent on destroying the true faith." In fact, White's desire was to reform, not destroy,
religion. "Since the roots of our [environmental] trouble are so
largely religious," he noted at the conclusion of the 1967 essay, "the
remedy must also be essentially religious." What he had in mind was
a revolution in ethics with religion, as a basic determinant of morality, on its cutting edge. "Religious values," White's knowledge of
history led him to believe, "are fundamental in the dynamics of cultural and social change."[17]

But what religious values could help the West work toward an
environmental ethic? White knew that the concept of the rights of
animals, plants, and even rocks was not foreign to many faiths. "To
an ancient Greek, to an American Indian, or perhaps to certain kinds
of Buddhists, the [idea] would have meaning." But from the tra-

ditional Christian perspective, White thought, the question "'Do people have ethical obligations toward rocks?' makes no sense at all." Yet it might if Christians like himself were willing to reinterpret their basic principles.[18]

White pointed to one possible direction for such rethinking in his proposal of Saint Francis of Assisi (1182–1226) as "a patron saint for ecologists." What led White to call Francis "the greatest spiritual revolutionary in Western history" was his forthright challenge to Christian anthropocentrism. Although the evidence from thirteenth-century Italy is fragmentary and interlaced with myth, it suggests that the saint subscribed to what might be called spiritual egalitarianism. Everything was equal in its derivation from God and its capacity to glorify God. Francis's thought held no hierarchies, no chains of being, no dualism. Worms and ants were just as much a part of his community of worshippers as the higher primates. And so, remarkably, were inanimate presences like rocks, water, fire, and wind. Expressing the ecological-like unity he perceived, Francis's canticles and prayers addressed nonhuman beings as "brother" and "sister." He preached sermons to birds, urging them as part of God's spiritual family to give thanks to their creator. Anticipating Albert Schweitzer by seven centuries, St. Francis commonly removed worms from paths where they might be crushed. In the village of Gubbio, Francis allegedly pacified a man-eating wolf by reminding him of his membership in the Christian community. And Francis used the adjective "mother" to characterize the earth. This way of thinking was completely unprecedented in Christian history, and it would be another seven centuries before religious leaders would recognize Francis's attitude toward nature as a starting point for an environmental ethic. In 1960 the University of Michigan zoologist, Marston Bates, declared that for Christians who loved nature, "St. Francis of Assisi rightfully is their patron." White's better-known proposal came seven years later. In 1980 the Vatican acted on these suggestions and officially dubbed the Assisi holy man the patron saint of ecologists.[19]

Francis of Assisi lived long before the age of the democratic revolutions, and he did not speak of the "rights" of birds, worms, wolves, and rocks. But he did remove them from the category of "things" by including them with humans in a single spiritual fellowship. Believing that they all independently praised and magnified God, Francis implicitly accorded to all creatures and natural processes a value entirely separate from human interest. Everything had a direct relationship with God. According to Francis the mere fact of something's existence was sufficient reason for its ethical consideration. While derived from sacred rather than secular premises, the thought of the medieval Christian radical paralleled that of later advocates of the rights of nature. But it is well to emphasize that within the Christian tradition Francis was unique in his point of view. He was the exception that proves the rule of Christian anthropocentrism. Had his Christian contemporaries fully recognized the radical quality of his ideas, Francis would quite likely have been condemned as a heretic rather than elevated to sainthood. As it was, orthodox Christians celebrated his love of God, his concern for the poor, and his disdain of things material while ignoring his bold challenge to other parts of the faith.

Lynn White, of course, was well aware that Francis of Assisi had failed in his attempt to persuade Christians to substitute "the idea of the equality of all creatures, including man, for the idea of man's limitless rule of creation." But White's study of Francis's thought inspired him to try again, and he felt he had an important ally in the new ecological perspective. "Fifteen years ago," White remarked in 1978, "almost no theologian knew what the word *ecology* meant." But with its axioms widely circulating in American thought, he hoped to construct a definition of Christian compassion grounded on "an ascetic and self-restraining conviction of man's comradeship with the other creatures." Perhaps, White reasoned, this concept of biological comradeship or interdependency could be "a viable equivalent to animism." If Christian-oriented Americans could not believe in the old pagan spirit of an organism, maybe they could acknowledge the importance of its presence in what White, following Aldo Leopold, called the "integrity" of the ecosystem. "Ecology," White felt, "provides us with new religious understandings of our own being, of other beings, and of being." [20]

In the manner of Joseph Wood Krutch, White believed that a meaningful ecotheology had to transcend prudence or enlightened self-interest. We should not protect the ecosystem and its component parts because they sustain us, he reasoned, just as "we should not be pleasant to people in order that they may treat us pleasantly." So much for the hallowed Golden Rule which underlay almost all ancient religious systems, including Judaism and Christianity. White even wondered "whether a prudential ethic can rightly be called an ethic." Instead he called for morality based on disinterested love of nature which, in turn, derived from nature's membership in God's world. St. Francis proved that this ethical system could emerge in a

Christian individual; White called for its reappearance on a cultural scale. Indeed he believed that such an intellectual development was imperative if technological civilization was to have a chance of co-existing with the natural order that sustained it. This sense of urgency led White to conclude that "Christian ethics is in the greatest crisis of its history of two millennia."[21]

Most critics of Lynn White did not read beyond his 1967 condemnation. In point of fact, he was not anti-Christian. His later essays showed the potential for a Christian perspective to generate a far-reaching environmental ethic. Indeed, White's concept of a "spiritual democracy" stands out as one of the most radically inclusive ethical systems yet evolved. His sense of community literally knew no bounds. "We can sense our comradeship," he wrote in 1978, "with a glacier, a subatomic particle or a spiral nebula." All of these, as well as living things, were humankind's spiritual equals, with whom we needed to coexist. As a motive for self-restraint in the species with the most potential for disrupting the ecosystem, ethics could help. White looked forward to a world in which humans exercised their rights to satisfy biological needs with an eye to the identical rights of other organisms. He wrote about "spiritual . . . courtesy" and "cosmic manners" which would promote such coexistence.[22]

To cap his argument, White even dared to defend the rights of life-forms undeniably hostile to his own species, like the smallpox virus, *Variola*. At a time when ecologists were beginning to raise ethical questions about the extermination of germs, White asked theological ones. Noting in 1978 that modern medicine had reached the point of being able to exterminate smallpox, White studied the implications. "From our standpoint, the advisability of the action is beyond debate. *Variola* could not be consulted because of a communication gap. What the God who created both *homo sapiens* and *Variola* thinks about all this, we do not yet know."[23] The implication was that a thoroughgoing Christian sense of morality must include smallpox, just as St. Francis included man-eating wolves. Perhaps White hoped for a latter-day saint who could instruct *Variola* in cosmic courtesy. More likely, he simply recognized that in killing people the smallpox virus was only performing its appointed role in the ecosystem God created.

Lynn White's theology stood out for its ethical egalitarianism. The more common approach of those who would make American religion environmentally responsible was to reinterpret traditional doctrine in light of the idea of stewardship. Rereading the Old Testament they found a directive to protect rather than a license to exploit nature. The "dominion" granted in Genesis 1:28 did not connote despotism, they said, but trusteeship. As God's most favored beings, humans were charged with overseeing the welfare of all the rest of creation—in a sense, completing creation. This halfway doctrine allowed for human superiority in the Christian hierarchy, acknowledged that God had "given" nature to humans, but used these concepts as reasons for protecting the natural world from exploitation. For biblical support the stewardship contingent went to Genesis 2:15, according to which God placed the first man in the Garden of Eden "to till it and keep it."[24] This, they contended, constituted a directive to humankind to take care of or serve the rest of God's creation.

Through their understanding of the creation myth, the stewards reinvested the environment with a sacredness once associated with animism and pantheism. Abuse of nature became, once again, sacrilegious. Of course abuse of nature also could endanger human existence, and the stewardship doctrine has been termed little more than enlightened self-interest. From a theological perspective, God could be thought of as punishing humans through the impact of neglected nature on human life. But the bottom line of stewardship was that the world belonged to God. Nature was holy. Therefore it was not only prudent but right to respect the environment. In a sense the myriad forms of life, as well as the earth itself, had rights that originated from their being the work of the deity. It followed that the stewards could interpret Christianity as being in league with environmental ethics.

Modern ecotheologians liked to point out that stewardship had an old and respected place in the Christian religion. The historical evidence for this characterization, however, is, at best, scanty. Still, it is interesting that René Dubos called attention to Benedict of Nursia as a pioneer practitioner of what Dubos called "a theology of the earth." A Christian of the sixth century, Saint Benedict founded the abbey of Monte Cassino in Italy. His followers spread the monastic system throughout medieval Europe. The busy monks drained swamps, cleared forests, improved fields, and tended their gardens with diligence and devotion. Dubos found them exemplifying the best of Christian stewardship and displaying an "ethical attitude" toward their environment. He added, in reply to Lynn White, "I believe that ecologists should select St. Benedict as a much truer symbol of the human condition than Francis of Assisi." What bothered Dubos about St. Francis was that he had rejected the hierarchical concept central to the idea of stewardly responsibility. Francis regarded all life-forms and even inanimate matter as brothers and sisters in the family of God. Dubos, on the contrary, accepted enlightened anthropocentrism as the basis of his ethical philosophy. Mankind was in charge of the world and could and should "manipulate nature to his best interests" but always with a feeling of reverence for what was ultimately not his possession but God's.[25]

Stewardship was notable chiefly by its absence in the thousand years of Christian thought following St. Benedict. Finally in the seventeenth century a minor motif of dissent to anthropocentrism began to surface in the work of John Ray and Alexander Pope. God, Pope wrote, had not created anything solely for the good of people. Humans were accountable to God for their treatment of his creation. Henry David Thoreau and John Muir in the nineteenth century and Edward Evans and Liberty Hyde Bailey in the early twentieth were the first Americans to apply this principle to human-environment relations.

Then in the 1930s a little-known forester and hydrologist named Walter C. Lowdermilk (1888–1974) used stewardship to rationalize the developing resource conservation movement. In 1922 Lowdermilk began a five-year residence in China to investigate problems of soil erosion and forest management. The Chinese, he concluded, had neglected intelligent land use to their extreme peril. In the next decade Lowdermilk became Assistant Chief of the Soil Conservation Service and traveled more than 25,000 miles by automobile in the Mediterranean Basin, the same ecologically depleted region that inspired George Perkins Marsh to call for a moral relationship to land. In June 1939, in the heart of the Holy Land, Lowdermilk made a speech on Jerusalem radio entitled "The Eleventh Commandment."[26] He reasoned that if God could have foreseen the ravages that centuries of thoughtless forestry and agriculture would bring to his creation, he would have been moved to add to the Ten Commandments. The eleventh, according to Lowdermilk, would "complete the trinity of man's responsibilities—to his Creator, to his fellow men, and to Mother Earth." The text Lowdermilk proposed for the new commandment read:

> XI. Thou shalt inherit the holy earth as a faithful steward, conserving its resources and productivity from generation to generation. Thou shalt safeguard thy fields from soil erosion, thy living waters from drying up, thy forests from desolation, and protect the hills from overgrazing by thy herds, that thy descendants may have abundance forever. If any shall fail in this stewardship of the

land, thy fruitful fields shall become sterile stony ground and
wasting gullies, and thy descendants shall decrease and live in poverty or perish from off the face of the earth.

Although Lowdermilk, writing in the utilitarian climate of the
1930s, grounded the appeal of his message in human self-interest, the
concept of a commandment from God through Moses to humankind
carried with it a strong ethical implication. Drawing on the very
source of Christian ethics (the human–God relationship), Lowdermilk succeeded in making conservation a moral matter. For him responsible land use was not just the key to "physical" progress but to
"higher spiritual . . . development" as well. Aldo Leopold had used
ecology; Lowdermilk took religion to be the foundation of environmental ethics.[27]

A few American churches began to explore the implications of
stewardship before the modern environmental era. The observance
of Rogation Days, which dates to the Middle Ages and acknowl-
edges human dependence on planting and harvesting, provided a
conceptual basis for modern dedications such as Rural Life Sundays
and Soil Stewardship Sundays. The dramatic exposure given soil erosion problems by the great dust storms that plagued the Middle West
in the 1930s supported these tentative beginnings. In the 1940s the
National Catholic Rural Life Commission of Des Moines, Iowa, endeavored to bring the force of religion behind careful land use. A decade later the National Council of Churches launched a program
called "A Christian Ministry in the National Parks," but its emphasis
was largely on human appreciation of the beauty of God's world.
Few religious leaders or, for that matter, anyone took the rights of
nature seriously before 1960. But the rising tide of interest in ecology
and a parallel anxiety about environmental problems created new
perspectives. In the 1970s and 1980s the ethics of the human–nature
relationship became a major preoccupation of American theologians
and, to a lesser extent, of ordinary churchgoers.

A necessarily brief history of this development can begin with
Joseph Sittler, a professor of systematic theology at Chicago Lutheran
Theological Seminary. Sittler was one of the first professional theologians in the United States to attempt to base an environmental
ethic on Christian faith. He began the effort in 1954 in a key article
entitled "A Theology for Earth." Rejecting the notion of mother
earth (as a Christian Sittler had to accept God, not nature, as the creative power), he advocated, a decade before Lynn White, following
St. Francis in regarding nature as "man's sister." The environment

was part of the created community; there were no grounds for dualism in Sittler's reinterpretation of the Judeo-Christian tradition.
"God-man-nature," he explained, had to be understood as a unity.[28]
In 1960 Sittler presented the core of his theology in an address to the
World Council of Churches. The purpose of God, he said, is "cosmic
redemption." Not only human souls but "all things" were potential
objects of God's saving grace. Extending this idea to the limit, Sittler
argued that even atoms belonged within the circle of salvation. He
opposed nuclear bombs for this reason, suggesting that the atoms
used to destroy people and nature be "reclaimed for God."[29] Sittler's
widely read 1962 sermon, "The Care of the Earth," drew a distinction between "use" and "enjoyment," and he urged Christians to let
the latter guide them in their dealings with nature. The point was to
take "joy in the things themselves," not in what they could do for
people. Sittler believed that abuse of the environment was an insult to
God; hence the care of the earth was a religious imperative. In this
attitude Sittler was among the first theologians to rise above simple,
anthropocentric stewardship. Environmental responsibility became a
matter of obeying Christ, not providing for human needs.[30]

Theologians had not been common contributors to conservation
journals, but in 1971 Joseph Sittler told the readers of the *National
Parks and Conservation Magazine* that "dominion" meant not enslavement of but tender caring for nature. Another significant essay,
"Ecological Commitment as Theological Responsibility," developed
his early idea that nature was a participant in salvation along with humans. Consequently, ecological interdependence became not just a
scientific description but the only appropriate worldview for Christians who accepted God's omnipresent love. According to Sittler the
pantheism or animism that Lynn White regretted losing was not essential for environmental responsibility. Sittler dismissed pantheism
and salvaged respect for nature in a single sentence: "The world is not
God, but it is God's." All the thoughtful modern Christian needed as
a reason to include nature in his or her moral circle was the belief that
God, too, wanted it in the redeemed heavenly kingdom. Grace created the interlocked relationship of theology and ecology.[31]

Along with the writing of Charles Hartshorne[32] and Daniel Day
Williams,[33] Joseph Sittler's work encouraged a number of younger
theologians and clergymen to apply their faith to environmental
problems. Richard A. Baer, Jr., is representative. Trained in the late
1950s at the Princeton Theological Seminary, Baer later added a Harvard doctorate in the history and philosophy of religion. In 1966,
even before Lynn White's controversial essay, Baer published "Land

Misuse: A Theological Concern" in *Christian Century,* one of the nation's oldest and most respected outlets of religious thought. His paper challenged American religion to become involved with environmental issues. "The church today," he wrote, "stands at a time of decision. If she is to remain true to her prophetic heritage, she must confront the power structures of society with a fresh and cogent ethic of land usage." He made it plain that he was not just interested in academic study but in "action—involvement." Significantly for the natural-rights tradition, Baer argued that religion's concern for race relations in the 1960s created a precedent for attention to exploitation of the environment.[34]

In welcome contrast to many of his colleagues, Baer took pains to simplify his case for deriving an environmental ethic from the Christian tradition. His first assumption was that *"the world belongs to God,"* not human beings. Baer developed the point in the language of political theory: Because God is the highest authority of earth, no member of his world can "dictate the destiny" of any other member. It was a clever stance, for it permitted Baer to retain the traditional Christian belief in human distinction from and superiority to nature but still argue for environmental responsibility. His point, in a nutshell, was that humans may be lords of nature but God is lord over humanity. It followed that "man's freedom to 'subdue' nature is always limited and under a higher authority." Baer believed that in this respect the Bible supported the same conclusion as "ecology texts" concerning the limits of the earth and the consequent necessity for human restraint.[35]

The second foundation of an ecotheology, according to Baer, is *"God likes the world he created."* He cited passages from the Bible indicating that nature "praises and honors God," that it "witnesses to his glory and majesty" and that "God delights in nature and cares for it quite apart from its importance for man." As the clincher for this interpretation, Baer cited Genesis 1:31: "And God saw everything that he had made, and behold, it was very good." This meant for Baer that nature in its totality had intrinsic value for God, and he emphasized *"all* of nature, both the living and the non-living; the human and non-human; plants as well as animals; sticks, air, water, stones: *everything."* Perhaps St. Francis of Assisi, but not many Christians before or since, would have understood Baer's universalism. Its implication was that the basic fact of their being created by God endowed every part of nature with rights that humans ought to respect. Americans familiar with their nation's history would immediately recognize the similarity of Baer's system to Lockean natural-rights liberalism, but for the theologian it stemmed from a sacred rather than a secular imperative and extended far beyond the limits of traditional liberal philosophy.[36]

Baer's third principle drew heavily on his knowledge of the ecological sciences. It held that not just every object in nature but the interrelationships between them were part of God's creation. God valued systems, processes, smoothly functioning wholes, and what Baer called the "web of life." The ethical precept Baer derived from this amalgamation of ecology and theology was that "wantonly to destroy the relational and holistic qualities of our environment is to sin against the very structure of the world which God has created." Here was another reason for religious condemnation of pollution and exploitation, another argument for involving the church in the environmental movement.[37]

Baer's three principles shed new light on the chronic Judeo-Christian "dominion" problem. As a practicing Christian he did not try to escape the central import of Genesis 1:26–28. Scripture clearly set humans apart from and placed them in dominance over nature. "Man cannot be man," he wrote in 1971, "and cease ruling over nature." The control of fire, the advent of herding and agriculture, and mechanical and electrical technology all proved to Baer that "whether he wants to or not man will rule over nature." But having thus stated what he knew would be "an obscenity for many environmentalists," Baer quickly reminded his readers that the important question was not the fact but the quality of human rule. Arrogance and anthropocentrism had to be avoided. Nature was not merely a utilitarian object with only instrumental value. As an antidote to this attitude, Baer suggested thinking of the environment as the home of a host and of humans as guests. Never forget that the earth is "property that does not belong to us." From Baer's perspective *Homo sapiens* rents an apartment called nature. God is, quite literally, the landlord. He expects compliance with basic "principles of etiquette" in the use of his creation. As Baer reinterpreted the controversial passage in Genesis, humankind does not have unconditional freedom to conquer and exploit what it could never, in the final analysis, own.[38]

Like others seeking to develop a modern ecotheology based on the reinterpretation of Christianity, Baer took the responsibility of stewardship very seriously. "Failure to fulfill our obligations as faithful trustees of the gifts of God's creation," he warned, "will inevitably bring God's judgment upon us. The earth itself will rebel against our greedy and thoughtless exploitation of nature and our irresponsible fecundity."[39] This linkage of ecological and theological

catastrophe had the flavor of a jeremiad intermixed with new ecological insights. Baer spoke for a growing number of theologians
who believed that environmental degradation, human suffering, and
divine retribution were closely related.

Richard Baer also probed the meaning of the alleged desacralization of nature by the Christian faith. A year before Lynn White publicized the issue, Baer recognized that a fundamental change had occurred about 2,500 years ago when Greek philosophers and Jewish
theologians substituted a single, supreme deity for the myriad gods
earlier cultures had found in virtually every natural object. Baer was
among the first American theologians to recognize that this switch
from pantheism to monotheism brought about "the disenthrone-
ment of the nature deities" and a consequent callousness toward the
environment that favored exploitation. But the remedy did not lie in
restoring nature worship. Speaking again as a Christian, Baer reasoned that, although nature is not a deity, it is the creation of the supreme deity and therefore is holy. The import for human attitude and
action is the same in either case; the spoliation of nature is "essentially irreligious." Baer concludes his argument with the observation
that "a mature Christian position would permit one neither to worship nature nor to despise it."[40]

In his attitude toward monotheism, as in his ideas about hierarchy and dominion, Baer pointed the way for those who would save
both their Christian faith and the environment. Working on the intellectual borderland of theology and ecology, he succeeded in giving
new meaning to nonhuman rights and human moral obligations. But
his interest extended beyond articulation to the implementation of a
Christian land ethic. In his most optimistic moments Baer hoped that
religious institutions could "draw into the conservation battle thousands, even millions, of committed churchmen."[41]

The Faith-Man-Nature Group, which Baer enthusiastically supported, was a notable institutional expression of this ideal. At one
time or another it included most of the early environmental theologians. Taking shape in 1963 and 1964 within the National Council of
Churches, the group's stated aim was "to understand man's relationship with nature in the light of religious faith, and to spell out ethical
imperatives for the conservation of natural resources."[42] Philip N.
Joranson, a biologist and consultant on forestry education, was the
catalyst around which clergymen, theologians, and scientists gathered
to discuss problems in human-environment relationships. Baer believed Joranson was "one of the first persons in America to see clearly
the need for developing a new environmental ethic."[43] Debatable as

this might be, Joranson had urged the church as early as 1954 to move beyond "standard stewardship" and recognize that the "moral activity of man is continuous with the process of the universe." He implied that the modern world needed reverence for, not simply conservation of, nature. Beginning in 1965 the Faith-Man-Nature Group convened at least annually to consider the possible contributions of religion to such concerns as population control, pollution, excessive resource consumption, and world community. It published the proceedings of its 1967 conference under the title *Christians and the Good Earth*. The 1969 meetings resulted in *A New Ethic for a New Earth*. In addition three regional gatherings produced written records.[44]

The primary message of the Faith-Man-Nature Group was that the earth and its resources are gifts of God which humans have thoughtlessly abused. The group's alternative recommendation was stewardship—human caretaking of God's good earth. Undeniably much of the force of this appeal stemmed from anthropocentric considerations. Time and again the clergymen and religious scholars anchored their case on the welfare of human beings, present and future. Several theologians, notably Conrad Bonifazi, argued that perception by the human mind was a necessary precondition for any object's having value. Yet an important theme in the Faith-Man-Nature books concerned God's creation and, in a sense, ownership of the earth. This viewpoint led some contributors to speak of stewardship as a "moral responsibility"—not of people to other people but of people to God.[45] A few went further. Citing St. Francis and Aldo Leopold, they argued for the transcendence of utilitarianism. "Things have a value and integrity in themselves," Daniel Day Williams of the Union Theological Seminary explained, because they are part of the process that is "ongoing reality." Environmental exploitation is therefore not only "bad for man" but also "bad for Nature" apart from any human interest.[46] This sense of the intrinsic worth of every part of the environment led one Faith-Man-Nature participant, H. Paul Santmire, to declare that "in the eyes of God nature has its own value, its own rights for life and fulfillment."[47] Such language indicates that theology was just as feasible a route to ethical egalitarianism as were ecology, philosophy, and environmental activism.

Despite its bold resolves to change the world, the Faith-Man-Nature Group did little other than prepare more studies and reports than it had originally condemned. In 1974, beset by the lack of regular funding and volunteer burnout, the organization disbanded.[48] But its leaders were justifed in feeling that they had nourished a trend. Given the nearly total absence of environmental ethics in previous

American religious life and thought, the simple fact that Faith-Man-Nature existed for a decade on a national level is remarkable enough. Philip Joranson continued to be active in ecotheology. In 1984 he published *Cry of the Environment: Rebuilding the Christian Creation Tradition,* which argued that the modern Christian's calling must be "to liberate the earth from the threat and the reality of its slow and steady execution at the hands of humanity." The idea of liberating nature from human domination linked environmental theology—or what Joranson called "eco-justice"—with earlier movements for human liberation.[49]

Paul Santmire, the most radical of the ecotheologians associated with Faith-Man-Nature, also went the farthest in developing and publishing his ideas on the Christian basis for environmental ethics. At Harvard, where Santmire took his doctorate in divinity in 1966, the reinterpretation of Christianity in the interest of ecological responsibility was a major preoccupation.[50] Richard Baer was a fellow graduate student, and Frederick Elder (see p. 109) also did graduate work in Cambridge at the end of the 1960s. In 1970, while serving as chaplain of Wellesley College, Santmire published a popularized version of part of his Harvard thesis under the title *Brother Earth: Nature, God and Ecology in Time of Crisis.* This was the year of the National Environmental Policy Act and the first Earth Day, when America's obsession with the "Age of Ecology" approached cult proportions. Santmire's book reflects the new concerns. "The earth," he declares in his opening sentence, "is in danger of destruction." One of the reasons, we learn, is the state of human values, and Santmire pays the by then almost obligatory homage to Lynn White and his 1967 critique of Judeo-Christian morality. But the intent of *Brother Earth* is to salvage a basis for ecological responsibility from the West's dominant religious tradition. Santmire is convinced that the "ecological bankruptcy" of Western theology is indeed "alleged," and his writing constitutes proof of the point.[51]

The most creative part of Santmire's 1970 work is his adaptation of the old Judeo-Christian concept of the Kingdom of God to support ethical extension. Santmire contends that the kingdom idea, coupled with God's valuation of all nature, creates a theological basis for community embracing humanity and the environment. In making this point Santmire employs the language of political theory likely to appeal to Americans versed in natural-rights liberalism. Santmire's God is a ruler interested in the right treatment of all his subjects. According to the terms of the divine body politic, the dominant members of the community—humans—have no legitimate basis for oppressing and exploiting minority members, that is, nature. So when Santmire mentions "social justice" it is not in the usual sense of interpersonal relations but applies to the entire spectrum of life on earth. In this way Santmire gives a decidedly modern flavor to St. Francis's idea of mother earth.[52]

Santmire's argument depends heavily on the concept of rights. Rereading the account of creation in Genesis, he concludes that "nature . . . has its own rights before man." He adds that "the Kingdom of God validates the rights of both nature and civilization." This becomes an important point for Santmire. He is not attempting to divest humankind of its rights or even of its status as a special part of creation. But he is calling on people to recognize that other creatures are part of their community. "*Nature and civilization,*" Santmire states emphatically, "*are fellow citizens of the Kingdom of God.*" He takes this to mean that "each can enjoy certain inalienable rights."[53]

The problem of how humans are to live in a world of omnipresent rights occupied a substantial portion of Santmire's 1970 book and related essays. He made no effort to repudiate "dominion." Humans would and should use nature, but they must do so with full recognition of nature's intrinsic worth as part of God's kingdom. In effect, this limits human freedom with regard to nature. To enhance the point, Santmire used a metaphor from political theory. Humanity is like a mayor or governor over the populace of the environment but its authority is always subordinate to that of the king, whose concern is for the just treatment of all members of the realm. So "man's dominion is limited by the rights of nature."[54]

While Santmire endorsed the doctrine of stewardship, he gave it an unprecedented twist. Nature's membership in the Kingdom of God meant that humans were responsible to God for conducting themselves in such a way that nature can enjoy its own inherent rights to existence and, in Santmire's language, "fulfillment." The idea was not to care for nature for humankind's sake but to "take care of nature for nature's sake." Santmire did not fully develop the precise way in which humans can claim their own rights to material resources without violating nature's rights, but he suggested that the ecological concepts of balance and sustainability point in the proper direction. He was sure that a reduced level of affluence and environmental impact—a level determined by "justifiable human needs"— would be required.[55]

The defense of nature was also part of Santmire's concept of stewardship. He saw a Christian basis for preserving the wilderness. "One should so order one's life," he recommended, "that the whole of nature, including *wild* nature, can flourish. This means not only to respect nature's rights but to *act to preserve and to defend* those rights." People, then, have a God-directed "personal and social responsibility" for the welfare of every living thing. (Santmire did not extend his ethics to nonliving matter. Rocks apparently remained in the I-It category. "Nature," to Santmire, seems to mean nonhuman life.) Ethics, acting as a restraint, would allow "dominion without exploitation." The ecologists of Santmire's generation believed that this sort of environmental ethic stemmed from the membership of people in and their dependency on the natural community. Theologians of Santmire's persuasion, however, felt the important point was not that humans are part of nature but that both humans and nature are part of the Kingdom of God.[56]

The latest contribution of Santmire to environmental theology is *The Travail of Nature* (1985), a detailed history and analysis of the basic documents of the Christian tradition that bear on the meaning of nature. Santmire argues that an "ecological motif" exists in traditional Christianity which describes "a system of interrelationships between God, humanity, and nature." Nature is not merely irrelevant scenery against which the central drama of the human-God relationship is played out, but is a full participant in the basic Christian process of creation and redemption. *The Travail of Nature* thus stands as historical support for the vision of people and nature together as citizens in the Kingdom of God that Santmire broached fifteen years earlier.[57]

The "process" philosophy of Alfred North Whitehead and that of the French Catholic paleontologist-priest Pierre Teilhard de Chardin[58] stimulated several modern American theologians to investigate the consequences for nature of an expanded morality. Neither Whitehead nor Teilhard specifically discussed environmental ethics or the rights of nature. Teilhard's thought is at best ambiguous on these matters; nature appears to have value for him primarily as a springboard for the emergence, through the evolution of consciousness, of the "Omega Point" of supreme human development. But both thinkers lay the philosophical groundwork for the intrinsic value of all matter that others would use to construct an environmental ethic. Charles Hartshorne, a student of Whitehead, and Hartshorne's student, Daniel Day Williams, pioneered this development. Conrad Bonifazi, an English-born professor at the Pacific School of Religion, extended it with the idea that "things" possessed an "inwardness" or intrinsic value that legitimized their being loved for their own sake. Borrowing Aldo Leopold's phrase, Bonifazi urged people to develop an "ecological conscience" as well as a social one.[59]

Of the modern Whiteheadians, John B. Cobb, Jr., made the greatest contribution to environmental theology. A professor at the School of Theology in Claremont, California and a student of both Hartshorne and Williams, Cobb built upon Whitehead's notion that the universe is not composed of inert matter but is instead a continuous series of events or interactions; in other words, a process. Cobb understood Whitehead to mean that all things exist only in relation to their environment. Their very essence is determined by "taking account of" their surroundings, and this characteristic of all matter gives it "reality, value, and kinship." It followed, for Cobb, that everything from humans through the various forms of nonhuman life, right down to cells, atoms, and subatomic particles, had a purpose, a capability of being fulfilled or being denied that opportunity. God desires fulfillment as part of the requirement for divine perfection. Extrapolating from Whitehead's belief that all matter had significance for the universe, Cobb concluded that it also had intrinsic value in the eyes of God. In Cobb's view this fact invested the "subhuman world" with "rights" that humans, as the most intelligent form of life on earth, ought to respect.[60]

Cobb's conviction that human beings, alone among life-forms, are capable of love underlay his concept of ethical responsibility. People are partners with God in caring for nature. Cobb hastened to point out that in this sense "caring" had nothing to do with stewardship. He rejected enlightened self-interest and instrumental theories of value as a basis for ethics. As Cobb explained, "man will in fact care for the subhuman world sufficiently to heal it and to adjust himself to its needs only if he views it as having some claim upon him, some intrinsic right to exist and prosper." The basis of this claim, Cobb explained, is an extension of self-transcendent Christian love. Whitehead had made it possible to think of nature as having intrinsic value and being an appropriate object of love; Cobb demonstrated the potential of integrating Whitehead and traditional Christianity to build an environmental ethic.[61]

John Cobb wrote *Is It Too Late?* (1972) in the midst of what he called "the ecological crisis." His purpose, as a Christian, was to explore the role his faith might play in alleviating the "threat of doom" brought on by chronic environmental abuse. His first realization was that "the major past forms of Christianity are inadequate to our needs and must be superceded." But he also realized that "it is fruitless to seek the vision we need in primitive or Oriental religions." Instead Cobb proposed a "new Christianity" based on the expansion of morality to include recognition of the rights of nature. The modern Christian environmentalist, Cobb argued, should understand the significance to God of everything and every process in the universe. This is why it was possible to think of a "theology of ecology."[62]

At the conclusion of *Is It Too Late?* Cobb outlined his new vision. It renounced dualism in all its forms but still retained the conception, so necessary to Christianity, of human beings as the "apex and summation of nature." Cobb believed this self-image could coexist with environmental ethics because the fact that "man is of vastly greater worth than any other creature does not reduce the value of the others to nothing." Human life was sacred but only in the context of God's sacred world. Turning from theology to ecology to make the same point, Cobb employed Leopoldian terms to state that "the new Christianity must substitute a vision of a healthy biotic pyramid with man at its apex for the absoluteness of man." On these bases Cobb could finally contend that a Christian commitment to God necessarily involved a responsibility to cherish and promote life in all its forms. St. Francis and Albert Schweitzer, Cobb acknowledged, had pointed the way toward this environmentally sensitive Christianity while ecologists provided recent scientific grounding.[63]

In subsequent writings Cobb set forth the thesis that the "habitats" or "ecosystems" that sustain life also belong in the ethical circle.[64] In 1978, he stated that animals "have the right to have the value of their existence and happiness weighed seriously in the balance. They have the right not to be exploited casually for trivial human purposes."[65] Here was an emphasis on life and "happiness," and in 1981 Cobb added liberty. His book *The Liberation of Life,* coauthored with Australian process philosopher Charles Birch, took the widest possible view of ethical applicability. Cobb argued that all matter, from subatomic particles to human beings, had a "potential for richness of experience" that humans should respect. "If there is intrinsic value anywhere," he declared, "there is intrinsic value everywhere." Humans, obviously, had a lot of company in the ethical circle. Cobb's call for a "religion of life," and his willingness to extend his moral vision down to "cells" and up to "biospheres" and "ecosystems," marks a milestone in the greening of both Christianity and natural-rights liberalism.[66]

In view of the meager previous record, the early 1970s witnessed an impressively large religious contribution to the development and popularization of environmental ethics. Of course this was a time of unprecedented American concern in general for environment and ecology but the theologians, still smarting under Lynn White's critical lashes, were especially energetic. A whole generation of religious thinkers joined Richard Baer, Paul Santmire, and John Cobb in advancing the new moral vision. *Christian Century* devoted its entire October 7, 1970 issue to "The Environmental Crisis." *Time* magazine covered the Lynn White controversy on February 2, 1970, while *The New York Times* featured an essay on "The Link between Faith and Ecology" in its January 4 issue. *The Nation* published the plea of a leading Episcopalian to expand the "circle of fellowship" to include other creatures and the earth. Scott I. Paradise went on to suggest that the growing appeal of an environmental ethic in the United States carried with it the "seeds of revolution."[67] Journals such as *Zygon* featured articles contending that "traditional theological or moral ideas must be extended to include not only man and society but nature itself." From this perspective "man's violence toward his surroundings is just as sinful as his violence toward his fellows."[68] Allan R. Brockway defined a theology of the natural world as one that "declares that the non-human world has just as much right to its internal integrity as does the human world, that human beings transgress their divine authority when they destroy or fundamentally alter the rocks, the trees, the air, the water, the soil, the animals—just as they do when they murder other human beings."[69] It would be hard to imagine a more direct application of natural-rights ideology to environmental relations.

While few ecotheologians went to such radical lengths as Brockway, concern was undeniably growing for the application of ethics to environmental problems. Conferences of clergymen resulted in publications such as *Ecology: Crisis and New Vision* (edited in 1971 by Richard Sherrell) and *This Little Planet* (1970, edited by Michael Hamilton). Francis A. Schaeffer wrote *Pollution and the Death of Man: The Christian View of Ecology* (1970) and Paul Folsom contributed *And Thou Shalt Die in a Polluted Land* (1971). Christopher Derrick's *The Delicate Creation: Towards a Theology of the Environment* (1972) contained an introduction by a prominent cardinal and by René Dubos. Ian Barbour edited two anthologies for college and university audiences, *Earth Might Be Fair* (1972) and *Western Man and Environmental Ethics* (1973). The latter exposed a large audience to the controversy engendered by Lynn White. The panicky mood of environmentalism at this time was reflected in books like Frederick Elder's *Crisis in Eden* (1970) and Henlee H. Barnette's *The Church and the Ecological Crisis* (1972). A student in Harvard's Divinity School when he wrote his book, Elder called for America's churches to emerge from "ethical parochialism" and, following the teachings of Aldo Leopold and Albert Schweitzer, to lead the nation "back from the brink of ecological disaster." As Elder understood it, this was nothing new; saving the world from disaster had always been the mission of religious institutions. But Christian churches would have to abandon their "exclusionist" position and recognize that humankind was part of nature as nature was part of God. Barnette argued that "the zone of ethics . . . must be redefined to include man . . . in his relation to all creatures and things, the organic and the inorganic." [70]

Eric C. Rust is an example of an older scholar of Judeo-Christian thought who became radicalized by the environmental movement and redirected his writing in the 1970s to advance environmental ethics. His *Man and Nature in Biblical Thought* (1953) had no prescriptive import. But twenty years later Rust contended that nature must be included, along with humankind, in the process of redemption and that it was humankind's responsibility to advance this end by right treatment of the environment. People were "co-workers with God in the redemption of nature." Rust concluded a 1971 essay in environmental theology with the observation that just as the churches had become involved in racial issues, they must now become "the conscience of the community" in ecological matters. He even added a section on "Christian Ecotactics." [71]

Not only did American religion become environmentally aware in the 1960s and 1970s, but environmentalism itself acquired some of the characteristics of a religion. The new environmentalists displayed an intensity of commitment and a tendency to conceptualize issues in terms of right and wrong. They could be said to subscribe to a "gospel of ecology." [72] Greenpeace, for example, regarded "ecology as religion." [73] The term "ecotheology" made the same point, and Henryk Skolimowski, for one, considered it "a religion for our times." [74] Peter Borrelli felt that "a sense of the sacred in nature" must be the "driving force . . . of environmentalism." [75] The National Council of Churches sponsored an "eco-justice agenda," regarding it as expressive of "a major new insight of our time." [76] John Carmody's *Ecology and Religion* (1983) argued that "every creature" is a "presence of God" and that therefore "nature has an independent right to exist, live and flourish." Carmody's ecological religion led him to call on Christians to "love nature like a neighbor or relative." [77] Jesus had once urged his followers to love their human neighbor as they loved themselves; by the 1980s some Christians had come to understand the neighborhood as the ecosystem.

A number of environmentally conscious modern Christians chose to focus their attention on farmland and farming. Viewing the former as sacred and the latter as holy work ("Farming for the Lord," one Minnesotan put it), [78] they combed Scripture for passages supporting stewardship. Wendell Berry's *The Unsettling of America* (1977) and *The Gift of Good Land* (1981) were the most visible statements. Berry summarized his thesis for the Sierra Club's 300,000 members: "If 'the earth is the Lord's' and we are His stewards, then obviously some livelihoods are 'right' and some are not." Berry doubted, for instance, that there could be a Christian strip mine or a Christian atomic bomb.[79] In the same tradition was John Hart's *The Spirit of the Earth: A Theology of the Land* (1984). Hart, a Catholic, described the awakening of the leaders of his faith to land-use problems and reforms. He detailed the preparation of two manifestos: *This Land Is Home to Me* (signed by twenty-five Appalachian bishops in 1975) and *Strangers and Guests* (signed by seventy-three bishops from Midwestern states in 1980). Their message was, by now, a familiar one: The land is God's and people have a sacred trust to be responsible custodians.[80] Berry, Hart, and others inspired endeavors such as the Land Stewardship Project based in St. Paul, Minnesota. Organized in 1983, its purpose is "to develop and encourage a public dialogue on a sustainable land ethic in the Midwest."[81]

A large part of the Christian stewardship argument was anthropocentric in character: take care of the earth (meaning, generally, productive soil) or you will either perish or be punished by an angry God. Guilt figured as a mainstay of the appeal. But latent in modern stewardship was the idea that because the environment was God's, not man's, it was morally wrong to abuse it regardless of the consequences for humanity. Some clergymen made this recognition of intrinsic value and the rights of nature their principal concern. Reverend Dennis G. Kuby's Berkeley-based Ministry of Ecology, for instance, functioned from 1973 to 1981 on a platform that emphasized "the interconnectedness inherent in the universe." Kuby's associates signed a pledge committing them "to moral accountability to . . . the biotic community."[82]

The Eleventh Commandment Fellowship picked up Walter Lowdermilk's earlier concept and the essence of Kuby's crusade in 1984. The additional commandment read: "The earth is the Lord's and the fullness thereof; thou shalt not despoil the earth nor destroy the life thereon." Reverend Vincent Rossi, who inspired the group, reminded it to transcend self-interested stewardship. "The *deep* ecological task is . . . to awaken in human souls the sharpest possible awareness that belief in the existence of God absolutely demands the deepest respect and reverence for the rights of the Earth."[83] The same message colored the concluding pages of *Earthkeeping: Christian Stewardship of Natural Resources,* which Loren Wilkinson edited in 1980 for Calvin

College's Center for Christian Scholarship. Wilkinson pointed out that if "justice is done within a recognized community," then the ecological sciences have given people reason to think about new communities and new definitions of equity. It followed that "a society which meets all the subsistence and development needs of its people but which destroys or tortures all living things under its control is not a just society." Wilkinson was quick to add that he was not implying that "the needs of a tree, a wolf, or a cow are to be equated with the needs of a human," but "neither are they to be ignored." The needed balance seemed to lie in an appropriate level of human consumption that filled basic human needs while still respecting the rights of nonhumans to habitat and sustenance.

Finally, *Earthkeeping* turned to the question of why people should endeavor to implement environmental justice and concluded, "We are commanded by God to do so." We should seek justice for all the earth's creatures because "it is a working-out of our calling to be stewards. It is the command of the King—an obligation and a challenge placed on all Christians."[84]

While agriculture preoccupied Christian stewards, concern for the religious significance of wilder landscapes opened another ethical door. The idea that a place or particular environment was sacred had clear significance for traditional Native American beliefs. The American Transcendentalists, especially John Muir, understood wilderness appreciation as a religious act. But in the 1960s and 1970s increasing numbers of Americans began to think that wildernesses in general—and certain national parks in particular—were sacred spaces. People of this persuasion were inclined to believe that ethics should be extended to regulate action toward nature. A few even went so far as to suggest that freedom of religion connoted the right to worship where as well as how one chose. If wilderness was one's church, the argument ran, why not defend it on ethical grounds?[85]

Although less important in American thought than the reinterpretation of the Judeo-Christian tradition, another source of the greening of religion has been recent interest in the ethical implications of several Asian religions. Some Americans simply used non-Christian beliefs to inspire reassessment of their own faiths. Others, especially younger contributors to the countercultural energies of the 1960s, gladly exchanged discredited Christianity for Asian religions such as Taoism, Jainism, Shinto, Buddhism—particularly the Japanese variety known as Zen—and Hinduism. At the core of these faiths was a rejection of the dualism and anthropocentrism that so thoroughly colored traditional Christianity. Eastern religions assumed the ultimate oneness of all of nature's components. By advocating the submersion of the human self in a larger organic whole they cleared the intellectual way for environmental ethics. Ancient Eastern ideas closely paralleled the new assumptions of ecology. In both systems the biological and ethical gulf between humans and nature disappeared. "The ten thousand things," as Taoists phrased it, "are one with me."[86] The process of enlightenment (the Zen notion of *satori,* for example) included this perception as one of its major characteristics. Nature, as a consequence, could not be objectified, desacralized, or, in 1960s jargon, "used." These were precisely the grounds on which Lynn White and the others faulted Christianity.

Eastern religion and philosophy were notably devoid of the concept of individual rights which underlay much of environmental ethics in the West. The Oriental mind tended to regard nature as imbued with divinity rather than as something possessing rights. One root of the idea of rights in non-Asian cultures was the Judeo-Christian notion that all humans (but only humans) were made in the image of God;[87] therefore every human was sacred, possessed of a redeemable soul, and intrinsically valuable. The natural-rights philosophy of John Locke and Thomas Jefferson secularized this concept. In the East, on the other hand, intrinsic value extended to the limits of the universe. All beings and things, animate and inanimate, were thought to be permeated with divine power or spirit such as the Tao or, in Shinto, *kami*. Every one of Taoism's ten thousand things—that is, everything in nature—had a purpose, a potential, a significance for the universe. Mahayana Buddhists speak of the *dharma,* or Buddha-nature, of every object. The Eightfold Path of Buddhism uses this concept as a basis for outlining appropriate human conduct toward all creatures and things. It centers on the doctrine of harmlessness or *ahimsa* which the Jains carried to extremes in their desire to avoid the destruction of any life. In sharp contrast, the Ten Commandments, which anchor Western morality, concern themselves exclusively with human-to-God and human-to-human relationships. The notion of "neighbor" in Judeo-Christianity begins and ends with people. In the Asian doctrines, this circle of community knows no bounds.[88]

American interest in Asian religions began with Transcendentalists such as Henry David Thoreau, who read as widely as Harvard's English-language holdings permitted. According to Rick Fields's useful study of the history of Buddhism in America, "the Concordians were at odds with their age, and they looked to the Orientals as an example of what their own best lives might be."[89] The same analysis could be made of the dissident Americans of the 1960s

and 1970s, with whom much of the new environmentalism originated. Both groups held ethical ideals concerning human–nature relationships that their contemporaries, in general, did not share. John
Muir and Edward Evans might also be cited as Americans whose
critical stance toward the ethics of their society led them to profess
sincere if untutored Buddhist philosophy. Albert Schweitzer's all-
embracing ethics derived in part from his doctoral studies of Asian
religion.[90]

Much of the modern American attention to Oriental religion
traces back to the remarkable Buddhist scholar and teacher Daisetz
Teitaro Suzuki (1870–1966), who arrived in the United States from
Japan in 1897. For a half century Suzuki wrote and taught the Zen
philosophy to an increasingly receptive American audience.[91] Among
those Suzuki inspired, the Englishman Alan W. Watts stood out for
his influence on American thought about nature. Watts, a practicing
Buddhist, moved to the United States in 1938. Twenty years before
Lynn White's critique of Christian attitudes toward nature, Watts began explaining how Eastern and Western views differed in this regard. The most important of his twenty-five books, *The Way of Zen*
(1957) and *Nature, Man and Woman* (1958), became paperback best-
sellers and acquainted a generation with the idea that the world, humans included, was part of a "seamless unity."[92] Watts's readers came
away with an unmistakable message: a fully developed moral sense
must include everything in nature.

The rejection of Christianity in favor of Asian religions was a
major component of the so-called beatnik mentality of the 1950s.
Jack Kerouac's novels *On the Road* (1955) and *The Dharma Bums* (1959)
popularized the rebellious new attitudes. Kerouac had a vision of a
"great rucksack revolution" with "millions of young Americans"
forsaking established churches and "going up to mountains to pray."[93]
A leader in this new nature worship, and the inspiration for an important Kerouac character, was Gary Snyder. Born on the West
Coast in 1930 and empathetic with wilderness, Snyder's chance encounter with D. T. Suzuki's books in 1951 and his friendship with
both Kerouac and Watts led to ten years of study under a Zen master
in Japan. Returning to the United States in the late 1960s, Snyder began to work out an ethic that combined Buddhist and Native American principles with American natural-rights ideology. The result was
explicit personification of nature and its inclusion in a Lockean social
contract. "Plants and animals are also people," Snyder wrote, and
must be "given a place and a voice in the political discussions of the
humans." He applauded Native American cultures that practiced "a

kind of ultimate democracy." Nonhuman life was "represented," according to Snyder, through ritual, dance, and religion. It was essential, he noted, to rephrase the popular countercultural slogan, "Power to the people," as "Power to all the people." Snyder explained what he meant in 1970: "What we must . . . do . . . is incorporate the other people . . . the creeping people, and the standing people, and the flying people and the swimming people . . . into the councils of government." Aware of the American liberal tradition, Snyder carried this idea to its logical conclusion: If all these "people" were not represented, "they will revolt against us" just as the American colonists had revolted against a British government that refused them political equality. Snyder argued that an exploited environment would ultimately jeopardize human civilization just as colonial exploitation caused the disintegration of Great Britain's eighteenth-century empire. In Snyder's opinion an abused ecosystem was already submitting "nonnegotiable demands about our stay on earth." As a corrective he called for widening the moral community and incorporating "the rest of life in our democratic society."[94]

Snyder explicitly applied natural-rights liberalism to the human relationship with nature. He identified nature as an oppressed minority whose rights civilization violated. Snyder declared that as a poet and a Buddhist, he saw his role as that of spokesman "for a realm that is not usually represented either in intellectual chambers or in the chambers of government." His constituency would be "the wilderness," by which Snyder meant all nonhuman creatures and things.[95] Snyder came to this extrapolation of the American democratic tradition only after a long intellectual detour to the Orient. But he rooted his defense of nature in the bedrock of the American political tradition. Americans who were already aware of environmental problems were likely to be impressed by Snyder's logic. And in fact his statements became part of a collection, *Turtle Island,* that won the Pulitzer Prize for poetry in 1975. Just as Muir had been more popular than Thoreau, Gary Snyder received a degree of public acclaim notable for its absence three decades before when Aldo Leopold broached the idea of biotic rights in *A Sand County Almanac.* The times, as Bob Dylan told a generation, were changing, and environmental ethics was one beneficiary.

After winning the Pulitzer Prize, Snyder became a celebrated lecturer and a popular subject for interviews. In a 1976 interview he returned to the idea of being a spokesman for the rights of nature. Poets, Snyder thought, were uniquely positioned to "hear voices from trees." Poets could be the vehicles of expression that Christopher Stone was seeking in 1972 when he proposed that trees be given legal rights. Snyder was deeply interested in where this idea of "the rights of things, the potentiality of salvation of things" might lead. "Push it a generation or two in[to] the future," he felt, and you might produce people who "actually feel on a gut level that non-human nature has rights."[96] As a Buddhist, Snyder already held that conviction; as a poet he felt himself responsible for communicating the ideal to others.

Americans increasingly found Oriental religions a guide to improving human relationships to the environment. The bellwether periodical *Christian Century* began publishing articles on Zen as an alternative to Western attitudes.[97] In 1972 it printed an essay entitled "Ecology, Zen, and Western Religious Thought." The author, Hwa Yol Jung, disagreed with Lynn White and Frederick Elder, among others, in their feeling that Americans in search of environmental responsibility could not benefit from Eastern faiths and should, instead, revise Christianity. Zen Buddhism, Jung pointed out, could show any culture how to replace utilitarianism with reverence and respect. According to Jung, the most enlightened American environmentalists, such as Aldo Leopold, were articulating Zen principles in their affirmation of "the intrinsic value of land . . . and the right of every creature to live."[98] Robert Aitken, who learned about Zen Buddhism as a Japanese prisoner of war and later established a notable Zen center in Hawaii, wrote that "there is no barrier between human and non-human." All beings, even the grasses, were "in the process of enlightenment." Aitken took seriously "the right to life of stones and clouds." In his view environmental ethics must begin with "the cultivation of intimacy with all things." By "forgetting the self" the Buddhist made his or her mind open to close communal relations with everything in the universe.[99] Rajagopal Ryali contributed an examination of Hinduism's polytheism, mysticism, and transmigration of souls (reincarnation) as a basis of reverence for nature.[100] These arguments for looking to the East were persuasive, but some American theologians, notably Thomas Merton and John Cobb, attempted to remain firm in their Christian faith and still integrate Oriental wisdom. The most recent approach eschews "blaming" Christianity in favor of "constructive borrowing to the benefit of both East and West."[101]

On the more popular level, large numbers of American readers used Fritjof Capra's *The Tao of Physics* (1974) and *The Turning Point* (1980) as a start toward the development of alternatives to the Western world's mechanistic view of matter and the universe, a view traditionally hostile to environmental ethics. Capra was encouraged by the rise of ecology, which he took to be the Western equivalent of Taoism's organic sense of unity. Dolores La Chapelle provided guides to those who would build a sense of brotherhood and sister-hood with nature upon a rediscovery of religiously oriented celebra-tions and rituals.[102] The Universal Pantheist Society attracted people convinced that environmental ethics depended upon "a new recogni-tion of the sacredness of the natural world." In a sense this neo-pantheism was a response to the criticism Lynn White leveled at Judeo-Christianity for its desacralization of nature.[103] On the institu-tional level, Zen Buddhism continued to grow as an American reli-gion, particularly on the West Coast where the Zen Centers of Los Angeles and San Francisco instructed growing numbers in alter-natives to Christianity's conception of nature.[104]

A widely distributed 1960s "ecology" poster featured a Native American contemplating the degraded condition of the continent after only a few centuries of white occupation. A single tear trickled down the man's cheek. The image expressed the new environmen-talists' understanding that the first occupants of North America were better custodians of the ecosystem than the subsequent tenants. Like the Oriental varieties, Indian religions avoided the dualism that nar-rowed traditional Christian morality. Most white American environ-mentalists believed that nature had an important place in the Indians' moral community. This idea was subject to distortion—the first Americans were not "ecological saints"—but there is little doubt that they accepted more restraints in their relationship to their environ-ment than did the people who displaced them.[105]

Central to most Indian religions and ethical systems was the idea that humans and other forms of life constituted a single society.[106] In-dians regarded bears, for example, as the bear *people*. Plants were also people. Salmon constituted a nation comparable in stature and rights to human nations. A complex of rituals and ceremonies re-inforced the familial bonds between Indians and their environment. Skins were, in effect, the outer coverings of a common being. Chief Seattle of the Suquamish tribe utilized these ideas in an 1853 oration. The version most familiar to environmentalists of the 1960s and 1970s, and probably modernized in meaning, contained the idea that "the rocky crests, the juices in the meadows, the body heat of the pony, and man—all belong to the same family." The demarcation between the animate and inanimate was not important to Seattle. "Every part of the earth is sacred to my people," he continued. "Rivers are our brothers," he explained; the sky was a sibling and the earth, almost universally in these cultures, a mother. "All things are connected," the chief concluded, "like the blood which unites one family."[107] Luther Standing Bear of the Lakotas or Sioux spoke in 1933, near the end of his life, of "a great unifying life force that flowed in and through all things." Taoists and Buddhists would have understood Standing Bear's belief that "all things were kindred and brought together by the same Great Mystery."[108]

It followed that restraints derived from ethics applied to every aspect of the human–environment relationship. Respect and courtesy were mandatory in all interactions with nature. Even when Indians took another life to sustain their own, it was done ritually with reverence and gratitude. Traditional tribal culture professed incredulity at the white tendency to objectify, desacralize, and exploit nature. The idea of owning the land was especially unthinkable. Buying and selling a piece of the earth was as foreign to most Indian cultures as marketing a brother or mother. This point of view may well have contributed to making Native Americans such easy targets for white treaty-makers. The natives never understood how a mark on a paper and the exchange of a few beads and tobacco could convert land to property. They balked at the notion of exchanging habitat for money. Ownership of nature appeared in their eyes morally wrong, a form of slavery. Standing Bear made this connection explicit with regard to domesticating and keeping animals. It was better to hunt wild creatures, he wrote, because herding "enslaved the animal" and deprived it of its basic rights: "the right to live, the right to multiply, the right to freedom."[109] This remarkable expression in 1933 deserves inclusion with Aldo Leopold's statement of a "conservation ethic" of the same year among the milestones in the American extension of natural-rights liberalism to include the rights of nature.

Whites' rediscovery of Native American religious and ethical beliefs became a characteristic of modern environmentalism. Seeking to disparage technological civilization, Theodore Roszak's widely read *The Making of a Counter Culture* (1969) publicized the remarks of a Wintu Indian woman who believed that not only trees but even rocks pleaded for respect. The white exploiters paid no attention and so "the spirit of the land hates them." Roszak called for a revitalization of the Native Americans' "shamanistic world view" that would guide alienated American society back to a moral relationship with sacred nature.[110] Secretary of the Interior Stewart Udall's history of American conservation characterized Native Americans as the first American ecologists. Understanding interdependency, they proclaimed an ethic of respect for nature.[111] By the time Udall wrote,

Native Americans were becoming the most insightful publicists of their own moral philosophy. Along with Seattle and Standing Bear, Black Elk, Lame Deer, and Hyemeyohsts Storm published widely read accounts which left little doubt that Native Americans' ethical community included nature.[112] N. Scott Momaday, a Kiowa whose *House Made of Dawn* (1968) won a Pulitzer Prize, wrote "An American Land Ethic" in 1970. His point was that the "deep ethical regard for the land" of his ancestors needed to be resurrected and disseminated. Americans had to recover the feeling of love of the earth and the ethics attendant upon that emotional relationship. The Sierra Club featured the essay in a book about environmental protest and reform.[113] Vine Deloria, Jr., a Sioux, became the best-known Native American author of the 1970s with *Custer Died for Your Sins* (1969), *We Talk, You Listen* (1970), and *God Is Red* (1973). A vocal champion of Indian as well as environmental rights, Deloria predicted in 1971 that Indian ideas "are going to cut the country's whole value system to shreds."[114] In an unpublished 1974 essay he presented "the idea of legal rights of non-human nature" as an example. Adoption of this concept would, in Deloria's opinion, necessitate a radical and total change in the white American worldview. But, he explained, "the concept is self-apparent in the Indian scheme of things." It fit perfectly into the Indian sense of brotherhood with everything in the universe.[115]

In the 1960s American churches became concerned with the relevance of their message for social problems. Civil rights, the war in Vietnam, poverty, and women's liberation claimed a major share of clerical attention. The concern of religion for the rights of nonhuman life and of the earth in the 1970s and 1980s continued and extended this pattern. The reinterpretation of the Christian tradition and a simultaneous renaissance of interest in Oriental and Native faiths acquainted many Americans with environmental ethics. Theologians and clergymen became primary architects and publicists of the new idea that human ethical obligations must include nature.

To be sure, some highly placed religious leaders dissented. Even dedicated ecotheologians had serious blind spots, not altogether surprising in a field as new and radical as environmental ethics. For instance, Harold K. Schilling, the distinguished Pennsylvania State University scholar, could title an essay "The Whole Earth Is the Lord's: Toward a Holistic Ethic" and conclude it with the statement that mosquitoes, ticks, cockroaches, "rats that attack babies in their cribs" and "myriads of other kinds of vermin" are without useful purpose and are, in fact, "demonic." In Schilling's view there was "nothing good or sacred about them."[116] Evidently not quite the whole earth was the Lord's, and ethics was somewhat less than holistic.

In Los Angeles in 1973 Catholic Archbishop Robert Dwyer characterized "worship of the Environment" and "the new cult of Nature Unspoiled" as "anti-human." Follow the environmental theologians and "dogmatic Ecology," he warned, and humanity could succeed in self-extinction. Wilderness conditions would surely return to New York City and, at least in the archbishop's aroused imagination, mastodons would roam the ruins of Chicago. Better, he suggested, to maintain the view of "Nature as Enemy, the alien force, to be conquered and broken to man's will."[117] Richard Neuhaus contended that believers in the rights of nature were actually advocating a pagan nature-worshipping cult aimed at diminishing human rights. The environmental movement, according to Neuhaus, was an effort to distract radicalism from its proper concern—poor and oppressed people.[118] And it was still possible in 1983 to find occasional expressions such as one addressed to the newspaper column "Dear Abby." In the course of defending the trapping of fur-bearing animals for coats, the writer declared that "the Bible gave man dominance over animals, birds and fish. They are God's gifts to man—created for us to use."[119]

But by the 1980s such opinions sounded increasingly old-fashioned. From the seminaries to neighborhood churches, increasing numbers took it for granted that the human-nature relationship could not be excluded from the ethics of religious individuals. "Ecotheology" had not only become a new word but a compelling world view.

CHAPTER 5

The Greening of Philosophy

I am quite seriously proposing that we give legal rights to forests, oceans, rivers and other so-called "natural objects" in the
environment—indeed, to the natural environment as
a whole.
                                        —*Christopher D. Stone, 1972*

The expansion of the moral circle to non-human animals is only
just getting underway. It has still to gain verbal and intellectual
acceptance, let alone be generally practiced. Yet . . . in philosophy departments all over the English-speaking world, the moral
status of animals has become a lively topic of debate. . . . We are
witnessing the first stirrings of a momentous new stage in our
moral thinking. Will this new stage also be the final stage in the
expansion of ethics? Or will we eventually go beyond animals
too, and embrace places, or perhaps even mountains, rocks and
streams?
                                        —*Peter Singer, 1981*

Deep ecology goes beyond a limited piecemeal shallow approach
to environmental problems and attempts to articulate a comprehensive . . . philosophical worldview. . . . [Its] basic insight . . .
of biocentric equality is that all things in the biosphere have an
equal right to live and blossom and to reach their own individual forms of . . . self-realization.
                                        —*George Sessions and Bill Devall, 1985*

*P*hilosophy is among the most ancient of human intellectual endeavors. One of its most important components, ethics, seeks to clarify
the moral principles by which we determine what is right and wrong.
But just like theologians, Western ethicists have focused for two mil-

lenia almost exclusively on the conduct of people toward each other
and toward various deities. Traditional moral philosophy professed
little concern for the human relationship with nature. When philosophers did examine the moral status of animals and natural objects, it
was usually in the manner of Descartes, for the purpose of ruling
them out of ethical bounds. Well into the middle of the twentieth
century, environmental ethics was simply inconceivable as a subject
for philosophy. Its emergence in the 1970s represents the farthest extension of ethical theory in the history of thought. "Until the early
seventies," Eugene Hargrove writes, "environmental ethics was
something only environmentalists talked about. If you had asked a
philosopher what he knew about the subject, you would most likely
have been greeted by stunned silence. . . . Environmental ethics was
entirely alien to the normal kinds of things that philosophers talked
about."[1] But the intensity of environmental concern in the 1970s,
coupled with an unprecedented eagerness on the part of philosophers
to apply their craft to contemporary issues, created a new field: environmental philosophy.

It would be overstating the case, however, to imply that no philosopher was interested in the ethics of human-nature relationships
prior to the age of environmentalism. We have seen how distinguished philosophers such as Baruch Spinoza and Alfred North
Whitehead took an interest in the moral status of nature, but the full
implications of their ideas for environmental ethics have only recently been drawn and applied. Jeremy Bentham, Charles Darwin,
and Henry Salt all made important contributions to the theory of
ethical extension. With his principle of "reverence for life," Albert
Schweitzer anticipated modern environmental philosophy, but his
approach tended toward mysticism rather than logic. Probably because of its close connection with natural-rights liberalism, American
intellectual history nurtured important roots of environmental ethics. Henry David Thoreau and John Muir developed far-reaching
moral systems that transcended humans' duties to other humans.
Edward P. Evans and J. Howard Moore deserve more recognition
than they have received as the first professional philosophers in the
United States to look beyond anthropocentrism. In the 1920s a theologian and philosopher named Royal Dixon tried to call Americans'
attention to the idea that all animals have "the inalienable right to life,
liberty and the pursuit of happiness."[2] Although Aldo Leopold was
trained as a resource manager and ecologist, many consider him a
pioneering philosopher of holistic ethics. And in 1950, a year after

the publication of *A Sand County Almanac,* Paul Weiss, the Yale philosopher, observed that "even a disease germ, playing havoc on all about, has value in itself. To exterminate it is relatively right, but inseparable from an absolute wrong."[3]

But philosophical attempts to widen the moral circle were few, far-between, and relatively unnoticed compared to the sudden burgeoning of environmental philosophy in the 1970s. About a decade after American religion began to "green," philosophy as a profession started a major exploration of the proposition that moral standing did not begin and end with human beings. Thinking historically, what is remarkable is the size and pace of this development. American philosophers joined colleagues in England, Canada, Norway, and Australia to create, in just a few years, an entire new discipline. Significantly, these international architects of environmental ethics had in common cultures with strong liberal traditions based on natural-rights ideology. This made the conceptual leap from recognizing oppressed people to recognizing exploited nature less difficult.

The growing perception of an environmental crisis in the 1970s spurred the philosophers into full intellectual gallop. New scholarly periodicals appeared, including *Environmental Ethics, Ecophilosophy, The Deep Ecologist, Between the Species,* and *Ethics and Animals,* while established philosophical journals such as *Ethics, Inquiry,* and *Philosophy* published numerous articles concerning environmental ethics. In 1980 George Sessions compiled a seventy-one page bibliographic essay on the new field, and the literature has grown substantially since that time. A 1981 bibliography "on animal rights and related matters" contained 3,200 entries.[4] Conferences with titles such as "The Rights of Nonhuman Nature" (1974), "The Humanities and Ecological Consciousness" (1980), and even "Environmental Ethics and the Solar System" (1985) brought scholars together to exchange ideas. *The Environmental Professional,* a journal concerned with environmental planning and impact assessment, devoted extensive attention in its 1987 numbers to the ethics of human-nature relations. Courses in environmental ethics appeared in many departments of philosophy and at a few universities it became possible to earn a graduate degree in the field. Textbooks such as George Kieffer's *Bioethics* (1979), Kristin Shrader-Frechette's *Environmental Ethics* (1981), Donald Scheorer and Tom Attig's *Ethics and the Environment* (1983), Robin Attfield's *The Ethics of Environmental Concern* (1983), Robert Elliot and Arran Gare's *Environmental Philosophy* (1983), Tom Regan's *Earthbound: New Introductory Essays in Environmental Ethics* (1984), and Holmes Rolston's

Philosophy Gone Wild (1986) aided the teaching and learning of this new venture in moral philosophy. Two collections of original essays entitled *Deep Ecology* appeared in 1985.

Most of this activity, to be sure, was academic and esoteric. With the exception of a few essays in national periodicals, most of the philosophers' work did not attract widespread popular attention. Yet just as a handful of radical social thinkers had used new philosophical ideals to rationalize a colonial revolution, the writings of environmental philosophers lent substance and respectability to radical environmentalism. In both eras philosophy helped theory converge with practice. Many of the environmental philosophers, moreover, did not rest with objective commentary and analysis; they wanted to change the status quo. As it had in colonial Massachusetts and Virginia, an atmosphere of crisis thrust philosophy onto the cutting edge of American liberalism.

As philosophers began to delineate it in the early 1970s, "environmental ethics" came to have several, sometimes contradictory, meanings. Almost all the creators of the new field agreed that there was no right and wrong in nature. Whether derived from a deity, evolved from experience, or deduced from logic, ethical norms were human constructs. Other forms of life might be the subjects of ethics, but they lacked the mental capacity to think of their behavior in terms of right and wrong or to enter into a reciprocal ethical relationship with humans. Morals existed in the human mind; they were self-imposed restraints on people's freedom of action. Humans determined ethical eligibility and, in a sense, dispensed rights. But at this point the consensus deteriorated rapidly. Much of the controversy turned on the question of whether environmental ethics were utilitarian and instrumental—derived from human self-interest—or whether nature possessed interests, value, or, perhaps, rights which people ought to respect even at considerable personal sacrifice.

Another division in the philosophical community concerned moral eligibility. Was everything in the environment to be included in humankind's moral community? If not, where did the ethical cutoff fall? The most traditional environmental philosophers extended ethics only so far as domestic mammals, in keeping with the old humanitarians. But more radical thinkers, notably the self-styled "deep ecologists" or "ecophilosophers," widened their circle to include all life. Going farther still, some holistic ethicists saw no reason to draw a moral boundary at the edge of life and argued for ethical consideration of rocks, soil, water, air, and the biophysical processes that constitute ecosystems. The Gaia hypothesis led a few philosophers to the conclusion that the planet and even the universe had rights superior to those of its most precocious life-form. Philosophical disagreement over such propositions was intense in the 1970s and 1980s, but from an historical perspective it was most remarkable that after a silence of two thousand years such controversy could occur at all.

One of the earliest indications of the awakening of American philosophy to environmental issues was a February 1971 conference at the University of Georgia. William T. Blackstone, a professor of philosophy there, organized the meeting and later edited its papers for publication. The book's title, *Philosophy and Environmental Crisis*, revealed that just as with the theologians, philosophers were starting to relate their craft to one of the central public concerns of the early 1970s. Blackstone believed that philosophers could analyze the significance of ecology for "social, ethical, political, and legal values." Not content to be merely commentators, the scholars who met in Georgia sought to advance value transformation. They hoped their work would constitute "a philosophical prolegomenon to the development of an environmental ethic."[5]

Published after some delay in 1974, *Philosophy and Environmental Crisis* exhibited the conservatism one would expect in one of the first ventures of the philosophy profession into environmentalism. Blackstone's own paper defined the ethical issue solely in terms of humans' right to a "liveable environment." He contended that environmental health should be regarded as a subset of "an inalienable . . . basic right to equality and freedom which are recognized in our political traditions." Here, surely, was the natural-rights tradition enlisted on behalf of environmental quality, but the approach was strictly anthropocentric. Blackstone simply followed the reasoning of President Richard Nixon, whose January 22, 1970, state of the union address defined "the great question of the seventies" as how to secure an unpolluted environment as "the birthright of every American." In the same manner Senator Gaylord Nelson, the originator of Earth Day (April 22, 1970), called for a constitutional amendment guaranteeing every American "an inalienable right to a decent environment." As Blackstone interpreted the meaning of these statements, they were logically consistent with the Lockean philosophy of limiting the freedom of the individual "in the interest of the freedom, rights, and welfare of all." Blackstone did admit the rights of future humans into his system, but other forms of life remained outside the moral circle. Rights had meaning only with reference to people.[6]

The most important paper of the 1971 conference became a touchstone for a large share of subsequent philosophical inquiry into the legitimacy of extending rights. Its author, Rockefeller University professor Joel Feinberg, asked the essential question: What sort of beings or things could be said to possess rights? His formula for answering it depended on "the interest principle." Something had to possess the ability to be harmed or benefited (and to be aware of such treatment) in order for people to think meaningfully about its rights. As Feinberg put it, "without awareness, expectation, belief, desire, aim, and purpose, a being can have no interests; without interests, he cannot be benefited; without the capacity to be a beneficiary, he can have no rights." This principle restricted the category of rights-possessors to people (including idiots, babies, and future generations) and to animals. The latter, Feinberg explained, were not moral "agents," but they did have an interest and a right to its satisfaction. Understanding the violation of one's interest and personally pressing a claim, he explained, were not requirements for the possession of rights. If a trustee embezzled money left to an animal, people could assert the creature's rights just as they might in the case of an inarticulate human baby.[7]

Feinberg excluded plants from the rights community on the grounds that they had insufficient "cognitive equipment" to be aware of their wants, needs, and interests. People might have a concern for the welfare of a particular plant and even impose laws for its protection, but in Feinberg's eyes this was a category of human interest (in the plant) and of human rights to benefit from it. Consistently, Feinberg also denied rights to incurable "human vegetables." Using the same logic he disqualified species. Collections of creatures could not have wants and desires; protection of rare and endangered species became the protection of the rights of humans to enjoy and benefit from them. Even less deserving of rights, Feinberg argued, were "mere things." He felt it was "absurd to say that rocks can have rights . . . because rocks belong to a category of entities of whom rights cannot be meaningfully predicated."[8]

Joel Feinberg wanted to advance the cause of environmental responsibility, and he believed his 1971 essay contributed to that end by making a case for the rights of animals and of future human generations. But Feinberg's ethical discrimination on the basis of "interests" left many unconvinced. The followers of Alfred North Whitehead had reason to believe that everything in nature, down to cells and atoms, had a potential for fulfillment. Ecologists hesitated to draw moral boundaries on the basis of an organism's cognitive ability. Descartes, after all, had ruled animals out of the moral community on the same grounds that Feinberg disqualified plants. Finally, Feinberg displeased adherents to the holistic ideas of Muir, Schweitzer, and Leopold with his opinion that "we have no choice" but to deny rights to animal "pests." But this was 1971, and the philosophical community was just beginning to stretch its newly found environmental wings.

One expression of the new theories was in the context of legal rights and the extent to which they might be applied to nature. As early as 1964 Clarence Morris, a professor of law at the University of Pennsylvania, published a remarkable essay on "nature's legal rights." According to Morris conservation laws should be thought of as expressing a "presumption in favor of natural" as opposed to "dislocated" environments. It would help reduce humans' impact on the environment, he thought, to assume that antipollution and protective measures "confer primary legal rights on nature," rights that could be advocated by "nature's lobbyists" and enforced in the courts. Morris was quite serious about giving legal rights to "birds, flowers, ponds . . . feral beasts, outcroppings of stone, primeval forests and sweet country air."[9] Such willingness to abandon the anthropocentrism of thousands of years of legal theory was a direct anticipation of Christopher Stone's better-known 1972 proposal to give trees and other natural objects legal standing.[10]

Morris's concepts did not attract attention in 1964, but six years later environmental activists called for "a Bill of Rights for all wild creatures, everywhere."[11] This did not mean human rights to experience or enjoy wildlife but the rights of the creatures themselves. Also in 1970 poet Gary Snyder raised the possibility of bringing the interests of wilderness and its inhabitants into the "chambers of government." Although he wrote from a Buddhist rather than a Western legal perspective, Snyder's conclusions paralleled Morris's and Stone's. He began his essay with an account of a climb of Glacier Peak in Washington's Cascade Range. His Japanese companion, overawed by the view of thousands of square miles of peaks and forests, asked about the American form of government. On hearing Snyder's reply, he exclaimed, "You mean, there is a senator for all this?" Sadly Snyder explained that nothing they could see was represented in the political order. But he added that he "would like to think of . . . a new definition of democracy that would include the non-human, that would have representation from those spheres."[12]

Similar thoughts came from a 1971 gathering at the San Francisco Ecology Center for the purpose of conducting the "First Constitutional Convention to recognize the existence and rights of the Great Family." As reported by environmentalist/journalist Harold

Gilliam, its purpose was "to ask how the Bill of Rights might be re-written by the national bicentennial in 1976 to affirm not only the rights of man but the rights of all living things—members of the Great Family. What are the rights of a pelican? A redwood? A stream?" Gilliam also reported how the Mendocino Institute of Man in Nature encouraged individuals and families to assume "totem protectorates" for particular species. Here was, at the same time, a throwback to American Indian philosophy and a modern application of ecologi-cal consciousness. American thought had come a long way in a quarter century. In the 1940s Aldo Leopold had written vaguely about biotic rights and wondered why philosophy and religion ig-nored the subject. By the 1970s lawyers and philosophers, as well as poets and ecologists, were making specific proposals for transform-ing American government in the interest of accommodating the rights of nature.[13]

The most visible statement came from Christopher D. Stone, a professor of legal philosophy at the University of Southern Califor-nia, who saw no logical or legal reason to draw any ethical bounda-ries whatsoever. Why, he wondered, should the moral community end with humans or even animals? Surely the tradition of natural rights that evolved in the United States, and the legal system erected upon it, were capable of further expansion.

The issue that inspired Stone to write his landmark essay with the arresting title "Should Trees Have Standing?" was a proposal in the late 1960s to develop a valley high in California's southern Sierra called Mineral King. The Sierra Club, a long-time guardian of this region, entered a protest against Walt Disney Enterprises' plans for a massive ski resort, but on September 17, 1970, the U.S. Court of Appeals of California ruled that since the Club was not itself injured it had no "standing," or legal reason, to sue against the development. But *something*, Stone reasoned, was going to be injured, and the courts should be receptive to its need for protection. Writing quickly late in 1971, hoping to influence the Supreme Court in its review of the Sierra Club's appeal, Stone used the *Southern California Law Review* to set forth the unprecedented argument that his society should "give legal rights to forests, oceans, rivers and other so-called 'natu-ral objects' in the environment—indeed, to the natural environment as a whole."[14]

Stone took it for granted that although the environmental move-ment was in full cry in 1972, many would find his proposal in-credible. He noted that throughout history, ideas once regarded as "unthinkable" were eventually incorporated into law. Jews in the

thirteenth century, black slaves, Chinese in California in the nineteenth century, children, women, and some animals had all gained a
measure of legal rights. Now, Stone thought, it was nature's turn.
Why not remove the environment from the category of "thing" and
afford it some protection from unconditional human exploitation?
Having boldly stated his thesis, Stone hastened to point out that giving the environment rights would not mean immediate cessation of
all human use of nature. People, after all, "used" other people (as laborers, for example) without denying their rights. Stone hoped that
environmental ethics would make possible similar kinds of use without abuse. Conferring rights on nature would give it more legal
weight than it had traditionally in human systems of justice.

A perceptive philosopher, Stone turned at once to objections that
might be raised against his idea. First, rivers, trees, and ecosystems
could not institute proceedings on their own behalf. Feinberg would
say they had no interest. How were they to be represented before the
law? Stone responded by citing the familiar legal notion of guardianship or trusteeship. The interests of infants or human incompetents were commonly represented legally by guardians. Stone felt
that an extension of this principle could give lakes and forests and the
land itself "standing" in the American judicial system. Going beyond
Feinberg, he contended that natural objects had definite needs, the
denial of which resulted in perceptible deterioration. Polluted air or
water turned trees brown, for example. It followed for Stone that
damages could be calculated and collected by the human guardians
of nature.[15]

What made Stone's 1972 proposal remarkable in American environmental and intellectual history was that it defined "injury" not
merely in human terms but with regard to nature. Biocentrism set it
apart from the familiar American practice of conserving national
parks and national forests (for tourism or natural resources) or reim-
bursing property owners for pollution damages. Stone argued in all
seriousness that trout and herons and cottonwood trees should be
thought of as the injured parties in a water-pollution case. Fines
would be assessed and collected (by guardians) on behalf of these
creatures and used to restore their habitat or create an alternative to
the one destroyed. Environmental damage so severe as to be considered "irreparable" would be completely prohibited. In effect this
gave natural objects absolute rights comparable to those inalienable
ones used to justify the American Revolution.

Christopher Stone's ethical system personified the environment
to an unprecedented extent. St. Francis of Assisi had regarded birds

and wolves as spiritual brothers and Henry David Thoreau had called sunfish and skunks his neighbors, but Stone wanted his society to think of a legal arrangement in which nature was actually treated as if it were a person. He said it would not be "unthinkable" to provide legislative apportionment that took wildlife into account. Alaska, for instance, should have more congressional representatives than Rhode Island on account of *"all those trees and acres, those waterfalls and forests."* Lest his readers dismiss this notion too quickly, Stone reminded them that prior to emancipation the American political system counted a slave as three-fifths of a man for purposes of apportioning representatives. Nature, in Stone's view, deserved as much in the 1970s and possibly more—just as the slaves eventually received. He was fully prepared to expand the boundaries of his community, to enlarge the scope of Lockean social philosophy from which much of American liberalism stemmed. His objective was nothing less than "to bring the environment into the society as a rightsholder." [16]

Stone's hope of influencing policy depended on Justice William O. Douglas reading "Should Trees Have Standing?" before the Supreme Court acted on the Sierra Club's Mineral King protest. Douglas was not only an advocate of human freedom but a long-time champion of wilderness. He had even published *A Wilderness Bill of Rights* (1965), although it concerned human rights to wilderness experiences rather than the rights of wilderness itself. Stone and the editor of the *Southern California Law Review* rushed a set of page proofs to Douglas's office and anxiously awaited the Court's action. When it came on April 19, 1972, Stone had mixed emotions. The majority of the Court rejected the Sierra Club's appeal for standing in the Mineral King issue on the traditional grounds that it had suffered no economic injury. But Justice Douglas had read and been persuaded by Stone's argument. Citing "Should Trees Have Standing?" on the first page of his dissenting opinion, Douglas stated that the proper name for the case was not *Sierra Club v. Morton* (Rogers C. B. Morton was Secretary of the Interior in 1972) but *Mineral King v. Morton*. In Douglas's mind this amounted to a "conferral of standing upon environmental objects to sue for their own preservation." Why not, he continued, open the American courts to "rivers, lakes, estuaries, beaches, ridges, groves of trees, swampland, or even air." Of course humans would have to represent these interests, and Douglas proposed a criterion for their selection: "those who have [an] intimate relation with the inanimate object about to be injured, polluted, or otherwise despoiled are its legitimate spokesmen." [17]

Aided by Stone, Douglas had clearly moved beyond his 1965

position that wilderness rights meant human rights. In the 1972 opinion he implied that many other forms of life, including ecosystems, had rights that people ought to respect. A river, he explained, sustained and nourished "fish, aquatic insects, water ouzels, otter, fisher, deer, elk, bear, and all other animals, including man." But humans, as the most articulate of these life-forms, must, according to Douglas, "speak for the entire ecological community." People, in effect, would be the moral voice of the river.[18]

In view of his acceptance of the ecological perspective and the intrinsic rights of the environment, it is not surprising that Douglas concluded his minority opinion with a reference to Leopold's *A Sand County Almanac*. Douglas was interested in Leopold's belief that a "land ethic," which enlarged the boundaries of the moral community, would logically expand the application of justice. That, Douglas stated, was the crux of the issue of "standing" in the Mineral King controversy. Although the Sierra Club lost its appeal to speak for Mineral King, ultimately it won the war. The cost of long delays discouraged Walt Disney Enterprises, and in 1978 Congress added the controversial valley to Sequoia National Park.

The idea initially raised by Morris in 1964 and popularized by Snyder, Stone, and Douglas penetrated the philosophical and legal communities as well as popular thought. Two paperback editions of Stone's article reached a large audience under the same title: *Should Trees Have Standing?* As a result of the Mineral King case, the media took unprecedented notice of environmental ethics. Stone appeared, somewhat uncomfortably, on radio and television talk shows. "Do Trees Have Rights Like People?" the *National Observer* asked in 1974 in an article on the implications of Stone's ideas for wilderness preservation. The newspaper's answer to its rhetorical queston was that, yes, the "far out" idea was being taken seriously by increasing numbers of environmentalists.[19]

After Stone and Douglas located the conceptual door to the rights of nature in 1972, philosophers and legal theorists were quick to push it open. One indication of their growing interest was the application of John Rawls's *A Theory of Justice* (1971) to environmental issues. Rawls's highly influential book was written in the late 1950s and early 1960s, well before American concern for the environment began to "green" philosophy. He specifically restricted his argument to human interests in equal liberty, justice, and opportunity.[20] But many philosophers who read Rawls in the 1970s seized on his theories to make a case for nature. The more conservative simply contended that Rawls could be understood as supporting a moral obligation to resist environmental degradation in the interests of future generations of humans.[21]

Others extended Rawls more radically. In 1974 Laurence H. Tribe, a Harvard law professor, proposed adding nature to the contractual arrangements between people that Rawls presumed occurred at the beginning of any society. Tribe contended that Rawls's principle of maximum liberty (applied equally, Rawls stipulated, to all members of the community) would maximize the benefits for all life as well as for human life. Noting Christopher Stone's work, Tribe pointed to the recent growth of the idea that "persons are not the only entities in the world that can be thought to possess rights." Although it was possible to understand this concept as a "legal fiction," Tribe preferred to see it as evidence of the capacity of humans to develop "new possibilities for respect and new grounds for community." In the manner of Darwin, Tribe wrote about a "spirit of moral evolution" that had recently spread to include blacks and women and was beginning to incorporate animals, plants, and might, in the distant future, include "canyons . . . a mountain or a seashore." Here, just three years after Rawls's anthropocentric theory, was evidence of the capacity of philosophy at least to discern what Tribe called the "distant shores" of morality.[22]

The belief that nonhuman organisms had legal rights struck responsive chords among animal liberationists in the 1970s. For example John Lilly, the preeminent defender of dolphins and other cetaceans, pointed out in 1976 that people have "evolved through certain stages, from unconscious acceptance of lack of rights, to the conscious awareness of the need for an adequate expression of an intolerable situation . . . to the demand for . . . relief . . . to the law and its adequate administration." Lilly knew from his study of history that demands for the liberation of oppressed groups of humans had frequently come from persons outside the group needing relief. Most abolitionists, for example, were whites. So for Lilly the Stone thesis that humans could represent the rights of other living things made perfect sense and led him to conclude his statement with an unequivocal manifesto: "Individual dolphins and whales are to be given the legal rights of human individuals. Human individuals and groups are to be given the right to sue in behalf of . . . cetacean individuals placed in jeopardy by other humans."[23]

The same idea surfaced in an even more specific form in David F. Favre's 1979 proposal in the journal *Environmental Law* to enact a new constitutional amendment on behalf of wildlife. Favre, a professor at the Detroit College of Law, correctly questioned the widespread use of the phrase "animal rights." As a lawyer Favre knew that the interests of nonhuman creatures might be defended as a category of human rights, but in existing legal systems they as yet possessed no rights. Favre sought to correct this with an addition to the document that provided the basis for rights in the American political system. His suggested amendment to the Constitution stated that "all wildlife . . . shall have the right to a natural life." Humans must not "deprive any wildlife of life, liberty or habitat without due process of law." Favre explained that human survival interests could override wildlife rights, and he knew enough about ecology to recognize that in the absence of natural predation people might need to check excessive wildlife populations in the interests of those creatures. Thus his system tended to focus on the rights of species and habitats rather than individual organisms. Like Stone, he understood that humans would be the actual defenders of inarticulate wildlife in the courts. Central to Favre's argument was the history of constitutional amendments as vehicles for extending the limits of American liberalism. Blacks attained full legal rights only after additions to the fundamental law of the land, and women still seek an equal rights amendment. The idea of including nonhumans and habitats in what Favre called "the ever-widening circle" marked the boldest legal application of environmental ethics to date.[24]

This kind of reasoning was so radical in terms of traditional notions of justice in the United States that it inevitably engendered opposition. One attorney, astonished at Stone's proposal to give trees standing in courts, used verse to make his point:

> If Justice Douglas has his way—
> O come not that dreadful day—
> We'll be sued by lakes and hills
> Seeking a redress of ills.
> Great mountain peaks of name prestigious
> Will suddenly become litigious.
> Our brooks will babble in the courts
> Seeking damages for torts.
> How can I rest beneath a tree
> If it may soon be suing me?
> Or enjoy the playful porpoise
> While it's seeking habeas corpus?
> Every beast within his paws
> Will clutch an order to show cause.
> The courts, besieged on every hand,
> Will crowd with suits by chunks of land.

Ah! But vengeance will be sweet,
        Since this must be a two-way street.
I'll promptly sue my neighbor's tree
        For shedding all its leaves on me.[25]

On a more serious philosophical level Mark Sagoff, a professor of philosophy at the University of Pennsylvania, crossed swords with Stone and Tribe shortly after publication of their unusual proposals. Writing in the *Yale Law Journal* in 1974, Sagoff ridiculed the idea that "all of nature marches forward in legal equality, with rights for all, without regard to race, creed, color, sex, leaf structure, or atomic number." How, Sagoff wondered, did Stone purport to know what inarticulate natural objects wanted? It seemed reasonable to him that wildness (or an undeveloped condition) might not be the preference of creatures struggling for survival in a tooth-and-claw world. Turning to Stone's case in point, Sagoff asked: "Why wouldn't Mineral King want to host a ski resort, after doing nothing for a billion years?" Perhaps the Disney developers, not the Sierra Club, had the valley's interests in mind. The way out of the dilemma for Sagoff was to accept anthropocentric morality forthrightly. He preferred to argue that people have a right to wild mountain valleys for their cultural, spiritual, and aesthetic value—to people.[26]

In 1984 P. S. Elder, a Canadian professor of law, launched similar attacks on Stone's argument. "The only stone which could be of moral concern and hence deserving of legal rights," he began, "is one like Christopher." Elder's objections to the extension of rights beyond humans reduced to his belief that trees and canyons are not "self-conscious beings." Bad treatment does not matter to them. Elder agreed with Joel Feinberg that rights were not relevant to anything less sophisticated than animals. But he quickly added that he fully supported responsible treatment of all nature. The way to achieve it was through the familiar formula of human rights. If some people feel that a certain treatment of nature is wrong, then they (not nature) should be permitted to use the courts for redress. All that need be done to achieve Stone's ends, Elder concluded, is to give new rights (to environmental integrity, beauty, and so forth) to people. In this way humans can extend morality to rocks without worrying about whether rocks have rights or what that means.[27]

Stone was not convinced, however, that the courts would be sufficiently moved by just another human interest. He believed nature would have a much better chance of obtaining legal protection if humans assumed that it actually had rights which they must respect. Yet Stone was persuaded by objections that rocks and mountains and rivers cannot be supposed to care what happens to them; that they have no feelings or interests. Why, then, should people represent, or even presume to know, their rights? In 1985 Stone reentered the debate over environmental ethics with a long article reconsidering his thirteen-year-old thesis that trees should have standing. He admitted at the outset that the direct extension of rights and legal standing from people to, say, places like Mineral King oversimplified a complex question. But Stone was not persuaded on these grounds to reject natural objects as members of humankind's moral community nor to define their rights strictly in terms of human rights and interests. His task thus became devising a way to include what he called "unorthodox" entities, such as those that lacked discernable interests, in ethical and judicial systems.[28]

Stone's solution, "moral pluralism," presumed that ethical activity could exist on several different logical planes. He illustrated his point with an analogy to maps that reveal different information about the same area and meet different needs. "There is no one map that is right for all the things we want to do with maps," Stone explained, "nor is one map more right than another." In the same way he envisioned various ethical systems that could direct human behavior toward other people, the environment, and also embryos, clones, robots, and other unconventional entities. This was the ethical frontier which, Stone hoped, philosophers would make bold to enter. As a starting point, he suggested the presumption for all objects and even *qualities* of objects if not human-type natural rights, then "*legal considerateness.*" This depended on the assumption that a lake had value in its undisturbed or "whole" condition "simply because the universe is better for containing it" in that state. If a specified condition of the lake (say being unpolluted or ecologically intact) were changed, the lake's human guardians could bring legal action and seek remedial attention. In effect this was a backdoor way of giving the lake legal rights without using either human interests or a supposition of the existence of interests on the part of the lake. For those who found the idea far-fetched, Stone noted that in 1975 a federal court allowed a suit to be brought in the name of the Byram River in New York and Connecticut against a polluting community on its banks. He was also encouraged that contemporary philosophy was at least seriously considering ways of incorporating very unconventional environmental entities into ethical discourse. And that, he knew, was a necessary prelude to making those radical leaps of moral reasoning which, to recall a word from his 1972 essay, people initially regarded as "unthinkable."[29]

While the legal-rights controversy stimulated some philosophers to consider justice for nature, others found their inspiration in psychology. Harvard's Lawrence Kohlberg in particular attracted attention when he postulated that moral motivation passes through stages of growth in the human mind. Beginning with the pure self-interest of an infant, the normal human progresses through higher levels of morality that initially include mother and father and the immediate family and eventually extend to the neighborhood, town, nation, and species—all humankind. Children mature ethically just as they do biologically. They increasingly accept the restraints of conscience on their freedom of action. They have at least the potential to learn that, much as they would like to, it is morally wrong to take a playmate's toy, their fellow citizen's wallet, or the land of a foreign nation. Coming to recognize that others have rights helps the morally maturing individual deal with the problems of existence in a world of expanding social horizons. Eventually, Kohlberg believed, a very few humans evolve to a stage that, in diametric opposition to the first, is pure altruism. At this point self-imposed ethical principles direct every action.[30]

Kohlberg's theories of the late 1960s involved strictly human-to-human relationships. But a few years later environmental philosophers took note of them, recalled the Darwinian idea that ethics had evolved over time, and contended that Kohlberg opened the way for assuming that ethics could extend beyond humanity. Thus Ernest Partridge used Kohlberg to suggest reasons for believing that in their ecologically inspired need to get along with nature as well as other people, humans might reach a new stage of moral evolution.[31] From a very different perspective, an environmental activist working with Earth First! used Kohlberg to explain why self-sacrifice, indeed violence, in the defense of mother earth made as much ethical sense as self-sacrifice in defense of one's human mother. The radical environmentalists, he contended, had simply attained a higher moral stage.[32]

Writing in the early 1980s, Tom Regan observed that the volume and intensity of the discussion of extended ethics within the philosophical community "would have been unthinkable twenty, even ten years ago." Regan supposed that even a non-philosopher would have cause to "wonder whether we are not now on the cutting edge of a significant development in our moral and cultural evolution."[33] Regan was most impressed with the outpouring of both emotional and analytical writing and speaking on the subject of animal rights and its corollary, animal liberation. Other philosophers, as we shall see, felt concentration on animals was far too limiting, but it was the issue around which the profession of philosophy first began to green. The intellectual barrier that had to be removed before the philosophical river could flow in wider channels was the idea that morality began and ended with people.

Recognition that rights extended beyond the human sphere at least to the higher animals had extensive roots in Anglo-American thought.[34] As we have seen, Nathaniel Ward may have had this in mind as early as 1641 and Jeremy Bentham certainly did in the 1780s. John Lawrence in 1796, Edward Nicholson in 1879, and Henry Salt in 1891 made explicit reference to the "rights," including the legal rights, of nonhumans. On the American side, John Muir pioneered in recognizing that the rest of creation might have rights comparable to its dominant member. At the turn of the century Edward Evans and J. Howard Moore possessed clear conceptions of the applicability of the rights idea beyond human beings. And the idea of "biotic right" for nonhumans and nature was the heart of Aldo Leopold's land ethic of the 1940s. Yet the mainstream of the humanitarian or animal welfare movement before 1970 generally avoided the natural-rights approach in favor of what was considered a more practical emphasis on preventing cruelty, and hence callousness, in people. For most of the nineteenth and twentieth centuries humanitarians were notably quiet about animal rights. But in the 1970s both the volume and intensity of concern for this subject increased remarkably. In retrospect it seems clear that the attention paid in the 1960s to the rights of blacks, women, Vietnamese, and, to a lesser extent, Native Americans, homosexuals, fetuses, the elderly, and students stimulated renewed interest in the place of animals in American liberal thought. The pattern was similar to one witnessed earlier in American history when a wave of concern for the rights of white males emboldened a few philosophers and activists to push the limits of liberalism into uncharted social waters.

The most influential early statement in the modern discussion of animal ethics was a review essay by the Australian philosopher and activist Peter Singer, published in 1973 in the *New York Review of Books* and the *National Observer,* both highly influential periodicals. In fact, the impact of Singer's article, "Animal Liberation," on the greening of American philosophy can be compared to the effect of Lynn White's 1967 paper on environmental theology. As his arresting title implied, Singer sought to link the defense of animals to recent liberation movements benefiting human minorities such as women, blacks, and gays. The genesis of Singer's interest in animals was his 1972 Oxford University thesis concerning the legitimacy of civil and criminal disobedience when directed toward achieving equality, justice, and liberty for all people.[35] While neither animals nor the environment figured in the dissertation, Singer was clearly pursuing a line of philosophical inquiry that would readily raise questions about oppressed nonhuman minorities.

"A liberation movement," Singer explained at the outset of his 1973 essay, "demands an expansion of our moral horizons." Once that occurs "practices that were previously regarded as natural and inevitable are now seen as intolerable." The "practices" that impelled Singer to write were the treatment of animals raised for food and used in laboratory experiments. His point was that if it was morally wrong to treat humans—even noncognizant infants or impaired adults—in such a way as to cause pain, suffering, and death, then it was wrong to do the same to animals. Animals, in a word, should not be killed under any circumstances. Singer's philosophy mandated vegetarianism. Singer accused those who disagreed with these conclusions of "speciesism," which he defined as "the belief that we are entitled to treat members of other species in a way in which it would be wrong to treat members of our own." Comparable prejudices, labeled "racism" and "sexism," had led white males to discriminate against blacks and women. This practice had been vigorously challenged, but, Singer believed, "Animal Liberation will require greater altruism on the part of mankind than any other liberation movement" because the beneficiaries could not protest on their own behalf. So Singer and his colleagues, like Christopher Stone's guardians of trees and valleys, must articulate animals' interest in ending exploitation.[36]

Singer's review praised pathbreaking books by activists such as Ruth Harrison's *Animal Machines* (1964). The latest in a long line of English humanitarians, Harrison focused on the most abusive forms of animal husbandry. She was not a philosopher, but she questioned the right of humans to place economics over ethics in agriculture and coined the phrase "factory farming." In the introduction to *Animal Machines* Rachel Carson recalled the philosophy of Albert Schweitzer and raised "the question of how far man has a moral right to go in his domination of other life."[37] Singer did not share such a sweeping ethical perspective, but he was very bold when it came to defending animals he believed capable of suffering. In response to the common rebuttal that rats sometimes eat human children, Singer simply pointed out that according to his logic "rats have interests too." Of all Singer wrote, this statement in particular proved too extreme for other philosophers. Donald VanDeVeer, of North Carolina State University, proposed discriminating between the "basic" and "peripheral" interests of both humans and nonhumans. He also felt that great "psychological" or mental differences (say between people and protozoa) created a basis for discrimination. VanDeVeer's formula for "interspecific justice" (that is, justice between species) derived from a recognition of these differences. He argued that humans were not acting unethically in killing rats that sought to eat their progeny, but using rats for target practice would be morally wrong.[38] Still, for Singer, the interests of any being capable of experiencing pain and pleasure had to be considered *equal* to that of any other. He found particularly persuasive the way Patrick Corbett, philosophy professor at the University of Sussex, drew the full meaning of animal rights for Anglo-American liberalism. We must, Corbett argued, "extend the great principles of liberty, equality, and fraternity over the lives of animals. Let animal slavery join human slavery in the graveyard of the past."[39] It was this kind of "rights" approach to animal welfare, heavily influenced by the various civil and social rights movements of the 1960s, that set the animal liberation movement apart from earlier humanitarianism.

Two years after his opening salvo in the *New York Review of Books,* and in response to the extensive controversy it generated, Singer expanded his arguments in a book, *Animal Liberation* (1975). His preface admitted that "five years ago I myself would have laughed at the statements I have now written in complete seriousness." An example was in the opening paragraph: "The tyranny of human over nonhuman animals . . . is a struggle as important as any of the moral and social issues that have been fought over in recent years." The subtitle of the first chapter read "Why supporters of liberation for Blacks and Women should support Animal Liberation too." Equality, Singer explained in the manner of Jeremy Bentham, entailed consideration of the interests of all beings and, particularly in the case of animals, the elimination of suffering. So the creatures included in Singer's moral community had to possess nervous systems of sufficient sophistication to feel pain. Philosophers call such beings "sentient." Following this rule Singer condemned animal husbandry (he repeatedly likened herding to slavery) and experimentation on animals (he drew several analogies between animal laboratories and Nazi death camps). Eating "slaughtered nonhumans" was clearly unethical, and Singer explained his own vegetarianism in a final chapter, "Cooking for Liberated People." From his perspective ethics ceased to apply "somewhere between a shrimp and oyster."[40] Many environmental philosophers find this statement absurd, but Singer deserves credit for helping liberate moral philosophy from its two-thousand-year fixation on human beings. Moreover, the appearance of *Animal Liberation* in a briskly selling paperback edition moved the discussion of ethical extension beyond professional philosophers to thoughtful members of the general public in England, Australia, and the United States.

After the publication of *Animal Liberation,* Singer went on to make a career in the philosophical examination of ethical extension. Although he was based in several Australian universities, his work had its widest circulation in the United States. Its hallmark was an effort to cast off the "sloppy sentimentalism" that had so often characterized the earlier humane movement and instead portray animal liberation as "an awakening of the conscience of the tyrant species to the nature of the tyranny we exercise over other species."[41] At the core of Singer's philosophy was the principle of equality: human and animal interests count equally. His main argument was that just as a human being values his or her own life and perceptions, so does a cat or a deer. The fact that a deer does not think like a person was no more relevant in the assignation of rights than the advanced quality of Einstein's thought compared to an average person's. Consciousness (but not necessarily self-consciousness) and sentience were the key requirements for ethical consideration. Intelligence was no more proper as a basis for discrimination between the rights of people than it was between the rights of human beings and other beings.

Singer amplified these ideas in a series of important philosophical treatises. *Practical Ethics* (1979) discussed the reasons for and consequences of acting on the basis of equality of interests. *Animal Factories* (1980), coauthored with James Mason, attacked agribusiness, the human institution Singer considered least susceptible to reform and replacement. In *The Expanding Circle: Ethics and Sociobiology* (1981) Singer explored the origins and possible futures of ethics with special attention to biological determinists such as Edward O. Wilson. Near the conclusion of this book he turned to the question of how far ethics might evolve. Were animals the end or just the beginning of ethical expansion? Albert Schweitzer and Aldo Leopold, Singer noted, carried their moral systems beyond animals, and he was aware that there were advocates of ethical consideration of "mountains, rocks and streams." But while admitting that "today's enlightened thinking often turns out to be tomorrow's hidebound conservatism,"

Singer stuck with his conviction that ethics ended at "the boundary of sentience." A tree or a mountain, or a rock being kicked down a road by a schoolboy, did not feel anything, therefore possessed no interests, nor rights. Since they could not be harmed by human action they had no place in ethical discourse. "There is nothing we can do," he concluded, "that matters to them." Yet Singer had been led into his career by the growing environmental movement, and he was anxious to make a place for environmental protection in his moral philosophy. His way out of the dilemma was the concept of habitat. The mountain or the stream, Singer reasoned, was the home of many animals whose rights ought to be respected. On this basis, then, human impairment of the environment could be said to be unethical.[42]

In 1985 Peter Singer edited a collection of hard-hitting essays which he understood as "a platform for the new animal liberation movement." The old humanitarian movement, Singer felt, opposed cruelty in humans, whereas the modern version stressed the rights of animals. He took it to be "part of a far-reaching ethical revolution" that was "expanding the circle of ethics." By the mid 1980s Singer expanded his own concerns from laboratory and food animals to zoos, whaling operations, and endangered species. He increasingly paid attention to the activists who were engaged in translating their ethical concern for animals into political, legal, and illegal actions. "The 1980s," Singer wrote, "will be remembered as the decade in which the defense of animals began to make headlines around the world." He praised the people who were bringing to animal rights crusades "the kind of commitment and political outlook more commonly associated with struggles for human rights than with the cozy conservatism of the older and more traditional animal welfare organizations."[43]

Returning to the pages of the *New York Review of Books* in 1985 to write "Ten Years of Animal Liberation," Peter Singer commented on the sudden emergence of the movement. "Before the publication of [my] *New York Review* essay in 1973, the question of the ethical status of animals was scarcely mentioned by academic philosophers." While exaggerating the influence of his own article, Singer is right about the timing. When philosophers did address the issue before 1970, it was generally to make categorical denials of animal rights.[44] Singer singled out Roslind Godlovitch's 1971 essay in *Philosophy* as the "pioneering article" that "broke the silence."[45] The scholarly din became much louder in the next decade. Entire issues of the prestigious journals *Ethics* (January 1978), *Philosophy* (October 1978), and *Inquiry* (Summer 1979) concentrated on the issue of the moral status of animals. One periodical, *Ethics and Animals,* had no other

focus. Massive bibliographies appeared.[46] Not all the philosophers
were in agreement as to the nature of animal rights (or even whether
they had them at all), but no observer of the field could doubt that
the issue was, for the first time, being actively debated. Conferences
facilitated this debate by bringing together the leading theorists and
disseminating the results in published proceedings such as *Animal
Rights: A Symposium* (1979) and *Ethics and Animals* (1983).[47]

Numerous books expanded the discussion. The volume Singer
reviewed in 1973, *Animals, Men and Morals* (1972), was the first modern treatment of animal rights in serious philosophical terms. Indeed
it would be necessary to look back as far as 1892 and Henry Salt's
Animals' Rights to find a comparable degree of radicalism concerning
life-forms other than human beings. The editors of *Animals, Men and
Morals*, young Canadian and English philosophers, featured a powerful essay by the clinical psychologist and reformed animal experi-
menter Richard Ryder, which protested the abuses of animal subjects
in British and American laboratories. In the manner of the American
abolitionists, Ryder made his most telling points by simply listing
factual reports of experiments with cats, dogs, mice, and monkeys.
In his concluding paragraphs he noted that the racism that sanctioned
violations of black rights had been largely overcome. Ryder's hope
was that "it may come to pass that enlightened minds may one day
abhor 'speciesism' as much as they now detest 'racism.'"[48] Although
ungainly, Ryder's term—"speciesism"—stuck in academic and activist discourse because it linked the cause of nonhuman rights to
those of human groups who had recently experienced a measure of
liberation. The word suggested the possibility of ethical extension
from people to at least part of nature, as did the English novelist Brigid
Brophy's proposal in *Animals, Men and Morals* for "A Declaration of
Independence on Behalf of the Other Animals." Drawing directly on
the natural-rights tradition, so meaningful in both Great Britain and
the United States, Brophy argued that "once we acknowledge life and
sentiency in the other animals, we are bound to acknowledge . . . the
right to life, liberty and the pursuit of happiness."[49]

Correctly taking it to be the critical intellectual hurdle before further ethical expansion, philosophers gave major emphasis to animal
rights in the 1970s and 1980s. Andrew Linsey's *Animal Rights* and
Tom Regan and Peter Singer's *Animal Rights and Human Obligations*
both appeared in 1976. Stephen R. L. Clark, the Scottish philosopher, wrote *The Moral Status of Animals* in 1977 and followed five
years later with *The Nature of the Beast: Are Animals Moral?* In 1978
Richard Knowles Morris and Michael W. Fox edited *On the Fifth*

Day: Animal Rights and Human Ethics. Published by the venerable Humane Society of the United States, it showed that even the conservative wing of the animal welfare movement was responding to the new rights-and-liberation approach. Indeed, Morris's introduction went far beyond animals in calling for "an ethics that looks at the entire biosphere of the planet earth—and beyond—and defines man's obligations and duties toward the inorganic, the plant, the animal and [the] human." Fox, a veterinarian, argued that "if a human has a natural right, by virtue of his very being, to be free . . . to seek self-actualization in an optimal environment, then surely this right should be extended to all other living creatures." But most of *On the Fifth Day*, which took its title from the Scriptural interpretation of the timing of the creation of animals, was confined to sentient beings and featured philosophers such as Joel Feinberg.[50]

In terms of productivity and professional influence, the only philosopher who ranks with Peter Singer in the discussion of animal rights and their implications is the American Tom Regan. A philosopher at North Carolina State University, Regan began to consider the problems of ethical extension at the same time as Singer, in 1972, as an outgrowth of a study of nonviolence and Mahatma Gandhi. Regan admired the Indian's extreme pacifism, but believed that for Western audiences a more meaningful approach to extending ethics would be found in natural-rights philosophy. His initial paper, published in 1975, set forth his premise that animals, like humans, are creatures capable of valuing their lives and consequently possessed of "intrinsic worth" and "an equal natural right to life." All the arguments defending respect for the natural rights of people, Regan contended, apply equally well to animals; the comparison of animals to oppressed groups of humans was a staple in Regan's discussions. "The truth we must emphasize," he wrote in 1979, "is that just as blacks do not exist for whites, or women for men, so animals do not exist for us. *They* have a life, and a value, of their own. A morality that fails to incorporate this truth is empty."[51] It followed, for Regan, that being cruel to or killing animals in laboratories or farming operations was wrong—not, as most humanitarians believed, because of its harmful effect on humans, but because it violated animals' rights. His approach in the 1970s clearly reflects the rhetoric and arguments of those who worked to liberate social groups in the previous decade. In *The Case for Animal Rights* (1983), which is the most thorough philosophical examination of the subject to date, Regan states unequivocally that "the animal rights movement is a part of the human rights movement."[52]

The initial focus of modern moral philosophy on animal rights was an understandable way station on the road from anthropocentric ethics to broader conceptions of moral applicability. A culture steeped from its beginnings in Lockean liberalism could be expected to appeal to the same natural-rights philosophy that had extended respect to all classes of humans. But pegging environmental ethics to rights left many philosophers and the more radical environmentalists unsatisfied. Why did Singer draw a circle that included domesticated animals but cut off oysters and all less sophisticated creatures? Why did Regan end his moral community with mentally normal mammals? Ecology had opened new horizons that extended to the totality of the biophysical world. Glimpsing them, some philosophers became eager to explore the ethical implications of the human relationship to the totality of life and beyond. Perhaps natural communities—ecosystems or, in the old vocabulary, "nature"—deserved ethical consideration as well. These thoughts led away from the traditional natural-rights approach with its emphasis on individual beings (human or nonhuman) and directed the attention of philosophers to processes, systems, and wholes. It meant widening the circle to think, as Aldo Leopold had advised, like a mountain.

It is intriguing at this juncture to speculate that if the abolition of slavery and, more recently, the civil rights movement created the most compelling historical precedents for animal liberationists, it was the women's liberation movement that proved especially inspiring to exponents of a broader environmental ethic.[53] The reason is the connection many feminists as well as environmentalists discerned between exploited femininity and exploited nature. "The hatred of women and the hatred of nature," Ynestra King wrote, "are intimately connected and mutually reinforcing."[54] At the heart of this analogy is the image of the natural environment as a female, nurturing, passive presence—Mother Nature, or as the Greeks named their earth goddess, "Gaia." The threat to both women and nature, so the analogy runs, is traditional male domination or patriarchy and, particularly, the tendency of male sexists to conquer, master, manipulate, oppress, and exploit what they fear, hate, and perceive to be less powerful than themselves. King finds misogyny to be at the root of the dualism that separated civilization from nature. Rosemary Radford Ruether adds that "we cannot criticize the hierarchy of male over female without ultimately criticizing and overcoming the hierarchy of human over nature."[55] Carolyn Merchant has commented perceptively on this "affiliation" and entitled the first chapter of her book, *The Death of Nature* (1980), "Nature as Female."[56] She goes on to remind readers that the nuturing and mothering image of the natural world, which for a time constituted an argument for restraint of human appetites, gave way in the seventeenth century to a conception of nature as wild, uncontrolled, and threatening. A concerted effort at mastery followed, and the scientific and technological revolutions facilitated the drive for domination. Almost every feminist writer noted the parallels between the "rape" of the "virgin" land and abuse of women.[57] Consequently the women's movement of the 1960s and 1970s—coupled with growing public understanding of ecology, Indian religions, and Asian yin-yang theology—focused attention on nature as an exploited female presence.

If nature and women were perceived as partners in subjugation, campaigns for their ethical consideration could be mutually supportive. Indeed many bridged the two causes under labels such as "ecofeminism," "ecosophy," and "gyn/ecology."[58] According to Ynestra King, "ecology, feminism, and liberation for all of nature, including ourselves, are joined." But how did this connection work? Many contended that because of their role in the creation of life, women have traditionally been "closer" to nature than men. The feminine mind knows best how to think about the human-nature relationship. "Ecology," King writes, "requires a feminist perspective," and Jim Cheney believes that "holistic deep ecology is somehow feminist."[59] Susan Griffin makes the point more poetically: "woman speaks with nature . . . she hears voices from under the earth . . . wind blows in her ears and trees whisper to her."[60] The whispered message, according to Griffin and most feminist writers on environmentalism, is that interrelatedness, not hierarchy, is the way of nature and should become the central support of a new moral philosophy.

In a book strikingly entitled *Why the Green Nigger?* Elizabeth Dodson Gray declared that "The new understanding of life must be systemic and interconnected. It cannot be linear and hierarchical, for the reality of life on earth is a whole, a circle . . . in which everything has its part to play and can be respected and accorded dignity."[61] Women were, allegedly, in a better position to understand this because of their tendency to deemphasize the individual self in preference for a conception of identity that put primary emphasis on relationships, networks, and webs. On this point feminist philosophers drew on the work of Carol Gilligan, who broke from her mentor, Lawrence Kohlberg, to argue that men and women have radically different conceptions of their selves. "Women," in the words of one interpreter of Gilligan, "define the self through relationships of care and responsibility. Men define the self in terms of individual achievement. . . . Women [seek] safety in affiliation and men [find] it in independence."[62] It follows that women reject the idea of an isolated, atomistic, and competitive ego so dear to the male heart. They also shy away from that staple of the liberal credo, individual rights. It is better, some ecofeminists contend, to drop the entire framework of natural rights in cases where nature is involved, in favor of one in which people are inextricably related to each other and to the environment.[63] According to this kind of holistic or organic moral philosophy, it makes no more sense to assert the rights of, say, trees or animals against humans than it does to claim that the heart has rights in its relationship with the bloodstream or lungs. Ariel Kay Salleh has even asserted that most systems of morality that concern nature are weakened by a masculine preference for a hierarchy of rights of competing individuals. Ecofeminism, she asserts, is deeper than deep ecology.[64]

Deep ecology, as George Sessions has pointed out, owes much to Norwegians. As early as 1941 Peter Zapffe outlined a nonanthropocentric theory of human-environment relations that he called "biosophy." And in 1974 another Norwegian, Sigmund Kvaloy, coined "ecophilosophy" in an article in *North American Review*.[65] But it remained for Arne Naess, the eminent Norwegian philosopher, Nazi resister, and mountaineer to exert the most impact on the new American environmentalism when he proposed "deep ecology." Naess also believed that ecologists and philosophers should pool their wisdom in a new discipline called "ecosophy." He first announced his concepts in a lecture in 1972 and published the paper in English the following year.[66] The year 1973, then, saw the genesis of both the modern animal-rights approach to ethical extension (Peter Singer's essay was also published in that year) and deep ecology. Although professional philosophers inspired both perspectives, the two viewpoints proved, as we shall see, to be uneasy allies in the new environmentalism.

For Arne Naess and the American exponents of deep ecology whom he inspired, notably George Sessions and Bill Devall, the rise of ecology entailed philosophical and religious principles that completely undermined traditional ways of understanding the human-environment relationship, or what deep ecologists frequently called the "dominant paradigm" of Western thought regarding nature. The most radical component of the new paradigm was what Naess calls "ecological egalitarianism." Other deep ecologists commonly used "biocentrism" or "anti-anthropocentrism" to refer to the same philosophy, and Naess spoke of "a core democracy in the biosphere." The central idea was the right of every form of life to function normally in the ecosystem or, in Naess's words, "the equal right to live and blossom."[67]

It is significant for the link between Western liberalism and environmental ethics that Naess and other deep ecologists based this axiom on the "inherent," "intrinsic," or, as older philosophers might have said, "natural" right of all beings to life, to freedom from excessive human interference, and to the opportunity to pursue their own definition of happiness. Here, of course, was an explicit application of the familiar tripartite foundation of American liberalism, dressed in new ecological language and extended not only to all living things but, as Sessions and Naess explained after a 1984 camping trip to Death Valley, California, to "rivers, landscapes [and] ecosystems."[68] Naess thought of happiness as the opportunity of a life-form to "blossom" or "flourish." Alternately he termed this the right to "self-realization."[69] Rivers had a right to be (or function as) rivers, mountains to be mountains, wolves to be wolves, and, the deep ecologists frankly admitted, humans to be humans. The last point clearly posed philosophical problems.

As synthesizers of ecology and philosophy, the deep ecologists were quite familiar with food chains and the inevitability of life taking other life to sustain itself. Naess forthrightly admitted that human participation in an ecosystem "necessitates some killing, exploitation and oppression."[70] Animal liberationists, such as Singer and Regan, found it hard to square this fact with their fundamental belief in the right of individuals to their interests or lives. But the deep ecologists, following Aldo Leopold, thought in terms of processes. So Naess and Sessions could explain in 1984 that environmental impact, even killing, was ethically acceptable so long as it was done "to satisfy *vital* needs." The antipode of "vital" or "basic" in the minds of deep ecologists was "peripheral," "excessive," or "nonvital."[71] The central liability of modern technological civilization was that it had lost the ability to distinguish between these antipodes. In unmodified ecosystems, as would be found under wilderness conditions, predator and prey coexisted in a balance of vital needs. Hierarchy, domination, exploitation, and power—all hated words in the deep-ecology lexicon—did not exist in nature. In Africa, Kirkpatrick Sale explained in a review of two books entitled *Deep Ecology,* "the lion is not regarded as the 'king of the jungle' and does not think of himself as such, and in fact lives daily in careful balance with such other life-forms as the tsetse fly and the antelope."[72] Antelope kill grass, lions kill antelope, flies or pre-civilized humans kill lions—all in the course of a series of what Naess would call self-realizations.

For Devall and Sessions a wilderness was "a natural self-organizing ecosystem state."[73] Even if lions or antelope had a sense of right and wrong, it would not be necessary in such a biotic equilibrium. But technological humans, unlike their own hunting and gathering ancestors, possessed the power to alter ecosystems beyond their vital or legitimate need to survive.

This line of thought raised the inevitable question of whether *Homo sapiens* could have civilization (arguably, the human form of self-realization and blossoming) without violating the basic deep ecological principle of ecological egalitarianism. If people had evolved intellectually and technologically to the point where they could alter much of the earth, was their doing so any different than a lion using its speed and strength to charge and kill? The deep ecologists' answer was that while some human impact was acceptable, modern humanity had grossly exceeded appropriate levels, as might a lion that killed fifteen antelope in a day. Both in terms of population and resource consumption, especially human utilization of the habitats of endangered species, people stood guilty in the eyes of deep ecologists of ever more serious violations of the rights of the rest of nature. This was why environmental ethics became essential as a restraining device. The lion who killed excessively could not restrain itself with ethics, but humans possessed not only power but the mental potential to control power. They alone could conceptualize the rights of other creatures to self-realization and judge their own actions in terms of these rights. This ability made possible a biocentric perspective and a holistic environmental ethic. The deep ecologists hoped these world views would lead to a significant reduction in population, to a massive, voluntary diminution of human impact on the ecosystem, and to fundamental, revolutionary changes in prevailing economic, political, social, and technological systems. Their objective was the end of dualism; humankind would step back into the life community as a member and not the master. For some ecophilosophers the means to this end was "bioregionalism" or "reinhabitation." People would cultivate love for a particular region and structure their style of life so as to live gently within that place.[74]

The deep ecologists raised sharp criticism not only of traditional Western civilization but of the traditional conservation movement. Following Naess they characterized old-style conservation as "shallow" and anthropocentric. Naess explained that the struggle against pollution and resource depletion had as its central objective "the health and affluence of people in the developed countries."[75] Traditional conservation operated under the familiar utilitarian rationale for protecting nature: people took better care of the environment so that the environment would take better care of them. Even the accepted rationale for establishing national parks and wilderness areas struck the deep ecologists as anthropocentric, rather than biocentric, because it stressed human needs for recreation rather than the needs of other species for a habitat in which they could blossom and flourish. "A wilderness area," Naess declared, "has a value independent of whether humans have access to it."[76] Bill Devall, a sociologist and environmental philosopher from northern California, asked "Why wilderness?" and offered an answer rarely encountered in the politics of wilderness preservation. According to Devall, only Henry David Thoreau, John Muir, and, in our own time, Sierra Club leader David R. Brower understood that keeping land wild meant more than helping people enjoy the good life. Brower said simply that "I believe in the rights of creatures other than man" and that wilderness offered them an opportunity to realize those rights.[77] The existence of wilderness for Devall was a manifestation of restraint on the part of the planet's dominant life-form. "Wilderness," he explained, "is the habitat of other beings which have a right to live and blossom for themselves." Humans should understand wilderness areas not as settings for outdoor recreation but as gestures of planetary modesty, expressions of respect and reverence for the intrinsic value of nature. Seen in this way, wilderness preservation demonstrates a human commitment to share the environment with present and what Devall called "future generations of all creatures, rocks and trees."[78]

Holmes Rolston, a philosopher from Colorado State University, devoted several essays to demonstrating that humans did not create the wild world; it created them. As a "generating matrix," wilderness and its community of wild organisms had intrinsic or existential value and deserved a place in human ethics. Like most deep ecologists, Rolston understood that in widening the definition of community the ecological sciences created a new, expanded meaning for ethics. Wilderness for Rolston was a focal point of the effort to implement this radical new philosophy.[79] But another philosopher contended that since wilderness had no "consciousness" or "desire," it was neither useful nor logical to say that it had rights. Better to rest the defense of wild places on the rights of present and future human generations to experience wildness and on the importance of undisturbed ecosystems to human spiritual and physical welfare.[80]

Continuing their criticism of traditional conservation, the deep ecologists contended that even the stewardship argument, the staple of many ecotheologians, was wrong-headed because it left intact the idea of humanity as a master (albeit a gentle one) over subservient nature. Indeed, the whole utilitarian philosophy of conservation struck deep ecologists as analogous to campaigns for better care of slaves on antebellum plantations. The only meaningful reform was the abolition of slavery. In the environmental movement nothing really mattered except the liberation of nature from the system of human dominance and exploitation. What Devall termed "reform environmentalism" was worse than useless because by correcting short-term symptoms it postponed the necessary reconstruction of the entire human relationship with the natural world.

Devall and his colleagues were especially critical of the turn-of-the-century Progressive conservationists and their concern for "natural resources," a term that seemed unremittingly anthropocentric to the deep ecologists. Utilitarian conservation might have begun the process of taming the pioneer ego by admitting the interests of posterity into environmental policy, but the new environmentalists wanted to reject the whole idea of using anything *for* anything else. They hoped to achieve an economy and a government based on the principle that every part of nature and all natural systems had intrinsic value and rights that humans must respect. Good treatment of the environment, Arne Naess and George Sessions explained in 1985, must be "independent of the usefulness of the nonhuman world for human purposes." John Muir had said as much in the 1860s, but that was long before the rise of conservation. To attack it as part of the problem, as deep ecologists did, caused understandable bitterness in the contemporary environmental community. But the deep ecologists' repudiation of both the exploitation and the conservation of natural resources underscored their radical stance in a striking manner.[81]

The traditional American conservation movement had relied almost exclusively on human self-interest. Society was exhorted to take care of nature so that nature would take care of society's material and recreational needs. Contemporary environmental philosophers scrutinized this proposition with varying results. Richard A. Watson of the Washington University Department of Philosophy argued that it was possible to attain ecologically responsible behavior without assuming the intrinsic value or rights of nonhuman life. All humans needed to know was that their own survival depended on the preservation of the integrity and health of the ecosystem. Enlightened self-interest, in other words, could bring about the same results as widening the ethical community and with considerably less intellectual gymnastics. Why bother with all the theoretical and practical problems associated with granting nature rights when a simple extension of human rights to include the right to survive could suffice?[82] From this point of view there need be no evolution of ethics beyond the very first tier of Figure 1 (see above, p. 5).

To this the deep ecologists had two responses. The first noted that since some life-forms and ecosystems were perceived to have (and perhaps actually had) no value for human survival, more than enlightened self-interest was necessary if they were to retain their rightful place in the ecosystem.[83] The second response was more complex and depended on the new vision of reality advanced by both the ecological sciences and the "new" physics as interpreted by process philosopher Alfred North Whitehead and, more recently, Fritjof Capra in books such as *The Tao of Physics* (1975). The heart of the theory was the idea that identity of the individual was indistinguishable from the identity of the whole, interrelated cosmos. Therefore selfishness, rightly understood, could embrace the interests and rights of all life and matter. "The deep ecology sense of self-realization," George Sessions and Bill Devall explained, "goes beyond the modern Western sense of 'self' as an isolated ego striving for hedonistic gratification. . . . Self, in this sense, is experienced as integrated with the whole of Nature." Human self-interest and the interest of the ecosystem were one and the same. Illustrating the point, they mentioned Gandhi's belief that in extending aid to others "altruism was unnecessary because his self embraced the whole village."[84] The ecophilosophers simply defined the new village as global, coterminous with the planet. They were fond of quoting Robinson Jeffers's 1938 advice to submerge the ego and love the organic wholeness of the universe and "not man apart from that."[85] In the 1960s Alan Watts restated the idea as "the world is your body."[86] Of course this kind of organicism had long been a staple of Eastern faiths, and many new environmentalists saw ecology as the Western equivalent. It expressed what Warwick Fox called "awareness of the fundamental interrelatedness of all things—or, more accurately, all events."[87] Coming full circle, it appeared that deep ecologists could accept self-interest as the basis for environmental policy so long as "self" was seen to be indistinguishable from the greater, all-inclusive "Self." Yet since few humans attained this state of final enlightenment, environmental ethics were necessary as everyday restraints on ordinary selfishness.

Like no other issue, the differences between animal rightists and exponents of more comprehensive ecological ethics divided the American philosophical community into hostile camps. The factions might have recognized that together they had a much more potent

common enemy in the dominant moral philosophy that judged
everything apart from humans as irrelevant to ethics. Thinking in
terms of intellectual history, they might have seen themselves as colleagues in the step-by-step extension of ethics away from its traditional fixation on people. Instead they energetically attempted to un-
dermine each others' philosophical position. Mark Sagoff thought
animal liberation and environmental ethics made a "bad marriage,"
and he called for a "quick divorce." His reason: The environmentalist, thinking holistically, would sacrifice the individual organism
to the ecological community. The animal liberationist, however,
must defend all individual lives, domesticated and wild, even at the
expense of normal ecosystemic processes.[88]

John Rodman, a political theorist at California's Claremont Graduate School, became a central figure in the debate when he began, as
early as 1970, to point out that liberalism had to be dynamic and
ongoing. When it set limits on the rights it would defend, it became
static, property-conscious, and conservative. Nature, in Rodman's
opinion, offered an exciting new frontier for American liberalism.[89]
But he felt that many moral philosophers stopped their ideas short
and sold out the liberal cause. The animal liberationists in particular
offended Rodman. Writing in *Inquiry* in 1977, he found "patronizing
and perverse" the whole idea that "*we* can liberate *them*." Rodman
protested the whole notion of extending human-type rights to nonhumans. Doing so, he thought, categorized them as "inferior human
beings" and "legal incompetents" who need human guardianship.
This was the same kind of mistake, although Rodman did not note it,
that some white liberals in the 1960s made with regard to blacks.
Rodman recommended respecting animals and everything in nature
"for having their own existence, their own character and poten-
tialities, their own forms of excellence, their own integrity, their own
grandeur." Instead of giving nature rights or legal standing within
the present political and economic order, Rodman urged environmentalists to become more radical and to change that order. As a
start, all forms of domestication must end along with the entire institutional apparatus associated with owning the land.[90]

Elsewhere, writing as a self-styled "radical environmentalist,"
Rodman intensified his criticism of what he labeled "moral exten-
sionism." This way of thinking employed a "conventional hierarchy
of moral worth" or a "moral pecking order" based on intelligence,
consciousness, or sentience. It destroyed the ideal of equal moral
worth (ecological egalitarianism) and opened the way for humans to
override the interests of "subhumans" in cases of conflict. The mere

extension of rights to creatures most like us, Rodman thought, left "the vast bulk of nature . . . in a condition of unredeemed thinghood." Turning around Richard Ryder's and Peter Singer's accusation of "speciesism," Rodman charged them with "sentientism" or prejudice based on the ability to feel pain, which he said established too narrow a moral circle. For example, in Singer's philosophy "the sole value of rainforest plant communities consists in being a natural resource for birds, possums, veneer manufacturers, and other sentient beings." What Rodman recommended was an ethic based on the "ecological sensibility" that all living things and natural systems have "a *telos* or end of [their] own," hence intrinsic value and rights to exist. From his viewpoint the area of ethical applicability included the entire ecosystem. Environmental ethics was a mechanism regulating the most powerful member in a community of moral equals.[91]

Rodman was not alone in his impatience with the animal rightists and his desire to drive a wedge between them and the more inclusive biocentric philosophers. In 1980 J. Baird Callicott, a philosopher from the University of Wisconsin and an admirer of Aldo Leopold's all-inclusive land ethic, declared that the animal liberation movement was not even allied with environmental ethics. The former was "*atomistic*"; it emphasized the rights of individual organisms. The land ethic, on the other hand, was "*holistic*" and had as its highest objective "the good of the community as a whole." This constituted a revolutionary new perspective because traditional ethics located moral value only in individuals. Natural-rights philosophy was a good example. The animal-rights advocates simply added individual animals to the category of rights holders. Other philosophers urged inclusion of all forms of life, regarded as individuals. Callicott's "ethical holism" calculated right and wrong in reference not to individuals but to the biotic community. The whole, in other words, carried more ethical weight than any of its component parts. "Oceans and lakes, mountains, forests, and wetlands are assigned a greater value than individual animals," Callicott explained, and he certainly included humans in the latter category. It followed that from the standpoint of the integrity of the ecosystem, the life of a single organism of an endangered species would be more valuable, more worthy of ethical respect by people, than the life of a person or even a substantial part of the large *Homo sapiens* population. He agreed with Edward Abbey's well-known opinion that he would rather kill a man than a snake. From Callicott's ecocentric perspective even soil bacteria and oxygen-generating oceanic plankton carried more ethical weight than beings at the tops of the food chains such as humans.[92]

This moral philosophy, building on the egalitarian thrust of deep ecology, was truly unprecedented. Even Aldo Leopold, whose land ethic laid the foundation of Callicott's thought, had not drawn such radical anti-human implications. Nor had the extreme ecologists who defended the rights of germs admitted the necessity of sacrificing a few designated human carriers so that the endangered smallpox virus could make its contribution to the integrity of the ecosystem. But this was the conclusion to which Callicott's philosophy pointed. Humans, as the only self-restraining moral agent on earth, could logically be expected to make the ultimate denial of self-interest, surrendering their lives for the greater good of nature. Most environmental philosophers sidestepped this conclusion, preferring to understand ethics as cumulative: you could have human rights *and* the rights of the biosphere. Callicott, however, did not avert his eyes from the radical implications of his philosophy. "The extent of misanthropy in modern environmentalism," he believed, "may be taken as a measure of the degree to which it is biocentric." But in a recent essay Callicott has attempted to integrate the liberal tradition's classical respect for the individual human being with respect for nature as a whole. His argument centers on the idea that the health and integrity of the ecosystem is "literally essential to . . . the individual's well-being."[93]

Although few pushed environmental ethics this far, support for Callicott's position appeared frequently in contemporary philosophy. Holmes Rolston, whose respect for wilderness led him to deep ecological viewpoints, was not only prepared to recognize "the intrinsic value of every ecobiotic component" but proposed that nature be looked upon as a "commonwealth" whose rights trumped those of its living components. This view led Rolston to formulate "duties to species" and "duties to ecosystems" with higher ethical priority than to individual organisms. Well aware of the opposition to this concept among his colleagues, Rolston granted that neither a species nor an ecosystem had a "self" or was a "subject of life" with definable "interests." For some philosophers this meant such collections could have no legitimate place in individually conceived ethics. But Rolston believed that a "biologically sounder ethic" would value the species and the ecosystem more than the individual. Survival was the key. Individuals survived *as* species *in* ecosystems; for Rolston, "the appropriate survival unit is the appropriate level of moral concern." By the same standards, the life process—evolution—always took moral precedence over "ephemeral and dispensable" individuals. The bottom line for Rolston was the continuation of the biotic community. "The systemic process," he explained, "is an overriding value, not because it is indifferent to individuals, but because the process is both prior to and productive of individuality." Consequently the ecosystem, or nature in general, is a legitimate holder of rights and an object of human duty.[94]

To take just one more example of biocentric environmental ethics from a growing volume of American, Australian, English, and Norwegian philosophical literature, Paul W. Taylor of Brooklyn College began to explore what he called "life-centered" or "biocentric" morality in 1981. His philosophy rested on the now familiar assumption of absolutely equal inherent value, and hence moral merit, of all forms of life, including humans. He eschewed ethical hierarchy. Indeed Taylor went so far as to say that, given the history of his own race's adverse impact on the environment, it seemed reasonable that the *complete* disappearance of the human race would not be a moral catastrophe at all but rather something that the rest of the "community of life," were it articulate, would applaud with "a hearty 'Good riddance!' "[95] Returning two years later to a defense of his "egalitarian type of biocentrism," Taylor addressed the charge that in his system killing a human was no more a moral wrong than crushing an insect or uprooting a plant. Yes, Taylor commented, he really did stand behind this shocking idea, provided it be understood that there could be "adequate moral reason" for swatting a fly off food or picking a plant to eat or killing a human attacker in self-defense. Without such extenuating circumstances, "the killing of a wildflower . . . is just as much a wrong . . . as the killing of a human." Moreover, "in some situations it is a *greater* wrong to kill a wildflower than it is, in another situation, to kill a human." The situations Taylor had in mind were taking the flower's life "wantonly" versus killing a person in self-defense.[96]

In a book-length summary of his studies entitled *Respect for Nature* (1986), Taylor explained the practical applications of his egalitarian biocentrism. Humans had the responsibility of calculating their own "basic" and "nonbasic" needs as well as those of other life-forms. As a life-form themselves, humans had a biotic right to eat and create shelter and also to realize their own special potential in such activities as the arts, medicine, and technology. But respect for nature meant according all beings a similar opportunity to fulfill their various potentials. As the only moral agent in the biosphere, as well as the most powerful, humans were ethically obligated to restrain their environmental impact. This meant choosing "ways of life that minimize habitat destruction," particularly when endangered species were involved. Humans should "locate and construct their buildings, highways, airports, and harbors with the good of other species in mind." They should also "control their own population growth, change their habits of consumption, and regulate their technology."[97] The ideal for Taylor, as it had been for Leopold, was an extended life community whose members necessarily affected each other, but were regulated by the restraining force of ethics.

Taylor was under no illusion that such restraint would come easily. It would require "nothing less than a revolution in our ordinary ethical vision." But he drew encouragement from the knowledge that a similar revolution had once occurred "with respect to egalitarian principles governing the moral relations among human persons." Natural-rights theory and liberal-democratic systems of government and justice were the result. Another ethical leap—to nature—was, in Taylor's estimation, "now our highest and noblest moral calling."[98]

Biocentric ethics, particularly the concept that nonhuman life, nonliving matter, and biophysical communities had rights that humankind ought to respect, became the focus of much contemporary philosophical debate. Some thinkers, like the Australian philosopher John Passmore, rejected the notion as so much "rubbish." Passmore, whose book *Man's Responsibility for Nature* (1974) was a landmark in early ecophilosophy, declared that "the idea of 'rights' is simply not applicable to what is non-human." The inability of nonhuman life to communicate and "recognise mutual obligations" meant that only people participated in the moral community. Wilderness, for Passmore, had only instrumental value (for human enjoyment). He further challenged deep ecological ideas by welcoming a world "purged of flies." Still, Passmore wanted humankind to be responsible for nature and he was prepared to discuss environmental ethics as a matter of human morality. Nature, in other words, did not have rights, but it was right for people to protect nature for their own well-being. This, in Passmore's opinion, was what the humane movement had been about for two hundred years when it stated that it was wrong for people to be cruel to animals. He simply could not understand contemporary defenses of the rights of animals, still less the rights of rivers, mountains, and nature in general.[99] Kenneth Goodpaster held similar reservations when he stated his support of environmentalism but added that "the *last* thing we need is simply another 'liberation movement'—for animals, trees, flora, fauna, or rivers."[100]

Several philosophers opposed to holistic ethics fell back on the old argument that moral considerability was conferred by virtue of the capacity to feel pain. Edward Johnson of the University of New Orleans declared that the pain and suffering of individual, sentient beings was the only dependable criterion for separating right action from wrong. It distressed him to find Callicott arguing that there is "nothing wrong with pain," and even death, because they are natural parts of the evolutionary process. According to Johnson, it was *only* pain that mattered; those who believed that plants, rocks, and "the Whole" had interests and rights were talking nonsense.[101] William K. Frankena, a widely respected philosopher from the University of Michigan, expressed a similar point of view in asking, "Why, if leaves or trees have no capacity to feel pleasure or to suffer, should I tear no leaf from a tree? Why should I respect its location any more than that of a stone in my driveway, if no benefit or harm comes to any person or sentient being by my moving it?" Frankena added that he saw no way "to consider the Whole" in a moral community, "at least not if the Whole is not itself a conscious, sentient being."[102]

On the other hand some philosophers and scientists were prepared to entertain precisely this possibility. Although the roots of the idea that the earth is a living being are very old in Western thought, James Lovelock, an English atmospheric chemist, made the most dramatic modern statement of the idea in the mid-1970s with his Gaia hypothesis. The ancient Greeks used the term "Gaia" to refer to the nurturing earth goddess. Lovelock removed the theology and dressed this concept in the clothing of biochemistry. The planet, he believed, gradually created and presently maintains a self-regulating environment which not only sustains the life of its components but is itself alive. From this perspective individual beings and species such as *Homo sapiens* were to the earth as cells and organs were to their own bodies—parts of indivisible wholes. It followed that just as it made no sense to value or respect a brain cell or a liver apart from the entire organism on which it depended for life, so a proper environmental ethic demanded assigning value to the whole earth. Since humans were the only morally conscious members of this community, the brain cells of Gaia, they had the unique capability of restraining themselves in a manner consistent with the continuing welfare of the earth-being to which they belonged. All this implied that the planet possessed the traditional requirements for ethical considerability: consciousness, the ability to feel pain, and an interest or capacity for what might be termed happiness. The earth, in short, was regarded as a super-being with rights primary to those of the lesser beings, and the most far-reaching of the biocentric environmentalists called upon humankind to acknowledge and act upon this reality.[103]

Theodore Roszak, for example, wrote in 1978 about "the rights of the planet," which he understood as deriving from "the person-hood of the Earth." According to Roszak, meaningful environmental reform would not occur without "a sense of ethical respect, if not reverence, that can only exist between persons." The point, then, was to view the earth as a person—Mother Gaia—and to expand ethics to include her. "Nature," Roszak concluded, "must also have its natural rights."[104] Michael J. Cohen wrote a *Guidebook for the Liberation of Self and Planet*. The director of several education programs aimed at integrating humankind and nature, Cohen believed that if the planet and, indeed, the universe were alive, then so were all their components: "rocks and mountains, sand, clouds, wind, and rain . . . nothing is dead." As part of the same cosmic being nothing was beyond ethical consideration. Cohen understood environmental ethics to be an expression of "the planet trying to protect itself and, in turn, myself."[105] Holmes Rolston contributed the idea that nature or the earth was the "originating matrix" or "parental environment" of all matter whether organized into what we call life or displayed as "crystals . . . rivers . . . mesas, canyons." Everything was created by nature and, for Rolston, "there is value wherever there is positive creativity." Using this principle, he found no reason to limit ethics to earth. Was not the universe the "originating matrix" of the planet we occupied? Should it not be included as the ultimate ethical circle?[106] In 1986 Rolston, along with other philosophers, theologians, and scientists, contributed the papers that the Sierra Club published under the title *Beyond Spaceship Earth: Environmental Ethics and the Solar System*. The collection explicitly addressed the "nonanthropocentric dimension," asking whether it was moral to conduct an experimental nuclear meltdown on the moon or to strip-mine a neighboring planet. If the answers to such questions were still sketchy, here were thinkers at least willing to inquire whether a moral philosophy that ended with the boundaries of the planet was a manifestation of "terra-centrism" or "Earth chauvinism."[107]

The implication of all biocentric and, literally, universal ethical philosophy from Aldo Leopold onwards is that the whole is more important than any of the parts. As Stephen R. L. Clark put it in 1983, "What matters is the maintenance of Gaia and her constituent ecosystems, not the preservation at all costs of any single line (even our own)."[108] Indeed the Gaia hypothesis connoted for many thinkers the capacity of the earth organism to purge itself of disruptive elements just as a simpler organism removed potentially poisonous liquid and solid wastes and tried to destroy cancers and infections.

The point of this line of reasoning was to imply that humankind, as the most formidable contemporary poison on the planet, might be excreted if the species did not clean up its technological act. Perhaps, some suggested, Gaia might choose to let *Homo sapiens* self-destruct with nuclear weapons. In 1986 British television featured a three-part special on a revolutionary environmental action group, called Gaia, whose members believed that human beings were an unhealthy force in the ecosystem and must be eliminated from the earth-organism. There can be no more graphic example of the ability of environmental ethics to transcend human self-interest. But as biocentric philosophers were quick to explain, individual self-interest was indistinguishable, to the Gaian perspective, from the interest of the whole because the self, like the cell, has no being at all outside the environmental context.

Although fully prepared to concede that part of nature had rights, the animal-liberation wing of contemporary environmental philosophy mounted a surprisingly vicious rebuttal to the biocentrists and to holists such as the advocates of Gaia. Tom Regan, for example, characterized the holism of Aldo Leopold and contemporary biocentrists such as J. Baird Callicott as "'environmental fascism.'" He meant that just like some twentieth-century totalitarian governments, the ecocentrists favored a system in which the good of the community, group, or nation-state superceded that of the individual. When pressed, environmental fascism demanded the sacrifice of the interests and even the lives of individuals to the ecosystem, planet, and universe. This is what Regan, writing in the tradition of natural-rights liberalism with its emphasis on the intrinsic value of every individual—animal as well as human—could not accept.[109] But there is another side to Regan. The holistic critics who scorned Regan's concentration on mentally normal mammals[110] overlooked the fact that in 1976 he had argued that according to the principle that all things had a "good of their own," one could ascribe rights concerning the retention of that good to "nonconscious, inanimate things (trees, sagebrush, rivers)." He went on to say that an "ethic of the environment" based on the goodness principle "would . . . commit us to a far larger view of what individuals, and possibly what groups of individuals (e.g., ecosystems) are of direct moral significance."[111] So, it would seem, Regan was capable of holistic moral philosophy, and Peter Singer does not appear to oppose the idea of including "mountains, rocks and streams" in the ethical community at least as habitats. Admittedly it is possible to find less comprehensive definitions of moral eligibility in the work of the animal liberationists, but it is clear that at least on occasion they deserve credit as architects of more comprehensive environmental ethics.[112]

In traditional American liberalism, ethics had always functioned to protect individual lives against aggregates such as states or nations. Philosophers assumed that first some humans, then all humans, then some nonhumans (animals), and, as the circle widened, all nonhumans (plants, insects, viruses), had intrinsic value and, it followed for some thinkers, natural rights to life, liberty, and the pursuit of their own style of happiness. But the land ethic (Leopold), ethical holism (Callicott), an egalitarian type of biocentrism (Taylor), and deep ecology (Naess) led the most radical moral philosophers of recent times to conclusions that devalued the individual life relative to the integrity, diversity, and continuation of the ecosystem. This understandably offended many proponents of animal rights, not to speak of those liberals whose moral community began and ended with human society.

In one sense ecological ethics did push traditional liberal philosophy past its conceptual limits. The circle of moral considerability became so large as to call into question the legitimacy of its earlier, individual components. Perhaps ethics was not sequential after all. But from another perspective environmental ethics created entirely new definitions of what liberty and justice meant on planet earth. It recognized that there can be no individual welfare (or liberty) apart from the ecological matrix in which the individual life must exist. A biocentric ethical philosophy could be interpreted as extending the esteem in which individual lives were traditionally held to the biophysical matrix that created and sustained those lives. It can be understood, then, as both the end and a new beginning of the American liberal tradition.

• CHAPTER 6 •

Liberating Nature

———————◆———————

If . . . the machine of government . . . is of such a nature that it
requires you to be the agent of injustice to another, then, I say,
break the law.

—Henry David Thoreau, 1849

Humanistic value systems must be replaced by supra-humanistic
values that bring all plant and animal life into the sphere of legal,
moral and ethical consideration. And in the long run, whether
anyone likes it or not, force will eventually have to be brought
to bear against those who would continue to desecrate the
environment.

—Greenpeace Chronicles, 1979

The Marine Mammal Protection Act [and] the Endangered Species Act [embody] the legal idea that a listed nonhuman resident
of the United States is guaranteed, in a special sense, life and
liberty.

—Joseph Petulla, 1980

Free shackled rivers! . . . The finest fantasy of eco-warriors in
the West is the destruction of [Glen Canyon] Dam and the liberation of the Colorado [River].

—Dave Foreman, 1981

As Americans have discovered frequently in their history, the denial
of natural or "inalienable" rights creates a sense of moral outrage that
can escalate theory into action. When issues are defined ethically—
phrased, that is, in terms of right and wrong—it is hard to remain
indifferent. People seldom consciously compromise their ethical convictions, and in the context of American liberalism, "oppression" is

among the cardinal sins. "Liberty" and "freedom" are sacred. Identify a minority that is oppressed by denial of its rights and you immediately create a strong argument for its liberation. Economic issues, even elections, generate comparatively little heat, but the failure to honor basic rights elicits crusade-like zeal with the power to transform reformers into radicals and even revolutionaries. Women, Indians, blacks, and fetuses have benefited from that zeal in the last quarter-century, and so has nature.

Domesticated or captured animals were logically the first non-human creatures to be included in the extension of ethics. Efforts to improve their treatment and even to liberate them from research laboratories have made recent headlines. Wild animals, such as whales, seals, dolphins, and endangered species in general, were also in the news as humans began to champion their rights. At the antipode of anthropocentricity, the most radical of the new environmentalists followed the philosophers of holistic ethics into defenses of the rights of wildernesses, rivers, rocks, ecosystems, and even nature and the planet in general. Such "ecological resisting" pushed American liberalism into forms that its original architects would have found hard to recognize. But the founders knew well that freedom was a force not easily contained. Noting that eighty-seven years elapsed from the Declaration of Independence to the Emancipation Proclamation, Donald Worster surveyed the ethically powered environmentalism of the 1980s and simply observed that "it is now nature's turn to be liberated."[1]

Many of the ecologists, philosophers, and theologians reviewed in the previous three chapters were also environmental activists. Some believed that nature had rights which humans, as both the primary violators and only moral agents on earth, should respect and uphold. Others preferred to argue that it was right to protect and wrong to abuse nature simply from the standpoint of human interests. Either route made environmentalism a moral issue, linked it to American liberalism, and, as a consequence, gave it more potency than ever before. Some chose to implement their ethical convictions within the framework of existing American legal and judicial institutions. The Animal Welfare Act (1966), the Marine Mammal Protection Act (1972), the Endangered Species Act (1973), and lawsuits featuring birds, fish, and plants as plaintiffs exemplified efforts to modify human conduct in the interest of the rights of other species. But this piecemeal and partial reform of the established order—or, as some deep ecologists preferred to say, the dominant paradigm—left the more radical exponents of environmental ethics unsatisfied. They ex-

pressed their displeasure through acts of nonviolent civil disobedience, which the black rights movement had employed so visibly
after 1955. Some occupied nuclear test sites, placed their bodies in
front of logging trucks, and chained themselves to whalers' harpoons
and, in one instance, to the bank of a wild river being flooded by
a dam. Others went further, destroying property and comparing
themselves to the participants in the Boston Tea Party of 1773. The
Animal Liberation Front freed monkeys from research facilities;
Greenpeace tried to stop nuclear tests and, in turn, had its own ship
sunk; the Sea Shepherd Conservation Society rammed pirate whalers
and vandalized whale-processing stations; and Earth First! spiked
trees (to thwart saws) and tore up survey stakes in wilderness areas.
This kind of "monkeywrenching"—a term adopted by the radical
environmentalists from a 1975 novel about pro-environment sabotage—took pains to avoid direct confrontation with or injury to
people. But the line between the perpetrators' avowedly illegal activity and outright warfare was philosophically and pragmatically
thin. The Boston radicals had reached a similar point at the dawn of
American liberalism two centuries ago.

Liberation necessarily entails overriding the laws and customs
that deny the rights of the oppressed minority. In the case of nature
those laws and customs included a tradition of human ownership and
exploitation already ancient at the time of colonization of the New
World.[2] Property was often taken to be a natural right in itself. The
right of nonhuman nature to life, liberty, and the opportunity to pursue its own kind of happiness ran directly against human rights to
possession and exploitation of real estate and livestock. The potentially devastating impact of the liberation of nature on the foundations of the established order made it imperative for the new ethically
oriented environmentalists to find not only a moral philosophy but
a justification for attacking the legal and legislative instruments of
what they considered oppression. The abolitionists had faced a similar problem (slaves were someone's property) in their efforts to extend the blessings of liberty. The American ideal of liberty made it
conceptually difficult to stop with half loaves in the 1850s. For the
same reason the gradual and partial improvement of existing institutions (what biocentrists scorned as "the conservation of natural resources" and "reform environmentalism") did not please the more
radical environmentalists. Earlier liberals had likewise scorned proposals to make slavery more humane or to improve, rather than replace, the British colonial empire. The first American revolutionaries
had John Locke, John Trenchard, Thomas Paine, and other liber-

tarian theorists to justify lawbreaking. The revolutionary environmentalists sought justification of their efforts to implement the rights of nature with the most persuasive contemporary philosophers of disobedience.[3] Their thinking helped take environmental ethics out of libraries and into the streets and forests.

For time spent laboring in the trenches of radical environmental theory, Murray Bookchin (also known by his pseudonym Lewis Herber) has few equals. As early as 1952 Bookchin published a paper on the problems that pesticides and other synthetic products created for food.[4] But Bookchin was interested in more than the chemistry of pollution. He also wrote about the "social origins" of such problems, meaning the human attitudes, values, and institutions that explained pollution on a fundamental level. In 1963, at the beginning of modern American environmentalism, Bookchin explored the interface between human ideas and environmental quality under the title *Our Synthetic Environment*. Although Rachel Carson's *Silent Spring* (1962) stole much of Bookchin's thunder, it was his book rather than hers that most clearly advanced the thesis that "the domination of nature by man stems from the very real domination of human by human."[5] Bookchin meant that the rise of civilization, the Western variety in particular, brought with it an obsession with hierarchy and the mechanisms of power politics and power economics. These made possible the chronic domination, oppression, and exploitation of women by men, of the young by the old, one ethnic group by another, and the poor by the rich.

Karl Marx, of course, had studied this last form of hierarchy and proposed a revolutionary remedy. Bookchin began where Marx stopped. He recommended discarding ecological as well as economic class distinctions along with the governments that sanctioned and sustained them. This meant revolution and, here again, Bookchin transcended Marx. The nineteenth-century revolutionary called for a government of and by the working class; Bookchin wanted no government at all. His objective was not to seize power for one group or another but to dissolve it entirely as an apparatus by which people related to each other and, as a species, to nature. As early as 1965 Bookchin linked anarchism and ecology. Both perspectives, he believed, stressed the equal value of every part of the community and the necessity of maximizing individual freedom so that every component could fulfill its potential. "I submit," Bookchin wrote in "Ecology and Revolutionary Thought" (1965), "that an anarchist community would approximate a [normal] ecosystem; it would be diversified, balanced and harmonious."[6] The means to this end, he explained in his major work, *The Ecology of Freedom* (1982), was through an "ethics of complementarity" derived from an "ecological vision of nature." Bookchin's utopia was not only based on ecological models; it *included* the ecosystem. He sought a "new and lasting equilibrium with nature" just as he did with other humans.[7]

Bookchin was under no illusion about the fact that his ecoanarchism necessitated the wholesale replacement of his civilization's "institutional and ethical framework."[8] He also knew that this was another word for revolution. "I would like to ask," he wrote in 1974, "if the environmental crisis does not have its roots in the very constitution of society as we know it today, if the changes that are needed . . . do not require a fundamental, indeed revolutionary, reconstitution of society along ecological lines?"[9] It was from this perspective that Bookchin, like the deep ecologists whom he anticipated, criticized most manifestations of American conservation and even large parts of modern environmentalism. As one of the first of the radical environmentalists, and as an avowed revolutionary, Bookchin remained profoundly suspicious of those who would save the world by banning aerosol cans or staging Earth-Day cleanups. He regretted that by 1980 "ecology is now fashionable, indeed faddish— and with this sleazy popularity has emerged a new type of environmentalist hype."[10] It featured anti-pollution campaigns but did not challenge the mental pollution that Bookchin regarded as the root of the problem. Dismissing charges that environmentalist demands were too radical, he argued "they are not radical enough." Specifically, Bookchin continued, "'environmentalism' does not bring into question the underlying notion of the present society that man must dominate nature; it seeks to facilitate domination by developing techniques for diminishing the hazards caused by domination."[11] The only meaningful, long-term solution was to replace the modern world's "odious morality" with a holistic, environmental ethic that had as its basis respect for all people and all nature. Armed with new definitions of right and wrong, ecoanarchists could tear down the old order and erect the new. Unless this happened soon, Bookchin warned, a poisoned, lifeless earth would be "a dead witness to [the] cosmic failure" of its most advanced life-form.[12] Murray Bookchin disappointed readers seeking practical programs for action, but his bitter indictment of contemporary ethics and his forthright call for revolutionary changes emboldened the liberators of nature.

For more than a century after Karl Marx's manifesto of the 1840s, socialist advocates of universal human liberation said little about the oppression of nature. But in the second half of the twentieth century the rising tide of opposition to the exploitation of nature—and the perception, noted by Bookchin, that it was closely linked to human exploitation—opened many eyes to the possibility of a transcendent libertarianism. For instance, after thirty years of protesting the dehumanizing effects of capitalism, science, and technology, Herbert Marcuse added nature to the category of subjects deserving freedom. Indeed Marcuse was the first well-known American radical to see nature as humanity's slave and to use the phrase "the liberation of nature."[13] Capitalism, Marcuse continued, reduced both nature and people to raw materials with strictly utilitarian value. But capitalism was in its death throes and the "coming revolution" would bring "universal liberation" including "a new relation between man and nature." Its basis, Marcuse thought, was the recognition, later publicized by the deep ecologists, that everything existed first and foremost "*for its own sake.*" This led Marcuse to advocate a reduction of human impact on animals and plants, and he concluded his essay with a widely quoted phrase: "nature, too, awaits the revolution!"[14] As it turned out, some American environmental activists were also waiting to be revolutionaries.

One of the most characteristic ideas of the 1960s concerned the need for fundamental changes in American life and thought. At its deepest level, the so-called counterculture advocated a new morality and the wholesale dismantling of many established institutions. The decade began with an emphasis on human rights, but by its end, as perception of an environmental crisis increased, the stakes began to widen to include nature. "There is a revolution coming," Charles Reich wrote in 1970. "Its ultimate creation will be a new and enduring wholeness . . . a renewed relationship of man to himself, to other men, to society, to nature, and to the land." Reich said his revolution "will not require violence to succeed,"[15] but as government-sanctioned oppression of nature continued, many of his readers remembered Henry David Thoreau's advice to "be men first and subjects afterwards." Explaining his own resistance in the 1840s to slavery and the Mexican War, Thoreau declared that "it is not desirable to cultivate a respect for the law, so much as for the right."[16]

True, Thoreau rested content with refusal to pay a Massachusetts tax and a night in the Concord jail—gestures that became classics in the American tradition of nonviolent civil disobedience. But on one occasion Thoreau endorsed what the radical environmentalists would later call ecological sabotage. The object of his moral indignation was a new dam on the Concord River that prevented fish from completing their accustomed spawning run. In *A Week on the Concord and*

Merrimack Rivers (1849) Thoreau anguished over the "poor shad!" whose instinct to swim upstream was thwarted, and asked "who hears the fishes when they cry?" Evidently Thoreau did, and he was sufficiently moved by the shad's "just cause" to contemplate violence. "I for one am with thee, and who knows what may avail a crowbar against that Billerica dam?"[17] Although they thought in terms of explosives rather than crowbars, contemporary opponents of Glen Canyon and other Western dams are one with Thoreau in their moral outrage and their willingness to transcend the law on behalf of oppressed nature. In 1981 Dave Foreman, a noted environmental activist. urged his colleagues to "free shackled rivers" and remarked that "the finest fantasy of eco-warriors in the West is the destruction of [Glen Canyon] Dam and the liberation of the Colorado [River.]"[18] As the first American "monkeywrencher," Thoreau would have likely been sympathetic to both the ends and means of modern environmental radicals.

Like Reich, Theodore Roszak's studies of the counterculture also led him to anticipate the "disassembling" of urban-industrial society and its "earth-rape" ideology. In its place, Roszak hoped, would arise a "visionary commonwealth" embracing "a new ecology, a new democracy," and ethical consideration of the nonhuman world.[19] By 1978 Roszak was calling for human acceptance of an "ethical obligation to the Earth" and recognition of "the rights of the planet." For this to occur, he thought, there must be a "life-affirming rebellion" leading to the "creative disintegration of industrial society."[20] Few, as yet, were advocating open, violent rebellion in the name of nature, but the recommendation by John Rodman of "ecological resistance" and by George Sessions and Bill Devall of "ecological resisting" skirted very close to the idea.[21] In the history of liberating, after all, resistance movements had frequently involved outright guerilla warfare against oppressive, totalitarian regimes. From the perspective of the most radical environmentalists, human domination of nature fitted this pattern closely.

Edward A. Abbey was the most visible spokesman for nature liberation in the 1970s and 1980s. A self-styled "desert rat," sometime employee of the National Park Service, and occasional visiting professor of English, Abbey wrote a collection of essays, *Desert Solitaire,* which attracted widespread attention in 1968 for its uncompromising defense of the wilderness qualities of the Southwest. In 1975 Abbey published a rambling novel entitled *The Monkey Wrench Gang,* source of the term "monkeywrenching." Its headquote from Walt Whitman—"Resist much. Obey little"—and its dedication to Ned Ludd, whose sabotage temporarily slowed England's industrial revolution in the eighteenth century, set the tone. In a sense the book was a fictional enactment of Abbey's University of New Mexico master's thesis, "Anarchism and the Morality of Violence." The book described the adventures of a small group of desert-lovers who came out of the mesas and canyons to throw the proverbial monkey wrench into the gears of modern American environmental exploitation. The targets of their raids ranged from the bulldozers of roadbuilders to the helicopters of law enforcers and the railways that carried strip-mined coal. The gang even contemplated blowing up Glen Canyon Dam and "liberating" the Colorado River from the stillness of Lake Powell. After considerable debate, Abbey's protagonists resolved not to kill people, but their commitment to the rights of nature brought them to the brink of such extreme action.

Edward Abbey left no doubt that he fantasized about pro-environment sabotage himself. It seemed the only effective way to stop what he regarded as morally wrong. As George Washington Hayduke, Abbey's foul-mouthed ex-Vietnam explosive expert, put it, the environmentalists "tried everything else. . . . They tried lawsuits, big fucking propaganda campaigns, politics."[22] So the time had come, in Hayduke's opinion, for direct, illegal violence on behalf of nature. *The Monkey Wrench Gang* was light on the philosophical underpinnings of such disobedience, but in 1979 Abbey explained that environmentalism, and particularly environmental ethics, should be understood as the way in which nature demanded its rights. The human mind evolved to defend the intrinsic value of the inarticulate earth. "The logical extension of the traditional Christian ethic," Abbey continued, goes beyond the "narrowly human to include the living creatures that share the planet with us." But ethics also should extend "to the nonliving, the inorganic, to the springs, streams, lakes, rivers and oceans, to the winds and clouds and the air, to the very rocks which form the foundation of the land, [to] the hills, mountains, swamps, deserts, plains and seashores."[23] At the deepest level this was what the Monkey Wrench Gang defended.

In 1982 Abbey expressed his basic belief that humans had no right to use more than a portion of the planet and that they had already passed that limit. Wild places must be left wild. This was not only or even primarily in the interest of humans who valued such places for recreation or renewal. Nature preservation expressed "a recognition . . . of the right of nonliving things—boulders, for example or an entire mountain—to be left in peace."[24] He was completely serious about the desirability of placing nature on a moral par with, if not above, human beings, who had "multiplied to the swarming stage" and become "Man the Pest." There were, he granted, defensible levels of human impact on the environment—"the reasonable needs of a reasonable number of people on a finite continent." But considering how modern technological civilization had exceeded that standard, Abbey concluded, "I could no more sink the blade of an ax into the tissues of a living tree than I could drive it into the flesh of a fellow human." [25] This made perfect sense to ecoactivists such as Dave Foreman, a leader of Earth First! who praised *The Monkey Wrench Gang* as "exactly what the staid environmental movement needed [something that] would kick us in our plump, comfortable butts." [26] Foreman hoped that Abbey's writing would help advance environmental ethics on both the theoretical and the practical level.

Thinking about the options facing the ethical individual who belongs to a society that engages in what he regards as wrongdoing, animal liberationist Peter Singer attempted to sort out the alternative philosophies of action. Singer was most concerned about the problem of disobedience in a democracy where the moral consensus of the majority is, theoretically, embodied in the law. In 1973 in *Democracy and Disobedience,* Singer addressed this subject strictly from the standpoint of human oppression. Six years later in *Practical Ethics* he turned to what the ethical person should do when confronted with the abuse of animals. "Are we under any moral obligation to obey the law," Singer asked, "if the law protects and sanctions things we hold utterly wrong?" He approached this dilemma by observing at the outset that "law and ethics are distinct." The abuse of animals and of the environment, for instance, might be legal, but many citizens still regarded it as wrong. Yet Singer knew that the law carried "moral weight." Particularly in republican forms of government, where the majority rules, the deliberate violation of the law could not be undertaken lightly. So Singer felt that the first recourse of any dissenter should be to try to change offensive laws or enact new, protective ones. Failing here, "we must assess each case on its merits in order to see if the reasons for disobeying outweigh [the] reasons for obedience." [27]

This ethical relativism, the pragmatic case-by-case approach in which the context of the deed determines its moral status, had been given wide publicity in the United States by Joseph Fletcher's *Situation Ethics* (1966). Quickly appreciated in the anti-normative climate of the counterculture, Fletcher's moral philosophy had special relevance to liberators of nature. As Garrett Hardin wrote, "situation ethics is ecological ethics. Fletcher's creation is the only ethics that meshes with ecological insight."[28] Peter Singer also based his ideas about environmental activism on the concept of "situations." He believed that some justified nonviolent civil disobedience. Passive resistance, and the willingness to accept punishment for it, dramatized a perceived evil but at the same time expressed respect for the prevailing political system. It was harder, Singer understood, to find situations in which illegal action was morally appropriate. Subjectivity was inevitable. The decision to act illegally, even violently, depended on the actor's sense of the magnitude of the evil involved and also on his assessment of the consequences of the action. In general Singer disapproved of violence, but he admitted that "it would be one-sided to say that violent revolution is always absolutely wrong, without taking account of the evils that the revolutionaries are trying to stop."[29] Violations of basic rights and liberties, for example, might in the Anglo-American context be regarded as evils of sufficient magnitude to warrant extraordinary resistance.

Turning specifically to the abuse of animals in laboratories and on farms, Singer contended that violence against property, as when groups break into laboratories to free captive animals, could be justified if the liberators regarded animal oppression as an intolerable moral wrong; if no human was killed or injured during the raid; and if, as a consequence of the action, significant pressure could be applied to public attitude and governmental policy. These were criteria with which many activists could agree. While dressed in academic jargon, Singer's situational or, as he termed it, "consequentialist" approach legitimized illegal action on behalf of animals. Activists with wider ethical horizons than Peter Singer's found no problem using similar logic to justify more extensive liberations of nature.

Although some environmentally oriented philosophers had opened the logical door to disobedience, the first recourse of most environmentalists was legal or legislative remedy. In the 1970s and 1980s proponents of ethical extension could point to significant accomplishments by American courts and legislatures. The whole national park movement, beginning with Yellowstone in 1872, represented at least in part a determination to leave parts of the natural world unimpaired. Granted, considerations of human pleasure figured almost exclusively in the early park rationale; predators were routinely killed in the parks until 1936. But thereafter the new idea gained ground that the parks were sanctuaries where all wildlife could be free to pursue their own kinds of happiness.

The nation's wildlife refuge system reflected this idea even more directly. Significantly, in view of the importance of marine mammals to later environmentalists, the first refuge was established in 1892 to protect seals, walruses, and sea otters, as well as salmon and marine birds, on Alaska's Afognak Island. The first unit in the National Wildlife Refuge System was Florida's Pelican Island, which Theodore Roosevelt reserved in 1903 as a "preserve and breeding-grounds for native birds." In contrast to the national parks, human recreation was not always a primary motive in creating the refuges. Concern for tiny Pelican Island, for example, developed as a result of protests over the wholesale slaughter of nongame birds for hat plumage.[30] After 1960, as "environment" and "ecology" became household words, public agitation resulted in significant revisions of American policies respecting wildlife. The trapping of fur-bearing animals and the deployment of poisons such as the chemical known as 1080 came in for intensive criticism and some degree of legislative control. Wild horses and burros, wolves, eagles, coyotes, and mountain lions all benefited from a more liberal morality.[31] The Wilderness Act of 1964, although worded anthropocentrically, seemed to some persons a legislative guarantee of freedom from human interference for wild creatures and ecosystems.[32]

Those who would use existing political systems on behalf of nature drew encouragement in the 1960s and 1970s from these American laws and, on the international level, from the appearance of "green" politics. Beginning in West Germany, political parties whose members called themselves Greens spread rapidly in Europe on a platform emphasizing peace, anti-nuclear policy, women's rights, and environmental ethics.[33] In Australia in July 1983 a coalition of green activists skilled in civil disobedience succeeded in reversing a government decision to dam a river previously placed on the World Heritage List of protected sites. As Australian "Greenies" flexed their political muscles, a prime minister fell and the nation's constitution was altered to minimize the generally pro-development power of the several states.[34] While less effective in the two-party, nonproportional system of the United States, green politics surfaced in campaigns for and against specific congressmen and senators. The Sierra Club, with 410,000 members, took pride in being "a mighty builder of the Green vote" in America. In August 1987 representatives of seventy-five American Green organizations convened in Amherst, Massachusetts. They espoused deep ecology as their "philosophical back bone" and "bioregionalism" as their guideline to proper living and proclaimed that "we are neither [politically] left nor right; we are in front."[35]

For those who chose to advance the rights of nature by changing the nation's laws, the various endangered species acts provided the most encouragement. As Joseph Petulla puts it, endangered species legislation expresses the belief that "a listed nonhuman resident of the United States is guaranteed, in a special sense, life and liberty."[36] Although some philosophers argued that species—as opposed to the individual organisms that constituted them—could not have interests or rights,[37] most environmentalists after 1960 understood human action that brought about the irrevocable disappearance of a life-form to be morally wrong. The near-extinction of the buffalo in the 1890s and the death of the last passenger pigeon, personified as "Martha," in 1914 shocked large numbers of Americans. For the same reasons American environmentalists showcased the rescue of the whooping crane from the brink of extinction as evidence of the new, ecological morality.[38]

The movement for regulations protecting endangered species began in the United States in 1964 in the context of growing public awareness of ecology and environmentalism. A provision in the Land and Water Conservation Fund Act of that year allocated funds to purchase habitats for certain threatened species. At the same time the Committee on Rare and Endangered Wildlife in the Department of the Interior's Fish and Wildlife Service published the first "Redbook" listing species that were in trouble.[39] In 1966 Congress passed with little controversy or fanfare the Endangered Species Protection Act. Limited to native vertebrates and focused on established wildlife refuges rather than on the environment in general, the bill created no new power or program and was so vague as to be meaningless. Nonetheless it marked the first recognition by an American legislature of an issue that would soon acquire strong ethical overtones. The Endangered Species Conservation Act of 1969 was also weak, applying only to the importation of a few rare foreign species. Exemptions to the law were easy to obtain. Economic and political "realities" still took precedence over morality, and when ethics did enter the discussion it was with regard to human rights to have useful species available. Few people, as yet, were thinking about the rights of nonhuman life. But the climate of opinion was changing. Congressmen and their constituents became increasingly concerned about the plight of fur-bearing animals. Animal-welfare groups took strong moral stands against the use of the skins of endangered species for fashion. Television brought millions *The Undersea World of Jacques Cousteau,* which did for marine mammals what Rachel Carson's book, *Silent Spring* (1962), had done for birds. The children's television serial *Flipper* acquainted Americans with dolphins. Soon flyers protesting the death of dolphins in tuna fishermen's nets asked, "Would you kill Flipper for a tunafish sandwich?"

This kind of popular concern, along with more scientific analysis that revealed a worldwide crisis in biological diversity, bore fruit in 1972 with the passage of the Marine Mammal Protection Act. For the first time congressional hearings revealed a sharp disagreement between those who considered whales, seals, and dolphins important for human welfare and those who felt the mammals had a right to exist regardless of their utilitarian value. The former advocated careful "management" of species in the manner of the old Progressive conservationists such as Gifford Pinchot; the latter argued for strict preservation and biotic right in the tradition of John Muir. This schism made for emotional testimony. John Dingell, chairman of the House Subcommittee on Fisheries and Wildlife Conservation, noted in his opening remarks on September 9, 1971, that the issue under consideration was highly charged because "critics of present programs relating to marine mammals argue that the killing of any animals for any purpose ultimately involves moral or ethical questions."[40] He was correct in his assessment. The advocates of a tough, protectionist policy contended that killing any marine mammal, rare or not, was morally wrong. For example, Gretchen Wyler of the World Federation for the Protection of Animals implored the subcommittee to "hear our plea, that the murder of ocean mammals, no matter how useful, be legally and morally banned."[41] Alice Herrington, representing Friends of Animals, told the Representatives that Leonardo da Vinci once said, "'The time will come when men . . . will look on the murder of animals as they now look on the murder of man.'" In Herrington's opinion "this prediction was correct; that time has arrived; the great mass of Americans, now aware of the brutality being inflicted upon innocent animals, have demanded that the laws of this country reflect this new morality." She wanted an act based on the principle that "ocean mammals should be left alone. They should be neither harassed, killed, managed, nor harvested."[42] The corollary of this position was the end of the traditional wise-use, sustained-yield approach of natural resource managers. Killing even a single marine mammal seemed to the animal-rights radicals as morally repugnant as killing a human being.

The unprecedented appearance of this kind of reasoning in debates over American wildlife policy surprised and dismayed utilitarian conservationists and professional wildlife managers. They came to the 1971 hearings prepared to support the protection of marine mammals as species, not as individuals. Professional philosophers had not yet disentangled these contradictory ethical theories. Aldo Leopold had consistently placed the integrity of the ecosystem ahead of the welfare of the individual organism. Indeed his whole theory of scientific game management depended on periodically bringing populations into line with the carrying capacities of their habitats. Adapting this perspective to the ocean, even the preservation-minded Audubon Society and Sierra Club argued against a policy of absolute protection of marine mammals. As long as the survival of the species was insured, they asked, why not use its "surplus" members for the benefit of people? For example, the testimony of Thomas L. Kimball of the venerable National Wildlife Federation included phrases such as "renewable resources," "stewardship," and "professional wildlife management." His organization believed that "harvesting of surplus wildlife populations is an . . . important management tool if the continuing long-range well being of an animal population is the ultimate objective."[43] That it was not for the animal-rightists identifies the schism in the environmentalists' ranks.

An early version of the Marine Mammal Protection Act, H.R. 6558, would have established an absolute ban on all killing of ocean animals, but in the end the viewpoint of the animal-rightists lost out. The 1972 act did not place the life of every marine mammal on a par with a human's, but it did give the preservation of the integrity of the marine ecosystem top priority. Species would not be "permitted to diminish beyond the point at which they cease to be a significant functioning element in the ecosystem of which they are a part."[44] To this end the legislation transferred authority for managing marine mammals from the states to the federal government and established tight controls over hunting. It also involved the United States in the necessarily international dimensions of marine mammal protection. This was a significant advance for applied environmental ethics. Only the most extreme animal-rightists could take exception to an action that legally affirmed the right of at least some members of a species to exist.

The momentum generated by the enactment of the Marine Mammal Protection Act led directly to two landmark actions in the implementation of environmental ethics. On March 3, 1973, over eighty nations gathered in Washington to sign the Convention on International Trade in Endangered Species of Wild Fauna and Flora (known as CITES). It created procedures for identifying species facing extinction and restricting the international trade that in many cases had decimated their populations. Recognizing CITES as a milestone in the history of Western liberalism, a writer in *Audubon* proclaimed it the "Magna Carta for Wildlife."[45] Lewis Regenstein, a strong advocate of ethical consideration for animals, called the treaty "the single most important international conservation measure ever agreed upon."[46]

CITES amounted to a pledge by the signatory nations to accept the principle that endangered species deserved protection. Enforcement procedures were left to the individual governments. The U.S. response was the Endangered Species Act of 1973, the strongest American legal expression to date of environmental ethics. It would be inaccurate to understand the act as entirely the product of deep-ecological, biocentric philosophy which, after all, was still inchoate in American thought at that time. Both the hearings on and the text of the act express a mixture of rationales. Most of those who testified in 1972 and early 1973 stressed the less radical idea that the extinction of species was wrong from the standpoint of human self-interest. "It is impossible to know," a spokesman from Defenders of Wildlife told the House subcommittee, "which species . . . will, in the future, become of value as a source of nutrition or in the production of some vital drug."[47] Senator Alan Cranston of California came to the hearing with the idea that "survival of man himself may ultimately depend on the survival of a diversity of flora and fauna." But Cranston could also say that "in addition to his concern for his own survival, man has an ethical and moral responsibility to protect other life forms." Quoting Albert Schweitzer and Lynn White in support of this position, Cranston suggested that "the ethic of reverence for all life" must be included among "man's basic moral tenets."[48] Cranston tried to bridge the differences between what would soon be called "shallow" and "deep" ecology by pointing out that in the long run, safeguarding human welfare necessitated extending ethics to the limits of the ecosystem. Ultimately human rights coincided with the rights of nature.

Alan Cranston was the first U.S. senator to lend such direct support to the cause of ethical extension. Moreover, he revealed an understanding, sophisticated for 1972, of the role of individual lives and of species in ecosystemic integrity. Protecting endangered species, Cranston thought, did not necessitate human interference "in the continuous cycle of life and death." Organisms would and should die, but Cranston knew that "the death of entire species is profound." What it means, he told the subcommittee, is that "nature has lost one of its components, which played a role in the interrelationship of life on earth." Extinction "creates a void" that can never be filled. It was on these Leopoldian grounds of the integrity of the ecosystem that Cranston based the human moral obligation to protect endangered species.[49]

Advocates of the 1973 endangered species bill who shared Cranston's holistic perspective found themselves in a somewhat uneasy alliance with old-line humanitarians and more recent animal rightists who protested any killing. For example, on behalf of the Society for Animal Protective Legislation Christine Stevens submitted for the record photographs of animals, or parts of them, caught in steel leghold traps. The images were gruesome, but none of the species shown was endangered. Indeed, trapped dogs and cats were part of Stevens's exhibit. This did not detract from her moral outrage in the least. "We have no right," she thundered, "to inflict this degree of suffering on animals for any purpose."[50]

Since Congress invariably justifies its actions in terms of the public interest, it is understandable that the opening sentences of the Endangered Species Act of 1973 had a decidedly anthropocentric ring. The law's purpose was stated as preserving species that are "of aesthetic, ecological, educational, historical, recreational, and scientific value to the Nation and its people."[51] The nonhuman beings' value to themselves and their right to exist may have been present in at least some of the lawmakers' minds, but it did not make the final version of the law. This created a loophole for later violations of the act; if other human values could be found that were allegedly superior to those listed, then a way was opened to discounting the rights of an endangered species.

Nonetheless, taken as a whole and judged relative to previous legislation, the Endangered Species Act gave an unprecedented degree of legal protection to the existence rights of at least some nonhuman beings. First, the law applied to all animals (even invertebrates), insects, and plants. Only bacteria, viruses, and insect pests that "present an overwhelming and overriding risk to man" were excluded.[52] Once placed by the Secretary of the Interior on the "endangered" or "threatened" lists, they were, in theory, secure. Never before had American law demonstrated a concern for such an extended group. Utility to humankind was not a criterion for the 1973 lists; in fact, most of the creatures included could not be used or harvested in any way; many were almost completely unknown. But they were protected simply because they were part of what the ecologists and ecotheologians, in their separate ways, thought of as creation.

The second innovation of the Endangered Species Act of 1973 was its willingness to define harm to a species not only as killing its

members but as disturbing the environments on which they depended. The act introduced the term "critical habitat" into American
wildlife law. It came close to saying that ecosystems, not just organisms, had a legal right to exist. Fines and imprisonment were to be
levied on those who violated this right. Section 7 gave the law more
bite by prohibiting federal agencies from conducting or even funding
activities detrimental to endangered species and their habitats. A
clause also invited private citizens and environmental organizations
to nominate species for inclusion on the lists and gave them the right
to enter lawsuits for this purpose.

Finally, in assessing the significance of the Endangered Species
Act it is important to understand that it did not apply only to wildlife
refuges or federal lands, as had previous legislation of this type. The
whole nation was involved; even private landholders would be compelled to recognize the rights of nonhumans to exist. Former New
York Senator James L. Buckley spoke for many when he declared that
the Endangered Species Act "represents a quantum jump in man's ac-
knowledgment of his moral responsibility for the integrity of the
natural world."[53] On a more popular level science fiction writers
played with the idea that in the future the assumption that "every creature, however small, has a right to live its own life" could lead to bans
on household disinfectants, many medicines, and even mouthwash.[54]

Christopher Stone had argued in 1972 for including the interests
of animals, plants, and even places in the American system of justice,
and the Endangered Species Act of 1973 could be regarded as the first
step in that direction. It encouraged legal action in defense of the
rights of nature. As Stone later noted, between 1974 and 1979 citizens used the courts to file complaints in the name of a polluted river,
a marsh, a brook, a beach, a species, and a tree.[55] The species was a
small Hawaiian bird, the palila, whose habitat had been reduced to a
small section of the slopes of the volcano Mauna Kea. On January 27,
1978, the Sierra Club Legal Defense Fund and the Hawaiian Audubon Society entered a suit on behalf of the few hundred remaining
palila to stop the grazing of cattle, sheep, and goats in the bird's habitat. The case was filed as *Palila v. Hawaii Department of Land and
Natural Resources*. For the first time in American legal history a nonhuman became a plaintiff in court. Moreover, the bird won! In June
1979 a federal judge ruled for the palila. Hawaii was given two years
to eliminate livestock grazing on Mauna Kea.[56]

Despite its success in defending the right to habitat of the palila,
the Endangered Species Act was too strict and comprehensive not to
be challenged. The most publicized confrontation with economic

and political interests occurred simultaneously with the palila case. It also involved an obscure, nongame species that had just been discovered in 1973. The snail darter, a three-inch minnow, was found to live on the gravel shoals of a section of the Little Tennessee River and, apparently, nowhere else. In 1975 it was added to the endangered species list and thereby placed on a collision course with the Tennessee Valley Authority's nearly completed Tellico Dam. Under Section 7 of the Endangered Species Act, environmentalists filed a suit to prevent completion of the $116 million dam. After extensive legal battles, on June 15, 1978, the U.S. Supreme Court ruled in favor of the fish. Congress, by now chafing under the restrictions of its 1973 action, immediately moved to amend the Endangered Species Act so as to introduce what was called "flexibility" into its protective mechanism. This translated into granting exemptions to the requirement to protect threatened species in cases where doing so would clash with overriding economic interests. Proponents of the amendment were determined that a minnow would not take precedence over a multimillion-dollar dam. The attitude of Representative John Duncan of Tennessee was typical. "I have a picture of the snail darter," he told the House subcommittee. "You cannot eat it. It is not much to look at. It is a slimy color."[57] Duncan also alleged that 3,000 people who worked on the Tellico project were unemployed as a result of the controversy over the minnow.

What Duncan eventually obtained was an amendment under which a seven-member committee of high-ranking federal officials could grant exemptions to the Endangered Species Act. Immediately dubbed the "God Committee," its first action was a ruling in the snail darter controversy. On January 23, 1979, much to the chagrin of the amenders of the act, the committee voted unanimously to kill the dam and preserve the fish. Outraged, Duncan turned to more subtle methods. On June 18, 1979, in a nearly empty House he offered a short rider to the annual energy and water-development bill and immediately moved that its reading be waived. A voice vote in favor followed. The whole procedure took forty-two seconds. Only after reading the *Congressional Record* the next day did environmentalists realize that Duncan's amendment had exempted the Tellico project from the requirements of the Endangered Species Act. Senator Howard Baker of Tennessee initially failed to move a similar measure through the Senate, but on September 11 he forced a four-vote victory. A veto by President Jimmy Carter was the last hope of the snail darter and its advocates, but the controversial rider was part of a whole year's public works budget and political pressures were too strong. Carter signed the bill, regretfully, on September 25, 1979. Zygmunt Plater, the lawyer who had worked for the minnow since 1974, summarized the feelings of the environmental community with a quote from Will Rogers to the effect that anyone who cares about laws and sausages should not watch them being made.[58]

Although a series of annual extensions have kept the Endangered Species Act in force, its failures in test cases such as the snail darter's discouraged those who thought legislative reform could implement environmental ethics. The *Los Angeles Times* believed Tellico was obtained at "too high a price." Restraints on human impacts on nature had no meaning, the editorial implied, if they could be overridden whenever inconvenient. *The New York Times* felt that "the affair of the Tellico Dam shows why millions of Americans have come to despair of politics."[59] Those Americans who preferred to defend the rights of nature within existing legal frameworks also deplored the failure of the United States to sign the United Nations Charter for Nature. Proposed by Zaire and adopted by the General Assembly in 1982, its preamble stated that "every form of life is unique, warranting respect regardless of its worth to man, and, to accord other organisms such recognition, man must be guided by a moral code of action."[60]

Faced with these disappointments and with the knowledge that on the global level the natural world was fighting a losing battle against the civilized one, environmental radicals turned to more direct forms of action and protest. Greenpeace was the first organization to represent their interests. Today it has offices in seventeen nations and claims a membership of 2.5 million, including 750,000 Americans. Greenpeace took shape in 1969 when American and Canadian anti-war and anti-nuclear activists staged a protest in Vancouver, British Columbia over the testing by the United States of an atomic bomb at Amchitka Island, Alaska.[61] *Greenpeace I* was the name of the boat sent into the Amchitka test zone in 1971. Two years later *Greenpeace III* sailed to Mururoa Atoll in the South Pacific to protest a French atmospheric nuclear test. When cameras caught the boat's skipper, David McTaggart, being severely beaten by soldiers, Greenpeace discovered the surest way to gain public sympathy.[62] In 1974, just as environmental ethics was gaining attention, Greenpeace widened its concern, in the words of founding member Robert Hunter, "from the concept of the sanctity of human life to the sanctity of all life." The crucial relationship, Hunter explained, is not between human and human but between humankind and the earth. "We must seriously begin to inquire into the rights of rabbits and turnips, the rights of soil and swamp, the rights of the atmosphere, and, ultimately, the rights of the planet."[63] The "Greenpeace Philosophy," which appeared regularly in its fundraising appeals and newspaper, declared that "Humankind is not the center of life on the planet. Ecology has taught us that the whole Earth is part of our 'body' and that we must learn to respect it as we respect ourselves."

The rights of sea mammals, particularly whales and seals, became a major concern of Greenpeace in the mid-1970s. The mammals' welfare had first drawn environmentalists' concern in the late 1960s, when Montreal-based Artek Films documented the Labrador seal hunt for the Canadian Broadcasting Corporation. The film's intent was to portray stalwart hunters carrying on an age-old frontier tradition. But this was the 1960s, and what many American as well as Canadian viewers saw was incredible brutality against cute, defenseless creatures. Controversy flared in the media, and Brian Davies, a Canadian humanitarian, along with the New York author Cleveland Amory, organized a massive protest. For Davies, who believed that animals should "be given the right to live," the only ethical response was stopping the hunt. Borrowing a word from the anti-slavery crusade of the previous century, he called for the "*abolition*" of sealing.[64] Operating under the aegis of the International Fund for Animal Welfare, Davies engineered boycotts of Canadian marine products that by the mid-1980s brought the sealing industry to a virtual standstill.

When Greenpeace joined the protest against sealing as well as whaling, it adopted the traditional Quaker method of nonviolent "witnessing" of injustice. Teams traveled to the Labrador ice and observed the seal slaughter. Off the coast of California in 1975 Greenpeace employed quick-moving inflatable boats to confront Russian whalers. Determined to remain nonviolent, they simply let the Russians know their ethical position as the great animals died. Photographs told the story to Greenpeace members. On one occasion in 1981 a Greenpeace member chained herself to a whaler's harpoon. The public responded to such displays of ultimate commitment; here was a human being willing to die to save the life of a whale.[65]

On July 10, 1985, Greenpeace made headlines around the world when its ship, *Rainbow Warrior,* was bombed and sank at a wharf in Aukland, New Zealand.[66] A member of the crew drowned in the incident. Clearly the introduction of ethics had raised environmentalism to the brink of violence. Although Greenpeace maintained its nonviolent stance after its ship sank, more radical defenders of the rights of nature were prepared to fight fire with fire. In Zimbabwe, for instance, park rangers have begun a policy of shooting on sight poachers of the rare black rhino.[67]

The career of Paul Watson, known to some as "the most famous eco-radical in the world," illustrates how easily nonviolent witnessing can slip over to direct and violent action after one accepts nonhuman rights.[68] A Canadian, born in 1951, Watson joined in Earth Day protests in 1970 as well as in the anti-nuclear and Indian-rights movements. He participated in the formation of Greenpeace and in the mid-1970s led the open-ocean demonstrations against Russian whalers. In 1976 and 1977 Watson picked up the work of Cleveland Amory and Brian Davies and turned his attention to Canada's annual hunt of harp seals on the ice floes off Labrador. Using helicopters, Watson and the Greenpeace team observed and photographed seal pups being skinned alive in front of their distressed mothers. Their initial response was to spray dye on the pups to make their coats valueless to the sealers. But as the slaughter continued Watson resorted to covering pups with his body to protect them from clubbing. He also handcuffed himself to a winch cable used to lift the pelts to the factory ship. The sealers retaliated by dousing Watson in the icy waters, dragging him through piles of seal carcasses and eventually leaving him, unconscious and near death, on the ice. He recovered in a hospital only to find that he had been voted out of Greenpeace for violating Canadian laws regarding the seal hunt and allegedly engaging in violent activities. Watson did not deny the charge that he had become a "vigilante," only replying that "it takes outlaws to stop outlaws." He would, he vowed, continue to "defy authority whenever I considered it wrong—and whenever its policies worked against sea mammals."[69]

Having proved too radical for Greenpeace, Watson formed his own organizations, Earthforce (1977) and the Sea Shepherd Conservation Society (1979). Their philosophy of action reflected Watson's belief that although "violence is morally wrong . . . nonviolent action alone has seldom produced beneficial change on our planet." So he would compromise "by allowing myself violence against property but never against life, human or otherwise."[70] This stance distressed Greenpeace but appealed to more radical environmentalists in the United States and in England. With financial assistance from Cleveland Amory's Fund for Animals and the Royal Society for the Prevention of Cruelty to Animals, Watson acquired at the end of 1978 a 206-foot-long ship which he named *Sea Shepherd*. Its first action was to head for Labrador and the annual spring seal hunt. In the aftermath Watson was accused of resisting arrest and obstructing justice. Police and citizen brutality in the course of the arrests came close to taking his life. Undeterred, he sailed for Portugal with the intention of ramming and disabling the pirate whaling ship *Sierra*. Watson proved as good as his word. On July 16, 1979, the *Sea Shepherd* crashed into *Sierra*, leaving an eight-foot gash in her bow and exposing the contraband whalemeat in her hold. A few months later bombs sank the *Sierra* and Watson scuttled *Sea Shepherd* to prevent her from being taken by Portuguese authorities. There were legal complications, but Watson retained the support of the Sea Shepherd Conservation Society, and Cleveland Amory provided him with another ship. Watson declared that he would continue "fighting for the whales until there are either no more whalers or no more whales."[71]

With an international membership of 10,000 in the mid-1980s, the Sea Shepherd Conservation Society continued what seemed to many to be a holy war against the killers of sea mammals. Watson characterized *Sea Shepherd II* as the "flagship of Gaia's whale navy"[72] and in 1983 it was back in Labrador to stop the seal hunt. But this time Watson's boat was rammed—by the Canadian Coast Guard—and he found himself fined and jailed. Far from being a deterrent, however, such action only raised more support for radical environmentalism. Campaigns followed against Russian whalers in Siberian waters, against wolf eradication in British Columbia, and against Japanese fishermen who killed dolphins. Then on November 9, 1986, the Sea Shepherds were back in the headlines after sabotaging an Icelandic whale processing station and sinking two unoccupied whale-catching ships at Reykjavik. The event, which was timed to coincide with the U.S.-Soviet summit talks in Iceland, transcended symbolic pranksterism; the loss to the whaling industry totaled $4.6 million. The men responsible for the raid, Californian Rodney Coronado and British citizen David Howitt, slipped away on a commercial airplane and remain confident that they will not be extradited because Iceland's whale operation was in violation of agreements reached with the International Whaling Commission. Watson felt no crime was involved because "whaling is a crime against nature."[73] On another occasion he argued that the destruction of property was nonviolent if it was aimed at disabling the tools that caused violence to living things. And he consistently maintained, following Thoreau, that "*natural* law always takes precedence over *national* law."[74] The right of an organism to exist, in other words, could not be legislated away.

Along with Greenpeace and the Sea Shepherds, Cleveland Amory's Fund for Animals emerged in the 1970s as a leading American defender of wildlife. A well-known social historian who moved easily among the wealthy and powerful, Amory used their influence to protest the hunting and trapping of animals for sport and fashion. From his perspective any killing of wildlife other than for food was wrong. The shift in national attitudes on these matters appeared clearly in the uproar surrounding the CBS News documentary "The Guns of Autumn," which exposed barbaric behavior of American hunters. Amory supported the film as a protest against human cruelty in the manner of the traditional humanitarians, but he gradually changed his appeal to emphasize animal "rights." His book *Man Kind?* appeared in 1974 in the context of Peter Singer's well-publicized call for animal liberation and Tom Regan's argument for animal rights. Along with numerous stories of atrocities, it described how the Fund for Animals prepared an advertisement featuring America's most attractive female entertainers clad in synthetic furs. The text expressed strong feelings. Doris Day declared that "killing an animal to make a coat is a sin . . . we have no right to do it." Jayne Meadows added that nobody could wear real fur "without feeling, literally, like a murderer." Both Angie Dickinson and Mary Tyler Moore stated that animals have a right to live. This idea was new in the humanitarian crusade, and it reflected the public emergence of environmental ethics. A Fund for Animals pamphlet juxtaposed a quotation from Albert Schweitzer with horrible pictures of trapped animals: "We need a boundless ethics which will include the animals also." A lapel button saying "Animals Have Rights, Too" made the point another way.[75]

Law-abiding animal rights advocates had some tangible gains to celebrate as the movement for the extension of ethics began to gather momentum. The Humane Slaughter Act of 1958 had mandated the elimination of needless suffering in the butchery of livestock. The rights of animals was not an issue this early, but one of the bill's primary sponsors, Senator Hubert Humphrey of Minnesota, defended it as an application of traditional American liberal values. "Whenever we shut our eyes to cruelty and suffering, whether among people or among animals, we are shutting out part of the spirit that has made America . . . stand apart in the world as a nation that puts moral principles and decency above sheer material value."[76] Established organizations like the American Anti-Vivisection Society and the Humane Society of the United States lobbied aggressively for the 1958 legislation and continued to press for additional laws governing the handling of animals prior to slaughter for food. Partial success came in 1978 with the passage of amendments to the Humane Slaughter Act.

Meanwhile, the condition of animals used in research received in-

creasing attention from activists. The first significant legislation that
broke a long drought in American humanitarianism came in 1966
with passage of the Laboratory Animal Welfare Act. Its initial intent
was to outlaw the alleged stealing and sale of millions of pet dogs and
cats annually for experimental purposes.[77] Groups such as the Animal
Welfare Institute and the Society for Animal Protective Legislation
had been active in this cause since the early 1950s, but political action
awaited public perception of the link between oppressed humans and
oppressed animals. A landmark essay published in *Life* simultaneous
with the 1966 hearings made the key connection: a vanished family
pet was likely to end up in "unspeakably filthy compounds that seem
scarcely less appalling than the concentration camps of World War
II."[78] The other common analogy was to the "animal slave trade."
But the most telling parts of the *Life* story were heartbreaking, full-
page photographs of abused animals. For Americans who had recently shuddered at news photos of blacks in Alabama and Mississippi under the clubs, water hoses, and attack dogs of the white
establishment, *Life*'s pictures carried a strong moral message.

In 1970, 1976. and 1985 Congress amended the basic Laboratory
Animal Welfare Act of 1966 in an effort to meet growing public demand to end abuses, not just in the research animal trade but in the
conduct of the research itself. The Improved Standards for Laboratory Animals (or Dole-Brown) Act of 1985 significantly expanded
the number of species protected and established tougher humane-
treatment requirements.[79] Clearly the American political system had
the capability of outlawing human cruelty and reducing animal suffering. For more than a century organizations such as the American
Society for the Prevention of Cruelty to Animals (established 1866)
and the American Humane Association (1874) had based their efforts
on this possibility of reforming the system. The Humane Society of
the United States, reorganized from the old AHA in 1954, carried the
movement for the reform of animal treatment into the modern era
and, as noted above, realized tangible legislative results. By the time
of the Dole-Brown Act the Humane Society's national umbrella included hundreds of state and local groups, an impressive political-
action budget, and 600,000 members.[80] Although derided as a "dog
and cat" organization by broader-thinking environmentalists, the
Humane Society has become involved in the protection of rodeo animals, wild horses and burros, marine mammals, and fur-bearing animals. In 1978 it published *On the Fifth Day: Animal Rights and Human
Ethics,* which stated that "what we seek . . . is an ethics that looks at
the entire biosphere of the planet earth—and beyond."[81] Although

according to Dale Hilton, a Humane Society staffer, the organization preferred the old-style concept of "animal welfare" to the newer one emphasizing "animal rights," the society's president, John Hoyt, stated in 1979 that "all life has intrinsic value and is, therefore, deserving of those same considerations we generally reserve for mankind." Modern humanitarians, Hoyt continued, believe "that man has no right, either divine or otherwise, to exploit creation for his own benefit." He characterized his efforts as part of the American "crusade for right and justice."[82] And even Dale Hilton acknowledged that "rights" rhetoric carried significant advantages in the United States because "it is the language with which Americans are familiar."[83] Despite attempts to split them apart,[84] these ideas appear to link the modern humane movement with both environmentalism and environmental ethics. The connection with American liberalism is clearer yet.

Still, for some pro-animal activists the reform humanitarianism exemplified by the Humane Society was not enough. The more extreme critics contended that a well-treated captive animal was still a captive, just as a healthy slave was still enslaved. If animals had rights not just to life but to liberty and fulfillment, as some philosophers were contending by the 1970s, then it was wrong for humans to hold them against their wills for other than absolutely essential purposes. It made sense from this point of view to talk about animal liberation, to use the phrase Peter Singer popularized in 1973, in the sense of actually freeing captive creatures. The issue came to a head over animals used in research, and dolphins were the first beneficiaries.

John C. Lilly, a neurophysiologist, began to study the behavior of these cetaceans in 1955. Two sophisticated laboratories in Florida and the Virgin Islands held dolphins in order to study their communication abilities. Lilly arrived at some startling conclusions: in several respects, including size, the dolphin's brain was superior to that of humans. Could it be that in capturing dolphins for research the scientists were actually enslaving life-forms that possess sensitivity and intelligence impressive even by human standards? The subtitle of one of Lilly's books made the point explicit: dolphins were "humans of the sea."[85] Lilly also came to the conclusion in the early 1960s that ethical principles, such as the Golden Rule, could not begin and end with human beings. Doing unto others as you would have them do unto you made sense only when "the others are to include other species, other entities, other beings in the universe." It was at the time of this realization, in 1967, that Lilly "suddenly realized that I must stop the dolphin research."[86] He could not "continue to run a concentration camp for my friends, the dolphins."[87] And he also perceived that several of his captive dolphins had, as he put it, "committed suicide." Before the rest killed themselves, he liberated them into the Atlantic and closed his laboratory.[88] A few years later Lilly wrote an essay proposing that "we must give [dolphins] rights as individuals under our laws." They should no longer be considered property or resources; they should have "complete freedom of the waters of the earth."[89] Research into cetacean behavior should continue, Lilly added, but it must be done with their full cooperation. To that end he proposed a laboratory tank with free access to the open ocean; the dolphins could come and go as they pleased, voluntary collaborators with humans in the research process.

In John Lilly's case the director of a research operation became an animal liberator. When subordinates or outsiders did the job, tensions mounted. On May 28, 1977, on the island of Oahu, two undergraduates freed a pair of dolphins that a University of Hawaii psychology professor had been training for eight years. Advised they might go to jail for grand theft of property, Kenny LeVasseur and Steve Sipman responded, "We know, man. We thought about that before we did it, and we decided it would be worth it if the dolphins were set free." On another occasion they said, "We didn't steal them; we gave them back." The courts did not agree; the liberators received six-month jail terms and five years' probation. But LeVasseur and Sipman became local celebrities in Hawaii. They called themselves "The Undersea Railroad," displaying knowledge of earlier American liberators, and they described how the released dolphins "just took off—free at last." As LeVasseur and Sipman must have known, Martin Luther King, Jr., used the same words in 1963 to express his dream of black liberation.[90]

Rising concern in the late 1970s over the ethics of other kinds of animal experimentation led to more direct action. Henry Spira, a New York high-school teacher, had worked in the 1960s civil rights and labor rights movements. In 1973 he read Peter Singer's essay on animal liberation in the *New York Review of Books* and concluded that this cause "was the logical extension of what my life was all about—identifying with the powerless and the vulnerable, the . . . dominated and oppressed." Spira's plan was to "adapt to the animal movement the traditions of struggle which had proven effective in the civil rights movement, the union movement and the women's movement." He would "focus sharply on a single significant injustice" that he felt capable of correcting. For civil rights activists in 1956 it had been discrimination against blacks on the public buses of Montgomery, Alabama; twenty years later Spira challenged the prestigious American Museum of Natural History's research program involving the behavior of deliberately maimed cats. After eighteen months of picketing and publicity, the federal government withdrew its support of the research and the laboratory closed.[91]

Spira's next target was the Draize Ophthalmic Irritancy Test, in which cosmetics are dropped into the eyes of rabbits to assess irritability which, in most cases, was extreme enough to cause blindness. This time he orchestrated the efforts of several hundred animal welfare and animal rights groups with a combined membership that he judged to be "in the millions." The turning point of the campaign was a full-page advertisement in a 1980 issue of *The New York Times* showing a blinded white rabbit and the caption, "How many rabbits does Revlon blind for beauty's sake?" Demonstrations took place outside Revlon's New York offices and also at international locations. The company responded by dismissing personnel involved in the Draize procedure and funding research that used different testing measures. The LD (lethal dose) 50 test, which took the lives of an estimated five million laboratory animals annually, also became a victim of Spira's activism when the U.S. Food and Drug Administration withdrew its requirement for the data the test provided. Spira felt he had demonstrated to American scientists that "you don't go around ordering 1,000 rabbits or 10,000 mice in the way you order a case of light bulbs on a Monday morning."[92]

Henry Spira worked to influence public opinion and corporate policy in familiar, legal ways, but the American animal rights movement did not always stop at the boundaries of the law. In this course it followed, as American humanitarianism had so often, the example of Great Britain. As early as 1974 Ronnie Lee attracted attention in England for breaking into laboratories, destroying facilities, and freeing animals. Four years and several jail terms later, Lee and his colleagues formed the Animal Liberation Front. By the mid-1980s the English group had nearly 2,000 members and conducted hundreds of illegal actions annually. According to one commentator, "animal liberation is arguably *the* youth movement of the '80s." Lee said he could foresee a time "when a cruel [director of animal research] could be shot on his doorstep" and argued that "direct action" was not a substitute for but an encouragement to "parliamentary change."[93] Meanwhile in the United States direct action on behalf of animals began to receive various expressions. Alex Pacheco, co-founder in 1980 of People for the Ethical Treatment of Animals (PETA), gained entrance to Dr. Edward Taub's Institute for Behavioral Research in Silver Springs, Maryland, as a volunteer. His testimony and photographs convinced Maryland authorities to act under the state's Animal Cruelty Law. On September 11, 1981, detectives holding search warrants entered the laboratory and seized Taub's monkeys. Taub was convicted on minor charges, but the adverse publicity surrounding the raid cost him first his funding and then his institute itself. PETA, which in 1987 claimed 200,000 members, is still trying to find a satisfactory home for the liberated primates.[94]

While Alex Pacheco used the courts to protect animal rights, some of his colleagues in animal liberation were less patient and less respectful of the law. Beginning in March 1982 Americans organized in a state-side Animal Liberation Front broke into a series of laboratories and released the captive animals. The raids caught the attention of the press. *Newsweek* noted that many of the activists were "veterans of the wars against racism and sexism who see animals as the next oppressed group awaiting liberation." They were no longer concerned "about animal welfare—improved living conditions for lab animals—but about animal 'rights'—the right not to be experimented on at all."[95] In a front-page story *The New York Times* reported that the newest liberators believed that "animals have inherent rights to a full life in a natural society and that it is immoral to exploit them, whatever benefits might accrue to humans."[96] Eric Malnic's front-page article for the *Los Angeles Times* on the Animal Liberation Front stated that the group's members "share a common concept—that all animals, not just humans, have inalienable rights as individuals . . . that all creatures hold positions of equal relevance in the overall scheme of life."[97] Writing in *Audubon,* Douglas Starr declared that although it was once "extremist," animal rights had become "mainstream" and was in a position to become a major political force. The movement, he thought, was inevitable: "Having weathered civil rights and women's liberation, many Americans were ready to broaden their conceptions of who deserves rights."[98]

National publicity followed an Animal Liberation Front raid on the University of Pennsylvania's Head Injury Laboratory on May 26, 1984. Although for obvious reasons the identity of the raiders was carefully guarded, they were anxious to publicize their cause. After guarantees of anonymity, a journalist was permitted to witness the break-in at the Head Injury Lab. His article[99] identified one of the raiders as a survivor of a Nazi concentration camp who in later life transferred his concern from oppressed humans to oppressed animals. The raid itself resulted in the destruction of equipment used to inflict head injuries on the captive primates, but none of the animals was liberated. Instead the Animal Liberation Front stole sixty hours of videotape documenting the research. Released to the media through Alex Pacheco and PETA, it revealed improperly anesthetized primates writhing in pain and researchers casually smoking as they operated on fully conscious subjects. The camera even recorded one scientist remarking that he hoped the animal rights groups never obtained the tape. But they had, and the explosion of public indignation ultimately resulted in a suspension of National Institutes of Health funding and the closing of the laboratory.[100]

The Animal Liberation Front's illegal and direct action on behalf of the rights of animals continues to be a dramatic, if still minor, part of American liberalism. A raid against the University of California's Riverside campus in 1985 resulted in the release of 467 animals and the destruction of equipment worth $680,000. At the University of California, Davis in 1987 the Front apparently celebrated the approach of Earth Day (April 22) and Animal Rights Day (April 24) by burning an animal-research building valued at $2.5 million. Seventeen university vehicles were also disabled.[101] While some Americans regarded such actions as little better than vandalism, others compared them to John Brown's 1859 raid on Harper's Ferry. The animal liberators had no doubt about their historical antecedents. "It's like the Underground Railroad and slavery," one declared, "sometimes people have to go outside the law . . . for social change."[102]

While Greenpeace, the Sea Shepherds, The Fund for Animals, and the Animal Liberation Front concentrated on the rights of individual organisms, other groups preferred to act on the basis of a more holistic philosophy. Earth First!, publisher of a self-styled "*radical* environmental journal" and institutional home base of the "no-compromise environmental movement," led the way in "translating the biocentric paradigm of Deep Ecology into political action."[103] Although the organization rejected hierarchy and centralization, it would be difficult not to identify Dave Foreman as a prime mover in its establishment. Before his thoughts and actions took a radical turn, Foreman, who was born in 1946, had strong establishment associations. These included a fourth-generation white New Mexican heritage, Eagle Scout training, a college degree, campaign experience for Barry Goldwater, enlistment in the U.S. Marines, and, in 1973, a job with a mainstream conservation group, The Wilderness Society. But in 1979, after a disappointing Forest Service decision on wilderness protection, Foreman resigned in disgust at the whole politically responsible environmental movement including, up to that point, himself. "The early conservation movement in the

United States," he wrote in *The Progressive,* "was a child . . . of the Establishment."[104] Even in the late 1970s American environmentalism seemed to Foreman to be linked too closely to anthropocentrism and utilitarianism. Only a few deep ecologists were pointing out that beneficent human control of nature was still control, and no one was acting on the assumption that nature had rights just like those of human beings. In the first mimeographed publication of Earth First! (November 1, 1980), Foreman declared that "we will not make political compromises. Let the other outfits do that. EARTH FIRST will set forth the pure, hard-line, radical position of those who believe in the Earth first."[105]

The example of 1960s defenders of human rights was very much in Foreman's mind as he formulated his initial manifesto in defense of the rights of nature. Lobbying, lawsuits, press releases, outings, and research papers were fine, he said, but insufficient. The new organization would extend its activities to "demonstrations, confrontations, and more creative tactics and rhetoric." "It is time," Foreman concluded, "to be passionate. It's time to be tough. It's time to have the courage of the civil rights workers who went to jail. It's time to fight for the Earth first."[106] In his second newsletter Foreman quoted Henry David Thoreau's recommendation to break unethical laws and asked: "Did the civil rights and anti-war activists keep their profiles low?"[107] In calling American environmentalism "timid," Foreman meant that in an effort to be reasonable, moderate, and effective within the established governing framework, environmentalists had sold their souls to the forces they should oppose. By being strategic they had compromised their integrity. Foreman's crusade was to add ethics and radical action to environmentalism, and the masthead of his newspaper soon carried the banner: "No Compromise in the Defense of Mother Earth!" A century and a half earlier William Lloyd Garrison's *Liberator* declared "No Compromise with Slaveholders." Garrison's liberalism impelled him to a radical stance against human slavery; Foreman's extended to uncompromising opposition to the enslavement of the earth.

The determination of Earth First! to make environmental protection a moral issue in the biocentric sense crystallized behind a policy of ecological militancy. Foreman and colleagues such as Howie Wolke, Mike Roselle, Susan Morgan, and Bart Koehler determined to be as radical as necessary to achieve their ends. They would work legally when possible but, remembering the success of the abolitionists and the civil rights advocates, would not eschew civil disobedience and even outright violence. Edward Abbey's novel *The*

Monkey Wrench Gang became their blueprint for action. They applauded its protagonists, who had the courage to stand up and fight for their ethical convictions. Foreman, who believed "all the Earth is sacred,"[108] stated that "monkeywrenching is an extremely moral way of resisting the industrialization of natural places . . . It's one tool. Sometimes you lobby; sometimes you write letters; sometimes you file lawsuits. And sometimes you monkeywrench."[109] Such attitudes, obviously, put Earth First! on one extreme in the spectrum of American environmentalism. Like the early abolitionists its members would not be universally applauded, even by other environmentalists, but like Garrison and his followers they would be heard.

Although it was not called "monkeywrenching" back then, ecological sabotage of the Earth First! type began at the height of American perception of an environmental crisis. A few zealots went beyond the law to dramatize their demands for responsible treatment of nature. In the early 1970s in the Chicago area "The Fox" plugged factory smokestacks and, on one occasion, diverted liquid toxic waste from a U.S. Steel plant to a location inside the chief executive's private office. Once, over the telephone, he responded to an interviewer who asked if his tactics were illegal or immoral by observing, "No more so than if I stopped a man from beating a dog or strangling a woman."[110] The "ecological Lone Ranger," as the press dubbed The Fox, successfully concealed his identity; he has never been unmasked.

In 1971 Michigan environmentalists dubbed "Billboard Bandits" made the headlines by chainsawing roadside signs. Arrested, one defended the vandalism in familiar liberal terms: "When the state is negligent in its duty, then someone has to act."[111] About the same time in Oregon, locals alerted by Rachel Carson's writing slashed vehicle tires and burned a helicopter involved in the spraying of pesticides. In 1978 on the Minnesota prairie a group of farmers known as the "Bolt Weevils" dismantled electrical powerlines and blocked survey and construction crews.[112] The next year in the foothills of California's Sierra the Corps of Engineers completed the New Melones Dam on the Stanislaus River. Mark Dubois, a leader of Friends of the River, had exhausted every legal option, including an unsuccessful 1974 referendum, in an effort to save from inundation a place he considered holy. Finally, on May 20, 1979, Dubois turned to civil disobedience. Under the cover of darkness he bound himself with a lock and chain to a cliff at a hidden location along the bank of the river and threw the key into the water. A letter from Dubois to the Corps of Engineers stated his intent to drown as the lake rose. "Part of my spirit dies as the reservoir fills," Dubois declared, and he felt he had

no choice but to defend the Stanislaus with his own life. Despite fran-
tic efforts authorities failed to locate and remove him. On May 28
California agreed to intercede against the Corps and Dubois emerged
from his hiding place. The media attention embarrassed the soft-
spoken river guide, but many Americans found compelling the story
of a man prepared to give his life in defense of a river.[113]

Before 1980 public understanding of environmental ethics was in
its infancy, and "ecotage" was linked more to human interests in an
unpolluted environment than to the rights of nature. But from its beginnings Earth First! understood itself to be defending the "'rights'
of trees, rivers, grizzly bears, mountains, meadows, and flowers to
exist—regardless of their perceived value to human uses."[114] As
Foreman put it in 1985, "every living thing in the ecosystem has intrinsic worth and a nature-given right to be here." Two years later he
declared that "we must constantly extend the community to include
all" because "the other beings—four-legged, winged, six-legged,
rooted, flowing, etc.—have just as much right to be in that place as
we do." Foreman added "they are their own justification for being,
they have inherent value, value completely apart from whatever
worth they have for . . . humans."[115]

Earth First! implemented this philosophy for the first time on
March 21, 1981, when Edward Abbey, Dave Foreman, and seventy
others gathered at Glen Canyon Dam on the Colorado River, diverted the attention of guards, and unrolled a 300-foot black plastic
"crack" down the concrete wall. Shouting "Free the Colorado!" and
"Liberate the River!" they left no doubt that their motives had to do
with the integrity of natural ecological processes rather than human
recreational interest in those processes. The "cracking of Glen Canyon Dam" received extensive media coverage, some of which dismissed the event as a meaningless prank. But Earth First! membership jumped to over a thousand and Foreman could state that he
"sensed a growing environmental radicalism in the country."[116]

As it grew to 10,000 members in the five years after the Glen
Canyon demonstration, Earth First! discovered imaginative new
ways to display its militancy. Some were in the classic tradition of
civil disobedience. One of the group's symbols was a tree stump
rising into the clenched-fist salute that black power advocates popularized twenty years earlier. And just as civil rights and anti-war protestors had physically blocked roads and buildings, Earth First! followers lay down in front of logging and mining trucks and, in one
instance, joined hands around a tree to thwart advancing chain saws.
The ensuing arrests interested the press and sometimes resulted in

delays and injunctions against the lumber companies.[117] In 1985 Earth First! took the civil-rights "sit-in" technique to a third dimension: climbers ascended 250-foot firs in Oregon's virgin Cathedral Forest, built platforms, and dared lumbermen to cut them down. When the sawyers moved to adjacent trees, the protestors created a spiderweb of ropes from tree to tree. The center point was their own necks.[118] An alternate technique to save trees began to lead some Earth First! members from civil to less legal forms of disobedience. They drove thousands of steel spikes into trees scheduled for cutting. This technique made chain-sawing impossible, and in Oregon, British Columbia, and Kentucky, tree spiking (and sometimes road spiking) succeeded in at least temporarily preserving wilderness. Facing ruined saws and thwarted sales, lumber companies and the U.S. Forest Service became incensed. But Mike Roselle, an Earth First! founder, defended the practice as consistent with the heart of American liberalism. "Monkeywrenching is an American tradition," he suggested. "Look at the Boston Tea Party—it's celebrated on a postage stamp. Someday we'd like to see tree-spiking celebrated that way."[119]

In 1985 Dave Foreman attempted to systematize environmental militancy in a book entitled *Ecodefense: A Field Guide to Monkeywrenching*. The dedicatory page of the second edition (1987) acknowledged The Fox, The Bolt Weevils, and newer radical groups like The Hardesty Mountain Avengers and The Tucson Ecoraiders. Edward Abbey contributed an introduction. "It is time," Foreman wrote, "to act heroically and admittedly illegally in defense of the wild, to put a monkeywrench into the gears of the machinery destroying natural diversity." He offered a tongue-in-cheek disclaimer saying that "no one involved with . . . this book . . . encourages anyone to do any of the stupid, illegal things contained herein," but he went on to offer very serious, detailed instructions on "Treespiking, Destroying Roads, Decommissioning Heavy Equipment, Pulling Survey Stakes, Trashing Billboards, Leaving No Evidence, [and] Security."[120] Foreman believed such "monkeywrenching not only can be *morally justified* but is morally *required.*" He added that "when you look closely at the unholy assault the industrial state is mounting against the public's wildlands, against natural diversity . . . it forces you to consider any and all means of resisting that destruction."[121] Indeed he saw environmental radicals as engaged in "the most moral of all actions: protecting life, defending the earth."[122] Foreman was not prepared to use violence against people, but machines were another story. In Hawaii monkeywrenchers "decommissioned" $300,000 worth of heavy equipment. In Wyoming interference with a wilderness survey operation cost the contractor $50,000 and resulted in a six-month jail term for Howie Wolke.[123]

Given their seriousness in defending nature and their willingness to include it in their moral circle, Earth First! members inevitably had to come to grips with the legitimacy of violence against property and ultimately against their human opponents. Everyone knew that defense of the rights of people had in the past occasioned bloodshed and even warfare. But how far should an uncompromising moral stand take defenders of nature? In 1983 in the Siskiyou National Forest near Grants Pass, Oregon, it had almost resulted in a pitched battle as a bulldozer operator, screaming "I'm going to kill you!" literally buried the blockaders of a lumber road in a pile of dirt. Dave Foreman was dragged one hundred yards behind a truck and suffered permanent knee damage.[124] In May 1987 George Alexander, the operator of a sawmill in northern California, was almost decapitated when a spiked log caused a fifteen-foot section of blade to break off and strike his face. Foreman commented that he was sorry about Alexander but, "I quite honestly am more concerned about old-growth forests, spotted owls and wolverines and salmon—and nobody is forcing people to cut those trees." Mike Roselle said, "I don't think people are more important than trees or trees are less important than people." He added that this did not mean "we should kill people the way we kill trees for lumber," but rather that "we have no right to kill trees with wanton waste." Even many dedicated environmentalists could not accept the implications of this logic. Harold Gilliam observed that "violence begets violence" and that "good intentions . . . do not sanctify destructive action." It made his "blood run cold" to think that there were environmental advocates "willing to risk maiming or killing people to save trees." A lumber company representative simply declared that the tree-spikers were "criminals."[125]

On another occasion after advising monkeywrenchers to "minimize any possible threat to other people" Foreman said that if equipment sabotage meant that "some fat guy has to walk a half mile to flag a ride and has a heart attack . . . that's an inherent risk."[126] Much Earth First! rhetoric gave the impression that a civil war was already underway. T. O. Hellenbach contributed a chapter to *Ecodefense* linking the monkeywrenchers to the radical colonists whose destruction of tea and British court records helped precipitate the American Revolution. He also noted the precedent of the Underground Railroad, which liberated the private property "of those who saw the slave as just another exploitable resource." Eventually, when the government did not acknowledge changing morals, "another war was needed to resolve the issues." Foreman added that "John Muir said that if it ever came to a war between the races, he would side with the bears. That day has arrived."[127]

There was disagreement about violence even among the new environmentalists. The editor of *Environmental Ethics* deplored Earth First!'s tactics as "paramilitary operations . . . closer to terrorism than civil disobedience." He noted that the sanctity of property was also one of John Locke's natural rights; ignoring it opened the possibility of a "terrible backlash" and the "undoing of all the good that has been done" in the environmental movement.[128] Jay Hair, chief executive officer of the huge National Wildlife Federation, similarly stated that "we're a nation of laws. Terrorism has no place in changing public policy."[129] Hair was unquestionably a mainstay of what Foreman called the ineffective environmental establishment, but the editor of the Earth First! newspaper resigned over the issue of publishing sympathetic accounts of tree and road spiking.[130] Even Gary Snyder, a pioneer in articulating the rights of nature and an Earth First! supporter, warned the organization that violence against property or people should only be undertaken as a last resort and then only "with a true warrior's consciousness," rather than beer-induced machismo or casual pranksterism. As a Buddhist, Snyder saw the hope of ending American civilization's violent relationship with nature in the rejection of violence in general. Violence should not be fought with violence.[131]

There was no consensus on this point. Some radical environmentalists tried to draw the line for acceptable violence between property and life. "Of course we have a moral right to act against lifeless 'property' to preserve the Earth," wrote an Earth First! correspondent from North Carolina. "Such acts of conscience are *not* violence; they are our *duty* if we are true stewards of this Earth." But, he cautioned, "all action must be *non-violent to life*."[132] Dave Foreman, for one, disagreed, admitting that while he admired the pacifism of a Gandhi or a Martin Luther King, Jr., he was "not by nature a pacifist." Turning the other cheek seemed to him "a good way to get a sore face." So Foreman, who had once been run down and badly injured by an irate lumber-truck driver, was fully prepared to respond in kind. He felt that "most of us have a point of no return where we'll fight back." As for himself, he would fight for the rights of nature with all the tools at his disposal, including violence. Foreman would not negotiate with the plunderers of the earth. In 1981 he drew an analogy for an undoubtedly shocked audience at the ultraconservative Mountain States Legal Foundation: "If you come home and find a bunch of Hell's Angels raping your wife, old mother, and eleven-year-old daughter, you don't sit down and talk balance with them or suggest compromise. You get your twelve-gauge shotgun and blow them to hell."[133] Evidently for Foreman the rape of the earth had become as morally intolerable as the rape of people one loved.

Howie Wolke, an Earth First! founder and frequent monkey-wrencher, thought "conventional tactics" and "non-violent direct action" were worthwhile techniques for environmentalists. Like Foreman, he did not presume to tell his colleagues what to do; the choice of means was a matter of individual conscience. But Wolke felt that "violence will soon become inevitable if we are to succeed in building an effective RADICAL environmental movement." People will get "downright militant . . . in defense of all living and non-living components of the biosphere." So Wolke welcomed, and associated himself with, "those individuals on the dark and shadowy fringes of society" who understood that "every major socio-political change has required some degree of violence." Violence, after all, "is as American as . . . apple pie."[134]

Wolke called nonviolence "unnatural" because "the most basic animal instinct is to fight back when under attack."[135] Variations on this idea have characterized the most recent discussions of violence within the Earth First! movement. A 1987 correspondent praised deep ecology but confessed his disappointment that most deep ecologists espoused and practiced nonviolence. Pointing out that "nearly all known organisms react with what can be called violence toward territorial encroachment and personal attack," he thought that environmentalists had every right to defend their habitat violently.[136] A year before Dave Foreman had told an interviewer that he considered "one hundred percent nonviolence as life-denying." Foreman regarded the idea of humankind overcoming its natural tendency to violence as "a bunch of new-age crap." Everything alive defended its vital interests, violently if necessary. Exempting humans from this biological imperative seemed to Foreman to contradict the basic premise of ecology that there was no separation between humans and nature. Yet it was not just a matter of defending human rights to a healthy habitat. Foreman argued that a specific river or wilderness or endangered species defends itself by "operating through you."[137] Radical environmentalism thus became, in the words of Stephanie Mills, "a sophisticated form of self-defense" on the part of non-human beings or natural objects.[138] Foreman liked to say that "I'm operating as part of the wilderness defending myself," and that monkeywrenching was "self-defense on the part of the Earth."[139] The idea of humans acting for nature depended on an understanding of the relationship of the individual self to the biophysical whole. In the minds of some Earth First! members, this legitimized any amount of illegality.

The history of American liberalism offered environmental radicals a way to justify violence. George Wuerthner told readers of the August 1985 issue of *Earth First!* that a culture, like Lawrence Kohlberg's individual, gained "moral maturity" when individuals aware of "universal truths" opposed "unjust laws." In the United States this process had not always been nonviolent. "It took a civil war," Wuerthner explained, "to extend certain inalienable rights to all people in our society." Now some were looking to violence as the only way to implement "the next major extension of rights . . . to the land."[140]

The almost unthinkable, global scale of destruction that nuclear war and "nuclear winter" would mean for the natural world received surprisingly little attention from anti-war activists. Most opposition to nuclear war has centered on the horror of nuclear weapons for human beings and their civilization. Yet a few commentators have recognized broader ethical implications. If humankind self-destructed, the species could be said to deserve its fate, but what about the other beings, species, and ecosystems that would be dragged into oblivion as well? This planetary perspective appeared in Jonathan Shell's best-selling book, *The Fate of the Earth* (1982), in which he pleaded not only for humans to save themselves from extinction but to have "respect for the earth" as the basis "of human as of other life."[141] In *Star Wars and the State of Our Souls: Deciding the Future of Planet Earth* (1985), Patricia M. Mische pointed out that modern weapons have created "a crisis of morality of ethics" because "we have new powers over life and death—not only human life but over the planetary processes in all [their] forms." This God-like power required, in her opinion, that "we become . . . more morally mature."[142] Lewis Thomas, who had compared the earth to a living cell, believed nuclear war would deal "the biosphere . . . a mortal or near-mortal blow." Life on the planet might survive, but as it did a billion years ago when bacteria topped the evolutionary tree.[143] Michael Allen Fox agreed that nuclear war could result in "*ecocide*." Apart from the decimation and possible termination of human life, a holocaust "must be regarded as morally worse in terms of its consequences for the non-human environment." On this point Fox noted the deep ecologists' belief that "other things have a right to continue existing even if we insist on obliterating ourselves."[144]

Carl Sagan and Paul Ehrlich, leaders in forecasting the ecological effects of nuclear war and publicizing the concept of "nuclear winter," preferred scientific to ethical arguments, but implicit in their work was the idea that atom bombs confronted humans with the awesome responsibility of being in charge of evolution. Linking people and nature in a single biological and ethical community, Sagan urged his generation to "cherish our fragile world as we do our children and our grandchildren."[145] Sagan turned to civil disobedience, as did scores of scientists and physicians. On several occasions in 1986 they illegally entered the Nevada Test Site to prevent detonation of nuclear bombs and were arrested for criminal trespass. Harvard psychologist John Mack cited the Boston Tea Party, Henry David Thoreau, and Martin Luther King, Jr., in a justification of his arrest in Nevada. "I recommend civil disobedience," he told cheering Harvard students, "for your spiritual health."[146]

Nuclear war and nuclear winter have the potential of focusing attention on the rights of both humans and nature as no other recent issue. The environmental movement has begun to recognize that what is at stake in disarmament is nothing less than the fate of the planet. Philosophers and scientists agree that the rights of any individual organism have no significance apart from the existence of a habitat, which alone assures existence, liberty, and the opportunity to pursue happiness. Some raise questions about the rights of the habitat itself. Ending the threat of nuclear holocaust is likely to become a major moral imperative for future liberators of nature as well as people.

Abolitionism, Environmentalism, and the Limits of American Liberalism

It was once considered stupid to think that colored men were really human and must be treated humanely. This stupidity has become a truth. Today it is thought an exaggeration to state that a reasonable ethic demands constant consideration for all living things down to the lowliest manifestations of life.
—*Albert Schweitzer, 1923*

Why the Green Nigger?
—*Elizabeth Dodson Gray, 1979*

There was an eighty-seven year hiatus from the Declaration of Independence to the Emancipation Proclamation and the freeing of American blacks from slavery. . . . The idea of an inalienable right of self-determination has moved with irresistible force to become what Jefferson claimed it was in 1776: a self-evident truth. . . . It is now nature's turn to be liberated.
—*Donald Worster, 1980*

We are like the Abolitionists, who are regarded as radicals, too. And we hope that a hundred years from now people will look back on the way animals are treated now with the same horror as we do when we look back on the slave trade.
—*Anonymous participant in a raid by the Animal Liberation Front, 1984*

*I*t is tempting to regard the extraordinary extension of ethics that radical environmentalists propose as unprecedented in American in-

199

tellectual history. For the same reason it is easy to judge their chances for changing traditional attitudes and institutions as poor to nonexistent. History, however, provides another perspective. As the preceding chapters have contended, there are grounds for regarding environmental ethics as a logical extrapolation of powerful liberal traditions as old as the republic. The American past contains a highly visible liberation movement with interesting similarities to contemporary environmentalism. If the abolition of slavery marked the limits of American liberalism in the mid-nineteenth century, perhaps biocentrism and environmental ethics are at the cutting edge of liberal thought in the late twentieth.

A century and a half ago a group of American reformers proposed a change in thought and action that, for its time, was no less radical than that mandated by biocentric ethics. The problem then was slavery, an institution socially and legally predicated on the denial of moral standing to black people. An initially tiny group of radical reformers known as abolitionists found this practice morally wrong. After exhausting other alternatives, they succeeded in persuading a majority of Northerners to support a civil war that ended the institution. What is intriguing for the present purposes is that the abolitionists faced an ethical and political situation directly comparable to that presently confronting the radical environmentalists. In both instances we find reformers who have identified an oppressed minority that they think possesses rights and is therefore entitled to liberty from exploitation. In each case we hear the argument that the laws and institutions supporting such exploitation are morally wrong and must be changed, legally if possible; otherwise, if necessary.

For the first eight decades of American independence all slaveholders, most Southerners, and a sizable number of Northern whites categorically excluded blacks from their ethical community. Recent scholarship has called attention to the diversity within the experience of American slavery.[1] Unquestionably some slaves were regarded as humans, rather than animals, and were treated well. Particularly in Southern cities a few slaves enjoyed an impressive degree of autonomy. But as John Boles notes, even at its best slavery was a "system based upon force . . . that defined persons as property."[2] Even under the moonlight and magnolias of legend, slaves were owned just as animals and land are today. They had no rights, natural or otherwise, and Southern law underscored the point. "The slave," a Virginia judge opined in 1858, "is not a person but a thing."[3] What this meant was that in Virginia and most slave states, even the murder of a slave by his or her master went unpunished. If someone other than the master did the killing, the slave laws of the South provided only for restitution of the value of the lost slave to the owner.[4] The logic was the same as that which now applies when a motorist runs over someone's dog or flower bed. The driver compensates the owner for his loss. The rights of the dog or the plants, like those of the slave, are legally irrelevant.

Historians have argued that while in other parts of the New World slavery was not a "closed," amoral system,[5] in the United States, in the words of sociologist Orlando Patterson, the black slave became "a nonbeing," "a socially dead person."[6] Oscar Handlin, and especially Stanley Elkins, feel strongly that, in Elkins's words, "unmitigated" or "unopposed capitalism" explains the severity of North American slavery.[7] Elkins also makes much of the anti-institutional character of American life. The points are related. The United States had no established national institutions—for example, a church, monarchy, aristocracy, dominant political party, or strong national bank—sufficiently powerful to restrain the profit-making urge. This meant that resources, including nature as well as human laborers, were left unprotected. Ruggedly individualistic and enormously ambitious, early nineteenth-century Americans pursued the main chance with little patience for the controls or restraints provided by ethics or institutions. Their success in exploiting available economic resources underwrote the young nation's accelerating prosperity. Progress, in these years, had overwhelming material connotations. Little stood between the greed of nascent capitalists and the fields and forests, beaver and buffalo, blacks and Indians.[8] Few paused in the race for riches to define their relationships to such entities in terms of right and wrong.

Slavery fitted into this interpretive framework nicely. It was essentially an economic institution, and while not free of costs, it had tangible economic advantages.[9] The exploitation of almost four million blacks underlay the prosperity and luxury of Southern life in the same way that the exploitation of other species and of the environment underwrote and continues to underwrite American affluence. The more radical contemporary environmentalists are well aware of this link. Most of them find the values associated with unrestrained capitalism to be at the root of modern environmental problems as well as continuing social discrimination. And they feel that any meaningful reform in environmental relations is predicated on changing the human relationship with nature from an economic to an ethical basis. Such a change obviously had antecedents in the antislavery crusade. Richard Ryder, the animal liberationist, observed in 1975,

"When we examine the arguments used by slave-owners in the past, we can see a striking similarity with the view expressed today by those who defend the exploitation of animals in factory-farms, the fur trade, [and] laboratories . . . above all else, it would be stressed [that animal] slavery was necessary for economic survival." [10]

When it did occur, humane treatment of slaves seldom reflected an ethical sensibility. It was good business, like skillful utilitarian management of livestock or good stewardship of fields. A sick or maimed slave could not work efficiently, a dead one not at all. It made economic sense to care for slaves in the same way that it did to care for the cattle and land one owned. The guiding principle behind this philosophy, stewardship, stemmed from an assumption of superiority and was, in actuality, the antipode of liberation. The new environmentalists who believe in the rights of nature dismiss conservation and stewardship as ethically meaningless just as abolitionists scorned kindly slavery. What the deep ecologists call "reform environmentalism" or "shallow ecology" seems to them just a more efficient form of exploitation and oppression. It compares to feeding slaves well or to buying women new dresses while refusing them the right to vote. Real reform, the radical environmentalists agree with the abolitionists, depends on replacing the entire exploitative system with one premised on the rights of the oppressed minority.

Slavery antedated antislavery by thousands of years. Human bondage existed for most of its history without significant opposition. Moreover, the slaves of antiquity, who could come from any race, were generally regarded as humans who had lost their natural rights through capture. To recall Aldo Leopold's anology, Odysseus's decision to hang his captive slave girls involved no question of ethics. This was not, as Leopold pointed out, because the slaveholders of ancient Greece had no morals. The boundaries of their moral community simply ended short of slaves.

Why, then, did the antislavery movement suddenly flower in the eighteenth century and, within a hundred years, eliminate almost all slavery in the Western world? The reason, as David B. Davis has demonstrated, was the emergence of liberal ideals in association with the democratic revolutions in England, France, and the United States. [11] Assuming one regarded slaves as people, the new natural-rights philosophy made a strong case for including them in the ethical community. The abolitionists quickly seized on this idea as a powerful argument for terminating an institution that denied slaves something all people possessed by birth and which could never be alienated— namely, their right to life and liberty. They had a clear sense that the tide of intellectual history was running in their favor. William Lloyd Garrison wrote in 1832 that the "Spirit of Liberty . . . is now shaking the world." He saw himself and his antislavery colleagues riding a "wave of revolution" that was producing "great and glorious and sudden . . . changes in the condition of the oppressed."[12] But Wendell Phillips, the consummate orator of abolitionism, put the idea most eloquently. "We are launched," he declared in 1859, "on the ocean of an unchained democracy."[13]

Six years later, the shores of Phillips's ocean expanded to encompass slaves. The possibility that "unchained" natural-rights principles might expand still further—even across the boundaries of species— would encourage subsequent environmental reformers. When they argued that nonhuman beings and nonsentient nature also possessed intrinsic value and rights regardless of being captured, conquered, and owned, they employed the same liberal faith that had served the antislavery partisans. It is thus possible to characterize both movements as conservative, rather than subversive, with reference to established ideas. Both sought to implement and extend the spirit of 1776.

The motives of the abolitionists were simple and straightforward. As Garrison saw it, the only documents necessary to make the case against slavery were the New Testament and the Declaration of Independence. Garrison understood the Declaration to express the core of the American liberal tradition, and in company with virtually every abolitionist he found slavery to be in direct violation. Indeed Garrison believed that six thousand years of human history could not produce "such a glaring contradiction as exists between our creed and practice."[14] For Wendell Phillips the reason slavery existed was that Americans "have never accepted our own civilization. We have held back," he added, "from the inference which we ought to have drawn from the admitted principles which underlie our life."[15]

The Bible offered abolitionists another way to fight human bondage. Using the New Testament, the anarchistic wing of American abolitionism could reject the Constitution because it supported slavery. Repeatedly the more radical abolitionists cited a "higher law," emanating from God, that justified resistance to slavery no matter what the nation's laws required.[16] John Brown drew on the higher law to justify his 1859 raid on Harper's Ferry and the several deaths it produced. After his capture and eventual hanging by a Virginia court, Brown became a martyr in antislavery circles. Emerson called him a saint. Thoreau thought his hanging compared to the crucifixion of Christ.[17]

The abolitionists' task was to resurrect slaves as human beings endowed with inalienable natural and God-given rights, and then to expose the disparity between slavery and American political and religious ideals. But even in a God-fearing nation founded on the principle that all men were created equal, antislavery encountered massive resistance. One root of the slavery dilemma was biological, just as it is with the contemporary controversy over the tension between human rights and the rights of other species and nature in general. A fundamental premise of proslavery thought held that an ethical code based on natural rights did not apply to blacks because they were not members of the human race. This was the only recourse for educated Southern slaveholders such as Thomas Jefferson, the only way to believe that all "men" were created equal and still own slaves. Jefferson, to his credit, agonized over the evidence to the contrary, but in the final analysis he had no other option. So we find Jefferson in his *Notes on the State of Virginia* (1782) laboring to place blacks in the biological netherland between whites and the more advanced monkeys. Unsophisticated proslavery apologists were considerably less tactful in their statement of this idea, which became a staple of the ugliest forms of racism.[18]

The position basing ethical inequality on biological inequality reappeared frequently in the modern argument against environmental ethics. Opponents of extending ethics outside the human community argued that nonhuman beings and the environment were incapable of understanding and following ethical rules or of having human-like "interests" or sensibility to pain. This inability, it was said, disqualified them from holding rights. Humans might find it imprudent to abuse nature, but no violation of its rights was involved. The abolitionist rejoinder to this kind of logic began with the idea that blacks and whites were not dissimilar. The most powerful abolitionist appeals, notably Harriet Beecher Stowe's *Uncle Tom's Cabin* (1852), presented dramatic evidence that slaves were actually superior in human qualities to the more brutal owners and overseers.

Clearly this kind of argument for the abolition of slavery was not fully applicable in the case humanitarians and environmentalists would later make for livestock, laboratory animals, trees, and ecosystems. No one could represent such beings as human. But many animal rightists fell back on Jeremy Bentham's reasoning that the ability to feel pain linked humans and the more advanced organisms into one ethical community. Animals suffer, they contend, just like people. The personification of ecosystems ("Mother Earth") and animals (the mother-child emphasis in the protest against butchery of baby seals) suggests parallels with antislavery. Some animal rights groups name the objects of their concerns in fund-raising appeals: one features a sad-eyed dog and the caption "This is *Clara;* she's going to be dissected alive tomorrow." Theodore Roszak called specifically for recognition of the "personhood" of nature in his appeals for environmental responsibility.[19] The Whale Rescue Project headlined its recent calls for resistance to the annual slaughter on the Faroe Islands: "When pilot whales are butchered alive, they scream in agony. Just like people." The Humane Society of the United States terms procurement of living subjects for scientific experimentation "the animal slave trade."

There is more relevance to environmentalism in the second kind of abolitionist rebuttal to the argument of biological inferiority. It granted that blacks were biologically different—even inferior—but insisted that those differences were not a barrier against moral considerability; blacks still possessed natural rights. Slavery was still wrong. This helped some white abolitionists out of the quandary of their own strong racist biases.[20] Although there were exceptions, the prevalent abolitionist attitude held that even though blacks could never attain intellectual and social parity with whites, that was no reason to deny them their natural rights.

In this stance the abolitionists became spokespersons for the rights of an oppressed and largely silent minority that they perceived to differ greatly from themselves and that, in fact, many knew only through hearsay and printed reports. It was their self-appointed role to advocate the rights of a group that they did not consider a part of their own society. In this attitude the antislavery advocates came very close to the position of recent environmentalists. The latter say that concerned humans must make the moral case for beings that cannot make it for themselves. No environmentalist seeks literal equality for the subjects of his or her concern, and many have as little firsthand experience with, say, whales and grizzly bears as most Northern abolitionists had with slaves. But the force of their moral outrage is not diminished by perceived biological differences.

The would-be liberators of slaves, like present-day advocates of nature liberation, faced the problem of changing a deeply rooted institution within their civilization. Slavery anchored a social order involving nearly four million slaves, four hundred thousand slaveholders, and eight million Southern whites. In the South, not unexpectedly, the moral absolutism of the abolitionists and their insistence that slaveholding was both a crime and a sin quickly aroused hostility and violence. However, most Northerners likewise determined not to let the slavery issue disturb domestic tranquility and prosperity and regarded the early abolitionists as somewhere between troublemakers and traitors. At the outset of their crusade they were widely regarded as a tiny, fanatical minority with ridiculous and dangerous ethical theories. On numerous occasions ridicule escalated into violence. Even in the free states abolitionists were mobbed, beaten, and, on one occasion, murdered by outraged Northerners. And the anti-abolitionist mobs were not social riffraff but, in the words of their primary historian, "gentlemen of property and standing."[21] The Northern "establishment," as the 1960s would have styled it, was clearly hostile to abolitionism until well into the 1850s. Consequently it would be hard to overstate the enormous odds against the success of American abolitionism when it began in earnest in the 1830s. Contemporary detractors of radical environmentalism would do well to remember this fact.

But if far from popular, the early abolitionists were driven by strong ethical convictions. They would not surrender their concern for the slaves to the prevailing ethics of their society. William Lloyd Garrison suggested the intensity of the abolitionist mind in 1831 in the first issue of *The Liberator*: "I am aware that many object to the severity of my language; but is there not cause for severity? I *will be* as harsh as truth, and as uncompromising as justice . . . urge me not to use moderation in a cause like the present." Here was a man out to right wrongs, an ethically oriented reformer who would give no quarter to his opponents. And he was nothing if not determined: "I am in earnest—I will not equivocate—I will not excuse—I will not retreat a single inch—AND I WILL BE HEARD." Garrison knew full well the depth of his unpopularity as he began his campaign of liberation. "The apathy of the people," he wrote in the initial *Liberator,* "is enough to make every statue leap from its pedestal, and to hasten the resurrection of the dead."[22] He liked to point out that in 1831 *The Liberator* had exactly zero subscribers and its editor was unknown. A decade later Garrison was a widely known, if still controversial figure, and the number of abolitionists in organized societies had reached 200,000. Thirty-four years after the inception of *The Liberator,* Garrison closed down his press: slavery no longer existed. He and his abolitionist colleagues had indeed been heard.

Confronted with the fact of an entrenched slave system and given the political realities of the United States, the abolitionists had four procedural options as they began their crusade against slavery. Similar ones are open to the new environmentalists. The first, reform, meant working within established institutions. It required patience, skill in compromise, and the ability to be satisfied with gradual gains that one hoped would lead to a final liberation. But slavery was not legislated out of existence. One reason was the reluctance of the political parties, including third parties, to violate the constitutional prohibition of federal interference with slavery where it existed at the time of the formation of the union.[23]

On a deeper level, however, slavery was not the kind of problem susceptible to compromise in the American political tradition. If the ownership and exploitation of black people was wrong, as the abolitionists believed, it was wrong at any given time, in any place, and in any form, however humane. A comparison on this point to the new environmentalism is tempting. Animal liberationists cannot, in good conscience, rest content with demands that laboratory animals have clean cages and be well fed. And deep ecologists must protest "natural resource management" no matter how efficient. Indeed, the deep ecologists' criticism of what they call "conservation" is precisely on the grounds of its superficiality and hyprocrisy. They argue that the entire system that subjugates nature to people must be replaced. For the same reason the more extreme abolitionists rapidly lost patience with efforts to reform slavery and with what they termed "gradualism." They did not want to improve slavery; they wanted its termination. So Garrison called for an immediate and total end to slavery and, after 1840, to the entire political process that gave it support. In 1843 he called the Constitution "a covenant with death and an agreement with Hell," and eleven years later, on the Fourth of July, he burned a copy of that venerable document in a public ceremony.[24]

For Garrison and his followers, freedom was not a negotiable issue. In the mind of the South, neither was slavery; it involved the relationship of an owner with his property. The would-be reform wing of the antislavery movement ran onto the shoals of this ethical impasse. So did several generations of national politicians in their efforts to solve the problem of slavery short of civil war. So also do contemporary philosophers and activists who would hope to arbitrate the thorny issues raised by environmental ethics. Of course, in contrast to all slaves not *all* of nature is privately owned or oppressed. Environmental reformers have been able to promote successful legislation on behalf of animals, endangered species, and wilderness areas. Up to a point human abuse of nature can be legislated away. For some, however, this point falls far short of the moral ideal.

The second option available to the abolitionists was ethical education, or what they called "moral suasion," which they hoped would lead to an ethical revolution on the subject of slavery. The idea was to disregard politics and appeal directly to the consciences of Americans. As Wendell Phillips put it in 1853, the abolition movement's "aim is to alter public opinion." Garrison said his objective was "to increase our moral power over the nation."[25] Men like this saw themselves in an evangelical role, exhorting the nation to expand its ethical circle and ultimately to change its laws and institutions. In this endeavor the abolitionists relied heavily on stories of atrocity. The most famous collection was Theodore Weld's *American Slavery as It Is: Testimony of a Thousand Witnesses,* which the American Anti-Slavery Society published in 1839. It was a devastating condemnation. Weld and his wife, Angelina Grimké, presented evidence that slaves were routinely branded with hot irons, boiled in salt brine, nailed by the ears to wooden fences, and whipped to death. The book sold spectacularly for its time: 100,000 copies in a year. Only *Uncle Tom's Cabin* had more readers; it, too, depended on graphic descriptions and lithographs of slave auctions and other atrocities to arouse moral outrage.

Environmentalists have employed similar techniques in building sympathy for nature. Pictures and descriptions of trapped animals, clearcut forests, and strip-mined land highlight their publications. In *Silent Spring* (1962), Rachel Carson began the new environmentalists' efforts at moral suasion with descriptions of the agony of poisoned birds and mammals. Media coverage of the Santa Barbara, California, oil spill of 1969 featured oil-soaked birds floundering helplessly as they died on the beach. Cleveland Amory, Peter Singer, and other animal rightists made effective use of pictures of abused laboratory and farm animals in their publications, and the seal and whale defense organizations appealed to the consciences and pocketbooks of Americans with photographs of the blood-stained carcasses of marine mammals.

The third option available to the abolitionists was separation. This meant the secession of the *free* states from a federal union perceived to be unholy and immoral. "It is the right and duty of the North," contended Charles C. Burleigh, "to cease supporting slavery. We have no right to help wrong-doing."[26] Many of his abolitionist colleagues felt that as long as they were part of a government with the slave states, they were guilty of the sin of slavery. In 1846, after spending a night in jail for refusing to pay taxes that supported the Mexican War and slavery, Henry David Thoreau declared, "I cannot for an instant recognize that political organization as *my* government which is the *slave's* government also." Explaining his civil disobedience further, Thoreau stated, "we should be men first and subjects afterwards."[27] Morals, in other words, had priority over laws.

Garrison simply put the slogan "NO UNION WITH SLAVEHOLDERS" on the masthead of *The Liberator.* In company with most abolitionists he was prepared to challenge the Constitution of 1787 with the Declaration of Independence. It was the familiar natural-rights stance: rebellion was justified if a government ceased protecting the inalienable rights of all who were entitled to them, and now slaves had entered the magic circle. But the abolitionists insisted that they were not the subversive element; it was the slaveholding states that perverted the sacred American creed. Abolitionism only sought to bring America back into conformation with the principles of its origins.

The separation option had the advantage of absolving the North from the guilt of association with a sinful political system. But separation did nothing for the slaves, just as contemporary withdrawals of ecologically responsible citizens into new bioregional communities do nothing about environmental exploitation in the old regimes.[28] Pollution proceeds as usual and may bring down the ecosystem that the new order necessarily shares with the old one. Nuclear devastation observes no boundaries. But to give the abolitionist secessionists their due, they expected that withdrawal of the North from the federal union would sooner or later bring about the downfall of the "unprotected" slave empire. Their logic was, at best, dubious, but separation, then and now, would make a dramatic statement.

The final and, as it turned out, the only effective alternative for the American antislavery movement was coercion. If institutions could not be changed legally through reform efforts, if ethical education did not persuade the South to abandon slaveholding, and if insufficient support could be found for secession of the free states, the only way to right a moral wrong was by force. The South would have to be *made* to give up slavery. Violence testified to the failure of American civilization to solve the slavery problem in other ways. After eighty years of detours the nation had reached a moral roadblock. Abraham Lincoln discerned this in his celebrated "house divided" speech of 1858, and summarized his view two years later in a letter to Alexander H. Stephens, a Georgian: "You think slavery is right and ought to be extended, while we think it is wrong and ought to be restricted. That, I suppose, is the rub."[29] Indeed it was. Lincoln explained the process in the 1858 oration: "A house divided against itself cannot stand. I believe this government cannot endure permanently half slave and half free. . . . It will become all of one thing or the other."[30] Of course the advocates of freedom could have relented, swallowed their moral outrage, and proceeded to live in peace with slavery. But people seldom relent on moral fundamentals; they do not compromise their deepest ethical convictions. Murder, rape, theft, and, especially for Americans, the oppression of minority rights and the denial of liberty constitute uncompromisable moral bedrock that people fight to defend.

George Santayana pointed out in 1920 that a necessary precondition for the existence of democratic forms of government is agreement on ethical fundamentals. "To put things to a vote, and to accept unreservedly the decision of the majority," he wrote, "are points essential to the English system but they would be absurd if fundamental agreement were not presupposed. . . . In a hearty and sound democracy all questions at issue must be minor matters; fundamentals must have been silently agreed upon and taken for granted when the democracy arose."[31] The North and South had lost such consensus by 1860 if, indeed, they ever shared it with regard to slavery. As a consequence American government was not "hearty and sound." A moral issue had entered the political arena, and suddenly a regular election, that of 1860, shattered the Union.

The historiography of the American Civil War reveals that well into the present century some scholars believed that slavery was not the cause of the sectional conflict. These "revisionist" historians characterized the war as needless and repressible. They criticized a "blundering generation" of politicians who could and should have found nonviolent solutions to the nation's problems.[32] They attributed the war to economic differences or to the states-rights theory of government, ignoring the fact that people do not normally fight their countrymen about such issues. Without slavery there was no reason for these matters to flare into war. The revisionists' short-range view found the war caused by the South's desire for independence and the North's determination to preserve the Union. Technically, this is an accurate assessment of the events of 1860 and 1861, but in the absence of slavery there would have been no compelling need for the South to secede, nor would there have been a strong reason for the North to resist secession. Wendell Phillips understood this more clearly than many subsequent scholars when he asked, soon after the Civil War began, "If it were possible to subjugate the South, and leave slavery just as it is, where is the security that we should not have another war in ten years?"[33] Phillips knew that the real reason the antebellum politicians blundered, and compromise was unattainable, was the absence of basic agreement on right and wrong with reference to slavery. "When a great number of persons," he wrote, "agree in a great number of things, that insures a union; that is not the case with the

North and South, therefore we separate; that is the case with the whole North, therefore we shall remain united."[34]

Antislavery advocates of Phillips's generation, who fought the war, never mistook its causes as did later commentators. For them it was cut-and-dried: take away slavery and you removed the need to force a new morality upon the South. Even Abraham Lincoln, who labored for several years to define his war aims without reference to slavery, eventually saw the war for what it was. When he issued the Emancipation Proclamation on September 22, 1862, freeing all slaves in rebel territory as of the following January 1, he finally defined the Civil War correctly. It was not a war for the preservation of the Union but a conflict about ethical ideas.

The Civil War adds evidence to the thesis that changes in ethics seldom occur peaceably. From the *Magna Carta* of 1215 on, force or the threat of force hammered out the Anglo-American philosophy of liberty. The advent of the commonwealth system in England in the 1640s involved a bloody civil struggle in the course of which Parliament asserted its authority over a reluctant (and eventually executed) monarch. The American Revolution was not accomplished at a negotiating table; a decade later, heads rolled in France as part of an effort to secure a broader basis of rights. Violence has long been part of the crusade for the rights of the laboring classes, as Karl Marx understood, and it reappeared during the American civil rights movement of the 1950s and 1960s. The history of liberty suggests that the economic and psychological benefits oppression carries for the oppressor are not easily surrendered. Liberation, as a consequence, has been closely associated with coercion.

Environmental advocates have found significant parallels between their crusade and that of the abolitionists. As early as the 1850s, Henry David Thoreau saw human slavery and the abuse of nature stemming from a common source: ethical myopia. After the Civil War, Harriet Beecher Stowe transferred her formidable talents from antislavery to the humane movement. Albert Schweitzer followed Charles Darwin and William Lecky in believing that the course of ethical evolution led in a logical progression from respect for black people to respect for all life. Aldo Leopold, whose holistic ethics bore the stamp of ecology, referred to the "enslavement of . . . earth" as early as 1933.[35] Present-day animal rightists such as Peter Singer continually link the liberation of animals to that of slaves in an effort to convince their readers that the limits of liberalism must extend beyond a concern for people.

Making the same point dramatically in the title of her 1979 book,

Elizabeth Dodson Gray simply asked *Why the Green Nigger?* Herbert Marcuse, Murray Bookchin, and Theodore Roszak, among others, have a ready answer. They see the green world (nature, environment, land, or earth) oppressed by the same exploitative, hierarchical values and institutions that once denied rights to slaves and continue to oppress many women, racial minorities, and laborers of all colors. Nature in their eyes is just the latest minority deserving a place in the sun of the American liberal tradition.

The comparison of those who liberated slaves over a century ago to those who would liberate nature today is at once encouraging and disturbing. On the one hand it might be heartening for the new animal rightists and biocentrists to remember that civil war and the abolition of slavery seemed just as unlikely in the 1830s as implementation of their moral ideals does a century and a half later. The abolitionists initially faced a culture united in the consensus that right and wrong did not apply to relations with slaves any more than they did to relations with cows or bacteria or rivers. The full weight of private property supported the slaveholders' cause, just as it does that of contemporary owners of nature. The ethical community ended then at the line between white and black; now it ends, for many, at the human–nature boundary. William Lloyd Garrison fully expected himself and his colleagues to be "ridiculed as fools, scorned as visionaries, branded as disorganizers, reviled as madmen, threatened and perhaps punished as traitors." But, Garrison added, "we shall bide our time." [36] He proved as patient as he was committed. In 1829, at the beginning of his abolitionist career, he characterized the established ethical system as higher than the Alps and spoke of the necessity of dismantling it "brick by brick, and foot by foot, till it is reduced so low that it may be overturned without burying the nation in its ruins." Garrison knew the length of time this might require. He understood in the 1830s that "the philanthropists who are now pleading in behalf of the oppressed may not live to witness the dawn which will precede the glorious day of universal emancipation." [37] Yet agitation continued and gradually the majority in the North came to accept the abolitionists' principal contention that slavery was incompatible with the American liberal tradition. Garrison did live to witness the end of slavery and the inclusion, at least by law, of all blacks in an extended ethical community. The price, to be sure, was high: four years of civil war and a loss of nearly a million human lives.

The chances of this process recurring on behalf of other species and nature itself seems to some as remote today as freedom for slaves did in the early nineteenth century. But some advocates of animals and nature don't agree. "The animal rights issue," notes Henry Holzer, "is at the same place now as the slavery issue was fifty years before Abolition."[38] In fact, most of the ingredients that sparked the Civil War presently exist. There is what many construe to be the denial of natural rights to exploited and oppressed members of the American ecological community. Ownership, what some even call the enslavement of nonhuman species and of the environment, is again the explosive issue. In the last two decades advocates of environmental ethics just as earnest as Garrison and as impassioned as Stowe have appeared. They have found their Thomas Jefferson in Aldo Leopold and their John Brown in Dave Foreman. Some are already acting on their ethical convictions. Radical environmentalism has produced both civil disobedience and violent resistance. As a spokesperson for the Animal Liberation Front declared, "It's like the Underground Railroad and slavery . . . sometimes people have to go outside the law to save lives. Any movement for social change has required disobedience."[39] An Earth First! publication of 1987 similarly noted that the "'Underground Railroad' was destructive of the private economic concerns of those who saw the slave as just another exploitable resource." The writer pointed out that disobedience was necessary when British administrators "refused to negotiate with radical colonists whom [they] associated with numerous attacks on public and private property." The upshot was the Boston Tea Party and eventually the American Revolution, because "the sluggish minds of men in government failed to acknowledge the changing times."[40]

When and if nuclear war is widely defined as a violation of the rights of nonhuman species and of the planet as well as of human rights, the potential for mass participation in ethically impelled environmentalism would increase enormously. On the other side are advocates of anthropocentric ethics and environmental exploitation who, like the nineteenth-century exploiters of black people, derive substantial material benefits from their limited ethics. Some of them will not voluntarily abandon their beliefs and behavior no matter how vigorously the radical environmentalists insist. If this situation, with its intellectual and political similarities to antebellum America, promises once again to endanger domestic tranquility, it is not the fault of history.

NOTES
◆
SELECTED BIBLIOGRAPHY
◆
INDEX

• Notes •

1. Curt Meine, *Aldo Leopold: His Life and Work* (Madison, Wis., 1988); Susan L. Flader, *Thinking Like a Mountain: Aldo Leopold and the Evolution of an Ecological Attitude toward Deer, Wolves and Forests* (Columbia, Mo., 1974).

2. Roderick Nash, *Wilderness and the American Mind* (New Haven, Conn., 1967, 1973, 1982).

3. "Rounding Out the American Revolution: Ethical Extension and the New Environmentalism," in Michael Tobias, ed., *Deep Ecology* (San Diego, 1984), 170–181, reprinted in Kendall E. Bailes, ed., *Environmental History: Critical Issues in Comparative Perspective* (New York, 1985), 242–257; "Do Rocks Have Rights?" *Center Magazine* 10 (Nov.–Dec. 1977), 2–12; "Thoughts on Environmental Ethics," in Florian Stuber and Michael Mooney, eds., *Small Comforts for Hard Times: Humanists on Public Policy* (New York, 1977), 120–134; "The Significance of the Arrangement of the Deck Chairs on the Titanic," *Not Man Apart* (mid-Oct. 1975), 7–9; "Environmental Ethics," in Ronald Clarke and Peter List, eds., *Environmental Spectrum: Social and Economic Views on the Quality of Life* (New York, 1974), 142–150; "Progress and Poverty: The Santa Barbara Story," in *Santa Barbara Oil Symposium* (Washington, D.C., 1972), 227–233; *The Santa Barbara Declaration of Environmental Rights* (Santa Barbara, Cal., 1969), reprinted in *Congressional Record* 116 (Jan. 20, 1970); "An '11th Commandment' Vital to Our Environment," *Santa Barbara News Press.* June 22, 1969, A16–17.

4. George Sessions, "Shallow and Deep Ecology: A Review of the Philosophical Literature," in Robert C. Schultz and J. Donald Hughes, eds., *Ecological Consciousness* (Washington, D.C., 1981), 422.

PROLOGUE
Ethical Extension and Radical Environmentalism

1. Richard Ryder coined the term in his essay, "Experiments on Animals," in Stanley and Roslind Godlovitch and John Harris, eds., *Animals, Men and Morals* (New York, 1972), 81. Ryder publicized it in two books, *Victims of Science: The Use of Animals in Research* (London, 1975), and *Speciesism: The Ethics of Vivisection* (Edinburgh, 1974).

2. The phrase is Richard and Val Routley's: "Human Chauvinism and Environmental Ethics," in Don Mannison, Michael McRobbie, and Richard Routley, eds., *Environmental Philosophy* (Canberra, Australia, 1980), 96ff.

3. Peter Singer, "Animal Liberation," *New York Review of Books* 20

(April 5, 1973), 17–21. See also Singer, *Animal Liberation: A New Ethic for Our Treatment of Animals* (New York, 1975).

4. Christopher D. Stone, *Should Trees Have Standing? Toward Legal Rights for Natural Objects* (Los Altos, Cal., 1974).

5. John Muir, *A Thousand-Mile Walk to the Gulf,* William F. Bade, ed. (Boston, 1917), 324.

6. Albert Schweitzer, *Out of My Life and Thought: An Autobiography* (New York, 1933), 188; Liberty Hyde Bailey, *The Holy Earth* (New York, 1915).

7. Aldo Leopold, *A Sand County Almanac* (New York, 1949), 201.

8. Herbert Marcuse, *Counterrevolution and Revolt* (Boston, 1972), 59.

9. Charles Birch and John B. Cobb, Jr., *The Liberation of Life: From the Cell to the Community* (Cambridge, England, 1981).

10. Theodore Roszak, *Person/Planet: The Creative Disintegration of Industrial Society* (New York, 1978), 31. See also James Lovelock, *Gaia: A New Look at Life on Earth* (New York, 1979).

11. Eugene C. Hargrove, ed., *Beyond Spaceship Earth: Environmental Ethics and the Solar System* (San Francisco, 1986).

12. Arne Naess, "The Shallow and the Deep, Long-Range Ecology Movement: A Summary," *Inquiry* 16 (Spring 1973), 96.

13. Michael J. Cohen, *Prejudice against Nature: A Guidebook for the Liberation of Self and Planet* (Freeport, Maine, 1983).

14. Lynn White, Jr., "The Future of Compassion," *Ecumenical Review* 30 (April 1978), 107; White, "Continuing the Conversation," in Ian G. Barbour, ed., *Western Man and Environmental Ethics* (Reading, Mass., 1973), 61.

15. H. Paul Santmire, *Brother Earth: Nature, God and Ecology in Time of Crisis* (New York, 1970), 132.

16. Gary Snyder, "Energy Is Eternal Delight," *The New York Times,* Jan. 12, 1973, 43.

17. David F. Favre, "Wildlife Rights: The Ever-Widening Circle," *Environmental Law* 9 (Winter 1979), 279.

18. As quoted, significantly, in Tom Regan, *The Case for Animal Rights* (Berkeley, Cal., 1983), vi.

19. Stone, *Should Trees Have Standing?* 6.

20. Aldo Leopold, "The Conservation Ethic," *Journal of Forestry* 31 (Oct. 1933), 635.

21. Editorial, *Greenpeace Chronicles* 3 (April 1979), 1.

22. Holly Jensen as quoted in Eric Malni, "Animal Liberation Front: Raids on Medical Laboratories Defended," *Los Angeles Times,* Dec. 30, 1984, I, 30.

23. Joseph Petulla, *American Environmentalism: Values, Tactics, Priorities* (College Station, Tex., 1980), 51.

24. Samuel P. Hays has documented the politics of the change in *Beauty, Health and Permanence: Environmental Politics in the United States, 1955–1985* (Cambridge, England, 1987); "From Conservation to Environment: Environmental Politics in the United States since World War II," *Environmental*

Review 6 (Fall 1982), 14–41; and "The Structure of Environmental Politics since World War II," *Journal of Social History* 14 (Summer 1981), 719–738. Also important are Warren Johnson, "Battling the Environment: Conservation Turns to Ecology," in Gerald R. Baydo, ed., *The Evolution of Mass Culture in America—1877 to the Present* (St. Louis, Mo., 1982), 197–209; Stephen Fox, *The American Conservation Movement: John Muir and His Legacy* (Madison, Wis., 1985), especially parts 2 and 3; Thomas R. Dunlap, "Conservationists and Environmentalists: An Attempt at Definition," *Environmental Review* 4 (1980), 29–31; Carrol Pursell, ed., *From Conservation to Ecology* (New York, 1973); Donald Fleming, "The Roots of the New Conservation Movement," *Perspectives in American History* 6 (1972), 7–91; and Thomas A. Heberline, "The Land Ethic Realized: Some Social Psychological Explanations for Changing Environmental Attitudes," *Journal of Social Issue* 28 (1972), 79–87.

25. Roderick Nash, ed., *The American Environment* (Reading, Mass., 1976), 225ff.; Samuel Hays, *Conservation and the Gospel of Efficiency: The Progressive Conservation Movement, 1890–1920* (Cambridge, Mass., 1959).

26. See Keith Thomas, *Man and the Natural World* (New York, 1983) and James Turner, *Reckoning with the Beast: Animals, Pain and Humanity in the Victorian Mind* (Baltimore, 1980).

27. For useful insights on this point see Louis Hartz, *The Liberal Tradition in America* (New York, 1955). Robert Bellah's *Habits of the Heart: Individualism and Commitment in American Life* (Berkeley, Cal., 1985) and *Varieties of Civil Religion* (San Francisco, 1980) are more recent arguments that liberalism works as a secular religion in America.

28. Paul Shepard, "Ecology and Man—A Viewpoint," in Shepard and Daniel McKinley, eds., *The Subversive Science: Essays Toward an Ecology of Man* (Boston, 1969), 9.

29. Lynton Caldwell, "New Legal Arena," *Science* 171 (Feb. 19, 1971), 665; Paul Sears, "Ecology—A Subversive Subject," *BioScience* 14 (July 1964), 11–13.

30. Shepard, "Ecology and Man," 9. The literary scholar Leo Marx elaborated on this point in "American Institutions and Ecological Ideals," *Science* 170 (Nov. 27, 1970), 945–952.

31. Murray Bookchin, *The Ecology of Freedom* (Palo Alto, Cal., 1982), 18, 366; Bookchin, *Toward an Ecological Society* (Montreal, 1980), 58, 68.

32. Marcuse, *Counterrevolution and Revolt,* 59.

33. William R. Catton, Jr., *Overshoot: The Ecological Basis of Revolutionary Change* (Urbana, Ill., 1980).

34. Roszak, *Person/Planet,* xix.

35. With this identification of a basis for environmental responsibility in the mainstream of Western intellectual history I am siding with John Passmore, whose *Man's Responsibility for Nature: Ecological Problems and Western Traditions* (New York, 1974) argued that environmentalists need not turn to the East—to pantheism, mysticism, and non-Christian religions—for a guiding philosophy. Instead he urged them to discount the chronic resis-

tance of Western philosophy to environmental responsibility and find solutions to ecological problems within Western philosophical, religious, and scientific traditions. But Passmore paid almost no attention to natural rights and the idea of liberating nature, probably because he rejected the idea that nonhuman beings can have rights and, therefore, be part of an extended ethical community.

Eugene C. Hargrove has recently picked up where Passmore left off, analyzing both resistance and receptivity to environmental ethics in Western intellectual history in *Foundations of Environmental Ethics* (New York, 1988). But he, too, ignores the natural-rights approach to environmental protection in favor of one that emphasizes very anthropocentric aesthetic values in nature.

CHAPTER 1
From Natural Rights to the Rights of Nature

1. William S. McKechnie, *Magna Carta,* 2d ed. (New York, 1958); J. C. Holt, *Magna Carta* (Cambridge, England, 1965); William F. Swindler, *Magna Carta: Legend and Legacy* (Indianapolis, 1965).

2. The most useful histories of natural rights are Ian Shapiro, *The Evolution of Natural Rights in Liberal Theory* (Cambridge, England, 1986); Richard Tuck, *Natural Rights Theories: Their Origin and Development* (New York, 1979); Leo Strauss, *Natural Rights and History* (Chicago, 1953); Frederick Watkins, *The Political Tradition of the West: A Study in the Development of Modern Liberalism* (Cambridge, Mass., 1948); Heinrich Rommen, *The Natural Law,* Thomas R. Hanley, trans. (St. Louis, Mo., 1947); and the classic study of David G. Ritchie, *Natural Rights* (London, 1894).

3. Ralph Henry Gabriel and Robert H. Walker, *The Course of American Democratic Thought,* 3d ed. (New York, 1986); Clinton Rossiter, *Seedtime of the Republic* (New York, 1953), especially ch. 12; and Bernard Bailyn, *Ideological Origins of the American Revolution* (Cambridge, Mass., 1967). Bailyn contends that the American revolutionaries actually knew Locke better through the work of publicizers and pamphleteers than in the original. For the modern analyses of rights theory see Jeremy Waldron, ed., *Theories of Rights* (Oxford, 1984); Joel Feinberg, *Rights, Justice and the Bounds of Liberty* (Princeton, N.J., 1980); John Finnis, *Natural Law and Natural Rights* (Oxford, 1980); David Lyons, ed., *Rights* (Belmont, Cal., 1979); Abraham I. Melden, *Rights and Persons* (Berkeley, Cal., 1977); and Melden, ed., *Human Rights* (Belmont, Cal., 1970).

4. John Locke, *Two Treatises of Government,* 2d ed., Peter Laslett, ed. (Cambridge, England, 1967), 289.

5. Thomas Hobbes, *Leviathan,* Henry Morley, ed. (London, 1885), 64.

6. Bailyn, *Ideological Origins,* 184.

7. James Otis, *A Vindication of the British Colonies* (Boston, 1765), 8.

8. See Carl Becker, *The Declaration of Independence: A Study in the His-

tory of Political Ideas (New York, 1922); Julian P. Boyd, *The Declaration of Independence: The Evolution of the Text* (Princeton, N.J., 1945).

9. Chilton Williamson, *American Suffrage from Property to Democracy, 1760–1860* (Princeton, N.J., 1960), is the definitive study.

10. Staughton Lynd has traced the driving force of the American revolutionary tradition in *Intellectual Origins of American Radicalism* (New York, 1968). See also Robert Bellah, *Varieties of Civil Religion* (San Francisco, 1980); Louis Hartz, *The Liberal Tradition in America* (New York, 1955); and Daniel Boorstin, *The Lost World of Thomas Jefferson* (Boston, 1948), ch. 2.

11. R. Robert Palmer, *The Age of the Democratic Revolution: A Political History of Europe and America, 1760–1800* (Princeton, N.J., 1959), vol. 1, 21.

12. For analysis of classical jurisprudence and ethics see Tuck, *Natural Rights,* and John Rodman, "Animal Justice: The Counter-Revolution in Natural Right and Law," *Inquiry* 22 (Summer 1979), 3–22.

13. As quoted in Allesandro Passerin d'Entreves, *Natural Law: An Introduction to Legal Philosophy* (London, 1951), 25.

14. John Passmore, *Man's Responsibility for Nature* (London, 1974), and Lynn White, "The Historical Roots of Our Ecological Crisis," *Science* 155 (March 10, 1967), 1203–1207, are the key studies of this trend. For extended discussions of these works see Chapters 4 and 5 below. Also relevant are Robin Attfield, "Western Traditions and Environmental Ethics," in Robert Elliot and Arran Gare, eds., *Environmental Philosophy* (University Park, Pa., 1983), 201–229; Clarence Glacken, *Traces on the Rhodion Shore: Nature and Culture in Western Thought from Ancient Times to the End of the Eighteenth Century* (Berkeley, Cal., 1967); Richard S. Westfall, *Science and Religion in Seventeenth-Century England* (New Haven, Conn., 1958); and Charles E. Raven, *Religion and Christian Theology* (Cambridge, England, 1953). Eugene C. Hargrove's *Foundations of Environmental Ethics* (New York, 1988) contains substantial historical material.

15. As quoted from Pufendorf's *De Jure Naturæ et Gentium* (1672) in Rodman, "Animal Justice," 9. Also useful is John Passmore, "The Treatment of Animals," *Journal of the History of Ideas* 36 (April–May 1975), 195–218.

16. René Descartes, *The Method, Meditations and Philosophy of Descartes,* John Veitch, ed. (New York, 1901), 170ff. For secondary commentary on Cartesian ethics see Tom Regan, *The Case for Animal Rights* (Berkeley, Cal., 1983), 3–25, and Walter H. O'Briant, "Man, Nature, and the History of Philosophy," in William T. Blackstone, ed., *Philosophy and Environmental Crisis* (Athens, Ga., 1974), 83–86.

17. Edward P. Evans, *The Criminal Prosecution and Capital Punishment of Animals* (London, 1906). For Evans, an important harbinger of environmental ethics in American thought, the purpose in writing the book was to challenge Descartes by demonstrating the kinship of humans and animals and the precedent of including animals in human systems of justice.

18. Christopher D. Stone, *Should Trees Have Standing? Toward Legal Rights for Natural Objects* (Los Altos, Cal., 1974).

19. "The Body of Liberties . . . 1641" reprinted in *Old South Leaflets* (Boston, 1896), vol. 7, no. 164, 273. See also Emily S. Leavitt, *Animals and Their Legal Rights: A Survey of American Laws from 1641 to 1978* (Washington, D.C., 1978), 11–12. Ward's life is treated in Samuel Eliot Morison, *Builders of the Bay Colony* (Boston, 1964), ch. 7.

20. John Locke, *The Educational Writings of John Locke,* James L. Axtell, ed. (Cambridge, England, 1968), 225–226.

21. Keith Thomas, *Man and the Natural World: A History of the Modern Sensibility* (New York, 1981), esp. ch. 4.

22. The quotations, and a discussion of More, appear in Donald Worster, *Nature's Economy: The Roots of Ecology* (San Francisco, 1977), 41–42. A very good example of a contemporary animism comes from the motion picture *Star Wars* and its sequels, where a mysterious and powerful "Force" pervades the universe.

23. George Sessions, "Spinoza and Jeffers on Man in Nature," *Inquiry* 20 (Winter 1977), 481–528, and Sessions, "Western Process Metaphysics: Heraclitus, Whitehead, and Spinoza," in Bill Devall and George Sessions, eds., *Deep Ecology* (Salt Lake City, Utah, 1985), 236–242. Sessions elsewhere characterizes Spinoza's thought as "biotic egalitarianism": *Ecophilosophy* 2 (May 1979), 29. See also Paul Wienphal, *The Radical Spinoza* (New York, 1979); Arne Naess, *Freedom, Emotion, and Self-Subsistence: The Structure of a Central Part of Spinoza's Ethics* (Oslo, 1975); and Stuart Hampshire, *Spinoza* (London, 1951).

24. John Ray, *The Widsom of God Manifested in the Works of Creation* (London, 1691), 127–128. Useful secondary discussions appear in Worster, *Nature's Economy,* 42ff., and Charles E. Raven, *John Ray, Naturalist* (Cambridge, England, 1950), 452ff.

25. As quoted in Thomas, *Man and the Natural World,* 166–167.

26. Alexander Pope, *Essay on Man,* in Herbert Davis, ed., *Pope: Poetical Works* (London, 1966), 249, 259, 260.

27. Clifford Dobell, *Anthony van Leeuwenhoek and His "Little Animals"* (New York, 1958), 174, 243.

28. As quoted and discussed in Worster, *Nature's Economy,* 47–50.

29. Humphrey Primatt, *A Dissertation on the Duty of Mercy and Sin of Cruelty to Brute Animals* (London, 1776), 7–8, 321–322.

30. Jeremy Bentham, *An Introduction to the Principles of Morals and Legislation,* Laurence J. LaFleur, ed. (New York, 1948), 311.

31. Ibid.

32. Jeremy Bentham, "Principles of Penal Law" in *The Works of Jeremy Bentham,* John Bowring, ed. (London, 1843), vol. 1, 562.

33. Lawrence's 1796 treatise is hard to find. A more convenient source is the reprinted chapters in Edward Byron Nicholson, *The Rights of an Animal: A New Essay in Ethics* (London, 1879). The quotations occur on pages 79 and 81.

34. Ibid., 84, 85.

35. Ibid., 83. It is worth noting that in 1792, four years before Lawrence

wrote, Thomas Taylor produced an anonymous tract entitled *A Vindication of the Rights of Brutes*. But the book was a spoof of Thomas Paine's *Rights of Man* (1791–1792) and Mary Wollstonecraft's *A Vindication of the Rights of Women* (1792). Taylor's purpose was to show the absurdity of extending natural rights ideals. He wrote, tongue in cheek, that "vegetables, minerals, and even the most apparently contemptible clod of earth" should be accorded rights. Undoubtedly, he would have been amazed at the seriousness of recent calls for a land ethic and for the rights of rocks: see Edward Johnson, "Treating the Dirt: Environmental Ethics and Moral Theory," in Tom Regan, ed., *Earthbound: New Introductory Essays in Environmental Ethics* (Philadelphia, 1984), 336–365. Taylor's statement may be found in *A Vindication of the Rights of Brutes,* Louise Schutz Boar, ed. (Gainesville, Fla., 1966), 103.

36. James Turner, *Reckoning with the Beast: Animals, Pain and Humanity in the Victorian Mind* (Baltimore, Md., 1980); E. S. Turner, *All Heaven in a Rage* (London, 1964), 125–129; and Wellesley Pain, *Richard Martin* (London, 1925). The first two are detailed explorations of many forms of cruelty to animals and its opposition in English society, primarily in the eighteenth and nineteenth centuries. Other useful general treatments are Richard D. Ryder's chapter, "A History of Compassion," in Ryder, ed., *Victims of Science: The Use of Animals in Research* (London, 1975), 178–247; Gerald Carson, *Men, Beasts and Gods: A History of Cruelty and Kindness to Animals* (New York, 1972); and Charles D. Niven, *History of the Humane Movement* (London, 1967).

37. John Stuart Mill, *Principles of Political Economy* (1848), M. M. Robson, ed. (Toronto, 1965), vol. 2, 952.

38. See Turner, *All Heaven in a Rage;* Arthur W. Moss, *Valiant Crusade: The History of the RSPCA* (London, 1961); Edward G. Fairholme and Wellesley Pain, *A Century of Work for Animals: The History of the RSPCA, 1824–1934,* 2d ed. (London, 1934); and Lewis Gompertz, *Moral Iniquities on the Situation of Man and Brutes* (London, 1824). Gompertz was the first secretary of the RSPCA.

39. Richard D. French, *Antivivisection and Medical Science in Victorian Society* (Princeton, N.J., 1975). Frances Power Cobbe's autobiography is *Life of Frances Power Cobbe* (Boston, 1894). See also Turner, *Reckoning with the Beast,* 83ff.

40. As quoted in Nicholson, *Rights of an Animal,* frontispiece.

41. Nicholson, *Rights of an Animal,* 19, 32.

42. Ibid., 7. The italics are Nicholson's.

43. The best biographical treatment is in George Hendrick, *Henry Salt* (Urbana, Ill., 1977) and Hendrick, "Henry S. Salt, the Late Victorian Socialists, and Thoreau," *New England Quarterly* 50 (Sept. 1977), 409–422. See also Stephen Winsten, *Salt and His Circle* (London, 1951). *Animal Rights* first appeared as a tract in 1892; it was later published in book form.

44. Henry S. Salt, *Animals' Rights Considered in Relation to Social Progress* (New York, 1894), 7, 8, 16, 92, 90. The book was reissued in 1980 by the

Society for Animal Rights under the same title (Clarks Summit, Pa., 1980). A laudatory review of this edition is George Russell, "Bookfind," *Orion* 2 (Winter 1983), 36–37.

45. David G. Ritchie, *Natural Rights* (London, 1894), 111, 108.

46. Joseph Rickaby, *Moral Philosophy* (1901), as quoted in Tom Regan and Peter Singer, eds., *Animal Rights and Human Obligations* (Englewood Cliffs, N.J., 1976), 179–180. For a satirical expression of the same point see Rupert Hughes, "Animal and Vegetable Rights," *Harper's Monthly Magazine* 103 (1901), 852–853.

47. Salt, *Animals' Rights,* 104, 88.

48. Henry S. Salt, "Humanitarianism: Its General Principles and Progress," in Henry S. Salt, ed., *Cruelties of Civilization: Program of Humane Reform* (London, 1897), vii.

49. Henry S. Salt, *The Life of Henry David Thoreau* (London, 1890).

50. Henry S. Salt, *Seventy Years among Savages* (London, 1921), 64.

51. Salt, *Animals' Rights,* 92–93, 96, 98.

52. Ibid., 66, 53, 78, 133–168. The Royal Buckhound issue is treated in Hendrick, *Henry Salt,* 63–67, and Turner, *All Heaven in a Rage,* ch. 17.

53. William E. H. Lecky, *History of European Morals from Augustus to Charlemagne* (London, 1869), vol. 1, 103.

54. Salt, *Animals' Rights,* 16–17; Henry S. Salt, *The Creed of Kinship* (New York, 1935), viii.

55. For the publicity Salt gave to Thoreau's ideas see Fritz Oehlschlaeger and George Hendrick, eds., *Toward the Making of Thoreau's Modern Reputation* (Urbana, Ill., 1979). The first edition of Salt's biography of Thoreau appeared in 1890, a time when Salt could aptly characterize the American's work as "comparatively little known." Salt, *Life of Thoreau,* v.

56. Edward P. Evans, *Evolutionary Ethics and Animal Psychology* (London, 1898), 99–100.

57. W J McGee, "The Conservation of Natural Resources," *Proceedings of the Mississippi Valley Historical Association* 3 (1909–1910), 379.

58. Aldo Leopold, *A Sand County Almanac* (New York, 1949), 204.

59. Michael W. Fox, "Man and Nature: Biological Perspectives," in Richard Knowles Morris and Michael W. Fox, eds., *On the Fifth Day: Animal Rights and Human Ethics* (Washington, D.C., 1978), 118.

60. Theodore Roszak, *Person/Planet: The Creative Disintegration of an Industrial Society* (New York, 1978), 32.

CHAPTER 2
Ideological Origins of American Environmentalism

1. Bernard Bailyn, *The Ideological Origins of the American Revolution* (Cambridge, Mass., 1967), 232. Staughton Lynd's *Intellectual Origins of American Radicalism* (New York, 1968) makes a similar point.

2. John Adams, *Diary and Autobiography,* L. H. Butterfield, ed. (Cam-

bridge, Mass., 1961), vol. 1, 282. For commentary on American liberalism see Ralph Henry Gabriel and Robert H. Walker, *The Course of American Democratic Thought*, 3d ed. (New York, 1986), and Louis Hartz, *The Liberal Tradition in America* (New York, 1955).

3. Michael W. Fox, "What Future for Man and Earth? Toward a Bio-spiritual Ethic," in Richard Knowles Morris and Michael W. Fox, eds., *On the Fifth Day: Animal Rights and Human Ethics* (Washington, D.C., 1978), 219–220.

4. Salt was Thoreau's first biographer: Henry S. Salt, *Life of Henry David Thoreau* (London, 1890). See also Fritz Oehlschlaeger and George Hendrick, eds., *The Making of Thoreau's Modern Reputation* (Urbana, Ill., 1979).

5. On this point see Roderick Nash, *Wilderness and the American Mind* (New Haven, Conn., 1982), especially chs. 1 and 2; Leo Marx, "American Institutions and Ecological Ideals," *Science* 170 (Nov. 27, 1970), 945–952; and Henry Nash Smith, *Virgin Land: The American West as Symbol and Myth* (Cambridge, Mass., 1950).

6. Ralph Waldo Emerson, "Ode, Inscribed to W. H. Channing," in *Poems* (Boston, 1847), 119. The full quote is "Things are in the saddle and ride mankind."

7. *The Writings of Henry Thoreau*, Bradford Torrey, ed. (Boston, 1906), vol. 14, 306–307.

8. Donald Worster, *Nature's Economy: The Roots of Ecology* (San Francisco, 1977), 33, 37, 192.

9. Nicholas Collin, "An Essay on Those Inquiries in Natural Philosophy, which are at present Most Beneficial," *Transactions of the American Philosophical Society* 3 (1793), xxiv.

10. The phrase is Ralph Waldo Emerson's in his 1836 *Nature,* Warner Berthoff, ed. (San Francisco, 1968), 13. Secondary commentary on Transcendentalism may be found in Nash, *Wilderness,* ch. 5; Worster, *Nature's Economy;* and Sherman Paul, *The Shores of America: Thoreau's Inward Exploration* (Urbana, Ill., 1958).

11. *Writings of Thoreau,* vol. 3, 165.

12. Ibid., vol. 14, 166.

13. Ibid., vol. 9, 210.

14. Henry David Thoreau, *The Maine Woods,* Joseph J. Moldenhauer, ed., (Princeton, N.J., 1972), 181.

15. *Writings of Thoreau,* vol. 11, 450.

16. Thoreau, *Maine Woods,* 121.

17. *Writings of Thoreau,* vol. 4, 422; vol. 3, 381.

18. Ibid., vol. 10, 51.

19. George Perkins Marsh, *Man and Nature; Or, Physical Geography as Modified by Human Action* (Cambridge, Mass., 1965), 36, 45, 46, 91–92. David Lowenthal, *George Perkins Marsh: Versatile Vermonter* (New York, 1958) is the definitive biography.

20. Muir's comments in the *Boston Recorder* for December 21, 1866, are quoted in Stephen Fox, *The American Conservation Movement: John Muir and*

His Legacy (Madison, Wis., 1985), 43–44. Muir's life and thought are interpreted in Fox and in Frederick Turner, *Rediscovering America: John Muir in His Time and Ours* (New York, 1985); Michael Cohen, *The Pathless Way: John Muir and the American Wilderness* (Madison, Wis., 1984); Nash, *Wilderness*, ch. 8; and Edith Jane Hadley, "John Muir's Views of Nature and Their Consequences" (Ph.D. diss., University of Wisconsin, 1956).

21. *John of the Mountains: The Unpublished Journals of John Muir*, Linnie Marsh Wolfe, ed. (Boston, 1938), 138. On Muir's idea that rocks might be "endowed with sensation," capable of happiness and perhaps even endowed with rights, see Scott Lehman, "Do Wildernesses Have Rights?" *Environmental Ethics* 3 (Summer 1981), 136.

22. John Muir, *Our National Parks* (Boston, 1901), 57–58.

23. John Muir, *A Thousand-Mile Walk to the Gulf*, William F. Badé, ed. (Boston, 1917), 343. In the original version of this journal entry Muir wrote "*side* with the bears:" Cohen, *Pathless Way*, 23.

24. Lisa Mighetto, "John Muir and the Rights of Animals," in Mighetto, ed., *Muir among the Animals* (San Francisco, 1986), xii.

25. Muir, *A Thousand-Mile Walk to the Gulf*, 324, 356.

26. Ibid., 354–356; John Muir, "Wild Wool," *Overland Monthly* 20 (April 1875), 364.

27. John Muir, *My First Summer in the Sierra* (Boston, 1911), 211. The book was a composite of Muir's much earlier journals, somewhat reworked. The first draft of this statement, written July 27, 1869, just after Muir had his first view from the rim of Yosemite Valley, seems even more striking: "When we try to pick out anything by itself, we find that it is bound fast by a thousand invisible cords that cannot be broken to everything in the universe. I fancy I can hear a heart beating in every crystal, in every grain of sand and see a wise plan in the making and shaping and placing of every one of them. All seems to be dancing in time to divine music." (As quoted in Fox, *American Conservation Movement*, 291).

28. For elaboration see Nash, *Wilderness*, chs. 8 and 10; Lee Clark Mitchell, *Witnesses to a Vanishing America* (Princeton, N.J., 1981); Kendrick A. Clements, "Politics and the Park: San Francisco's Fight for Hetch Hetchy, 1908–1913," *Pacific Historical Review* 48 (May 1979), 185–215; and Holway R. Jones, *John Muir and the Sierra Club: The Battle for Yosemite* (San Francisco, 1965).

29. For example, John Muir, *The Yosemite* (New York, 1912), 261–262.

30. Bill Devall has criticized Muir on these grounds in "John Muir as Deep Ecologist," *Environmental Review* 6 (Spring 1982), 63–86.

31. Muir, *Yosemite*, 261–262; Muir to Robert Underwood Johnson, Feb. 7, 1909, and March 23, 1913, as quoted in Nash, *Wilderness*, 167.

32. As quoted in E. S. Turner, *All Heaven in a Rage* (London, 1964), 162.

33. Charles Darwin, *The Descent of Man and Selection in Relation to Sex* (New York, 1874), 81; Francis Darwin and A. C. Seward, eds., *More Letters of Charles Darwin* (London, 1903), vol. 1, 114. Useful secondary literature includes Worster, *Nature's Economy*, part 3; A. G. N. Flew, *Evolutionary Eth-*

ics (London, 1967); Gertrude Himmelfarb, *Darwin and the Darwinian Revolution* (Gloucester, Mass., 1967); and Gavin de Beer, *Charles Darwin* (Garden City, N.J., 1964).

34. Muir, *Thousand-Mile Walk,* 357–358.

35. Thomas Huxley, *Evolution and Ethics* (London, 1893), 46–116.

36. *The Writings of William James,* John J. McDermott, ed. (Chicago, 1977), 669.

37. See Richard Hofstadter, *Social Darwinism in American Thought* (Boston, 1955).

38. As quoted in George Hendrick, *Henry Salt* (Urbana, Ill., 1977), 62.

39. *The Life and Letters of Charles Darwin,* Francis Darwin, ed. (New York, 1888), vol. 1, 368.

40. Darwin, *Descent of Man,* 145. A few years later the Russian social philosopher Peter Kropotkin would extend this theme in *Mutual Aid* (New York, 1902).

41. Darwin, *Descent of Man,* 137, 138.

42. Ibid., 138, 140, 141. For a discussion of the place of ethics in Darwin's philosophy see Theodosius Dobzhansky, "Ethics and Values in Biological and Cultural Evolution," *Zygon* 8 (1973), 261–281.

43. Worster, *Nature's Economy,* 181.

44. De Beer, *Darwin,* 259–260; Turner, *All Heaven in a Rage,* 205, 207; E. Westacott, *A Century of Vivisection and Anti-Vivisection* (Ashingdon, England, 1949), 75, 308; Richard D. French, *Antivivisection and Medical Sciences in Victorian Society* (Princeton, N.J., 1975), 112–178. Donald Fleming's "Charles Darwin, The Anaesthetic Man," *Victorian Studies* 4 (March 1961), 219–236, examines Darwin's ideas on cruelty to animals.

45. Muir, *Yosemite,* 261–262.

46. Theodore Roszak, *Person/Planet: The Creative Disintegration of an Industrial Society* (New York, 1978), 33.

47. William E. H. Lecky, *History of European Morals from Augustus to Charlemagne* (London, 1869), vol. 1, 143, 103; Darwin, *Descent of Man,* 140.

48. *The Complete Writings of Thomas Paine,* Philip S. Foner, ed. (New York, 1945), vol. 1, 512.

49. The best accounts of Bergh and his work are Alvin Fay Harlow, *Henry Bergh: Founder of the ASPCA* (New York, 1957) and Zelma Steele, *Angel in Top Hat* (New York, 1942). James Turner, *Reckoning with the Beast: Animals, Pain and Humanity in the Victorian Mind* (Baltimore, 1980) discusses Bergh and other nineteenth-century American humanitarians in the context of Anglo-American thought about animals. Along with the ASPCA (1866), the American Humane Association (1874) and the American Anti-Vivisection Society (1883) are key institutional landmarks of the movement.

50. Steele, *Angel in Top Hat,* 36–37.

51. Roswell C. McCrea, *The Humane Movement: A Descriptive Survey* (New York, 1910), 33–34. Emily S. Leavitt, *Animals and Their Legal Rights. A Survey of American Laws from 1641 to 1978* (Washington, D.C., 1978) is a comprehensive digest which reveals the wide variety of state laws that

attempted to regulate human conduct toward animals. As early as 1829 a New York law forbade cruelty to domestic animals, but it had never been enforced.

52. George T. Angell, *Autobiographical Sketches and Personal Recollections,* (Boston, 1898), 8–9, 94–97.

53. Stowe and Beecher are quoted in Steele, *Angel in Top Hat,* 286–290.

54. The secondary literature on early American humanitarianism includes Andrew N. Rowan, *Of Mice, Models and Men: A Critical Evaluation of Animal Research* (Albany, 1984); Turner, *Reckoning with the Beast;* Leavitt, *Animals and Their Legal Rights;* John Rodman, "The Liberation of Nature," *Inquiry* 20 (Spring 1977), 83–131; Charles D. Niven, *History of the Humane Movement* (London, 1967); William J. Schultz, *The Humane Movement in the United States, 1910–1922* (New York, 1924); and McCrea, *The Humane Movement.*

Turner is particularly critical of the humane movement, arguing that by the early part of the twentieth century it had become a "conventional reflex" reduced to an emphasis on dog and cat shelters: *Reckoning with the Beast,* 138 and 122–127. But such a dismissal ignores the important role humanitarianism played in widening the ethical circle beyond its conventional fixation on humans.

55. J. Baird Callicott, "Animal Liberation: A Triangular Affair," *Environmental Ethics* 2 (Winter 1980), 311–338. The quote, by Kenneth Goodpaster, appears on p. 315. Callicott has softened his position on the incompatibility of animal liberation and environmental ethics in a book review: *Canadian Philosophical Review* 10 (1986), 464–467. A balanced assessment of the relationship between the humane movement and environmental ethics, critical of Callicott, is Mary Anne Warren, "The Rights of the Nonhuman World," in Robert Elliot and Arran Gare, eds., *Environmental Philosophy: A Collection of Readings* (University Park, Pa., 1983), 109–134. For further commentary on this dispute see ch. 5, below.

56. Mark Sagoff, "Animal Liberation and Environmental Ethics: Bad Marriage, Quick Divorce," *Osgood Hall Law Journal* 22 (Summer 1984), 297–307.

57. See Roderick Nash, ed., *The American Environment: Readings in Conservation History* (Reading, Mass., 1976), 36–93 and Samuel Hays, *Conservation and the Gospel of Efficiency: The Progressive Conservation Movement, 1890–1920* (Cambridge, Mass., 1959).

58. As quoted in McCrea, *Humane Movement,* 250. See also Lisa Mighetto, "Wild Animals in American Thought and Culture, 1870s–1930s" (Ph.D. diss., University of Washington, 1986); James A. Tober, *Who Owns the Wildlife? The Political Economy of Conservation in Nineteenth Century America* (Westport, Conn., 1981); James B. Trefethen, *An American Crusade for Wildlife* (New York, 1975), ch. 13; and John F. Rieger, *The Passing of the Great West: Selected Papers of George Bird Grinnell* (New York, 1972).

59. McCrea, *Humane Movement,* 247.

60. Henry George, *Progress and Poverty* (San Francisco, 1879), 490–496.

61. Staughton Lynd, *Intellectual Origins of American Radicalism* (New York, 1968), 5ff.; Charles A. Barker, *Henry George* (New York, 1955); George Hendrick, "Henry S. Salt, the Late Victorian Socialists, and Thoreau," *New England Quarterly* 50 (Sept. 1977), 412.

62. W J McGee, "The Conservation of Natural Resources," *Proceedings of the Mississippi Valley Historical Association* 3 (1909–1910), 379. I have reproduced McGee's paper in *The American Environment,* 42–46.

63. Edward P. Evans, *Animal Symbolism in Ecclesiastical Architecture* (London, 1896) and *The Criminal Prosecution and Capital Punishment of Animals* (New York, 1906).

64. Evans's *Popular Science Monthly* essay appeared in his book, *Evolutional Ethics and Animal Psychology* (New York, 1897), 82–104; the references here are to pages 83, 88–99, and 91. The essay may also be found in an abridged form in Donald Worster, ed., *American Environmentalism: The Formative Period, 1860–1915* (New York, 1973), 198–208.

65. Evans, *Evolutional Ethics,* 99–100.

66. Ibid., 4

67. See Nash, *Wilderness,* ch. 9; Peter J. Schmitt, *Back to Nature: The Arcadian Myth in Urban America* (New York, 1969); and Hans Huth, *Nature and the American* (Berkeley, Cal., 1957).

68. Ernest Thompson Seton, *Wild Animals I Have Known* (New York, 1898), 357.

69. Henry S. Salt, *Company I Have Kept* (London, 1930), 110–112.

70. J. Howard Moore, *The Universal Kinship* (London, 1906), 107, 239, 297; Moore, *The New Ethics,* rev. ed. (Chicago, 1909), 215.

71. Moore, *Universal Kinship,* vii, 324; Moore, *New Ethics,* 15, 19.

72. Moore, *Universal Kinship,* 324, 273; Moore, *New Ethics,* 169.

73. Moore, *Universal Kinship,* 281, 324.

74. Ibid., viii, 329; Moore, *New Ethics,* 13.

75. Evans, *Evolutional Ethics,* 164.

CHAPTER 3
Ecology Widens the Circle

1. Donald Worster's *Nature's Economy: The Roots of Ecology* (San Francisco, 1977) is the definitive history of ecology as both science and philosophy. Sharon E. Kingsland, *Modeling Nature: Episodes in the History of Population Ecology* (Chicago, 1985); Robert P. McIntosh, *The Background of Ecology: Concept and Theory* (Cambridge, England, 1985); and Ronald C. Tobey, *Saving the Prairies: The Life-Cycle of the Founding School of American Plant Ecology, 1895–1955* (Berkeley, Cal., 1981) explore ecology from the history of science perspective. Older, but still useful, summaries are Charles S. Elton, *The Pattern of Animal Communities* (London, 1966), 29–44; Richard C. Brewer, "A Brief History of Ecology," *Occasional Papers of the C. C. Adams Center for Ecological Studies* 1 (1960); and W. C. Allee, et al.,

Principles of Animal Ecology (Philadelphia, 1949), 1–72. Thomas R. Dunlap, *"Interpreting Nature Aright"*: *Science and Wildlife Preservation in America* (Princeton, N.J., 1988), and Joseph V. Siry, *Marshes of the Ocean Shore: Development of an Ecological Ethic* (College Station, Tex., 1984) are important reviews of the contributions of ecologists to the understanding of the natural world.

2. Aldo Leopold, *A Sand County Almanac* (New York, 1949), 203.

3. Ronald Engels, *Sacred Sands: The Struggle for Community in the Indiana Dunes* (Middletown, Conn., 1983), 135–182; Andrew Denny Rodgers, *American Botany, 1873–1892: Decades of Transition* (Princeton, N.J., 1944).

4. Frederic Clements, *Plant Succession* (Washington, D.C., 1916); J. Arthur Thompson, *The System of Animate Nature* (London, 1920), vol. 1, 58–59.

5. Liberty Hyde Bailey, *The Holy Earth* (New York, 1915), 14, 24, 30–31. For secondary analysis see Stephen Fox, "Liberty Hyde Bailey: The Earth as Whole, the Earth as Holy," *Orion* 2 (Autumn 1983), 13–23; Philip Dorf, *Liberty Hyde Bailey: An Informal Biography* (New York, 1956); and Andrew Denny Rodgers: *Liberty Hyde Bailey: A Story of American Plant Science* (Princeton, N.J., 1949), 405ff.

6. Frederic Clements and Victor Shelford, *Bio-Ecology* (New York, 1939).

7. Charles Elton, *Animal Ecology* (New York, 1927), especially ch. 5.

8. Arthur G. Tansley, "The Use and Abuse of Vegetational Concepts and Terms," *Ecology* 16 (July 1935), 284–307; Leopold, *Round River: From the Journals of Aldo Leopold,* Luna Leopold, ed. (New York, 1935); Eugene Odum, "Environmental Ethics and the Attitude Revolution," in William T. Blackstone, ed. *Philosophy and the Environmental Crisis* (Athens, Ga., 1974), 10–15. For analysis of the impact of ecology on modern conceptions of the nature of biophysical reality and on metaphysics see J. Baird Callicott, "The Metaphysical Implications of Ecology," *Environmental Ethics* 8 (Winter 1986), 301–316.

9. Worster, *Nature's Economy,* ch. 13, entitled "The Value of a Varmint," is a skillful treatment of the predator issue. Also useful are Thomas R. Dunlap, "Values for Varmints: Predator Control and Environmental Ideas, 1920–1939," *Pacific Historical Review* 53 (May 1984), 141–161, and James B. Trefethen, *An American Crusade for Wildlife* (New York, 1975).

10. As quoted from manuscripts in Stephen Fox, *The American Conservation Movement: John Muir and His Legacy* (Madison, Wis., 1985), 267–268, and Worster, *Nature's Economy,* 283.

11. William Morton Wheeler, "Emergent Evolution of the Social," *Science* 64 (Nov. 5, 1926), 433–440. Wheeler's *Essays in Philosophical Biology* (Cambridge, Mass., 1939) amplifies his theories. Also useful is Mary Alice and Howard E. Evans, *William Morton Wheeler, Biologist* (Cambridge, Mass., 1970), especially 263ff.

12. Alfred Emerson, "The Biological Basis of Social Cooperation," *Transactions of the Illinois Academy of Science* 39 (May 1946), 9–18.

13. Walter P. Taylor, "Significance of the Biotic Community in Ecological Studies," *Quarterly Review of Biology* 10 (Sept. 1935), 296.

14. As quoted in Walter P. Taylor, "What Is Ecology and What Good Is It?" *Ecology* 17 (July 1936), 335–336.

15. Whitehead's principal books are *The Concept of Nature* (Ann Arbor, Mich., 1920), *Science and the Modern World* (New York, 1925), and *Process and Reality* (New York, 1929). A useful collection of so-called process philosophy, including statements by both Whitehead and his followers, is Jack R. Sibley and Pete A. Y. Gunter, eds., *Process Philosophy: Basic Writings* (Washington, D.C., 1978). For Whitehead's importance to ecotheology see below, pp. 106ff.

16. The most recent biography is James Brabazon, *Albert Schweitzer* (New York, 1975). See also George Seaver, *Albert Schweitzer: The Man and His Mind* (London, 1969); Henry Clark, *The Ethical Mysticism of Albert Schweitzer* (Boston, 1962); and Norman Cousins, *Doctor Schweitzer of Lambaréné* (New York, 1960).

17. Albert Schweitzer, *Out of My Life and Thought: An Autobiography* (New York, 1933), 185, 188.

18. Ibid., 188.

19. Albert Schweitzer, *Philosophy of Civilization: Civilization and Ethics,* John Naish, trans. (London, 1923), 254.

20. Schweitzer, *Out of My Life,* 271.

21. Albert Schweitzer, *The Animal World of Albert Schweitzer,* Charles R. Joy, trans. (Boston, 1950), 189–190.

22. Commentary on this point may be found in Herbert Spiegelberg, "Albert Schweitzer's 'Other Thought,' Fortune Obligates," *Africa: Thought and Praxis* 1 (1974), and in William T. Blackstone, "In Search of an Environmental Ethic," in Tom Regan, ed., *Matters of Life and Death* (Philadelphia, 1980), 299–335.

23. Schweitzer, *Philosophy of Civilization,* 264; Schweitzer, *Animal World,* 183, 187, 188.

24. Albert Schweitzer, *Indian Thought and Its Development,* C. E. B. Russell, trans. (New York, 1936), 261–262; Schweitzer, *Animal World,* 169.

25. Stewart L. Udall, *The Quiet Crisis* (New York, 1963), 206.

26. J. Baird Callicott, "Animal Liberation: A Triangular Affair," *Environmental Ethics* 2 (Winter 1980), 311.

27. Wallace Stegner, "Living on Our Principal," *Wilderness* 48 (Spring 1985), 15; Donald Fleming, "Roots of the New Conservation Movement," *Perspectives in American History* 6 (1972), 18; Clay Schoenfeld, "Aldo Leopold Remembered," *Audubon* 80 (May 1978), 79; Foreman as quoted in Mark Vaz, "Leaves of Green," *Sierra* 71 (May–June 1986), 56.

28. Van Rensselaer Potter, *Bioethics: Bridge to the Future* (Englewood Cliffs, N.J., 1971), v; René Dubos, *A God Within* (New York, 1972), 156.

29. Aldo Leopold, "Wherefore Wildlife Ecology?" undated lecture notes, Aldo Leopold Papers, University of Wisconsin Archives, Madison, Wis., Box 8; Leopold, *Round River,* 146–147. Biographical information may be found in Roderick Nash, *Wilderness and the American Mind* (New Haven, Conn., 1982), ch. 11; Edward Schriver, "Leopold's Land Ethic: Wishful Thinking or Workable Dream?" *Sierra Club Bulletin* 62 (March

1977), 9–11, 16; Worster, *Nature's Economy,* 271–274, 284–290; Nash, "Aldo Leopold," *Dictionary of American Biography* (New York, 1974), vol. 4, 482–484; Fleming, "Roots of the New Conservation," 18–27; and especially in Curt Meine, *Aldo Leopold: His Life and Work* (Madison, Wis., 1988), and Susan L. Flader, *Thinking Like a Mountain: Aldo Leopold and the Evolution of an Ecological Attitude toward Deer, Wolves, and Forests* (Columbia, Mo., 1974). Flader's *The Sand Country of Aldo Leopold* (San Francisco, 1973) also contains biographical data, as does Boyd Gibbons, "Aldo Leopold: A Durable Scale of Values," *National Geographic* 160 (Nov. 1981), 682–708. J. Baird Callicott, ed., *Companion to* A Sand County Almanac: *Interpretive and Critical Essays* (Madison, Wis., 1987), and Thomas Tanner, ed., *Aldo Leopold: The Man and His Legacy* (Ankeny, Ia., 1987) contain the most recent Leopold scholarship.

    30. Aldo Leopold, *A Sand County Almanac* (New York, 1949), 129–130.

    31. Leopold's 1923 essay was finally published, thanks to the efforts of Eugene C. Hargrove: "Some Fundamentals of Conservation in the Southwest," *Environmental Ethics* 1 (Summer 1979), 131–141.

    32. Peter D. Ouspensky, *Tertium Organum: The Third Canon of Thought, A Key to the Enigmas of the World,* E. Kadloubovsky, trans. (New York, 1981), 166.

    33. Ibid., 118, 166, 168; Leopold, "Some Fundamentals," 140.

    34. Leopold, "Some Fundamentals," 139–140.

    35. John Burroughs, *Accepting the Universe* (Boston, 1920), 32.

    36. Leopold, "Some Fundamentals," 140–141.

    37. Susan L. Flader, "Leopold's *Some Fundamentals of Conservation:* A Commentary," *Environmental Ethics* 1 (Summer 1979), 143.

    38. Ouspensky, *Tertium Organum,* 179.

    39. Aldo Leopold, "The Conservation Ethic," *Journal of Forestry* 31 (October 1933), 634, 635, 640.

    40. Ibid., 634; J. Baird Callicott, "The Land Aesthetic," *Environmental Review* 7 (Winter 1983), 345; J. Baird Callicott, "The Scientific Substance of the Land Ethic," in Tanner, ed., *Aldo Leopold,* 87.

    41. These were, in particular, "A Biotic View of Land," *Journal of Forestry* 37 (Sept. 1939), 727–730, and "The Ecological Conscience," *Bulletin of the Garden Club of America* (Sept. 1947), 45–53.

    42. Leopold, *A Sand County Almanac,* 203–204, 205, 218, 226, viii. The best analyses of this book as a work of literary craft are Dennis Ribbens, "The Making of *A Sand County Almanac,*" in Callicott, ed., *Companion,* 91–109, and Peter A. Fritzell, "Aldo Leopold's *A Sand County Almanac* and the Conflicts of Ecological Conscience," *Transactions of the Wisconsin Academy of Sciences, Arts and Letters* 64 (Fall 1976), 22–46. The Fritzell essay also appears, somewhat abridged, in the Callicott book. A related study, linking Leopold's ideas of beauty to ecology, is J. Baird Callicott, "The Land Aesthetic," *Orion* 3 (Summer 1984), 16–23.

    43. Leopold, *A Sand County Almanac,* 204, 209, 211.

44. The distinction between Leopold as a holistic ethicist and the animal liberationists has been emphasized by J. Baird Callicott in "Animal Liberation," 311–338, and Callicott, "Elements of an Environmental Ethic: Moral Considerability and the Biotic Community," *Environmental Ethics* 1 (Spring 1979), 71–81. Also pertinent are Callicott, "Hume's *Is/Ought* Dichotomy and the Relation of Ecology to Leopold's Land Ethic," *Environmental Ethics* 4 (Summer 1982), 163–174, and John Rodman, "The Liberation of Nature?" *Inquiry* 20 (Spring 1977), 83–131. For a rebuttal supporting the present thesis that proponents of animal liberation and holistic or land ethics are more complementary than contradictory, see Mary Anne Warren, "The Rights of the Nonhuman World," in Robert Elliott and Arran Gare, eds., *Environmental Philosophy: A Collection of Readings* (University Park, Pa., 1983), 109–134. Another perspective, also critical of Callicott, may be found in Marti Kheel, "The Liberation of Nature: A Circular Affair," *Environmental Ethics* 7 (Summer 1985), 135–149. Callicott has softened his position on the incompatibility of animal liberation and environmental ethics in a review in *Canadian Philosophical Review* 10 (1986), 464–467.

45. Leopold, "Conservation Ethic," 641; Leopold, *A Sand County Almanac,* 224–225. Leopold's first published version of the "integrity" axiom appeared in "The Ecological Conscience," 52, and it stressed the common membership of humans and other life-forms in one community. The 1947 version reads: "A thing is right only when it tends to preserve the integrity, stability, and beauty of the community, and the community includes the soil, waters, fauna, and flora, as well as people." Extensive analysis of this idea appears in Tom Regan, ed., *Earthbound: New Introductory Essays in Environmental Ethics* (Philadelphia, 1984), 268ff., 351ff., and James D. Heffernan, "The Land Ethic: A Critical Appraisal," *Environmental Ethics* 4 (Fall 1982), 235–247. Regan, who disagrees with Leopold's de-emphasis of the rights of individual organisms, comments on Leopold's thought in *The Case for Animal Rights* (Berkeley, Cal., 1983), 361ff.

Jon N. Moline has recently called attention to Leopold's alleged inconsistency in extending biotic rights to individuals while at the same time advocating a holistic "land ethic" that necessarily accepted sacrifice of one individual in the food chain to another. According to Moline it is incorrect—despite what Leopold wrote—to regard his ethics as a simple extension of natural rights from human to nonhuman organisms. He was, first and foremost, concerned with the welfare of the ecosystem as a whole, and he used the idea of rights to advance conduct that was conducive to that end. Jon N. Moline, "Aldo Leopold and the Moral Community," *Environmental Ethics* 8 (Summer 1986), 99–120.

46. Worster, *Nature's Economy,* 288.

47. Leopold, *A Sand County Almanac,* 214. For Leopold's ideas on wildlife control see his *Game Management* (New York, 1933). For extended commentary on his work as a game manager see Flader, *Thinking Like a Mountain.*

48. Leopold, "Some Fundamentals," 141; Burroughs, *Accepting the Universe,* 35.

49. Chauncey D. Leake, "Ethicogenesis," *Scientific Monthly* 60 (April 1945), 248.

50. Leopold, *A Sand County Almanac,* 209–210; Leopold, *Round River,* 155.

51. Leopold, "The Ecological Conscience," 53. Underscoring the importance of ecology to his ethical system, Leopold used the term "ecological conscience" synonymously with "the land ethic" in *A Sand County Almanac.*

52. Worster, *Nature's Economy,* 289–315, 331–332; Kingsland, *Modeling Nature,* chs. 7, 8.

53. McIntosh, *Background of Ecology,* 308–323.

54. Along with Joseph Wood Krutch, *More Lives than One* (New York, 1962), the best source for Krutch's life and thought is John D. Margolis, *Joseph Wood Krutch: A Writer's Life* (Knoxville, Tenn., 1980).

55. Joseph Wood Krutch, *The Modern Temper: A Study and a Confession* (New York, 1929), 249.

56. Ibid., p. 97.

57. Joseph Wood Krutch, *Grand Canyon: Today and All Its Yesterdays* (New York, 1958), 275.

58. Joseph Wood Krutch, "Conservation Is Not Enough," *American Scholar* 24 (Summer 1954), 297.

59. Ibid., 298, 301, 302.

60. Ibid., 296, 298, 302, 304.

61. Arthur O. Lovejoy's *The Great Chain of Being* (Cambridge, Mass., 1936) documents the history of this idea. Krutch discusses his own book in *More Lives than One,* 335ff.

62. Joseph Wood Krutch, *The Great Chain of Life* (Boston, 1956), 153.

63. Olaus Murie, "Ethics in Wildlife Management," *Journal of Wildlife Management* 18 (July 1954), 289–293.

64. Leopold, *A Sand County Almanac,* 109, 204.

65. As quoted in Anne Chisholm, *Philosophers of the Earth: Conversations with Ecologists* (New York, 1972), 15. Dubos's principal statements occur in *Man Adapting* (New Haven, Conn., 1965); *Mirage of Health, Utopias, Progress and Biological Change* (New York, 1959); and *Biochemical Determinants of Microbial Diseases* (Cambridge, Mass., 1954). Biographical information is available in Chisholm's book; in Fleming, "Roots of the New Conservation Movement," 34–39; and in John Culhane, *"En Garde,* Pessimists! Enter René Dubos," *New York Times Magazine,* October 17, 1971, 44ff.

66. René Dubos, "The Despairing Optimist," *American Scholar* 40 (Winter 1970–1971), 16–20.

67. René Dubos, *A God Within* (New York, 1972), 45.

68. For extended commentary on Stowe, abolitionism, and the Civil War as they shed light on modern environmentalism, see the Epilogue, below.

69. Biographical treatment may be found in Paul Brooks, *The House of Life: Rachel Carson at Work* (Boston, 1972), and Phillip Sterling, *Sea and Earth: The Life of Rachel Carson* (New York, 1970). Carol B. Gartner, *Rachel Carson* (New York, 1983) is primarily a literary analysis. Siry, *Marshes of the Ocean Shore,* 134ff., and Fleming, "Roots of the New Conservation Movement," 11ff. are also valuable.

70. Brooks, *House of Life,* 8.

71. Thomas R. Dunlap, *DDT: Scientists, Citizens, and Public Policy* (Princeton, N.J., 1981) is the definitive treatment of the pesticide controversy. Also informative is James Whorton, *Before Silent Spring: Pesticides and Public Health in Pre-DDT America* (Princeton, N.J., 1974).

72. Rachel Carson, *Silent Spring* (Boston, 1962), 12–13, 99–100.

73. Ibid., 251.

74. Brooks, *House of Life,* 243–244.

75. Carson, *Silent Spring,* 126, 189, 297.

76. Ibid., 275, 297. Carson's *The Sense of Wonder* (New York, 1965) also expresses these ideals.

77. As quoted in Brooks, *House of Life,* 315–317; Carson, *Silent Spring,* 297. It is interesting that, close as Rachel Carson's ideas were to those of Aldo Leopold, she never quoted nor even mentioned his writings, with which she must have been familiar. Albert Schweitzer remained her only acknowledged source of inspiration.

78. The debate over *Silent Spring* is analyzed in detail in Frank Graham, Jr., *Since Silent Spring* (Boston, 1970), 48ff. Ralph H. Lutts argues that public fear of nuclear fallout, peaking at the time of *Silent Spring*'s publication, increased the level of controversy over the book: "Chemical Fallout: Rachel Carson's *Silent Spring*, Radioactive Fallout and the Environmental Movement," *Environmental Review* 9 (Fall 1985), 211–225. Dunlap, *DDT,* 102ff. first discerned this connection.

79. Samuel P. Hays, "From Conservation to Environment: Environmental Politics in the United States since World War II," *Environmental Review* 6 (Fall 1982), 14–41; Hays, *Beauty, Health and Permanence: Environmental Politics in the United States, 1955–1985* (Cambridge, England, 1987).

80. Edward O. Wilson, *Biophilia* (Cambridge, Mass., 1984), 119.

81. The most convenient sources of Edward O. Wilson's ideas about the nature of ethics are *Sociobiology: The Abridged Edition* (Cambridge, Mass., 1980), 287–288, and *On Human Nature* (Cambridge, Mass., 1978). The quotations above are from Wilson, *Biophilia,* 121, 138 and Wilson, "Million-Year Histories: Species Diversity as an Ethical Goal," *Wilderness* 48 (Summer 1984), 14–15. Comparable statements of the instrumental value of species are Paul Ehrlich and Anne Ehrlich, *Extinction: The Cause and Consequence of the Disappearance of Species* (New York, 1981), and Norman Myers, *The Sinking Ark: A New Look at the Problem of Disappearing Species* (Oxford, 1979). See Chapters 4 and 6, below, for the ethical and political ramifications of the endangered species issue.

82. Wilson, *Biophilia,* 85, 139; Wilson, "Million-Year Histories," 13, 17. Wilson's most recent statement of these ideas is "The Biological Diversity Crisis," *BioScience* 35 (Dec. 1985), 700–706.

83. David Ehrenfeld, *The Arrogance of Humanism* (New York, 1978). An earlier statement of Ehrenfeld's ideas appeared as "The Conservation of Non-Resources," *American Scientist* 64 (Nov.–Dec. 1976), 648–656.

84. Ehrenfeld, *Arrogance of Humanism,* vii–viii, 208, 210; Ehrenfeld, "Conservation of Non-Resources," 655. At the time of Ehrenfeld's publications the furbish lousewort had received extensive publicity in connection with a Maine hydroelectric project that would have flooded its only known habitat.

85. Ehrenfeld, *Arrogance of Humanism,* 208–209; Bernard Dixon, "Smallpox: Imminent Extinction, and an Unresolved Dilemma," *New Scientist* 26 (Feb. 1976), 430–432. For Lynn White's use of smallpox to dramatize the meaning of extended ethics see below, p. 95.

86. See Potter, *Bioethics,* and George H. Kieffer, *Bioethics: A Textbook of Issues* (Reading, Mass., 1979).

87. George Sessions has investigated this relationship in "The Deep Ecology Movement: A Review," *Environmental Review* 11 (Summer 1987), 105–125. On the environmental implications of countercultural thinking see Nash, *Wilderness,* ch. 12.

88. Ehrenfeld, *Arrogance of Humanism,* 208, 210; Wilson, "Million-Year Histories," 14.

CHAPTER 4
The Greening of Religion

1. Aldo Leopold, *A Sand County Almanac* (New York, 1949), 209–210; Charles A. Reich, *The Greening of America* (New York, 1970).

2. Harold W. Wood, Jr., "Modern Pantheism as an Approach to Environmental Ethics," *Environmental Ethics* 7 (Summer 1985), 151.

3. Lynn White, Jr., "The Historical Roots of Our Ecologic Crisis," *Science* 155 (March 10, 1967), 1203–1207. White anticipated his thesis twenty years earlier in "Natural Science and Naturalistic Art in the Middle Ages," *American Historical Review* 52 (April 1947), 421–435. Ian McHarg's well-known *Design with Nature* (Garden City, N.J., 1969), 24–26, 44, contained an apparently independent analysis of Christianity that paralleled White's. Morris Berman, *The Reenchantment of the World* (Ithaca, N.Y., 1981) is one of several recent elaborations of White's insights.

White's 1967 essay was initially a lecture and admittedly a suggestive rather than definitive study. It touched off a storm of controversy in the late 1960s which must be understood as a function of so-called countercultural disenchantment with established institutions as well as misgivings in the Christian community about its own contributions to contemporary social and environmental problems. Eugene C. Hargrove has recently called on theologians to move "beyond the Lynn White debate" and edited a collection of papers to that end: Eugene C. Hargrove, ed., *Religion and Environmental Crisis* (Athens, Ga., 1986).

Edward P. Evans was the first American writer to anticipate White's thesis (see above, pp. 50ff.). In the nineteenth century Arthur Schopenhauer recognized the "unnatural distinction" Christianity made between humankind and animals. "Christianity," he wrote, "contains in fact a great and essential imperfection in limiting its precepts to man, and in refusing rights to the entire animal world." Arthur Schopenhauer, *Religion: A Dialogue and Other Essays,* 2d ed. (London, 1890), 112.

4. White, "Historical Roots," 1205.

5. Genesis 1:27–28 as translated in *The Holy Bible: Revised Standard Edition,* Thomas Nelson and Sons edition (New York, 1953), 2.

6. Genesis 9:2–3, Ibid., 8.

7. White, "Historical Roots," 1207. For a rebuttal to White, contending that orthodox Christianity is ecologically responsible, see Vincent Rossi, "Church and Ecology: Ecological Reformation or Patristic Renewal?" *The Eleventh Commandment Newsletter* 4 (1986), 4–5.

8. White, "Historical Roots," 1206.

9. Lynn White, Jr., "Continuing the Conversation," in Ian G. Barbour, ed., *Western Man and Environmental Ethics* (Reading, Mass., 1973), 61.

10. W. Lee Humphreys, "Pitfalls and Promises of Biblical Texts as a Basis for a Theology of Nature," in Glenn C. Stone, ed., *A New Ethic for a New Earth,* Faith-Man-Nature Papers, no. 2 (Andover, Conn., 1971), 100–101. Humphreys concludes that "man of this century will not find a ready-made theology of nature in the Bible; he must create and recreate his own" (p. 115). For discussions that differ from White on the meaning of Genesis 1:28 see James Barr, "Man and Nature: The Ecological Controversy and the Old Testament," in David Spring and Eileen Spring, eds., *Ecology and Religion in History* (New York, 1959) and Thomas S. Deer, "Religious Responsibility for the Environmental Crisis: An Argument Run Amok," *Worldview* 18 (Jan. 1975), 30–45.

11. For details on the Christian view of nature, historically conceived, see Keith Thomas, *Man and the Natural World: A History of the Modern Sensibility* (New York, 1983), 17ff.; John Passmore, *Man's Responsibility for Nature: Ecological Problems and Western Traditions* (New York, 1974); and Clarence Glacken, *Traces on the Rhodian Shore: Nature and Culture in Western Thought from Ancient Times to the End of the Eighteenth Century* (Berkeley, Cal., 1967), especially ch. 4. H. Paul Santmire's *The Travail of Nature: The Ambiguous Ecological Promise of Christian Theology* (Philadelphia, 1985) is a recent, comprehensive study of the meaning of nature in Christian thought. See also Robin Attfield, "Christian Attitudes to Nature," *Journal of the History of Ideas* 44 (July–Sept. 1983), 369–386, and George H. Williams, "Christian Attitudes toward Nature," *Christian Scholars Review* 2 (Fall 1971 and Winter 1972), 33–35, and 112–126. Attfield's "Western Traditions and Environmental Ethics," in Robert Elliot and Arran Gare, eds., *Environmen-*

tal Philosophy (University Park, Pa., 1983), 201–228, is also useful, as is Robert S. Brumbaugh, "Of Man, Animals and Morals: A Brief History," in Richard Knowles Morris and Michael W. Fox, eds., *On the Fifth Day: Animal Rights and Human Ethics* (Washington, D.C., 1978), 6–25. Jewish attitudes toward nature, traditional and contemporary, are studied in Jonathan Helfand, "The Earth Is the Lord's: Judaism and Environmental Ethics," in Hargrove, ed., *Religion and Environmental Crisis,* 38–52; David Ehrenfeld and Joan Ehrenfeld, "Some Thoughts on Nature and Judaism," *Environmental Ethics* 7 (Spring 1985), 93–95; and Albert Vorspan, "The Crisis of Ecology: Judaism and the Environment," in *Jewish Values and Social Crisis* (New York, 1970).

12. Martin Buber, *I and Thou,* Walter Kaufmann, trans. (New York, 1970). Robert E. Wood's *Martin Buber's Ontology: An Analysis of I and Thou* (Evanston, Ill., 1969) is a helpful comment.

13. Among the many titles concerning the meaning of the Bible for human-nature relations, the following proved particularly useful: Martin LaBar, "A Biblical Perspective on Nonhuman Organisms: Values, Moral Considerability, and Moral Agency," in Hargrove, ed., *Religion and Environmental Crisis,* 76–93; Richard H. Hiers, "Ecology, Biblical Theology, and Methodology: Biblical Perspectives on the Environment," *Zygon* 19 (March 1984), 43–59; Susan Power Bratton, "Christian Ecotheology and the Old Testament," *Environmental Ethics* 6 (Fall 1984), 195–209; Gerhard Hasel, *Old Testament Theology: Basic Issues in the Current Debate* (Grand Rapids, Mich., 1972); Gordon D. Kaufman, "A Problem for Theology: The Concept of Nature," *Harvard Theological Review* 65 (1972), 337–366; John Black, *The Dominion of Man: The Search for Ecological Responsibility* (Edinburgh, 1970), chs. 2–4; Walter Eichrodt, *Theology of the Old Testament* (Philadelphia, 1967); C. F. D. Moule, *Man and Nature in the New Testament* (Philadelphia, 1964); Gerhard von Rad, *Old Testament Theology* (New York, 1962); and Eric C. Rust, *Nature and Man in Biblical Thought* (London, 1953).

Mircea Eliade's *The Sacred and the Profane* (New York, 1959) remains an important investigation of what Eliade calls the "secularization of nature," while Berman, *The Reenchantment of the World* and Sam Keen, *Apology for Wonder* (New York, 1969) are more recent examinations of the same subject. D. H. Lawrence wrote a delightful essay on the implications of the end of animism: "Pan in America," in Edward D. McDonald, ed., *Phoenix: The Posthumous Papers of D. H. Lawrence* (New York, 1936), 22–31. According to Lawrence, the old Greek god of the mountain wilderness, called Pan, became the Christians' devil, complete with cloven hoofs and tail. There can be no more graphic evidence of Christians' attitude toward pantheism.

14. White, "Historical Roots," 1205.

15. Roderick Nash, *Wilderness and the American Mind* (New Haven, Conn., 1982), 13ff. 23ff.; George H. Williams, *Wilderness and Paradise in Christian Thought* (New York, 1962).

16. As quoted in Santmire, *Travail of Nature,* 3.

17. White, "Continuing the Conversation," 57, 60; White, "Historical Roots," 1207.

18. White, "Continuing the Conversation," 63.

19. White, "Historical Roots," 1207; Marston Bates, *The Forest and the Sea* (New York, 1960), 197. For the present purposes the most important studies of St. Francis of Assisi are Santmire, *Travail of Nature,* 106ff., and Edward A. Armstrong, *Saint Francis: Nature Mystic—The Derivation and Significance of the Nature Stories in the Franciscan Legend* (Berkeley, Cal., 1973). See also Roy Gasnick, *The Francis Book: Eight Hundred Years with the Saint from Assisi* (New York, 1980); J. R. H. Moorman, *Saint Francis of Assisi* (London, 1963); and C. W. Hume, *The Status of Animals in Christian Religion* (London, 1957). The most recent biography is Julien Green, *God's Fool* (New York, 1985). With reference to the legend of the wolf of Gubbio, Green reports that in 1873 construction workers in that Italian village unearthed the skull of an enormous wolf.

20. Lynn White, Jr., "The Future of Compassion," *Ecumenical Review* 30 (April 1978), 106–108; White, "Continuing the Conversation," 62.

21. White, "Future of Compassion," 107, 109; White, "Continuing the Conversation," 63.

22. White, "Continuing the Conversation," 61; White, "Future of Compassion," 107.

23. White, "Future of Compassion," 109.

24. Genesis 2:15, *Holy Bible,* 2. For commentary on stewardship in Christian history see Black, *Dominion of Man,* ch. 4. Evidence of stewardship in Judaism is discussed in Jonathan Helfand, "Ecology and the Jewish Tradition," *Judaism* 20 (Summer 1971), 330–335, and in Robert Gordis, "Judaism and the Spoliation of Nature," *Keeping Posted* 16 (Dec. 1970), 5–9.

25. René Dubos, *A God Within* (New York, 1972), 45, 153–74; René Dubos, "A Theology of the Earth," in Barbour, ed., *Western Man and Environmental Ethics,* 47. The first statement of Dubos's stewardship idea occurs in *So Human an Animal* (New York, 1968), 7–8; further development of the thesis may be found in his *The Wooing of Earth* (New York, 1980).

26. Walter Lowdermilk appears to be the first American to employ this concept in an argument for environmental responsibility. Subsequent uses include Roderick Nash, "An '11th Commandment' Vital to Our Environment," *Santa Barbara News Press* (June 22, 1969), A16–17; René Dubos, "The Eleventh Commandment," *Keeping Posted* 16 (Dec. 1970), 3–4; and the *Eleventh Commandment Newsletter,* which began publication in San Francisco in 1984. In 1986 two environmental educators proposed a series of ten "ecological commandments," patterned after the Bible's, that were designed to facilitate construction of a Leopoldian sense of community that includes nature: Paul A. Yambert and Carolyn F. Donow, "Are We Ready for Ecological Commandments?" unpublished manuscript submitted to the *Journal of Environmental Education,* March 1986.

27. Walter C. Lowdermilk, "The Eleventh Commandment," *American*

Forests 46 (Jan. 1940), 12–15; J. Douglas Helms, "Walter Lowdermilk's Journey: From Forester to Land Conservationist," *Environmental Review* 8 (Summer 1984), 133–145; personal communication from Inez M. Lowdermilk, July 5, 1969.

28. Joseph Sittler, "A Theology for Earth," *Christian Scholar* 37 (Sept. 1954), 367–374.

29. Joseph Sittler, "Called to Unity," *Ecumenical Review* 14 (Jan. 1962), 177–179.

30. Joseph Sittler, *The Care of the Earth and Other University Sermons* (Philadelphia, 1964), 89, 97–98. The essay can be found more readily in Franklin H. Littell, ed., *Sermons to Intellectuals* (New York, 1963).

31. Joseph Sittler, "Two Temptations—Two Corrections," *National Parks and Conservation Magazine* 45 (Dec. 1971), 21; Sittler, "Ecological Commitment as Theological Responsibility," *Zygon* 5 (June 1970), 178. Additional statements of Sittler's theology appear in his *Essays on Nature and Grace* (Philadelphia, 1972). For analysis see Nathan A. Scott, Jr., "The Poetry and Theology of Earth: Reflections on the Testimony of Joseph Sittler and Gerard Manley Hopkins," *Journal of Religion* 54 (April 1974), 102–120.

32. For example, *A Natural Theology for Our Time* (LaSalle, Ill., 1967) and *Beyond Humanism: Essays in the New Philosophy of Nature* (Chicago, 1937). See also John B. Cobb and Franklin I. Gamwell, eds., *Existence and Actuality: Conversations with Charles Hartshorne* (Chicago, 1984).

33. Representative works are *God's Grace and Man's Hope* (New York, 1949) and *The Spirit and the Forms of Love* (New York, 1968).

34. Richard A. Baer, Jr., "Land Misuse: A Theological Concern," *The Christian Century* 83 (Oct. 12, 1966), 1240. See also Baer's "Conservation: An Arena for the Church's Action," *Christian Century* 86 (Jan. 8, 1969), 40–43.

35. Richard A. Baer, Jr., "Higher Education, the Church, and Environmental Values," *Natural Resources Journal* 17 (July 1977), 485. A similar statement is Baer's "Ecology, Religion, and the American Dream," *American Ecclesiastical Review* 165 (Sept. 1971), 46–47. The essential ideas of both essays appeared initially in Baer's 1966 statement.

36. Baer, "Land Misuse," 1240; Baer, "Higher Education," 485–486; Baer, "Ecology," 47.

37. Baer, "Ecology," 49.

38. Ibid., 47, 53; Baer, "Higher Education," 486.

39. Richard A. Baer, Jr., "The Church and Man's Relationship to His Natural Environment," *Quaker Life* 12 (Jan. 1970), 421.

40. Baer, "Land Misuse," 1240; Richard A. Baer, Jr., "Conservation Problems More Human than Technological," *Conservation Catalyst* 2 (Summer 1967), 4–5.

41. Baer, "Conservation," 43.

42. "The Mission of the Faith-Man-Nature Group," n.d., and "Proceedings of Two Meetings which Led to the Formation of the Research Group on Theology and Ethics of Man-Nature-Resources," Nov. 1965,

both in the Baer Papers in the possession of Richard A. Baer, Jr., Secretary, Faith-Man-Nature Group, Ithaca, N.Y.

43. Richard A. Baer, Jr., to Edward G. Zern, Nov. 30, 1977, Baer Papers, Ithaca, N.Y. Philip N. Joranson's work includes "Biological Development and the Christian Doctrine of Man," *Christian Scholar* 37 (Dec. 1954), 530, and "The Faith-Man-Nature Group and a Religious Environmental Ethic," *Zygon* 12 (June 1977), 175–179.

44. Joranson, "Biological Development," 530; Alfred Stefferud, ed., *Christians and the Good Earth,* "Faith-Man-Nature Papers," no. 1 (Alexandria, Va., 1968); Glenn C. Stone, ed., *A New Ethic for a New Earth,* "Faith-Man-Nature Papers," no. 2 (New York, 1971). The three regional publications are Donald Scherer, ed., *Earth Ethics for Today and Tomorrow: Responsible Environmental Trade-Offs* (Bowling Green, Ohio, 1974); Philip N. Joranson and C. Alan Anderson, eds., *Religious Reconstruction for the Environmental Future* (South Coventry, Conn., 1973); and Dave Stefferson, Walter J. Herrscher, and Robert S. Cook, eds., *Ethics for Environment: Three Religious Strategies* (Green Bay, Wis., 1973).

45. Donald Williams, "Christian Stewardship of the Soil," in Stefferud, ed., *Christians and the Good Earth,* 22.

46. Daniel Day Williams, "The Good of All," Ibid., 75.

47. H. Paul Santmire, "Reflections on the Alleged Ecological Bankruptcy of Western Theology," in Steffenson, Herrscher, and Cook, eds., *Ethics for Environment,* 36. The essay is more readily available under the same title in *Anglican Theological Review* 57 (April 1975), 131–152.

48. "Minutes of the Faith-Man-Nature Executive Committee," Jan. 3, 1975 and Philip N. Joranson, "To the Members of the Faith-Man-Nature Executive Committee," Feb. 5, 1976, Baer Papers.

49. Philip N. Joranson and Ken Butigan, eds., *Cry of the Environment: Rebuilding the Christian Creation Tradition* (Santa Fe, N. Mex., 1984), 8, 9, 127, 241.

50. H. Paul Santmire, "Creation and Nature: A Study of the Doctrine of Nature with Special Attention to Karl Barth's Doctrine of Creation" (Ph.D. diss., Harvard University, 1966).

51. H. Paul Santmire, *Brother Earth: Nature, God and Ecology in Time of Crisis* (New York, 1970), 6; Santmire, "Reflections on the Alleged Bankruptcy of Western Theology," *Anglican Theological Review* 57 (April 1975), 131–152.

52. Santmire, *Brother Earth,* 101.

53. Ibid., 98, 132–133. Extended, if sometimes abstruse, commentary on Santmire's ideas may be found in Claude Y. Stewart, Jr., *Nature in Grace: A Study in the Theology of Nature,* "National Association of Baptist Professors of Religion Dissertation Series," no. 3 (Macon, Ga. 1983), 39–88.

54. Santmire, *Brother Earth,* 146, 149. Several essays developed and publicized Santmire's ideas to a wide audience, at least in the Christian community. His most important statements are "Ecology, Justice and Theology: Beyond the Preliminary Skirmishes," *Christian Century* 93 (May 12, 1976,

460–464); "The Struggle for an Ecological Theology: A Case in Point," *Christian Century* 87 (March 4, 1970), 275–277; "The Integrity of Nature," in Stefferud, ed., *Christians and the Good Earth,* 128–133; and "A New Theology of Nature?" *Lutheran Quarterly* 20 (Aug. 1968), 290–308.

55. Santmire, *Brother Earth,* 151, 185–186, 188. On the need for a life-style revolution away from affluence and in the direction of ecstasy see H. Paul Santmire and Paul E. Lutz, *Ecological Renewal* (Philadelphia, 1972), 119ff.

56. Santmire, *Brother Earth,* 150, 160, 179, 191.

57. Santmire, *Travail of Nature,* 9, 13–29, 189–218.

58. Teilhard died in 1955, but his work was not well known in the United States until the 1960s. The most important translations in English appeared as *The Phenomenon of Man* (New York, 1961) and *The Divine Milieu* (New York, 1960). Commentary is available in Thomas Berry, *Teilhard in the Ecological Age* (Chambersburg, Pa., 1982).

59. Conrad Bonifazi, *A Theology of Things* (Philadelphia, 1967), 24. See also Bonifazi's *The Soul of the World: An Account of the Inwardness of Things* (Lanham, Md., 1978) and "Biblical Roots of an Ecologic Conscience," in Michael Hamilton, ed., *This Little Planet* (New York, 1970), 203–233.

60. John B. Cobb, Jr., *Is It Too Late? A Theology of Ecology* (Beverly Hills, Cal., 1972), 109–116; Cobb, "The Population Explosion and the Rights of the Subhuman World," in John A. Day, F. F. Fost and P. Rose, eds., *Dimensions of the Environmental Crisis* (New York, 1971), 19–32. Cobb's earlier work, such as *A Christian Natural Theology: Based on the Thought of Alfred North Whitehead* (Philadelphia, 1965), ignored the ethical status of nature, but by 1970 it had become one of his major preoccupations. On Cobb and his significance see Stewart, *Nature in Grace,* 89–160, and David Ray Griffin and Thomas J. J. Altizer, eds., *John Cobb's Theology in Process* (Philadelphia, 1977). Alfred North Whitehead's importance to Cobb and other modern theologians and organicists is the subject of Jay McDaniel, "Christian Spirituality as Openness to Fellow Creatures," *Environmental Ethics* 8 (Spring 1986), 33–46, and David Ray Griffen, "Whitehead's Contribution to a Theology of Nature," *Bucknell Review* 20 (Winter 1972), 3–24. For the modern statement of process philosophy see Jack R. Sibley and Pete A. Y. Gunter, eds., *Process Philosophy: Basic Writings* (Washington, D.C., 1978).

61. Cobb, *Is It Too Late?* 48–52; Cobb, "Population Explosion," 31. Cobb also rejected stewardship as a guide to human-nature relations in "The Local Church and the Environmental Crisis," *Christian Ministry* 4 (Sept. 1973), 7.

62. Cobb, *Is It Too Late?* vii.

63. Ibid., 51–52, 55–56, 125, 127.

64. John B. Cobb, Jr., "The Hierarchy of Rights," manuscript presented to The Conference on Nonhuman Rights, Claremont, Cal., April 18–20, 1974.

65. John B. Cobb, Jr., "Beyond Anthropocentrism," in Richard Knowles Morris and Michael W. Fox, eds., *On the Fifth Day,* 147.

66. John B. Cobb, Jr., and Charles Birch, *The Liberation of Life: From the Cell to the Community* (Cambridge, England, 1981), 152, 154, 168, 170. Cobb's most recent statement is "Christian Existence in a World of Limits," in Hargrove, ed., *Religion and Environmental Crisis,* 172–187.

67. Scott I. Paradise, "The Vandal Ideology," *The Nation* 209 (Dec. 29, 1969), 729–732.

68. Donald E. Engel, "Elements in a Theology of Environment," *Zygon* 5 (Sept. 1970), 223, 227.

69. Allan R. Brockway, "A Theology of the Natural World," *Engage/ Social Action* 23 (July 1973), 37.

70. Frederick Elder, *Crisis in Eden: A Religious Study of Man and Environment* (Nashville, Tenn., 1970), 160–161; Henlee H. Barnette, *The Church and the Ecological Crisis* (Grand Rapids, Mich., 1972), 35.

71. Eric Charles Rust, *Nature—Garden or Desert? An Essay in Environmental Theology* (Waco, Tex., 1971), 132, 139–140.

72. Roderick Nash, *The American Environment: Readings in the History of Conservation* (Reading, Mass., 1976), 225ff.

73. Bob Hunter, "Environmentalism in the 1980s: Ecology as Religion," *Greenpeace Chronicles* 18 (Aug. 1979), 3.

74. Henryk Skolimowski, *Eco-Theology: Toward a Religion for Our Times* (Madras, India, 1985).

75. Peter Borrelli, "Epiphany: Religion, Ethics and the Environment," *Amicus Journal* 2 (Winter 1986), 35, 41.

76. *Land Stewardship Newsletter* 5 (Winter 1987), 3.

77. John Carmody, *Ecology and Religion: Toward a New Christian Theology of Nature* (New York, 1983), 119, 133, 166.

78. *Land Stewardship Newsletter* 4 (Spring 1986), 15.

79. Wendell Berry, "The Gift of Good Land," *Sierra* 64 (Nov.–Dec. 1979), 24. See also Wendell Berry, Wes Jackson, and Bruce Colman, eds., *Meeting the Expectations of the Land: Essays in Sustainable Agriculture and Stewardship* (San Francisco, 1984).

On the nuclear question Mark Hatfield, the Senator for Oregon and a devout Christian, proposed stewardship as the answer to those who would race toward nuclear armaments. It was wrong, he contended, for Christians to support something that could destroy God's creation. Mark O. Hatfield, "Finding the Energy to Continue," *Christianity Today* 24 (Feb. 8, 1980), 20–24.

80. John Hart, *The Spirit of the Earth: A Theology of the Land* (New York, 1984), 42–51, 122–123.

81. Joe Paddock and Nancy Paddock, eds., *The Land Stewardship Project Materials* (unpublished sourcebook, St. Paul, Minn., 1984). For a similar perspective applied internationally see Sean McDonagh, *To Care for the Earth: A Call for a New Theology* (Santa Fe, N. Mex., 1987).

82. *Ecology and Religion Newsletter* 1 (Jan. 1973); 47 (Nov. 1977); 78 (Summer, 1981).

83. Vincent Rossi, "The 11th Commandment: A Christian Deep Ecology," *The Eleventh Commandment Newsletter* 3 (1985), 3.

84. Loren Wilkinson, ed., *Earthkeeping: Christian Stewardship of Natural Resources* (Grand Rapids, Mich., 1980), 246–249. See also Loren Wilkinson, "Global Housekeeping: Lords or Servants?" *Christianity Today* 24 (July 27, 1980), 26–30.

85. The seminal study of sacred space is Mircea Eliade, *The Sacred and the Profane.* See also J. Donald Hughes and Jim Swan, "How Much of the Earth Is Sacred Space?" *Environmental Review* 10 (Winter 1986), 247–259; Robert S. Michaelsen, "Sacred Land in America," *Religion* 16 (1986), 249–268; J. Ronald Engel, *Sacred Lands: The Struggle for Community in the Indiana Dunes* (Middleton, Conn., 1983); Gary Snyder, "Good, Wild, Sacred," *Co-Evolution Quarterly* 39 (Fall 1983), 8–17; Roderick Nash, *Wilderness and the American Mind* (New Haven, Conn., 1982); Berman, *The Reenchantment of the World;* Ken Erickson, "Ceremonial Landscapes of the American West," *Landscapes* 22 (1977), 39–47; Linda H. Graber, *Wilderness as Sacred Space,* "Monograph Series of the Association of American Geographers," no. 8 (Washington, D.C., 1976); and Yi-Fu Tuan, *Man and Nature* (Washington, D.C., 1971).

86. The basic texts of Taoism are over two thousand years old. Americans of the 1960s popularized them as ethical guideposts in both social and natural relations. Two of the most popular American editions were Lao Tsu, *Tao Te Ching,* Gia-Fu Feng and Jane English, trans. (New York, 1972) and *Chuang Tze: Basic Writings,* Burton Watson, trans. (New York, 1964).

87. On this point see Ninian Smart, *Beyond Ideology: Religion and the Future of Western Civilization* (San Francisco, 1981), 290.

88. In making these broad generalizations I have relied upon J. Baird Callicott and Roger T. Ames, eds., *Environmental Philosophy: The Nature of Nature in Asian Traditions of Thought* (Albany, N.Y., 1988); Po-Keung Ip, "Taoism and Environmental Ethics," in Hargrove, ed., *Religion and Environmental Crisis,* 94–106; Peter Matthiessen, *Nine-Headed Dragon River: Zen Journals, 1969–1982* (New York, 1986); Huston Smith, "Tao Now: An Ecological Testament," in Ian G. Barbour, ed., *Earth Might Be Fair: Reflections on Ethics, Religion and Ecology* (Englewood Cliffs, N.J., 1972); 62–81; Theodore Roszak, *The Making of a Counter Culture* (Garden City, N.J., 1969), 124–154; Philip Kapleau, ed., *The Three Pillars of Zen* (Boston, 1967); Hajime Nakamura, *Ways of Thinking of Eastern Peoples,* Philip P. Wiener, ed., (Honolulu, 1964); Joseph Needham, *Science and Civilization in China,* 5 vols. (Cambridge, England, 1956); Daisetz T. Suzuki, "The Role of Nature in Zen Buddhism," in William Barrett, ed., *Zen Buddhism: The Selected Writings of D. T. Suzuki* (New York, 1956); and Herrlee Creel, *Sinism* (Chicago, 1929).

Particularly useful essays for the present purposes are Krishna Chaitanya, "A Profounder Ecology: The Hindu View of Man and Nature," *The Ecolo-*

gist 13 (1983), 127–135, and William La Fleur, "Sattva: Englightenment for Plants and Trees in Buddhism," *Co-Evolution Quarterly* 19 (Fall 1978), 47–52. Recent scholarship includes the entire issues of *Philosophy East and West* 37 (April 1987) and of *Environmental Ethics* 8 (Winter 1986), as well as Holmes Rolston, "Can the East Help the West to Value Nature?" *Philosophy East and West* 37 (April 1987), 172–190.

The fact that Asians have not always been able to live up to their ideals concerning the environment is the subject of Vaclav Smil, *The Bad Earth: Environmental Degradation in China* (London, 1984); Yi-Fu Tuan, "Discrepancies between Environmental Attitudes and Behavior: Examples from Europe and China," in David Spring and Eileen Spring, eds., *Ecology and Religion in History* (New York, 1974), 91–113; and Lewis W. Moncrief, "The Cultural Basis of Our Environmental Crisis," *Science* 170 (Oct. 30, 1970), 508–512.

89. Rick Fields, *How the Swans Came to the Lake: A Narrative History of Buddhism in America* (Boulder, Colo., 1981), 60–61.

90. Albert Schweitzer, *Indian Thought and Its Development,* C. E. B. Russell, trans. (New York, 1936).

91. Fields, *Swans,* 136ff. Suzuki's important works include *The Training of the Zen Buddhist Monk* (New York, 1934); *Zen and Japanese Culture* (New York, 1959); *An Introduction to Zen Buddhism* (New York, 1964); and *Zen Buddhism,* Barrett, ed.

92. Alan W. Watts, *Nature, Man and Woman* (New York, 1958), 7–8. On Watts see John Stark, "Alan Watts: A Case Study in the Appropriation of Asian Religious Thought in Post–World War II America" (Ph.D. diss., University of California, Santa Barbara, 1983); Fields, *Swans,* 186ff.; and David K. Clark, *The Pantheism of Alan Watts* (Downers Grove, Pa., 1978).

93. Jack Kerouac, *The Dharma Bums* (New York, 1959), 78.

94. Gary Snyder, "Energy is Eternal Delight," *The New York Times,* Jan. 12, 1972, 43, which also appears in Snyder's *Turtle Island* (New York, 1974), 103–105; Gary Snyder, "The Wilderness," *Center Magazine* 3 (Aug. 1970), 70–71.

For Snyder's life and significance see Fields, *Swans,* 212ff.; L. Edwin Folsom, "Gary Snyder's Descent to Turtle Island: Searching for Fossil Love," *Western American Literature* 15 (Summer 1980), 103–121; Robert Kern, "Recipes, Catalogues, Open Form Poetics: Gary Snyder's Archetypal Voice," *Contemporary Literature* 18 (Spring 1977), 173–197; Bob Steuding, *Gary Snyder* (Boston, 1976); and Roy K. Okada, "Zen and the Poetry of Gary Snyder" (Ph.D. diss., University of Wisconsin–Madison, 1973).

95. Snyder, "Wilderness," 70. Exploring the Marxist dimensions of this idea on one occasion, Snyder proposed that we regard bacteria and simple plants as the proletariat of the ecological community. Disregard of their rights would bring down the entire capitalist structure. The *real* workers of the world would revolt. Snyder found this analogy effective in discussing environmental reforms with communists on his several visits to China. Interview with Gary Snyder, Santa Barbara, Cal., Feb. 21, 1985.

96. Gary Snyder, *The Real Work: Interviews and Talks, 1964–1979* (New York, 1980), 72. Snyder seems to have been aware since the 1960s that full subscription to Buddhist-inspired ethics entailed a revolutionary attitude with reference to many Western institutions. His essay "Buddhism and the Coming Revolution" appeared initially in Snyder, *Earth Household* (New York, 1969). It has since been extensively reprinted and slightly revised under the title "Buddhism and the Possibilities of a Planetary Culture," in Bill Devall and George Sessions, eds., *Deep Ecology* (Salt Lake City, Utah, 1985), 251–253.

97. William R. Hoyt, "Zen Buddhism and Western Alienation from Nature," *Christian Century* 87 (Oct. 7, 1970), 1194–1196.

98. Hwa Yol Jung, "Ecology, Zen and Western Religious Thought," *Christian Century* 89 (Nov. 15, 1972), 1155. Jung extended his analysis of Leopold in "The Splendor of the Wild: Zen and Aldo Leopold," *Atlantic Naturalist* 29 (Spring 1984), 5–11. See also D. Barash, "The Ecologist as Zen Master," *American Midland Naturalist* 89 (1973), 214–217 and Hwa Yol Jung, "The Ecological Crisis: A Philosophic Perspective, East and West," *Bucknell Review* 20 (Winter 1972), 25–44.

99. Robert Aitken, "Thoughts on Buddhist Ecology," *Blind Donkey* (1985) 9, 14, 17, 19, 21.

100. Rajagopal Ryali, "Eastern-Mystical Perspectives on Environment," in Steffenson, Herrscher, and Cook, eds., *Ethics for Environment*, 47–56.

101. Thomas Merton, *Zen and the Birds of Appetite* (New York, 1968); John B. Cobb, Jr., *Beyond Dialogue: Toward a Mutual Transformation of Christianity and Buddhism* (Philadelphia, 1982); Eugene C. Hargrove, "Religion and Environmental Ethics: Beyond the Lynn White Debate," in Hargrove, *Religion and Environmental Crisis*, xvii, xviii.

102. Dolores La Chapelle and Janet Bourque, *Earth Festivals: Seasonal Celebrations for Everyone Young and Old* (Silverton, Colo. 1977); Dolores La Chapelle, *Earth Wisdom* (Los Angeles, 1978); Dolores La Chapelle, *Ritual: The Pattern That Connects* (Silverton, Colo., 1981).

103. Harold W. Wood, "Modern Pantheism," 151. Representative statements are Bill Devall, "Nature Mysticism and Neo-Paganism" (unpublished essay, 1979) and Universal Pantheist Society, *Pantheism and Earthkeeping* (Big Pine, Cal., 1975).

104. Field, *Swans,* especially chs. 12–16.

105. On this point see Peter Steinhart, "Ecological Saints," *Audubon* 86 (July 1984), 8–9, and Calvin Martin, "The American Indian as Miscast Ecologist," in Robert C. Schultz and J. Donald Hughes, eds., *Ecological Consciousness* (Washington, D.C., 1981), 137–148.

106. The most useful secondary sources for Indian religion as it affected environmental attitudes are Gerard Reed, "A Native American Environmental Ethic," in Hargrove, ed., *Religion and Environmental Crisis*, 25–37; Peter Matthiessen, *Indian Country* (New York, 1984); Richard White, "Native Americans and the Environment," in William R. Swagerty, ed.,

Scholars and the Indian Experience (Bloomington, Ind., 1984), 179–204; J. Donald Hughes, *American Indian Ecology* (El Paso, Tex., 1983); J. Baird Callicott, "Traditional American Indian and Western European Attitudes toward Nature: An Overview," *Environmental Ethics* 4 (Winter 1982), 293–318; Peter Nabakov, "America as Holy Land," *North Dakota Quarterly* 48 (Autumn 1980), 9–20; Christopher Vecsey and Robert Venables, eds., *American Indian Environments* (Syracuse, N.Y., 1980); Calvin Martin, *Keepers of the Game* (Berkeley, Cal., 1978); Walter H. Capps, ed., *Seeing with a Native Eye: Essays on Native American Religion* (New York, 1976); and T. C. McLuhan, ed., *Touch the Earth* (New York, 1971). Hughes's bibliography, in particular, will lead to the most important related literature. Also valuable for its survey of recent scholarship is Richard White, "Native Americans and the Environment," in Swagerty, *Scholars and the Indian Experience,* 179–204.

107. Chief Seattle, "The Land Is Sacred," *Counseling and Values* 18 (Summer 1974), 275–277. The story behind the preservation of Seattle's remarks is told in Rudolph Kaiser, *Indians and Europe,* C. Feest, ed. (Aachen, West Germany, 1987). The original translation of Seattle's speech, which lacks some of the holistic language, appears in W. C. Vanderwerth, ed., *Indian Oratory: Famous Speeches by the Noted Indian Chieftains* (Norman, Okla., 1971), 118–122. Regardless of what the chief actually said in 1853, it is significant that modern white Americans wanted to credit him with a biocentric philosophy.

108. Luther Standing Bear, *Land of the Spotted Eagle* (Boston, 1933) 193.

109. Ibid.

110. Roszak, *Making of a Counter Culture,* 245, 264–268.

111. Steward Udall, *The Quiet Crisis* (New York, 1964), 4ff.

112. Black Elk, *Black Elk Speaks: Being the Life Story of a Holy Man of the Oglala Sioux,* John G. Niehardt, ed. (Lincoln, Neb., 1961, originally published 1932); John Fire Lame Deer, *Lame Deer, Seeker of Visions: The Life of a Sioux Medicine Man,* Richard Erdoes, ed. (New York, 1972); Hyemeyohsts Storm, *Seven Arrows* (New York, 1972).

113. N. Scott Momaday, "An American Land Ethic," in John G. Mitchell, ed., *Ecotactics: The Sierra Club Handbook for Environment Activists* (San Francisco, 1970), 97–106. A related statement is Momaday's "A First American Views His Land," *National Geographic* 150 (July 1976), 13–18.

114. Vine Deloria, Jr., "Introduction" in Sam Steiner, *The New Indians* (New York, 1968), x.

115. Vine Deloria, Jr., "Toward a Planetary Metaphysics," manuscript presented to The Conference on Nonhuman Rights, Claremont, Cal., April 18–20, 1974, 1, 18.

116. Harold K. Schilling, "The Whole Earth Is the Lord's," in Barbour, ed., *Earth Might Be Fair,* 115.

117. Robert Dwyer, "Worship of the Environment Is the New Religion," *Los Angeles Times,* August 10, 1973, 27.

118. Richard Neuhaus, *In Defense of People: Ecology and the Seduction of Radicalism* (New York, 1971).
119. Santa Barbara, Cal., *News Press,* Oct. 23, 1983, 12.

CHAPTER 5
The Greening of Philosophy

1. Eugene C. Hargrove, ed., *Religion and Environmental Crisis* (Athens, Ga., 1986), ix. Hargrove's book, *Foundations of Environmental Ethics* (New York, 1988) is, in part, a history of philosophy's interest in environmental issues.
2. "Form First Church of Animal Rights," *The New York Times,* March 14, 1921, 11.
3. Paul Weiss, *Man's Freedom* (New Haven, Conn., 1950), 257.
4. George Sessions, "Shallow and Deep Ecology: A Review of the Philosophical Literature," in Robert C. Schultz and J. Donald Hughes, eds., *Ecological Consciousness* (Washington, D.C., 1981), 291–362; Charles R. Magel, *A Bibliography on Animal Rights and Related Matters* (Lanham, Md., 1981).
5. William T. Blackstone, ed., *Philosophy and Environmental Crisis* (Athens, Ga., 1974), 1, 9. On the concluding page (137) of Blackstone's book, Pete A. Y. Gunther, a professor of philosophy at North Texas State University, called for "a greening of the philosophers."
6. Ibid., 4, 32–33. Nixon's remark is quoted on page 29. In a later essay Blackstone appears to have extended his idea of a moral community to include some animals: William T. Blackstone, "The Search for an Environmental Ethic," in Tom Regan, ed., *Matters of Life and Death* (Philadelphia, 1980), 299–335.
7. Joel Feinberg, "The Rights of Animals and Unborn Generations," in Blackstone, ed., *Philosophy,* 47, 51, 61. Feinberg has extended his ideas in *Rights, Justice and the Bounds of Liberty* (Princeton, N.J., 1980).
8. Feinberg, "Rights of Animals," 44, 50, 52, 60.
9. Clarence Morris, "The Rights and Duties of Beasts and Trees: A Law Teacher's Essay for Landscape Architects," *Journal of Legal Education* 17 (1964), 189, 190, 191. Interestingly, Morris developed his essay as a guest lecturer in the class of the renowned University of Pennsylvania landscape architect, Ian McHarg.
10. Another anticipation of Stone's inquiry was Earl F. Murphy's essay, "Has Nature Any Right to Life?" *Hastings Law Journal* 22 (Feb. 1971), 467–484, although the title is more provocative than the text. David M. Atkinson's "The Relationship between Man and Nature: Moral Endorsement and Legal Recognition of Environmental Rights" (Ph.D. diss., University of Maryland, 1972) examines human rights *to,* rather than the rights *of,* nature. The same approach is taken by Victor J. Yannacone, Jr., Bernard S. Cohen, and Steven G. Davison, *Environmental Rights and Remedies,* (New York, 1972), 2 vols.

11. Garrett De Bell, ed., *The Voter's Guide to Environmental Politics* (New York, 1970), 76.

12. Gary Snyder, "The Wilderness and the Non-Verbal World," *Center Magazine* 3 (Aug. 1970), 70. Another 1970 proposal, by a philosopher, for attention to the implications of ecology was Thomas Colwell, Jr., "Some Implications of the Ecological Revolution for the Construction of Value," in E. Lazlo and J. Wilbur, eds., *Human Values and Natural Science* (New York, 1970), 245–258.

13. Harold Gilliam, "An Equinoctial Ceremony in a Nob Hill Cathedral," *San Francisco Examiner and Chronicle,* Oct. 17, 1971, 31.

14. Christopher D. Stone, "Should Trees Have Standing? Toward Legal Rights for Natural Objects," *Southern California Law Review* 45 (Spring 1972), 450–501. The essay was later published as a much-discussed book: *Should Trees Have Standing? Toward Legal Rights for Natural Objects* (Los Altos, Cal., 1974). The passage quoted appears on page 9 of the book; subsequent references will be to this source. The Mineral King controversy is comprehensively treated in John L. Harper, *Mineral King: Public Concern with Government Policy* (Arcata, Cal., 1982); also useful is Susan Schrepfer, "Perspectives on Conservation: Sierra Club Strategies in Mineral King," *Journal of Forest History* 20 (Oct. 1976), 176–191.

15. Stone, *Should Trees Have Standing?* 24ff.

16. Ibid., 27, 35, 40.

17. *Sierra Club v. Morton,* 405 U.S. 727 (1972), as reprinted in Stone, *Should Trees Have Standing?* 73, 74–75, 76. It should be noted that Justices Brennan and Blackmun joined Douglas in dissenting to the Court's majority, although on less ethically radical grounds. For more on Douglas see "Should Trees Have Rights? William O. Douglas Expands the Law," in Peter Wild, *Pioneer Conservationists of Western America* (Missoula, Mont., 1979), 141–149.

18. Stone, *Should Trees Have Standing?* 75, 83.

19. Wesley Pruden, Jr., "Do Trees Have Rights Like People?" *National Observer,* June 29, 1974, 17.

20. John Rawls, *A Theory of Justice* (Cambridge, Mass., 1971), 512. On Rawls see Robert Paul Wolff, *Understanding Rawls* (Princeton, N.J., 1977).

21. Representative statements are Russ Manning, "Environmental Ethics and John Rawls' Theory of Justice," *Environmental Ethics* 3 (Summer 1981), 155–165; Brian Barry, "Justice between Generations," in P. M. S. Hacker and J. Rax, eds., *Law, Morality and Society* (Oxford, England, 1977); Ernest Partridge, "Rawls and the Duty to Posterity" (Ph.D. diss., University of Utah, 1976); and two collections: Ernest Partridge, ed., *Responsibilities to Future Generations* (Buffalo, N.Y., 1981) and Richard Sikora and Brian Barry, eds., *Obligations to Future Generations* (Philadelphia, 1978).

22. Laurence H. Tribe, "Ways Not to Think about Plastic Trees: New Foundations for Environmental Law," *Yale Law Journal* 83 (June 1974), 1341, 1343, 1345. Tribe revised his essay a few years later in Laurence H. Tribe, Corinne S. Schelling, and John Voss, eds., *When Values Conflict: Es-*

says on Environmental Analysis, Discourse and Decisions (Cambridge, Mass., 1976), 61–91.

23. John Lilly, "The Rights of Cetaceans under Human Laws," *Oceans* 9 (March 1976), 67–68.

24. David F. Favre, "Wildlife Rights: The Ever-Widening Circle," *Environmental Law* 9 (Winter 1979), 279. Stephen R. L. Clark's "The Rights of Wild Things," *Inquiry* 22 (Summer 1979), 171–188, should be examined as a rebuttal to the conclusion some derived from wildlife-rights theory that human moral action should extend to regulating relations between predators and prey in the wilderness.

25. "Reflections on the Dissent of Douglas, in *Sierra Club v. Morton,*" *American Bar Association Journal* 58 (Dec., 1972), 820ff.

26. Mark Sagoff, "On Preserving the Natural Environment," *Yale Law Journal* 84 (Dec. 1974), 221–222, 265ff.

27. P. S. Elder, "Legal Rights for Nature: The Wrong Answer to the Right(s) Question," *Osgood Hall Law Journal* 22 (Summer 1984), 285, 290. Pages 281–348 of this journal issue were a symposium on the rights-of-nature issue.

28. Christopher D. Stone, "*Should Trees Have Standing?* Revisited: How Far Will Law and Morals Reach? A Pluralist Perspective," *Southern California Law Review* 59 (November 1985), 9ff; personal communication from Christopher D. Stone, November 2, 1986. Stone's 1985 essay has been expanded as *Earth and Other Ethics: The Case for Moral Pluralism* (New York, 1987).

29. Stone, "*Trees* Revisited," 24, 27, 52, 76–77.

30. Lawrence Kohlberg's comprehensive work is *The Philosophy of Moral Development* (New York, 1981).

31. Ernest Partridge, "Are We Ready for an Ecological Morality?" *Environmental Ethics* 4 (Summer 1982), 182–187. For another application of Kohlberg's thesis see George H. Kieffer, *Bioethics: A Textbook of Issues* (Reading, Mass., 1974), 36ff.

32. George Wuerthner, "Tree Spiking and Moral Maturity," *Earth First!* 5 (August 1985), 20.

33. Tom Regan, *All that Dwell Therein: Animal Rights and Environmental Ethics* (Berkeley, Cal., 1982).

34. A useful survey of the history of humanitarianism and the recognition of animal rights is Mary Midgley, *Animals and Why They Matter* (Athens, Ga., 1983).

35. The thesis was published as Peter Singer, *Democracy and Disobedience* (Oxford, England, 1973).

36. Peter Singer, "Animal Liberation," *New York Review of Books* 20 (April 5, 1973), 17, 18, 21. Singer's essay was a review of Stanley and Roslind Godlovitch and John Harris, eds., *Animals, Men and Morals: An Enquiry into the Maltreatment of Non-Humans* (New York, 1972). For professional philosophers Singer published a more academic version of his essay as "All Animals Are Equal," *Philosophic Exchange* 1 (Summer 1974), 103–116.

Objections to Singer's analogy between human and animal liberation movements may be found in David Lamb, "Animal Rights and Liberation Movements," *Environmental Ethics* 4 (Fall 1982), 215–233, and Christine Pierce, "Can Animals Be Liberated?" *Philosophical Studies* 36 (July 1979), 69–75. Lamb argues that what Singer is really describing is a *reform* movement; a liberation depends on communicative competence beyond the capability of animals. For similar reasons Pierce thinks that animal liberation cannot entail a right to liberty as humans would understand that idea. James Rachels, "Do Animals Have a Right to Liberty?" in Tom Regan and Peter Singer, eds., *Animal Rights and Human Obligations* (Englewood Cliffs, N.J., 1976), 205–223, attempts to define "liberty" in such a way as to support Singer's position. T. L. S. Sprague, "Philosophers and Antivivisectionism," *Alternatives to Laboratory Animals* 13 (1985), 99–106, analyzes the main positions in the debate.

37. Ruth Harrison, *Animal Machines: The New Factory Farming Industry* (London, 1964), viii.

38. Donald VanDeVeer, "Interspecific Justice," *Inquiry* 22 (Summer 1979), 55–79.

39. Singer, "Animal Liberation," 17, 21. Corbett's statement appears in Godlovitch and Harris, *Animals, Men and Morals,* 238.

40. Peter Singer, *Animal Liberation: A New Ethics for Our Treatment of Animals* (New York, 1975), vii, xii, 1, 188.

41. Regan and Singer, eds., *Animal Right and Human Obligations,* iii.

42. Peter Singer, *The Expanding Circle: Ethics and Sociobiology* (New York, 1981), 121–124. See also Singer, "Not for Humans Only: The Place of Nonhumans in Environmental Issues," in K. E. Goodpaster and K. M. Sayre, eds., *Ethics and Problems of the 21st Century* (Notre Dame, Ind., 1979), 191–205.

43. Peter Singer, ed., *In Defense of Animals* (New York, 1985), 1, 9, 10, 209, 211.

44. See, for example, H. J. McCloskey, "Rights," *Philosophical Quarterly* 15 (April 1965), 115–127. McCloskey extended his case against transferring human-type rights to animals or the environment in *Ecological Ethics and Politics* (Totowa, N.J., 1983).

45. Roslind Godlovitch, "Animals and Morals," *Philosophy* 46 (Jan. 1971), 23–33.

46. Magel, *Bibliography on Animal Rights.*

47. David Paterson and Richard Ryder, eds., *Animal Rights: A Symposium* (Fontwell, England, 1979); Harlan B. Miller and William H. Williams, eds., *Ethics and Animals* (Clifton, N.J., 1983).

48. Richard Ryder, "Experiments on Animals," in Godlovitch and Harris, eds., *Animals, Men and Morals,* 81. Ryder expanded his arguments in *Speciesism: The Ethics of Vivisection* (Edinburgh, 1974) and in *Victims of Science: The Use of Animals in Research* (London, 1975).

49. Brigid Brophy, "In Pursuit of a Fantasy," in Godlovitch and Harris, *Animals, Men and Morals,* 128.

50. Richard Knowles Morris and Michael W. Fox, eds., *On the Fifth Day: Animal Rights and Human Ethics* (Washington, D.C., 1978), 27, 118. Fox's *Animal Rights and Human Liberation* (New York, 1980) is notable for its argument that the recognition of animal rights would free humans from an illogical and outdated moral philosophy. See also his *Returning to Eden: Animal Rights and Human Responsibility* (Melbourne, 1986). Fox's most recent book, *Agricide: The Hidden Crisis that Affects Us All* (Cambridge, Mass., 1986) is a wholesale condemnation of the American way of food production with a major section on animal farming.

One interesting philosophical exercise derived a theory of animal rights from Robert Nozick's "minimal state" theory as developed in *Anarchy, State and Utopia* (1974): Robert W. Hanula and Peter Waverly Hill, "Using Metaright Theory to Ascribe Kantian Rights to Animals within Nozick's Minimal State," *Arizona Law Review* 19 (1977), 242–283. Hanula and Hill conclude that "animals share a moral space with human beings" (283).

51. Regan, *All that Dwell Therein*, 27, 29, 70–72, 93–95, 163.

52. Tom Regan, *The Case for Animal Rights* (Berkeley, Cal., 1983), xiii. An adequate understanding of Regan's contributions to contemporary ethical philosophy would be incomplete without mention of his three widely respected anthologies: Tom Regan, ed., *Earthbound: New Introductory Essays in Environmental Ethics* (Philadelphia, 1984); Tom Regan and Donald Van-DeVeer, eds., *And Justice for All* (Totowa, N.J., 1982); and Regan, ed., *Matters of Life and Death* (Philadelphia, 1980). The *Monist* 70 (Jan. 1987) is devoted to critical examination of Regan's ideas.

In the interest of objectivity, it is relevant to note at this juncture that some contemporary philosophers dismissed the whole notion that animals had a right to equal consideration of interests (Peter Singer's position) or a natural right to life (Tom Regan's). Canadian philosopher Michael Fox, for instance, argues that only humans possess the cognitive capacity and the potential for reciprocity necessary for possessing rights. Fox agrees that animals should not be made to suffer, but he finds the idea of their holding rights to be philosophically insupportable and a "bogus issue." Michael Fox, "'Animal Liberation': A Critique," *Ethics* (Jan. 1978), 107. Note that Michael Fox is not to be confused with Michael W. Fox, the American veterinarian associated with the humane movement, whose ideas on ethical extension are diametrically opposite to the Canadian's. Further confusion arises from the fact that Warwick Fox is an Australian philosopher of deep ecology and Matthew Fox an ecotheologian.

Singer responded to Michael Fox's critique in an essay pointedly entitled "The Fable of the Fox and the Unliberated Animals," in the same issue of *Ethics,* 119–125. Regan responded on pages 126–133 of the journal and Fox issued a final rebuttal on 134–138. The exchange is representative of the convoluted nature of modern philosophical discourse, an interesting trail but one that this history cannot afford the space to trace in its entirety. For the present purposes what is remarkable is that the debate occurred at all.

53. Americans began to learn about the connection between environ-

mentalism and feminism in Alan Watts, *Nature, Man, and Woman* (New York, 1970); Herbert Marcuse, *Counterrevolution and Revolt* (Boston, 1972); and Theodore Roszak, *Person/Planet: The Creative Disintegration of Industrial Society* (New York, 1978). More recent comment can be found in Karen J. Warren, "Feminism and Ecology: Making Connections," *Environmental Ethics* 9 (Spring 1987), 3–20; Murray Bookchin, *The Ecology of Freedom: The Emergence and Dissolution of Hierarchy* (Palo Alto, Cal., 1982); and Carolyn Merchant, "Earthcare: Women and the Environmental Movement," *Environment* 23 (1981), 2–13.

54. Ynestra King, "Toward an Ecological Feminism and a Feminist Ecology," in Joan Rothschild, ed., *Machina Ex Dea: Feminist Perspectives on Technology* (New York, 1983), 118.

55. Rosemary Radford Ruether, *Sexism and God-Talk: Toward a Feminist Theology* (Boston, 1983), 73. Her earlier book, *New Woman/New Earth: Sexist Ideologists and Human Liberation* (New York, 1975) is also valuable in this context.

56. Carolyn Merchant, *The Death of Nature: Women, Ecology and the Scientific Revolution* (San Francisco, 1980), xv, 1ff.

57. See Don Marietta, Jr., "Environmentalism, Feminism, and the Future of American Society," *The Humanist* 44 (May–June 1984), 15–18, 30; Elizabeth Dodson Gray, *Green Paradise Lost* (Wellesley, Mass., 1979); and Annette Kolodny, *The Lay of the Land* (Chapel Hill, N.C., 1975).

58. Jim Cheney, "Eco-Feminism and Deep Ecology," *Environmental Ethics* 9 (Summer 1987), 115–145; Donald Davis, "Ecosophy: The Seduction of Sophia?" *Environmental Ethics* 8 (Summer 1986), 151–162; Mary Daly, *Gyn/Ecology: The Metaethics of Radical Feminism* (Boston, 1978).

59. King, "Toward an Ecological Feminism," 127; Cheney, "Eco-Feminism," 121.

60. Susan Griffin, *Woman and Nature: The Roaring Inside Her* (New York, 1978), 1.

61. Gray, *Green Paradise Lost,* 58.

62. Claudia Card as quoted in Cheney, "Eco-Feminism," 120. Carol Gilligan's major work is *In a Different Voice: Essays on Psychological Theory and Women's Development* (Cambridge, Mass., 1982). See also Elizabeth Dodson Gray, *Patriarchy as a Conceptual Trap* (Wellesley, Mass., 1982), 52–56.

63. The most forthright exponent of this view is Michael E. Zimmerman, "Feminism, Deep Ecology, and Environmental Ethics," *Environmental Ethics* 9 (Spring 1987), 28ff. See also Cheney, "Eco-Feminism," and Zimmerman's "The Crisis of Natural Rights and the Search for a Non-Anthropocentric Basis for Moral Behavior," *Journal of Value Inquiry* 19 (1985), 43–53.

64. Ariel Kay Salleh, "Deeper than Deep Ecology: The Eco-Feminist Connection," *Environmental Ethics* (Winter 1984), 339–345.

65. George Sessions, "The Deep Ecology Movement: A Review," *Environmental Review* 11 (Summer 1987), 105–125. Kvaloy's essay is "Ecophiloso-

phy and Ecopolitics," *North American Review* 259 (Summer 1974), 17–28.

66. Arne Naess, "The Shallow and the Deep, Long-Range Ecology Movement: A Summary," *Inquiry* 16 (Spring 1973), 95–100. Naess developed his thesis most notably in *Ecology, Community and Lifestyle: Ecosophy T* (Cambridge, England, 1987), as well as in "The Deep Ecological Movement: Some Philosophical Aspects," *Philosophical Inquiry* 8 (1986), 10–29; "Basic Principles of Deep Ecology," in Bill Devall and George Sessions, eds., *Deep Ecology* (Salt Lake City, Utah, 1985), 69–76; "Identification as a Source of Deep Ecological Attitudes," in Michael Tobias, ed., *Deep Ecology* (San Diego, Cal., 1985), 256–270; "Intuition, Intrinsic Value and Deep Ecology," *The Ecologist* 14 (1984), 201–203; "A Defense of the Deep Ecology Movement," *Environmental Ethics* 6 (Fall 1984), 265–270; "The Arrogance of Anti-Humanism?" *Ecophilosophy* 6 (May 1984), 8–9; "Self-Realization in Mixed Communities of Humans, Bears, Sheep and Wolves," *Inquiry* 22 (Summer 1979), 231–241. Biographical data on Naess and a revealing interview may be found in Stephen Bodian, "Simple in Means, Rich in Ends: A Conversation with Arne Naess," *The Ten Directions* (Summer/Fall, 1982), 7, 10–15. *Ten Directions* is an occasional publication of the Zen Center of Los Angeles.

67. Naess, "Shallow and Deep Ecology," 96; Naess in Bodian, "Simple in Means, Rich in Ends," 11. George Sessions's ideas are most readily available in his article "The Deep Ecology Movement," 105–125.

68. Devall and Sessions, *Deep Ecology,* 71.

69. Naess, "Self-Realization in Mixed Communities," 231.

70. Naess, "Shallow and Deep Ecology," 95.

71. Devall and Sessions, *Deep Ecology,* 70; Naess, "Defense of Deep Ecology," 267; Naess, "Identification," in Tobias, ed., *Deep Ecology,* 266–267. The most important paper on this subject, which Naess cites approvingly, was VanDeVeer, "Interspecific Justice."

72. Kirkpatrick Sale, "Anarchy and Ecology: A Review Essay," *Social Anarchism* 10 (1985), 14. For a similar disavowal of any form of hierarchy and domination in nonhuman nature by another American anarchist see Murray Bookchin, *Toward an Ecological Society* (Montreal, 1980), 59–60.

73. Bill Devall and George Sessions, "The Development of Natural Resources and the Integrity of Nature," *Environmental Ethics* 6 (Winter 1984), 305.

74. Peter Berg, ed., *Reinhabiting Separate Country: A Bioregional Anthology of Northern California* (San Francisco, 1978); Kirkpatrick Sale, *Dwellers in the Land: The Bioregional Vision* (San Francisco, 1985).

75. Naess, "Shallow and Deep Ecology," 95.

76. Naess, "Identification," in Tobias, ed., *Deep Ecology,* 268.

77. As quoted in John McPhee, *Encounters with the Archdruid* (New York, 1971), 65.

78. Devall and Sessions, eds. *Deep Ecology,* 111, 120. For a similar perspective see Bev Driver, Roderick Nash, and Glen Haas, "Wilderness Benefits: State of Knowledge," in *Proceedings, National Wilderness Research Confer-*

ence, U.S. Forest Service, General Technical Report INT-212 (Ogden, Utah, 1987); Janna L. Thompson, "Preservation of Wilderness and the Good Life," in Robert Elliot and Arran Gare, eds., *Environmental Philosophy: A Collection of Readings* (University Park, Pa., 1983), 85–105; and Roderick Nash, "The Value of Wilderness," *Wild America* 4 (Spring 1980), 10.

79. Holmes Rolston, *Philosophy Gone Wild: Essays in Environmental Ethics* (Buffalo, N.Y., 1986), 118–142, 180–205.

80. Scott Lehman, "Do Wildernesses Have Rights?" *Environmental Ethics* 3 (Summer 1981), 135, 137. For similar points of view see William Godfrey-Smith, "The Value of Wilderness," *Environmental Ethics* 1 (Winter 1979), 309–319, and Roderick Nash, *Wilderness and the American Mind* (New Haven, Conn., 1982), 270–271.

81. Devall and Sessions, eds., *Deep Ecology,* 4, 51–61; Bill Devall and George Sessions, "The Development of Natural Resources and the Integrity of Nature," *Environmental Ethics* 6 (Winter 1984), 293–322; Bill Devall, "The Deep Ecology Movement," *Natural Resources Journal* 20 (Spring 1980), 300–322; John Rodman, "Four Forms of Ecological Consciousness Reconsidered," in Donald Scherer and Thomas Attig, eds., *Ethics and the Environment* (Englewood Cliffs, N.J., 1983), 82–92; Alan R. Drengson, "Shifting Paradigms: From the Technocratic to the Person-Planetary," *Environmental Ethics* 3 (Fall 1980), 221–240.

82. Richard A. Watson, "A Critique of Anti-Anthropocentric Biocentrism," *Environmental Ethics* 5 (Fall 1983), 245–256. A similar point of view appears in W. H. Murdy, "Anthropocentrism: A Modern Version," *Science* 187 (March 1975), 1168–1172.

83. Naess, "Defense of Deep Ecology," 265–266. Joseph Wood Krutch made a similar point in "Conservation Is Not Enough," *American Scholar* 24 (Summer 1954), 295–305.

84. Devall and Sessions, "The Development of Natural Resources," 302–303; Devall and Sessions, *Deep Ecology,* 66–68, 88–89, 197. See also Robert Aitken Roshi, "Gandhi, Dogen and Deep Ecology," in Devall and Sessions, *Deep Ecology,* 232–235, and Fritjof Capra, "Deep Ecology: A New Paradigm," *Earth Island Journal* 2 (Fall 1987), 27–30.

85. The verse, from Jeffers's poem, "The Answer," is reprinted in Devall and Sessions, *Deep Ecology,* 64 and regularly on the masthead of the Friends of the Earth's newsletter, *Not Man Apart.*

86. Alan Watts, *The Book: On the Taboo against Knowing Who You Are* (New York, 1966) as quoted in J. Baird Callicott, "The Metaphysical Implications of Ecology," *Environmental Ethics* 8 (Winter 1986), 313.

87. Warwick Fox, "Deep Ecology: A New Philosophy of Our Time," *The Ecologist* 14 (1984), 194–200. Fox also wrote a sixty-five page unpublished essay, "Approaching Deep Ecology: A Response to Richard Sylvan's Critique of Deep Ecology" (typescript courtesy of George Sessions and Edward Grumbine), which is the most comprehensive explication and defense of the philosophy to date. Fox's paper was circulated as *Environmental Studies Occasional Paper* 20 (1986) by the University of Tasmania.

88. Mark Sagoff, "Animal Liberation and Environmental Ethics: Bad Marriage, Quick Divorce," *Osgood Hall Law Journal* 22 (1984), 304. For analysis of the wild vs. domestic animal issue, see Midgley, *Animals and Why They Matter.*

89. John Rodman, "Liberalism and the Ecological Crisis: Some Tentative Reflections," unpublished paper presented at the Western Political Science Association's annual meeting April 4, 1970. In 1974 Rodman organized a conference entitled "The Rights of Nonhuman Nature" in Claremont, California. The first gathering to consider this theme formally, it brought together theologians, historians, biologists, and philosophers. Rodman hoped to publish their papers in a book to be called "The Rights of Nature: Essays toward a Radical Ecological Ethic," but in the mid 1970s, at the beginning of interest in this subject, he failed to find a publisher. Some of the essays eventually enjoyed publication, several in the *North American Review* 259 (Winter 1974).

90. John Rodman, "The Liberation of Nature?" *Inquiry* 20 (Spring 1977), 94–101.

91. John Rodman, "Four Forms of Ecological Consciousness," 87–89. A popular essay that used the same line of criticism against the animal rightists was David Quammen, "Animal Rights and Beyond: The Search for a New Moral Framework and a Righteous Gumbo," *Outside* (June 1984), 26.

92. For amplification and some qualification of Callicott's ecocentrism see his "Animal Liberation: A Triangular Affair," *Environmental Ethics* 2 (Winter 1980), 324, 326, 337. Edward Abbey's statement may be found in *Desert Solitaire* (New York, 1968), 20. For amplification of Callicott's position see his "Metaphysical Implications of Ecology," 301–316, and "Conceptual Foundations of the Land Ethic," in Callicott, ed., *Companion to* A Sand County Almanac, 186–217. Callicott published fifteen of his most important essays in an anthology, *In Defense of the Land Ethic: Essays in Environmental Philosophy* (Albany, N.Y., 1988).

93. Callicott, "Animal Liberation," 326; J. Baird Callicott and Frances Moore Lappé, "Marx Meets Muir: Toward a Synthesis of the Progressive Political and Ecological Visions," *Tikkun* 2 (1987), 18.

94. Holmes Rolston, "Is There an Ecological Ethic?" *Ethics* 85 (Jan. 1975), 101; Holmes Rolston, "Duties to Endangered Species," *BioScience* 35 (Dec. 1985), 723–724; Holmes Rolston, "Duties to Ecosystems," in J. Baird Callicott, ed., *Companion to* A Sand County Almanac (Madison, Wis., 1987), 272. Rolston's *Environmental Ethics: Duties to and Values in the Natural World* (Philadelphia, 1988) pulls together his writings on biocentric moral philosophy into a coherent system. For an examination of the various philosophical positions of species' rights and an extensive bibliography see Alastair S. Gunn, "Preserving Rare Species," in Tom Regan, ed., *Earthbound: New Introductory Essays in Environmental Ethics* (Philadelphia, 1984), 289–335.

95. Paul W. Taylor, "The Ethics of Respect for Nature," *Environmental Ethics* 3 (Fall 1981), 209.

96. Paul W. Taylor, "In Defense of Biocentrism," *Environmental Ethics* 5 (Fall 1983), 241–243. For related arguments see Taylor's "Are Humans Superior to Animals and Plants?" *Environmental Ethics* 6 (Summer 1984), 149–160.

97. Paul W. Taylor, *Respect for Nature: A Theory of Environmental Ethics* (Princeton, N.J., 1986), 270, 288. For an illuminating analysis of the moral problems involved in balancing human and nonhuman needs see William Aiken, "Ethical Issues in Agriculture," in Regan, ed., *Earthbound*, 247–288.

98. Taylor, "Are Humans Superior to Animals and Plants?" 160.

99. John Passmore, *Man's Responsibility for Nature: Ecological Problems and Western Traditions* (New York, 1974), 107, 116, 174. See also Passmore, "The Treatment of Animals," *Journal of the History of Ideas* 36 (April–May 1975), 195–218. Understandably, Passmore attracted the critical attention of biocentrists, for example in Val Routley, "Critical Notice of *Man's Responsibility for Nature,*" *Australasian Journal of Philosophy* 53 (1975), 171–185. But a year after the publication of his book Passmore apparently changed his mind and called for a nonanthropocentric basis for moral attitudes toward nature. "This," he declared, "is the only adequate foundation for effective environmental concern." John Passmore, "Attitudes toward Nature," in R. S. Peters, ed., *Nature and Conduct* (New York, 1975), 251ff.

100. Kenneth E. Goodpaster, "From Egoism to Environmentalism," in Kenneth E. Goodpaster and K. M. Sayre, eds., *Ethics and Problems of the 21st Century* (Notre Dame, Ind., 1979), 29. For another vote of support for Passmore see Robin Attfield, *The Ethics of Environmental Concern* (Oxford, England, 1983), 140–165.

101. Edward Johnson, "Animal Liberation versus the Land Ethic," *Environmental Ethics* 3 (Fall 1981), 266, 269. Callicott's statement appeared in his "Animal Liberation," 333.

102. William K. Frankena, "Ethics and the Environment," in Goodpaster and Sayre, eds., *Ethics and the Problems of the 21st Century*, 11, 15. See also Frankena's *Ethics* (Englewood Cliffs, N.J., 1973).

103. James Lovelock and Sidney Epton, "The Quest for Gaia," *New Scientist* 6 (Feb. 1975), 304ff.; James Lovelock, *Gaia: A New Look at Life on Earth* (New York, 1979). Two interesting histories of the Gaia idea are J. Donald Hughes, "Gaia: Environmental Problems in Chthonic Perspective," in Kendall E. Bailes, ed., *Environmental History: Critical Issues in Comparative Perspective* (Lanham, Md., 1985), 64–82, and, from a theological point of view, Conrad Bonifazi, *The Soul of the World* (Lanham, Md., 1978). Related applications of the hypothesis may be found in Peter Russell, *The Global Brain: Speculations on the Evolutionary Leap to Planetary Consciousness* (Los Angeles, 1983); Peter Vajk, *Doomsday Has Been Cancelled* (Culver City, Cal., 1978); and Lewis Thomas, *The Lives of a Cell* (New York, 1974). The most recent explication is the 1300-page mimeographed proceedings of a conference entitled "Is the Earth a Living Organism?" edited by Michael J. Cohen and Jim Swan, held in August 1985 and available from the National Audubon Society Expedition Institute, Sharon, Mass. Anthony Weston,

"Forms of Gaian Ethics," *Environmental Ethics* 9 (Fall 1987), 217–230, explores the meaning of the Gaia idea for morality.

104. Theodore Roszak, *Person/Planet: The Creative Disintegration of Industrial Society* (New York, 1978), 32, 41, 49.

105. Michael J. Cohen, *Prejudice against Nature: A Guidebook for the Liberation of Self and Planet* (Freeport, Me., 1983). Note also Cohen's editorship of and contribution to "Is the Earth a Living Organism?" From a historical perspective it is relevant that many Native American faiths subscribe to a similar idea. See also the belief of Peter D. Ouspensky that anything indivisible is a living being, which influenced Aldo Leopold's 1923 essay, "Some Fundamentals of Conservation in the Southwest," published in *Environmental Ethics* 1 (Summer 1979), 131–141, and Alan Watts's essay "The World Is Your Body," in his *The Book: On the Taboo.*

106. Rolston, *Environmental Ethics,* 197–199.

107. Eugene C. Hargrove, ed., *Beyond Spaceship Earth: Environmental Ethics and the Solar System* (San Francisco, 1986), xiii, 247. For the view that polluting and arming space is morally wrong see Gar Smith, "Space as Wilderness," *Earth Island Journal* 2 (Winter 1987), 24–27, and Patricia M. Mische, *Star Wars and the State of Our Souls* (Minneapolis, 1985).

108. Stephen R. L. Clark, "Gaia and the Forms of Life," in Robert Elliot and Arran Gare, eds., *Environmental Philosophy: A Collection of Readings* (University Park, Pa., 1983). 190.

109. Tom Regan, "Holism as Environmental Fascism," in James E. White, ed., *Contemporary Moral Problems* (St. Paul, Minn., 1985), 291–292; Regan, *Case for Animal Rights,* 361–362.

110. See, for example, J. Baird Callicott's review of Regan's *The Case for Animal Rights* in *Environmental Ethics* 7 (Winter 1985), 365–372.

111. Tom Regan, "What Sort of Beings Can Have Rights?" *Southern Journal of Philosophy* 14 (Winter 1976), 485–498. Regan's remark concerning trees, sagebrush, and rivers appeared in his introduction to this essay in Tom Regan, ed., *All That Dwell Therein: Animal Rights and Environmental Ethics* (Berkeley, Cal., 1982), 166.

112. Commentary on the debate between the animal rightists and the biocentrists is abundant. Mary Anne Warren's "The Rights of the Nonhuman World," in Elliot and Gare, eds., *Environmental Philosophy,* 109–134, attempts to mediate between the animal rightists and the proponents of holistic ethics on the grounds that in all but their extreme formulations they lead to the same goal: human environmental responsibility. Warren's intent is to show that "shallow" (instrumental) and "deep" ecology actually converge. On this see also Jon N. Moline, "Aldo Leopold and the Moral Community," *Environmental Ethics* 8 (Summer 1986), 99–120, and Marti Kheel, "The Liberation of Nature: A Circular Affair," *Environmental Ethics* 7 (Summer 1985), 135–149.

Commenting on the schism between the holists and the animal rightists, Eugene Hargrove has recently stated that "the trend today is to treat them as complementary, rather than antagonistic, approaches to parallel, and only slightly overlapping, sets of moral problems." Hargrove, ed., *Religion and Environmental Crisis,* xi.

CHAPTER 6
Liberating Nature

1. Donald Worster, "The Intrinsic Value of Nature," *Environmental Review* 4 (1980), 44.
2. Documentation of this tradition is abundant and includes Roderick Nash, *Wilderness and the American Mind* (New Haven, Conn., 1982); John Passmore, *Man's Responsibility for Nature: Ecological Problems and Western Traditions* (New York, 1974); William Leiss, *The Domination of Nature* (New York, 1972); John Black, *The Dominion of Man* (Edinburgh, 1970); Clarence Glacken, *Traces on the Rhodian Shore: Nature and Culture in Western Thought from Ancient Times to the End of the Eighteenth Century* (Berkeley, Cal., 1967).
3. Two useful collections of radical writings, many prompted by the crusades for human rights of the 1960s, are Jeffrie G. Murphy, ed., *Civil Disobedience and Violence* (Belmont, Cal., 1971), and Henry J. Silverman, ed., *American Radical Thought: The Libertarian Tradition* (Lexington, Mass., 1970).
4. Lewis Herber, "The Problems of Chemicals in Food," *Contemporary Issues* 3 (1952), 206–241.
5. Murray Bookchin, *The Ecology of Freedom: The Emergence and Dissolution of Hierarchy* (Palo Alto, Cal., 1982), 1.
6. Murray Bookchin, "Ecology and Revolutionary Thought" (1965), in Bookchin's *Post-Scarcity Anarchism* (Berkeley, Cal., 1971), 80.
7. Murray Bookchin, *The Ecology of Freedom: The Emergence and Dissolution of Hierarchy* (Palo Alto, Cal., 1982), 366; Murray Bookchin, *Toward an Ecological Society* (Montreal, 1980), 58.
8. Bookchin, *Ecology of Freedom,* 366.
9. Ibid., 58.
10. Ibid., 77.
11. Bookchin, *Toward an Ecological Society,* 58, 59.
12. Bookchin, *Ecology of Freedom,* 366.
13. Herbert Marcuse, *Counterrevolution and Revolt* (Boston, 1972), 59. William Leiss, who admired and analyzed Marcuse, also used the phrase in 1972: Leiss, *Domination of Nature,* 167. See also John Rodman, "The Liberation of Nature?" *Inquiry* 20 (Spring 1977), 83–131.
14. Marcuse, *Counterrevolution,* 59, 62, 72, 74. For analysis of Marcuse's contributions to environmental ethics see Janna L. Thompson, "Preservation of Wilderness and the Good Life," in Robert Elliot and Arran Gare, eds., *Environmental Philosophy: A Collection of Readings* (University Park, Pa., 1983), 93–101. Along with Bookchin, other socialist advocates of environmental ethics include Andre Gorz, *Ecology and Politics* (Boston, 1980), and Alan Roberts, *The Self-Managing Environment* (London, 1979).

15. Charles Reich, *The Greening of America* (New York, 1970), 4.

16. Henry David Thoreau, "Civil Disobedience," in H. A. Bedau, ed., *Civil Disobedience: Theory and Practice* (New York, 1969), 28.

17. Henry David Thoreau, *A Week on the Concord and Merrimack Rivers,* Carl F. Horde, ed. (Princeton, N.J., 1980), 37.

18. David Foreman, "Earth First!" *The Progressive* 45 (Oct. 1981), 42.

19. Theodore Roszak, *Where the Wasteland Ends: Politics and Transcendence in a Postindustrial Society* (Garden City, N.J., 1972), 231, 444.

20. Theodore Roszak, *Person/Planet: The Creative Disintegration of Industrial Society* (New York, 1978), 31, 251, 314.

21. John Rodman, "Theory and Practice in the Environmental Movement: Notes towards an Ecology of Experience," in *The Search for Absolute Values in a Changing World,* Proceedings of the Sixth International Conference on the Unity of the Sciences, (New York, 1978), vol. 1, 52ff.; Bill Devall and George Sessions, *Deep Ecology* (Salt Lake City, Utah, 1985), 193ff.

22. Edward Abbey, *The Monkey Wrench Gang* (Philadelphia, 1975), 150.

23. Edward Abbey, "Introduction," in Peter Wild, *Pioneer Conservationists of Western America* (Missoula, Mont., 1979), xvii.

24. Edward Abbey, *Down the River* (New York, 1982), 119.

25. Edward Abbey, *The Journey Home* (New York, 1977), 208. This essay was also read by thousands as "The Crooked Wood," *Audubon* 17 (Nov. 1975), 24–26. On Abbey see Wild, *Pioneer Conservationists,* 185–197, and Garth McCann, *Edward Abbey* (Boise, Idaho, 1977).

26. As quoted in Mark Vaz, "Leaves of Grass," *Sierra* 71 (May–June 1986), 57.

27. Peter Singer, *Practical Ethics* (Cambridge, England, 1979), 185, 187.

28. As quoted in Vaz, "Leaves of Grass," 61.

29. Singer, *Practical Ethics,* 197.

30. James B. Trefethen, *An American Crusade for Wildlife* (New York, 1975), 122–123, 139ff.; Michael Bean, *The Evolution of National Wildlife Law* (Washington, D.C., 1977).

31. Cleveland Amory, *Man Kind? Our Incredible War on Wildlife* (New York, 1974); Thomas R. Dunlap, *DDT: Scientists, Citizens, and Public Policy* (Princeton, N.J., 1981); Thomas R. Dunlap, *"Interpreting Nature Aright": Science and Wildlife Preservation in America, 1880–1985* (Princeton, N.J., 1988); Donald Worster, *Nature's Economy: The Roots of Ecology* (San Francisco, 1977).

32. Craig W. Allin, *The Politics of Wilderness Preservation* (Westport, Conn., 1982); Nash, *Wilderness,* chs. 12 and 13; Bill Devall and George Sessions, "Why Wilderness in the Nuclear Age?" in *Deep Ecology,* 109–129; Holmes Rolston, *Philosophy Gone Wild: Essays in Environmental Ethics* (Buffalo, N.Y., 1986), ch. 9.

33. Charlene Spretnak, *The Spiritual Dimensions of Green Politics* (Santa Fe, N. Mex., 1986); Charlene Spretnak and Fritjof Capra, *Green Politics: The Global Promise* (Santa Fe, N. Mex., 1986); Richard Porritt, *Seeing Green*

(London, 1985); "The Flowering of the Greens in Europe," *Newsweek* 103 (Aug. 31, 1987), 30–31.

34. William Steffen, "Furor over the Franklin," *Sierra* 69 (Sept.–Oct. 1984), 43–49.

35. "The Green Vote," undated mailing of the Sierra Club (c. 1984), 2; Ronnie Z. Hawkins, "Greens, Deep Ecology, Ecodefense, Bioregionalism, and Animal Rights," *Earth First!* 7 (June 21, 1987), 28–29. The best source of Green information in the United States is Brian Tokar, *The Green Alternative: Creating an Ecological Future* (San Pedro, Cal., 1987).

36. Joseph Petulla, *American Environmentalism: Values, Tactics, Priorities* (College Station, Tex., 1980), 51.

37. For a discussion of this issue see Alastair S. Gunn, "Preserving Rare Species," in Tom Regan, ed., *Earthbound: New Introductory Essays in Environmental Ethics* (Philadelphia, 1984), 289–335; Holmes Rolston, "Duties to Endangered Species," in Rolston, *Philosophy Gone Wild;* and Mark Sagoff, "On Preservation of Species," *Columbia Journal of Environmental Law* 7 (Fall 1980), 33–36.

38. Background on American concern for endangered species is provided in Dunlap, *"Interpreting Nature Aright"*; Bryan G. Norton, *Why Preserve Natural Variety?* (Princeton, N.J., 1988); Bryan G. Norton, ed., *The Preservation of Species: The Value of Biological Diversity* (Princeton, N.J., 1986); Paul Ehrlich and Anne Ehrlich, *Extinction: The Causes and Consequences of the Disappearance of Species* (New York, 1981); Lewis Regenstein, *The Politics of Extinction: The Shocking Story of the World's Endangered Wildlife* (New York, 1975); and Trefethen, *American Crusade for Wildlife.*

39. Detailed political history of endangered species legislation may be found in Laura L. Manning, "The Dispute Processing Model of Public Policy Evolution: The Case of Endangered Species Policy Changes from 1973 to 1983" (Ph.D. diss., University of California, Santa Barbara, 1986); Steven Lewis Yaffee, *Prohibitive Policy: Implementing the Federal Endangered Species Act* (Cambridge, Mass., 1982); Michael J. Bean, *The Evolution of National Wildlife Law* (Washington, D.C., 1977); William D. Palmer, "Endangered Species Protection: A History of Congressional Action," *Environmental Affairs* 4 (Spring 1975), 255–293.

40. U.S. Congress, House, Committee on Merchant Marine and Fisheries, Subcommittee on Fisheries and Wildlife Conservation, Hearings, *Marine Mammals,* 91st Cong., 1st sess. (September 9, 13, 17, 23, 1971), 2.

41. Ibid., 87.

42. Ibid., 88–89. The testimony of Cleveland Amory, head of The Fund for Animals and later the author of *Man Kind?* suggested that "an overwhelming majority," indeed an "animal army," supported this radical position. Ibid., 79.

43. Ibid., 65–66.

44. Public Law 92-522, 86 *U.S. Statutes at Large,* 1027.

45. Elizabeth N. Layne, "Eighty Nations Write Magna Carta for Wildlife," *Audubon* 75 (May 1973), 99–102.

46. Regenstein, *Politics of Extinction,* 156.

47. U.S. Congress, House, Committee on Merchant Marine and Fisheries, Subcommittees on Fisheries and Wildlife Conservation and the Environment, Hearings, *Endangered Species,* 93d Cong., 1st sess. (March 15, 26, 27, 1973), 309. For elaboration of what might be called the cure-for-cancer argument for endangered species see R. J. Hoage, ed., *Animal Extinctions: What Everyone Should Know* (Washington, D.C., 1985); Norman Myers, *A Wealth of Wild Species: Storehouse for Human Welfare* (Boulder, Col., 1983); and Norman Myers, *The Sinking Ark: A New Look at the Problem of Disappearing Species* (New York, 1979). Ehrlich and Ehrlich, *Extinction,* 35–100, analyze the utilitarian argument and compare it to the one that stresses intrinsic value.

48. U.S. Congress, House, Committee on Merchant Marine and Fisheries, Subcommittee on Fisheries and Wildlife Conservation, Hearings, *Predatory Mammals and Endangered Species,* 92d Cong., 2d sess. (March 20, 21, April 10, 11, 1972), 481, 484, 561, 562.

49. Ibid., 484.

50. Ibid., 170–186, 187.

51. Public Law 93-205, 87 *U.S. Statutes at Large,* 884.

52. Ibid., 885.

53. James L. Buckley, "In Defense of Snail Darters," *Washington Post,* Sept. 4, 1979, A20.

54. Joe Patrouch, "Legal Rights for Germs?" *Analog Science Fiction/Science Fact* 97 (Nov. 1977), 167–169.

55. Christopher D. Stone, *Earth and Other Ethics: The Case for Moral Pluralism* (New York, 1987), 6.

56. The palila case is reported in 471 *F. Supp.* 985 (1979). The case and its background are treated in J. O. Juvik and S. P. Juvik, "Mauna Kea and the Myth of Multiple Use: Endangered Species and Mountain Management in Hawaii," *Mountain Research and Development* 4 (1984), 191–202; Steve Yates, "On the Cutting Edge of Extinction," *Audubon* 86 (July–Aug. 1984), 62–84; Jack Nelson, "*Palila v. Hawaii Department of Land and Natural Resources:* State Governments Fall Prey to the Endangered Species Act of 1973," *Ecology Law Quarterly* 10 (1982), 281–310; and Charles van Riper, J. Michael Scott, and David M. Woodside, "Distribution and Abundance Patterns of the Palila on Mauna Kea, Hawaii," *The Auk* 95 (July 1978), 518–527.

57. U.S. Congress, House, Committee on Merchant Marine and Fisheries, Subcommittee on Fisheries and Wildlife Conservation and the Environment, Hearings, *Endangered Species—Part I,* 95th Cong., 2d sess. (May 24, 25, June 1, 15, 16, 20, 23, 28, 1978), 54.

The best account of the Endangered Species Act and its various amendments is U.S. Congress, Senate, Committee on Environment and Public Works, Committee Print, *A Legislative History of the Endangered Species Act of 1973 as Amended in 1976, 1977, 1978, 1979 and 1980,* 97th Cong, 2d sess. (February 1982). For details on the snail darter controversy see William Bruce Wheeler and Michael J. McDonald, *TVA and the Tellico Dam, 1930–*

1979 (Knoxville, Tenn., 1986); Peter Matthiessen, *Indian Country* (New York, 1984), 105–126; Yaffee, *Prohibitive Policy,* 13ff.; Eric Erdheim, "The Wake of the Snail Darter," *Ecology Law Quarterly* 9 (1981), 629–682; and Robert Cahn, *Footprints on the Planet: A Search for an Environmental Ethic* (New York, 1978), 3–20.

58. Interview with Zygmunt Plater, Ann Arbor, Michigan, Nov. 11, 1980.

59. "Too High a Price," *Los Angeles Times,* Oct. 1, 1979, pt. II, 6; "The Ultimate Corruption," *The New York Times,* Jan. 17, 1980, 23.

60. Quoted in Harold W. Wood, Jr., "The United Nations World Charter for Nature," *Ecology Law Quarterly* 12 (1985), 992.

61. The history of Greenpeace may be found in Robert Hunter, *Warriors of the Rainbow: A Chronicle of the Greenpeace Movement* (New York, 1979), and in the pages of the *Greenpeace Chronicle* and *Greenpeace Examiner.*

62. David McTaggart, *Outrage! The Ordeal of Greenpeace III* (Vancouver, 1973).

63. Hunter, *Warriors of the Rainbow,* 137, ix–x.

64. Brian Davies, *Savage Luxury: The Slaughter of the Baby Seals* (Toronto, 1970), 20, 21. For a discussion of the crucial role of the Artek film in launching the movement see Peter Lust, *The Last Seal Pup: The Story of Canada's Seal Hunt* (Montreal, 1967). Cleveland Amory's *Man Kind?* 283ff. supplies additional data.

65. Paul Watson and Warren Rogers, *Sea Shepherd: My Fight for Whales and Seals* (New York, 1982), 17ff; Robert Hunter, *To Save a Whale: The Voyages of Greenpeace* (San Francisco, 1978); Peter Dykstra, "Greenpeace," *Environment* 28 (July–Aug. 1986), 45ff.

66. John Dyson, *Sink the Rainbow! An Enquiry into the "Greenpeace Affair"* (London, 1986); Sunday *Times* Insight Team, *Rainbow Warrior: The French Attempt to Sink Greenpeace* (London, 1986); Elyse Chiland, "Sabotage and Sorrow: But the Spirit Survives," *Greenpeace Examiner* 10 (Sept. 1985), 10–14; Robert F. Jones, "Warriors Who Will Not Stay Down," *Sports Illustrated* 63 (Sept. 2, 1985), 28ff.

67. Maryanne Vollers, "The Rhino Wars: Zimbabwe Is Shooting Poachers Who Menace the Rare Black Rhino," *Sports Illustrated* 66 (March 2, 1987), 61–71.

68. *Earth First!* 6 (Sept. 23, 1986), 7.

69. Watson and Rogers, *Sea Shepherd,* 71ff., 152–153.

70. Ibid., 155.

71. Ibid., 171ff., 251. For the broader picture see Briton Cooper Busch, *The War against the Seals: A History of the North American Seal Fishery* (Kingston, Ontario, 1985); Farley Mowat, *Sea of Slaughter* (Toronto, 1984); David Day, *The Whale War* (San Francisco, 1987); Robert McNally, *So Remorseless a Havoc: Of Dolphins, Whales and Men* (Boston, 1981); and Regenstein, *Politics of Extinction.* Two useful articles are David Steinman, "A Shepherd of Wild Creatures," *Utne Reader* 19 (Jan.–Feb. 1987), 49–56 and Paul Dean, "Soldier with a Dangerous Task: 'Let There Be Whale,'" *Los Angeles Times,* February 3, 1982, V, 1, 4.

72. Paul Watson, "Occurrence in the Ferocious Isles: Sea Shepherd Takes on Whale Butchers," *Earth First!* 6 (Sept. 23, 1986), 1.

73. Paul Watson, "Raid on Reykjavik," *Earth First!* 7 (Dec. 21, 1986), 1, 6. See also "Whaling: The Iceland Caper," *Outside* 12 (Feb. 1987), 9–10, and "Protesters Sink 2 Iceland Whaling Boats," *Los Angeles Times,* Nov. 10, 1986, I, 7.

74. Interview with Paul Watson, Santa Barbara, Cal., April 22, 1987.

75. Amory, *Man Kind?* 231–232.

76. U.S. Congress, Senate, Committee of Agriculture and Forestry, Hearings, *Humane Slaughter of Livestock,* 85th Cong., 2d sess. (April 28, 1958), 11.

77. U.S. Congress, House, Committee on Agriculture, Subcommittee on Livestock and Feed Grains, Hearings, *Regulate the Transportation, Sale and Handling of Dogs and Cats Used for Research and Experimentation,* 89th Cong., 1st and 2d sess. (Sept. 2, 1965, March 7, 8, 1966).

78. "Concentration Camps for Dogs," *Life* 60 (Feb. 4, 1966), 22–29.

79. U.S. Congress, House, Committee on Agriculture, Subcommittee on Department Operations, Research, and Foreign Agriculture, Hearings, *Improved Standards for Laboratory Animals Act,* 98th Cong., 2d sess. (September 19, 1984). See also "Triumph for Dole-Brown Laboratory Animal Bill," *Animal Welfare Institute Quarterly* 4 (Winter 1985–1986), 1, 8–9; Christine Stevens, "Battles of the Animal Welfare Institute," *Alternatives to Laboratory Animals* 13 (Sept. 1985), 48–52; Andrew N. Rowan, *Of Mice, Models and Men: A Critical Evaluation of Animal Research* (Albany, 1984); and Emily S. Leavitt, *Animals and Their Legal Rights: A Survey of American Laws from 1641 to 1978* (Washington, D.C., 1978).

80. Patrick B. Parkes and Jacques V. Sichel, *The Humane Society of the United States, 1954–1979: Twenty-Five Years of Growth and Achievement* (Washington, D.C., 1979); interview with Dale Hilton, Humane Society of the United States, May 8, 1987. In England a Universal Declaration of the Rights of Animals received two *million* signatures in the late 1970s.

81. Richard Knowles Morris and Michael W. Fox, eds., *On the Fifth Day: Animal Rights and Human Ethics* (Washington, D.C., 1978), 27.

82. John A. Hoyt, "A Heritage for the Future," in Parkes and Sichel, *Humane Society,* 43.

83. Interview with Hilton.

84. See, for example, J. Baird Callicott, "Animal Liberation: A Triangular Affair," *Environmental Ethics* 2 (Winter 1980), 311–338.

85. John C. Lilly, *Lilly on Dolphins: Humans of the Sea* (Garden City, N.J., 1975). Earlier statements are John C. Lilly, *The Mind of the Dolphin* (New York, 1967), and John C. Lilly, *Man and Dolphin* (New York, 1961).

86. John C. Lilly, *The Center of the Cyclone: An Autobiography of Inner Space* (New York, 1972), 60, 61.

87. John C. Lilly, *Communication between Man and Dolphin: The Possibilities of Talking with Other Species* (New York, 1978), 257.

88. Lilly, *Center of the Cyclone,* 61–63.

89. John C. Lilly, "The Rights of Cetaceans under Human Laws," *Oceans* 9 (March 1976), 68.

90. Arthur Lubow, "Riot in Fish Tank II: The Abduction/Liberation in Hawaii of Two Dolphins Spotlights a Tricky Question for the Aquarian Age: Do Animals Have Rights?" *New Times* 7 (Oct. 14, 1977), 36ff.; *State v. LeVasseur*, 1 *Hawaii Appeals* 613 P.2d, 1328ff. For an illuminating, if hypothetical, use of dolphin intelligence to expose human biases see John Rodman, "The Dolphin Papers," *North American Review* 259 (Spring 1974), 13–29.

91. Henry Spira, "Fighting to Win," in Peter Singer, ed., *In Defence of Animals* (Oxford, 1985), 196, 197. See also Patricia Curtis, "New Debate over Experimenting with Animals," *The New York Times Magazine*, December 31, 1978, 18–23.

92. Spira, "Fighting to Win," 203, 205; Margaret Laurer, "A Champion of Animal Rights," *The Progressive* 48 (April 1984), 14–15.

93. Philip Windeatt, "'They Clearly Now See the Link': Militant Voices," in Singer, ed., *Defence of Animals*, 190–193; Hal Quinn, "Fighting to Free Animals," *Maclean's* 97 (Dec. 3, 1984), 58; Jolyon Jenkins, "Animal Rights: The New Politics?" *New Statesman* 111 (Feb. 21, 1986), 10–11.

94. Alex Pacheco and Anna Francione, "The Silver Springs Monkeys," in Singer, ed., *Defence of Animals*, 135–147; Constance Holden, "Scientist Convicted for Monkey Neglect," *Science* 214 (Dec. 11, 1981), 1218–1220; and Ronald D. White, "Police Raid Lab, Seize Animals," *Washington Post*, September 12, 1981, A1.

95. "Liberation in the Labs: Animal-Rights Groups Are Gaining Clout and Respect," *Newsweek* 104 (Aug. 27, 1984), 66.

96. William Robbins, "Animal Rights: A Growing Movement in the U.S.," *The New York Times*, June 15, 1984, A-1, A-14.

97. Eric Malnic, "Animal Liberation Front: 'Deep Ecology,'" *Los Angeles Times*, Dec. 30, 1984, I, 1, 30, 32.

98. Douglas Starr, "Equal Rights," *Audubon* 86 (Nov. 1984), 30.

99. Robert Weil, "Inhuman Bondage," *Omni* 9 (Nov. 1986), 65ff.

100. Barbara J. Culliton, "HIL Halts Animal Experiment," *Science* 229 (Aug. 2, 1985), 447.

101. Stephanie Chavez, "Animal Rights Group Takes the Credit for 'Freeing the Bunnies,'" *Los Angeles Times*, April 19, 1987, 1; "Arson Hint in UCD Vet School Fire: Shadow Animal Rights Group Is Suspected," *Sacramento Bee*, April 17, 1987, A-1.

102. As quoted in Malnic, "Animal Liberation Front," 32.

103. The quotations appear regularly in the newspaper *Earth First!* The last quote is from Bruce Hayes, representing the Earth First! Foundation, in a letter to the general membership of the organization, December 1, 1983.

104. Dave Foreman, "Earth First!" *The Progressive* 45 (Oct. 1981), 39; interview with Dave Foreman, April 22, 1987. For further analysis of the differences between traditional and radical environmentalism see Dick Russell, "The Monkeywrenchers," *Amicus Journal* 9 (Fall 1987), 28–42;

Fred Setterberg, "The Wild Bunch: Earth First! Shakes Up the Environmental Movement," *Utne Reader* 21 (May–June 1987), 68–76; Kirkpatrick Sale, "The Forest for the Trees: Can Today's Environmentalists Tell the Difference?" *Mother Jones* 11 (Nov. 1986), 25–29, 32–33, 58; and Dave Foreman, "Making the Most of Professionalism," *Earth First!* 4 (Aug. 1984), 16–17.

105. Dave Foreman, editorial, *Earth First* 1 (Nov. 1, 1980), 1. The exclamation mark that is associated with the organization's name did not appear until the second issue of the newsletter, December 21, 1980.

106. Ibid.

107. Dave Foreman, "Timid Environmentalism," *Earth First!* 1 (Dec. 21, 1980), 5.

108. As quoted in Peter Steinhart, "Ecological Saints," *Audubon* 86 (July 1984), 8.

109. As quoted in Joe Kane, "Mother Nature's Army: Guerrilla Warfare Comes to the American Forest," *Esquire* 107 (Feb. 1987), 99. See also Stewart McBride, "The Real Monkey Wrench Gang," *Outside* 7 (Dec.–Jan. 1983), 34–38, 69–73. Interview with Susan Morgan, March 24, 1986.

110. *Time* 96 (Oct. 5, 1970), 46; "When the Fox Stalked Polluters Trembled," *Mother Earth News* 91 (Jan.–Feb. 1985), 22.

111. *Time* 97 (March 22, 1971), 48.

112. *The New York Times,* Jan. 10, 1978, 25, 30.

113. Tim Palmer, *Stanislaus: The Struggle for a River* (Berkeley, Cal., 1982), 160–185; interview with Mark Dubois, Nov. 16, 1979.

114. George Wuerthner, "Tree Spiking and Moral Maturity," *Earth First!* 5 (August 1, 1985), 20.

115. "The Plowboy Interview: Dave Foreman," *Mother Earth News* 91 (Jan.–Feb. 1985), 18; Dave Foreman, "Reinhabitation, Biocentricism and Self Defense," *Earth First!* 7 (Aug. 1, 1987), 22.

116. *Earth First!* 1 (May 1, 1981), 1–9.

117. "Wilderness War in Oregon," *Earth First!* 3 (June 21, 1983), 1, 4; "Blockaders Roughed Up in Middle Santiam," *Earth First!* 4 (Aug. 1, 1984), 1. The most recent confrontation occurred in Northern California over old-growth lumbering on private lands: Ilana DeBare, "Old Redwoods, Traditions Felled in a Race for Profits," *Los Angeles Times,* April 20, 1987, Pt. I, 1, 14.

118. Kane, "Mother Nature's Army," 101; Ron Huber, "Treeclimbing Hero," *Earth First!* 5 (June 21, 1985), 1, 4; Mark A. Stein, "From Rhetoric to 'Ecotage': Environmental 'Fanatics' Try to Keep Things Wild," *Los Angeles Times,* Nov. 29, 1987, 1, 40, 41.

119. As quoted in Setterberg, "The Wild Bunch," 71.

120. Dave Foreman and Bill Haywood, *Ecodefense: A Field Guide to Monkeywrenching* (Tucson, 1987), 14. The first edition of *Ecodefense* sold 5,000 copies quickly.

121. "The Plowboy Interview," 21.

122. Foreman and Haywood, *Ecodefense,* 17.

123. "Howie Jailed! Earth First! Founder Gets Six Months," *Earth First!* 6 (March 20, 1986), 1.

124. "Blockaders Assaulted by Bulldozer," *Earth First!* 3 (June 21, 1983), 1.

125. As quoted in Larry B. Stammer, "Environment Radicals Target of Probe into Lumber Mill Accident," *Los Angeles Times,* May 14, 1987, 7, and in Harold Gilliam, "Tree Spiking: Can It Ever Be Right?" *San Francisco Chronicle,* Nov. 1, 1987, 8–9. See also Nagasaki Johnson, "Tree Spiking," *Earth First!* 7 (June 21, 1987), 34.

126. As quoted in Kane, "Mother Nature's Army," 102.

127. Foreman and Haywood, *Ecodefense,* 17, 19.

128. Eugene Hargrove, "Ecological Sabotage: Pranks or Terrorism?" *Environmental Ethics* 4 (Winter 1982), 292.

129. As quoted in Kane, "Mother Nature's Army," 102. David Brower, sometime executive of the Sierra Club and Friends of the Earth, offered the alternate viewpoint that "the real terrorists are the polluters and despoilers." Ibid.

130. Pete Dustrud, "Dear Readers," *Earth First!* 2 (Aug. 1, 1982), 2.

131. Gary Snyder, "Dear Dave," Ibid., 2–3.

132. Hank Fonda, "Violence," Ibid., 3.

133. Dave Foreman, "Earth First! and Non-Violence," *Earth First!* 3 (Sept. 23, 1983), 11; Dave Foreman, "Violence and Earth First!" *Earth First!* 2 (March 20, 1982), 4.

134. Howie Wolke, "On Violence," *Earth First!* 3 (Sept. 23, 1983), 12.

135. Ibid.

136. "Letter," *Earth First!* 7 (Feb. 2, 1987), 26, 30.

137. Bill Devall, "Interview with Dave Foreman, Jan. 4, 1986," typescript supplied by Bill Devall, 3, 17. The interview is intended for Devall's unpublished book, *Simple in Means, Rich in Ends: Practicing Deep Ecology.*

138. Stephanie Mills, "Thoughts from the Round River Rendezvous," *Earth First!* 6 (Feb. 2, 1986), 25.

139. As quoted in Kane, "Mother Nature's Army," 102; as quoted in "The Plowboy Interview," 21.

140. Wuerthner, "Tree Spiking," 20.

141. Jonathan Shell, *The Fate of the Earth* (New York, 1982), 177.

142. Patricia M. Mische, *Star Wars and the State of Our Souls: Deciding the Future of Planet Earth* (Minneapolis, Minn., 1985), 115, 120–121.

143. Lewis Thomas, "Foreword," in Paul Ehrlich, et al., *The Cold and the Dark: The World after Nuclear War* (New York, 1984), xxiii. A related title is Mark A. Hartwell, *Nuclear Winter: The Human and Environmental Consequences of Nuclear War* (New York, 1984).

144. Michael Allen Fox, "Nuclear Weapons and the Ultimate Environmental Crisis," *Environmental Ethics* 9 (Summer 1987), 170, 175, 178. See also Michael Allen Fox and Leo Groarke, eds., *Nuclear War: Philosophical Perspectives* (New York, 1985).

145. Carl Sagan, "Nuclear War and Climatic Catastrophe," in Lester

Grinspoon, ed., *The Long Darkness: Psychological and Moral Perspectives on Nuclear Winter* (New Haven, 1986), 59. See also Ehrlich, *The Cold and the Dark,* and Paul Ehrlich, et al., "Long-Term Biological Consequences of Nuclear War," *Science* 222 (Dec. 23, 1983), 1293–1300.

146. John E. Mack, "Action and Academia in the Nuclear Age," *Harvard Magazine* 90 (Jan.–Feb. 1987), 31.

EPILOGUE
Abolitionism, Environmentalism, and the Limits of American Liberalism

1. Understanding American slavery must begin with Kenneth M. Stampp, *The Peculiar Institution: Slavery in the Ante-Bellum South* (New York, 1956); Stanley M. Elkins, *Slavery: A Problem in American Institutional and Intellectual Life* (Chicago, 1959); and David Brian Davis, *The Problem of Slavery in Western Culture* (Ithaca, N.Y., 1966). More recent work includes John B. Boles, *Black Southerners, 1619–1869* (Lexington, Ky., 1984); John W. Blassingame, *The Slave Community: Plantation Life in the Ante-Bellum South* (rev. ed., New York, 1979); Lawrence W. Levine, *Black Culture and Black Consciousness: Afro-American Folk Thought from Slavery to Freedom* (New York, 1977); Claudia Golden, *Urban Slavery in the American South, 1820–1860* (Chicago, 1976); Herbert C. Gutman, *The Black Family in Slavery and Freedom* (New York, 1976); Howard Owens, *This Species of Property: Slave Life and Culture in the Old South* (New York, 1976); Willie Lee Rose, *A Documentary History of Slavery in North America* (New York, 1976); and Eugene D. Genovese, *Roll, Jordan, Roll: The World the Slaves Made* (New York, 1974).

2. Boles, *Black Southerners,* 80, 104.

3. Quoted in Bernard E. Rollin, *Animal Rights and Human Morality* (Buffalo, N.Y., 1981), 86.

4. The essential sources of slave law are John C. Hurd, *The Law of Freedom and Bondage in the United States,* 2 vols. (Boston, 1858); William Goodell, *The American Slave Code in Theory and Practice* (New York, 1853); and Helen T. Catterall, *Judicial Cases Concerning American Slavery and the Negro,* 2 vols. (Washington, D.C., 1926).

5. The initial work in the ongoing debate was Frank Tannenbaum, *Slave and Citizen: The Negro in the Americas* (New York, 1947).

6. Orlando Patterson, *Slavery and Social Death: A Comparative Study* (Cambridge, Mass., 1982), 38–39.

7. Handlin, *Race and Nationality in American Life* (Garden City, N.J., 1957), ch. 3; Elkins, *Slavery,* ch. 2.

8. These generalizations rest upon secondary studies such as Roderick Nash, *Wilderness and the American Mind* (New Haven, Conn., 1982); Richard Slotkin, *Regeneration through Violence: The Mythology of the American Frontier, 1600–1869* (Middletown, Conn., 1973); and John William Ward, *Andrew Jackson: Symbol of an Age* (New York, 1955).

9. See Robert W. Fogel and Stanley L. Engerman, *Time on the Cross:*

The Economics of American Negro Slavery, 2 vols. (Boston, 1974); Hugh Aitken, ed., Did Slavery Pay? Readings in the Economics of Black Slavery in the United States (Boston, 1971); and Elkins, Slavery. Analysis of the economics issue is available in Harold D. Woodman, "The Profitability of Slavery: A Historical Perennial," Journal of Southern History 29 (August 1963), 303–325.

10. Richard D. Ryder, Victims of Science: The Use of Animals in Research (London, 1975), 12.

11. David B. Davis, The Problem of Slavery in the Age of Revolution, 1770–1823 (Ithaca, N.Y., 1975) is the most extensive examination of the rise of abolitionism in the context of liberal-democratic social thought. Davis refers to "a profound transformation of moral perception" in the late eighteenth century that exposed slavery as an ethical wrong (p. 11). Also pertinent is Davis's Slavery and Human Progress (New York, 1984). Other historians who have commented on the conflict between slavery and the ideals on which American nationhood rested include Robert M. Cover, Justice Accused: Antislavery and the Judicial Process (New Haven, Conn., 1975); Edmund S. Morgan, "Slavery and Freedom: The American Paradox," Journal of American History 59 (June 1972), 14–29; Donald L. Noel, ed., The Origins of American Slavery and Racism (Columbus, Ohio, 1972); Winthrop D. Jordan, White over Black: American Attitudes toward the Negro 1550–1812 (Chapel Hill, N.C., 1968); Staughton Lynd, Intellectual Origins of American Radicalism (New York, 1968), ch. 4; and Bernard Bailyn, Ideological Origins of the American Revolution (Cambridge, Mass., 1967), 232ff.

12. George M. Fredrickson, ed., William Lloyd Garrison (Englewood Cliffs, N.J., 1968), 7, 27.

13. Louis Filler, ed., Wendell Phillips on Civil Rights and Freedom (New York, 1965), 97.

14. Fredrickson, Garrison, 15, 35–36.

15. Filler, Phillips, 96.

16. See Lewis Perry, Radical Abolitionism: Anarchy and the Government of God in Antislavery Thought (Ithaca, N.Y., 1973), and Aileen S. Kraditor, Means and Ends in American Abolitionism: Garrison and His Critics on Strategy and Tactics, 1834–1850 (New York, 1967).

17. Of the many John Brown biographies, the most detailed and balanced is Stephen B. Oates, To Purge This Land with Blood: A Biography of John Brown (New York, 1970). Chapters 20–22 analyze the reaction to Brown's raid at Harper's Ferry.

18. Jefferson's dilemma and his attempt to extricate himself are the subject of extensive analysis. See especially John Chester Miller, The Wolf by the Ears: Thomas Jefferson and Slavery (New York, 1977); and see Davis, The Problem of Slavery in the Age of Revolution, ch. 4; David B. Davis, Was Thomas Jefferson an Authentic Enemy of Slavery? (Oxford, 1970); Jordan, White over Black, ch. 12.

19. Theodore Roszak, Person/Planet: Toward the Creative Disintegration of Industrial Society (New York, 1978), 41.

20. See George M. Fredrickson, The Black Image in the White Mind: The Debate on Afro-American Character and Destiny, 1817–1914 (New York,

1971); Eugene H. Berwanger, *The Frontier against Slavery: Western Anti-Negro Prejudice and the Slavery Extension Controversy* (Urbana, Ill., 1967); William H. Pease and Jane H. Pease, "Antislavery Ambivalence: Imme-diatism, Expediency, Race," *American Quarterly* 17 (Winter 1965), 682–695; and Leon Litwack, *North of Slavery: The Negro in the Free States, 1790–1860* (Chicago, 1961).

21. Leonard L. Richards, *Gentleman of Property and Standing: Anti-Abolition Mobs in Jacksonian America* (New York, 1970). See also Lorman Ratner, *Powderkeg: Northern Opposition to the Antislavery Movement, 1831–1840* (New York, 1968). Also useful are Litwack, *North of Slavery,* and Pease and Pease, "Antislavery Ambivalence."

The abolitionists have been the subject of extensive historical investi-gation. In the present discussion I have relied upon the following works: Laurence J. Friedman, *Gregarious Saints: Self and Community in American Abolitionism, 1830–1870* (Cambridge, England, 1982); James B. Stewart, *Holy Warriors: The Abolitionists and American Slavery* (New York, 1976); Ronald G. Walters, *The Antislavery Appeal: American Abolitionism after 1830* (Baltimore, 1976); Merton Dillon, *The Abolitionists: The Growth of a Dis-senting Minority* (De Kalb, Ill., 1974); Donald G. Mathews, ed., *Agitation for Freedom: The Abolitionist Movement* (New York, 1972); Gerald Sorin, *Aboli-tionism: A New Perspective* (New York, 1972); Martin B. Duberman, ed., *The Antislavery Vanguard: New Essays on the Abolitionists* (Princeton, N.J., 1965); Louis Filler, *The Crusade against Slavery, 1830–1860* (New York, 1963); Dwight L. Dumond, *Anti-Slavery: The Crusade for Freedom in America* (Ann Arbor, 1961); David H. Donald, "Toward a Reconsideration of Aboli-tionists," in *Lincoln Reconsidered: Essays on the Civil War Era* (New York, 1956), 19–36; and Gilbert H. Barnes, *The Anti-Slavery Impulse, 1830–1844* (New York, 1933). There are, in addition, excellent interpretations of abo-litionism in Elkins, *Slavery,* and Lynd, *Intellectual Origins of American Radicalism.*

22. The quotations from *The Liberator,* Jan. 1, 1831, may be found in Hugh Hawkins, ed., *The Abolitionists: Immediatism and the Question of Means* (Boston, 1964), 32.

23. In some respects anti-slavery "third" parties before the Civil War, such as the Liberty Party (1840 and 1844) and the Free Soil Party (1848), can be compared to the "green" parties in contemporary Germany and Aus-tralia. Third parties have as yet made little inroad on the strong two-party tradition of the United States. But antislavery elements joined together in 1854 in a new party called Republican. In 1860 it elected its presidential can-didate, Abraham Lincoln, to office.

24. Russel B. Nye, *William Lloyd Garrison and the Humanitarian Reform-ers* (Boston, 1955), 143.

25. Filler, *Phillips,* 38; Fredrickson, *Garrison,* 54.

26. Donald G. Mathews, ed., *Agitation for Freedom,* 50.

27. Henry David Thoreau, "Civil Disobedience," in Henry S. Salt, ed., *Anti-Slavery and Reform Papers by Henry D. Thoreau* (London, 1890), 23, 25.

28. The best example of this sentiment in the new environmental move-

ment is contained in Ernest Callenbach's novel *Ectopia* (Berkeley, Cal., 1975), which describes the secession of the Pacific Northwest from the rest of the United States. On a smaller scale the contemporary attempt to "re-inhabit" wilderness areas, also known as "bioregionalism," involves physical separation but has not yet extended to a rejection of allegiance to the established government. See Kirkpatrick Sale, "Bioregionalism—A New Way to Treat the Land," *The Ecologist* 14 (1984), 167–233, and Sale, *Dwellers in the Land* (San Francisco, 1985).

29. John G. Nicolay and John Hay, eds., *Abraham Lincoln: Complete Works* (New York, 1894), vol. 1, 661.

30. Roy B. Basler, ed., *The Collected Works of Abraham Lincoln* (Springfield, Ill., 1953), vol. 2, 461–462.

31. George Santayana, *Character and Opinion in the United States* (New York, 1920), 205–206. A related analysis appears in Richard Hofstadter, *The American Political Tradition and the Men Who Made It* (New York, 1948). The same "consensus" thesis may be found in Louis Hartz, *The Liberal Tradition in America: An Interpretation of American Political Thought Since the Revolution* (New York, 1955).

32. The major statements are Avery Craven, *The Repressible Conflict, 1830–1861* (University, La., 1939), and James G. Randall, *Lincoln the Liberal Statesman* (New York, 1947), 36–64. An immediate, and still one of the best, rejoinders to the revisionists is Arthur Schlesinger, Jr., "The Causes of the Civil War: A Note on Historical Sentimentalism," *Partisan Review* 16 (Oct. 1949), 969–981. Schlesinger states that "when social conflicts embody great moral issues," they are not easily resolved short of violence. For Civil War historiography see Thomas J. Pressly, *Americans Interpret Their Civil War* (New York, 1962), and Kenneth M. Stampp, ed., *The Causes of the Civil War* (Englewood Cliffs, N.J., 1959).

33. Filler, *Phillips,* 148. Horace Greeley made the same point in "The Prayer of Twenty Million," *New York Tribune,* Aug. 19, 1862. This editorial, addressed to President Lincoln, pleaded that slavery be officially recognized as the "inciting cause" of the Civil War.

34. Filler, *Phillips,* 129.

35. Aldo Leopold, "The Conservation Ethic," *Journal of Forestry* 31 (Oct. 1933), 635.

36. Fredrickson, *Garrison,* 54.

37. Wendell Phillips Garrison, *William Lloyd Garrison* (New York, 1885), vol. 1, 135.

38. As quoted in Arthur Lubow, "Riot in Fish Tank II," *New Times* 7 (Oct. 14, 1977), 51.

39. Holly Jensen as quoted in Eric Malnic, "Animal Liberation Front: Raids on Medical Laboratories Defended," *Los Angeles Times,* Dec. 30, 1984, I, 30.

40. T. O. Hellenbach, "The Future of Monkeywrenching," in Dave Foreman and Bill Haywood, eds., *Ecodefense: A Field Guide to Monkeywrenching* (Tucson, Ariz., 1987), 19.

· Selected Bibliography ·

The heavy footnoting of the preceding text is the best place to gain familiarity with the literature essential to understanding the history of environmental ethics. The following comments will be limited to the key secondary material.

Bibliographies are the obvious place to begin and, fortunately, some very good ones exist. Loren C. Owings, *Environmental Values, 1860–1972: A Guide to Information Sources* (Detroit, 1976) is badly out of date for a rapidly evolving field such as environmental ethics, but it is still useful as a guide to general human-nature relations in the American context. Mary Anglemyer, Eleanor R. Seagraves, and Catherine C. Le Maistre wrote *A Search for Environmental Ethics: An Initial Bibliography* (Washington, D.C., 1980) in the late 1970s, but the simple alphabetical listing is hard to use. Better is the 1984 publication that Anglemyer and Seagraves compiled under the title *The Natural Environment: An Annotated Bibliography on Attitudes and Values* (Washington, D.C., 1984). It describes over eight hundred items. The most recent survey of the literature is Eric Katz's "A Select Bibliography of Environmental Ethics, 1983–1987," *Research in Philosophy and Theology* 9 (1988), pages to be determined upon publication. Indicative of the rapid growth of interest in a subject closely related to environmental ethics is Charles R. Magel, *A Bibliography of Animal Rights and Related Matters* (Lanham, Md., 1981). In 622 pages Magel describes over 3,200 items, some of which inevitably lap over from animal rights to a concern for nature in general. For a shorter list of key sources see Charles R. Magel and Tom Regan, "A Selected Bibliography on Animal Rights and Human Obligations," *Inquiry* 22 (Summer 1979), 243–247. A related bibliographic work that treats ethical concern as part of a broad survey of human attitude and action toward animals is Stephen R. Kellert and Joyce K. Berry, *A Bibliography of Human/Animal Relations* (Lanham, Md., 1985). With fifty topical areas and 4,000 entries, this is a research tool of extraordinary value.

George Sessions is the preeminent bibliographer of deep ecology and related ecocentric moral philosophy. Although copies are hard to find, *Ecophilosophy*, which Sessions distributed as an occasional newsletter from 1976 to 1984, comments on the literature of this field at the time of its emergence. Sessions also prepared "Shallow and Deep Ecology: A Review of the Philosophical Literature," in Robert C. Schultz and J. Donald Hughes, eds., *Ecological Consciousness: Essays from the Earthday X Colloquium, University of Denver, April 21–24, 1980* (Washington, D.C., 1981), 391–462. Sessions identifies all the key books and essays, but his treatment should be updated with his 1987 essay, "The Deep Ecological Movement: A Review," *Environmental Review* 11 (Summer 1987), 105–125. Investigators should proceed from Sessions's work to a perusal of the entire run of *Environmental Ethics:*

An Interdisciplinary Journal Dedicated to the Philosophical Aspects of Environmental Problems. It has been published quarterly under the editorship of Eugene C. Hargrove since 1979. Much of the technical philosophical debate over the meaning of environmental ethics has been carried on in the pages of *Environmental Ethics*, and its book review section is a critical guide to the longer treatments of the subject. Researchers should also review issues of philosophical journals such as *Ethics, Inquiry, American Philosophical Quarterly, Philosophy, Ethics and Animals, Ecophilosophy, Between the Species, Ecospirit*, and *The Trumpeter*, particularly for the last decade.

Several published anthologies of key statements in the search for wider ethical horizons ease the task of the researcher. Among the earliest is Herman E. Daly, ed., *Economics, Ecology and Ethics: Essays Toward a Steady-State Economy* (San Francisco, 1973, rev. ed., 1980). In 1976 Tom Regan and Peter Singer, the leading expositors of animal rights, edited *Animal Rights and Human Obligations* (Englewood Cliffs, N.J., 1976). Its thirty-four selections range from Aristotle and Saint Thomas Aquinas through Descartes and Darwin to ethicists of the 1970s. Ernest Partridge, ed., *Responsibilities to Future Generations: Environmental Ethics* (Buffalo, N.Y., 1981) and Richard Sikora and Brian Barry, eds., *Obligations to Future Generations* (Philadelphia, 1978) are the outstanding collections of secondary sources about projected concerns in mankind's relationship to nature. Their bibliographies open additional doors. Donald Scherer and Thomas Attig edited *Ethics and the Environment* (Englewood Cliffs, N.J., 1983) with more than twenty influential essays, most of which were previously published. In the same vein is Donald VanDeVeer and Christine Pierce, eds., *People, Penguins and Plastic Trees* (Belmont, Cal., 1986). Tom Regan, ed., *Earthbound: New Introductory Essays in Environmental Ethics* (Philadelphia, 1984) departs from this mold in that it contains fresh interpretations written especially for this collection. The footnotes to the ten contributions are designed to lead the reader into the heart of subjects ranging from the rights of rare species to the ethics of agriculture. Edward Johnson's contribution to the Regan collection, an essay entitled "Treating the Dirt: Environmental Ethics and Moral Theory," is a particularly insightful discussion of the roots and modern expressions of comprehensive ethics. Two other Regan anthologies merit passing comment. *Matters of Life and Death* (Philadelphia, 1980, 2d ed., 1986) deals with issues such as suicide and euthanasia but also contains important statements by Peter Singer, William T. Blackstone, and J. Baird Callicott on animal rights and environmental ethics. With Donald VanDeVeer, Tom Regan edited yet another collection: *And Justice for All: New Introductory Essays in Ethics and Public Policy* (Totowa, N.J., 1982). Several contributions concern the idea of rights as applied to nonhumans.

Philosophers have been particularly eager to anthologize papers dealing with ethics and the environment. The pathbreaking work was William T. Blackstone, ed., *Philosophy and the Environmental Crisis* (Athens, Ga., 1974). The humane movement and, more recently, animal liberation received attention in Richard Knowles Morris and Michael W. Fox, eds., *On the Fifth*

Day: Animal Rights and Human Ethics (Washington, D.C., 1978). In 1980 Australian environmental philosophers produced a collection of papers that influenced their American colleagues: D. S. Mannison, M. A. McRobbie, and R. Routley, eds., *Environmental Philosophy* (Canberra, 1980). This volume appeared under the imprint of the Department of Philosophy of the Australian National University and is not easy to locate. Two other Australians, Robert Elliot and Arran Gare, edited a more easily found collection entitled *Environmental Philosophy: A Collection of Readings* (University Park, Pa., 1983). K. E. Goodpaster and K. M. Sayre, eds., *Ethics and Problems of the 21st Century* (Notre Dame, Ind., 1979) gathers together papers about the human relationship to the environment including some directly concerned with the ethical dimension of that relationship.

In addition, three of the major contributors to contemporary nature-oriented moral philosophy have anthologized their own key statements. Tom Regan's *All that Dwell Within: Animal Rights and Environmental Ethics* (Berkeley, Cal., 1982) gathers his papers from the previous seven years. A more ecocentric thinker, Holmes Rolston, wrote *Philosophy Gone Wild: Essays in Environmental Ethics* (Buffalo, N.Y., 1986). The fifteen reprinted papers are essential for gaining an understanding of the farthest horizons of the field. This book should be supplemented with Rolston's *Environmental Ethics: Duties to and Values in the Natural World* (Philadelphia, 1988). J. Baird Callicott, another major architect of holistic ethics, collected his earlier work under the title *In Defense of the Land Ethic: Essays in Environmental Philosophy* (Albany, N.Y., 1988).

There are a few general discussions, or what could be called textbooks, in environmental ethics. Van Rensselaer Potter's *Bioethics: Bridge to the Future* (Englewood Cliffs, N.J., 1971) is one of the earliest. The book, of course, cannot reflect two decades of recent scholarship, but it is dedicated to Aldo Leopold and endeavors to explicate the ways in which moral reasoning relates to new insights offered by the ecological sciences. A related work is *Bioethics: A Textbook of Issues* (Reading, Mass., 1979) by George H. Kieffer. Henry Skolimowski has contributed *Ecophilosophy: Designing New Tactics for Living* (London, 1979). K. S. Shrader-Frechette, *Environmental Ethics* (Pacific Grove, Cal., 1981) discusses the problems and possibilities of applying ethics to new technological situations that affect humankind and the biosphere. Many professional philosophers consider Robin Attfield's *The Ethics of Environmental Concern* (New York, 1983) to be the best available text. Kristin Shrader-Frechette's "Four Land Use Ethics: An Overview," *Environmental Professional* 9 (1987), 121–132, is a useful summary of the most important schools of thought about environmental ethics.

Two journalistic accounts that advocate activism on behalf of the environment should not be dismissed as simplistic cheerleading. Albert J. Fritsch and the Science Action Committee are listed as the joint authors of *Environmental Ethics: Choices for Concerned Citizens* (Garden City, N.J., 1980). The book ranges over topics as diverse as the use of fossil fuels and pesticides, species extinctions, voluntarily simplistic lifestyles, and the theological foundations of environmental ethics. Robert Cahn's *Footprints on the Planet: A Search for an Environmental Ethic* (New York, 1978) contains some history of the environmental movement but features a number of vignettes of businesses and organizations that attempted to act on the basis of an ethical commitment regarding nature in the 1970s.

General histories of the human-nature relationship are the essential foundation of any study of environmental ethics and radical environmentalism. A basic book is Clarence Glacken, *Traces on the Rhodian Shore: Nature and Culture in Western Thought from Ancient Times to the End of the Eighteenth Century* (Berkeley, Cal., 1967). This is a monumental work that will acquaint the reader with the bulk of the primary sources. John Black's *The Dominion of Man: The Search for Ecological Responsibility* (Edinburgh, 1970), and William Leiss, *The Domination of Nature* (Boston, 1972) review the ideas, some dating to the Old Testament, that have contributed to present environmental problems. Although it is sometimes confused with ecofeminist tracts, Carolyn Merchant, *The Death of Nature: Women, Ecology and the Scientific Revolution* (San Francisco, 1980) is a valuable history of domination and hierarchy in Western thought.

John Passmore's *Man's Responsibility for Nature: Ecological Problems and Western Traditions* (London, 1980) makes contributions to both intellectual history and environmental philosophy. An Australian philosopher, Passmore tries to identify grounds for environmental responsibility in Western traditions and values, but in the process he gives detailed attention to the resistance this idea encountered in the West. (Passmore does not find credible the idea that rights can extend to nature nor the possibility of its liberation—concepts of central importance to this work.) Eugene C. Hargrove has continued Passmore's study of resistance and receptivity to environmental ethics in Western thought in *Foundations of Environmental Ethics* (New York, 1988).

The title of Keith Thomas's book, *Man and the Natural World: A History of the Modern Sensibility* (New York, 1983) promises more than it delivers. Actually, the book is about English attitudes toward pets, garden songbirds, and domesticated animals and is confined to the seventeenth, eighteenth, and nineteenth centuries. It is heavily anecdotal but occasionally rises to a generalization about the history of changing ideas towards a limited part of the natural world. In contrast, Donald Worster, *Nature's Economy: The Roots of Ecology* (San Francisco, 1977) concerns the history of thinking about the natural community and the human position within it. Worster digs deeply into both American and European thought primarily in the nineteenth and twentieth centuries, when the ecological perspective emerged. Roderick Nash's *Wilderness and the American Mind,* 3d ed. (New Haven, Conn., 1982) focuses on changing attitudes and actions toward one environmental condition.

In the field of environmental theology there are several indispensable secondary sources. Eugene C. Hargrove, ed., *Religion and Environmental Crisis* (Athens, Ga., 1986) is a collection of essays aimed at going beyond the criticism of Christianity fashionable in the 1960s and 1970s and taking a fresh look at the contributions that Western as well as Eastern faiths can make to modern environmentalism. J. Baird Callicott and Roger T. Ames are the editors of *Environmental Philosophy: The Nature of Nature in Asian Traditions of Thought* (Albany, N.Y., 1989). Since most Asian philosophies are not separable from Asian religions, their book is an aid to understanding ecotheology. Ian Barbour has put together two important collections of papers concerning the role of religion in shaping environmental attitude: *Earth Might Be Fair: Reflections on Ethics, Religion and Ecology* (Englewood Cliffs, N.J., 1972) and *Western Man and Environmental Ethics* (Reading, Mass., 1973). Lynn White's seminal 1967 essay, along with criticisms and rebuttals, is conveniently found in the second book. David and Eileen Spring, ed., *Ecology and Religion in History* (New York, 1974) is thinner.

Essential monographs in ecotheology include H. Paul Santmire's *The Travail of Nature: The Ambiguous Ecological Promise of Christian Theology* (Philadelphia, 1985), which may also be taken as a primary source, and Claude Y. Stewart, Jr., *Nature in Grace: A Study in the Theology of Nature* (Macon, Ga., 1983), which analyzes Santmire and other contemporary religious thinkers. Mircea Eliade's *The Sacred and the Profane: The Nature of Religion* (New York, 1959) is the groundbreaking work in the study of the meaning of nature for various religious traditions. Morris Berman, *The Reenchantment of the World* (Ithaca, N.Y., 1981) continues this investigation. The best secondary examination of American Indian religion is J. Donald Hughes, *American Indian Ecology* (El Paso, Tex., 1983). Linda Graber in *Wilderness as Sacred Space* (Washington, D.C., 1976) suggests that white people as well as Indians can regard parts of the natural world as holy. The definitive treatment of the impact of Buddhism on American thought is Rick Fields, *How the Swans Came to the Lake: A Narrative History of Buddhism in America* (Boulder, Colo., 1981). Carl Mitcham and Jim Grote have edited *Theology and Technology* (Lanham, Md., 1984), which contains a bibliography, "Religious Environmental Ethics," pp. 441–469.

As the 3,200 entries in the Magel bibliography suggest, there is a vast literature concerning ideas about how animals fit into human ethical systems. Good starting places for this subject are Mary Midgley, *Animals and Why They Matter* (Athens, Ga., 1984); Emily Leavitt, *Animals and Their Legal Rights* (Washington, D.C., 1978); and Gerald Carson, *Men, Beasts and Gods: A History of Cruelty and Kindness to Animals* (New York, 1972). Leavitt surveys American laws respecting animals from the seventeenth century to the late 1970s. The Morris and Fox anthology, *On the Fifth Day* and Michael W. Fox's own book, *Returning to Eden: Animal Rights and Human Responsibility* (New York, 1980), are valuable. Tom Regan's *The Case for Animal Rights* (Berkeley, Cal., 1983), and Peter Singer's *Animal Liberation: A New Ethics for Our Treatment of Animals* (New York, 1975), are, of course, primary sources, but in the course of making their arguments they present a valuable review of the entire issue. The newest arguments for animal rights are presented in Steve F. Sapontzis, *Morals, Reason, and Animals* (Philadelphia, 1987). More limited in focus are James Turner, *Reckoning with the Beast: Animals, Pain and Humanity in the Victorian Mind* (Baltimore, 1980), and E. S. Turner, *All Heaven in a Rage* (London, 1964). Both volumes explore cruelty to animals and its opposition in England during the eighteenth and nineteenth centuries. Charles D. Niven's *History of the Humane Movement* (London, 1967) is a start toward organizing a subject badly in need of a comprehensive, international history.

It is difficult to distinguish primary from secondary sources in environmental philosophy because most of those who contribute to this field tend to prescribe as well as analyze. For example, Bill Devall and George Sessions are both scholars of and major contributors to deep ecology. Their summary statement is *Deep Ecology: Living as if Nature Mattered* (Salt Lake City, Utah, 1985). Michael Tobias, ed., *Deep Ecology* (San Diego, Cal., 1985) is about the same subject. Other recent works that are both philosophies and commentaries on philosophy are Christopher D. Stone, *Earth and Other Ethics: The Case for Moral Pluralism* (New York, 1987); Paul W. Taylor, *Respect for Nature: A Theory of Environmental Ethics* (Princeton, N.J., 1986); and Rolston, *Environmental Ethics*. Arne Naess, the Norwegian ecophilosopher, has written *Ecology, Community and Lifestyle: Ecosophy I* (Cambridge, England, 1987). But most environmental philosophy is in the form of articles, rather than books. For a guide to this literature see the opening pages of this bibliography.

In the biographical literature several titles stand out for their insights into the meaning and development of environmental ethics and recent environmentalism. John Muir, in particular, has received extensive recent treatment in Frederick Turner, *Rediscovering America: John Muir in His Time and Ours* (New York, 1985); Michael P. Cohen, *The Pathless Way: John Muir and the American Wilderness* (Madison, Wis., 1984); and Stephen Fox, *The American Conservation Movement: John Muir and His Legacy* (Madison, Wis., 1985). Although it is a collection of Muir's writings, Lisa Mighetto has contributed a valuable introduction entitled "John Muir and the Rights of Animals" in her edited volume, *Muir among the Animals: The Wildlife Writings of John Muir* (San Francisco, 1986). We are fortunate that the centennial of Aldo Leopold's birth arrived in 1987 because it inspired two excellent collections of scholarly commentary on the land ethic and its significance: Thomas Tanner, ed., *Aldo Leopold: The Man and His Legacy* (Ankeny, Iowa, 1987), and J. Baird Callicott, ed., *Companion to* A Sand County Almanac (Madison, Wis., 1987). The definitive biography is Curt Meine, *Aldo Leopold: His Life and Work* (Madison, Wis., 1988).

Future opportunities for ethical extension are discussed in Stone, *Earth and Other Ethics;* Eugene C. Hargrove, ed., *Beyond Spaceship Earth: Environmental Ethics and the Solar System* (San Francisco, 1986); and Rolston, *Environmental Ethics*. Several books take into account the ethical implications of nuclear and planetary warfare: Lester Grinspoon, ed., *The Long Darkness: Psychological and Moral Perspectives on Nuclear Winter* (New Haven, Conn., 1986); Michael Allen Fox and Leo Groarke, eds., *Nuclear War: Philosophical Perspectives* (New York, 1985); and Patricia M. Mische, *Star Wars and the State of Our Souls* (Minneapolis, 1985).

• *Index* •

tionism, 42; feminism on, 144–46; journals of, 189, 190; justified, 136, 163–64, 196; legal remedies of, 170–79; and liberalism, 10, 11–12; as misanthropic, 154; Native American, 118; negativism in, 10–11; on nuclear war, 197–98; radical, 34, 136, 162, 163, 164–65, 166, 167, 171, 179–82, 189–98, 200, 201–2, 203, 213; reform, 150, 175, 202; as religion, 110; on stewardship, 202; violence in, 136, 167, 168, 181–82, 191, 192, 193–97, 213

Environmental Law, 6

The Environmental Professional, 123

Erosion, soil, 98

Erskine, Lord Thomas, 25

Ethical circle, 16, 95; in Asian religions, 113; blacks excluded from, 200; boundaries of, 43, 128, 141, 144, 156–57; democracy widens, 55–56; ecology widens, 32, 36, 56, 59, 124; of environmental ethics, 19–20; extended, 3–7, 27, 31, 83, 90, 140, 160; extended to animals, 37, 42, 43–44, 51, 117–18, 121, 162; extended to Earth and universe, 158; extended to nonequals, 202–3, 205; extended to nonhumans, 19–20, 37, 44, 48–49, 53, 55, 56, 75, 128, 135, 136; extended to slaves, 78, 202–3; humanitarians on, 47, 48–49; nature as, 39–40, 56, 104–6, 144; philosophy on, 124–25, 126, 128, 136–37; plants excluded from, 53

Ethics: of abolitionism, 206, 207; animal, 44, 137; anthropocentric, 134; change by force, 8, 211; Civil War fought over, 210–11; compromised, 41; of conservation, 49, 50, 65, 67; of ecology, 83–84, 155–56; education, 207–8; egalitarian, 95, 204; environmental (*see* Environmental ethics); evolution of, 4–6, 44–45, 52, 62, 68, 82–83, 132, 136, 197; extended (*see* Ethical circle); holistic, 66, 70, 122, 140, 153, 158, 211; on human-nature relationship, 4, 7, 17–18, 22, 38, 51, 65, 72; as human restraint, 10, 72, 84; of hunting, 76–77; kinship as basis of, 51, 53, 55–56, 62, 117–19; land,

6, 32, 55, 63, 66, 67, 69–70, 71–73, 77, 84, 85, 87, 118, 119, 131, 137, 153, 154; for nonhumans, 4, 7, 24, 25, 26–27; and organicism, 59; philosophy and, 121, 136–37; pluralistic, 135–36; prudential, 94; religion as custodian of, 88; of responsibility, 107; in revolution, 34, 50; situation, 169–70; Social Darwinism limits, 43; in stewardship, 111. *See also* names of individuals

Evans, Edward Payson, 32, 50–52, 97, 114, 122; on anthropocentrism, 51; Darwin influenced, 52, 54; on ethics, 51, 52; on metempsychosis, 91; on rights of nonhumans, 51–52, 56, 137

Evolution, 42–43; of ethics, 4–6, 44–45, 52, 62, 68, 82–83, 132, 136, 197

Exploitation: of humans, 164, 166, 201 (*see also* Slavery); of nature, 88–89, 103, 144–45, 163, 164, 165–66, 201; of women, 144–45

Faith-Man-Nature Group, 102–4

Farmland/farming, 110–11

Favre, David F., 132–33

Feinberg, Joel, 126–27, 129, 134, 143

Feminism, 144–46

Feuerbach, Ludwig, 92

Fields, Rick, 113

Flader, Susan, 67

Fleming, Donald, 63

Fletcher, Joseph, 169

Folsom, Paul, 109

Food and Drug Administration, 187

Food chain, 57

Foreman, Dave, 4, 63, 161, 167, 169, 189, 190–96, 213; on monkey-wrenching, 191, 193; on rights of nature, 190, 192; on violence/nonviolence, 195–96

Forest Service, 9

The Fox, 191, 193

Fox, Michael, 252*n*52

Fox, Michael Allen, 197

Fox, Michael W., 32, 34, 142, 143

Fox, Warwick, 151

Fox hunting, 19, 24, 26

Francis of Assisi. *See* St. Francis of Assisi.

Frankena, William K., 157